The O'Leary Series

Microsoft® Office Word 2003

Brief Edition

The O'Leary Series

Microsoft® Office Word 2003

Brief Edition

Timothy J. O'Leary
Arizona State University

Linda I. O'Leary

Boston   Burr Ridge, IL   Dubuque, IA   Madison, WI   New York   San Francisco   St. Louis
Bangkok   Bogotá   Caracas   Kuala Lumpur   Lisbon   London   Madrid   Mexico City
Milan   Montreal   New Delhi   Santiago   Seoul   Singapore   Sydney   Taipei   Toronto

MICROSOFT® OFFICE WORD 2003, BRIEF EDITION

Published by McGraw-Hill Technology Education, an imprint of the McGraw-Hill Companies, Inc. 1221 Avenue of the Americas, New York, NY, 10020. Copyright © 2004 by the McGraw-Hill Companies, Inc. All rights reserved. No part of this publication may be reproduced or distributed in any form or by any means, or stored in a database or retrieval system, without the prior written consent of The McGraw-Hill Companies, Inc., including, but not limited to, in any network or other electronic storage or transmission, or broadcast for distance learning.

Some ancillaries, including electronic and print components, may not be available to customers outside the United States.

This book is printed on acid-free paper.

2 3 4 5 6 7 8 9 0 QPD/QPD 0 9 8 7 6 5

ISBN 0-07-283533-8

Editor-in-Chief: *Bob Woodbury*
Sponsoring editor: *Don Hull*
Developmental editor: *Jennie Yates*
Manager, Marketing and Sales: *Paul Murphy*
Media producer: *Mark Christianson*
Project manager: *Jim Labeots*
Manager, new book production: *Heather Burbridge*
Coordinator freelance design: *Artemio Ortiz Jr.*
Photo research coordinator: *Ira C. Roberts*
Supplement producer: *Matthew Perry*
Senior digital content specialist: *Brian Nacik*
Cover design: *Asylum Studios*
Interior design: *Artemio Ortiz Jr.*
Typeface: *10.5/13 New Aster*
Compositor: *Rogondino & Associates/Cecelia G. Morales*
Printer: *Quebecor World Dubuque Inc.*

Library of Congress Control Number 2003108662

www.mhhe.com

McGraw-Hill Technology Education

At McGraw-Hill Technology Education, we publish instructional materials for the technology education market—in particular, for computer instruction in post secondary education that ranges from introductory courses in traditional four-year universities to continuing education and proprietary schools. McGraw-Hill Technology Education presents a broad range of innovative products—texts, lab manuals, study guides, testing materials, and technology-based training and assessment tools.

We realize that technology has created and will continue to create new mediums for professors and students to use in managing resources and communicating information to one another. McGraw-Hill Technology Education provides the most flexible and complete teaching and learning tools available and offers solutions to the changing needs of the classroom. McGraw-Hill Technology Education is dedicated to providing the tools for today's instructors and students, which will enable them to successfully navigate the world of Information Technology.

- McGraw-Hill/Osborne—This division of The McGraw-Hill Companies is known for its best-selling Internet titles, Harley Hahn's *Internet & Web Yellow Pages* and the *Internet Complete Reference*. For more information, visit Osborne at www.osborne.com.

- Digital Solutions—Whether you want to teach a class online or just post your "bricks-n-mortar" class syllabus, McGraw-Hill Technology Education is committed to publishing digital solutions. Taking your course online doesn't have to be a solitary adventure, nor does it have to be a difficult one. We offer several solutions that will allow you to enjoy all the benefits of having your course material online.

- Packaging Options—For more information about our discount options, contact your McGraw-Hill Sales representative at 1-800-338-3987 or visit our website at **www.mhhe.com/it**.

McGraw-Hill Technology Education is dedicated to providing
the tools for today's instructors and students.

Brief Contents

Labs

	Introduction to Microsoft Office 2003	I.1
	Overview of Microsoft Office Word 2003	WDO.1
1	Lab 1: Creating and Editing a Document	WD1.1
2	Lab 2: Revising and Refining a Document	WD2.1
3	Lab 3: Creating Reports and Tables	WD3.1
	Working Together 1: Word 2003 and Your Web Browser	WDWT1.1
	Command Summary	WDCS.1
	Glossary of Key Terms	WDG.1
	Reference 1	WDR1.1
	Reference 2	WDR2.1
	Index	WDI.1

Detailed Contents

Introduction to Microsoft Office 2003   I.1

What Is Microsoft Office System 2003?   I.2
Office Word 2003   I.2
Office Excel 2003   I.4
Office Access 2003   I.7
Office PowerPoint 2003   I.9
Office Outlook 2003   I.10
Common Office 2003 Features   I.11
Starting an Office 2003 Application   I.11
Using Menus   I.12
Using Shortcut Menus   I.15
Using Shortcut Keys   I.17
Using Toolbars   I.17
Displaying Toolbars on Separate Rows   I.17
Using Task Panes   I.21
Using Office Help   I.21
Using the Help Table of Contents   I.25
Exiting an Office 2003 Application   I.26
Lab Review   I.27
Key Terms   I.27
Command Summary   I.27
Step-by-Step   I.28
On Your Own   I.28

WORD

Overview of Microsoft Office Word 2003   WDO.1
What Is Word Processing?   WDO.1
Word 2003 Features   WDO.1
Case Study for Office Word 2003 Labs   WDO.3
Before You Begin   WDO.4
Microsoft Office Shortcut Bar   WDO.5
Microsoft Office Language Bar   WDO.5
Instructional Conventions   WDO.5

Lab 1 — Creating and Editing a Document   WD1.1

Objectives   WD1.1
Case Study   WD1.2
Concept Preview   WD1.4
Introducing Office Word 2003   WD1.4
Starting Office Word 2003   WD1.4
Exploring the Word 2003 Window   WD1.5
Creating New Documents   WD1.7
Viewing and Zooming a Document   WD1.8
Developing a Document   WD1.10
Entering Text   WD1.11
Typing Text   WD1.11
Using Backspace and Delete   WD1.12
Ending a Line and Inserting Blank Lines   WD1.13
Revealing Formatting Marks   WD1.14
Moving Through Text   WD1.15
Moving Using the Keyboard   WD1.16
Moving Using the Mouse   WD1.17
Identifying and Correcting Errors Automatically   WD1.18
Checking Grammar   WD1.18
Using AutoText and AutoComplete   WD1.21
Checking Spelling   WD1.22
Using AutoCorrect   WD1.25
Using Word Wrap   WD1.28
Using Smart Tags   WD1.29
Saving, Closing, and Opening Files   WD1.30
Saving a File   WD1.30
Closing a File   WD1.33
Opening a File   WD1.34
Navigating a Document   WD1.36
Scrolling a Document   WD1.36
Editing Documents   WD1.39

Ignoring Spelling Errors	WD1.40
Inserting Text	WD1.40
Deleting a Word	WD1.42
Selecting and Deleting Text	WD1.43
Undoing Editing Changes	WD1.46
Changing Case	WD1.48
Formatting a Document	WD1.50
Revealing Document Formatting	WD1.50
Changing Fonts and Font Sizes	WD1.51
Applying Character Effects	WD1.55
Setting Paragraph Alignment	WD1.57
Working with Graphics	WD1.60
Inserting a Picture	WD1.60
Deleting a Graphic	WD1.64
Sizing a Graphic	WD1.66
Previewing and Printing a Document	WD1.67
Previewing the Document	WD1.67
Printing the Document	WD1.68
Setting File Properties	WD1.69
Documenting a File	WD1.69
Exiting Word	WD1.71
Focus on Careers	WD1.71
Concept Summary	WD1.72
Lab Review	WD1.74
Key Terms	WD1.74
MOS Skills	WD1.74
Command Summary	WD1.75
Lab Exercises	WD1.78
Screen Identification	WD1.78
Matching	WD1.79
Multiple Choice	WD1.79
True/False	WD1.80
Fill-In	WD1.81
Hands-On Exercises	WD1.82
Step-by-Step	WD1.82
On Your Own	WD1.88

Lab

2 Revising and Refining a Document WD2.1

Objectives	WD2.1
Case Study	WD2.2
Concept Preview	WD2.4
Revising a Document	WD2.4
Spell-Checking the Entire Document	WD2.5
Using the Thesaurus	WD2.10

Moving and Copying Selections	WD2.12
Using Copy and Paste	WD2.13
Using Cut and Paste	WD2.15
Using Drag and Drop	WD2.16
Copying Between Documents	WD2.17
Controlling Document Paging	WD2.20
Inserting a Hard Page Break	WD2.21
Finding and Replacing Text	WD2.21
Finding Text	WD2.22
Replacing Text	WD2.25
Inserting the Current Date	WD2.26
Modifying Page Layout	WD2.29
Changing Margin Settings	WD2.30
More Paragraph Formatting	WD2.33
Indenting Paragraphs	WD2.33
Setting Tab Stops	WD2.38
Adding Tab Leaders	WD2.41
Changing Line Spacing	WD2.42
More Character Formatting	WD2.44
Adding Color Highlighting	WD2.45
Underlining Text	WD2.46
Copying Formats with Format Painter	WD2.48
Applying Formats Using the Styles and Formatting Task Pane	WD2.48
Creating Lists	WD2.50
Numbering a List	WD2.51
Bulleting a List	WD2.53
Using AutoText Entries	WD2.53
Inserting an AutoText Entry	WD2.53
Creating an AutoText Entry	WD2.54
Adding and Modifying an AutoShape	WD2.55
Inserting an AutoShape	WD2.56
Filling the AutoShape with Color	WD2.57
Adding Text to an AutoShape	WD2.58
Moving an AutoShape	WD2.60
Editing While Previewing	WD2.61
Previewing Multiple Pages	WD2.61
Editing in Print Preview	WD2.62
Using Document Versions	WD2.64
Creating Versions	WD2.65
Opening a Version	WD2.66
Focus on Careers	WD2.67
Concept Summary	WD2.68
Lab Review	WD2.70
Key Terms	WD2.70
MOS Skills	WD2.70
Command Summary	WD2.71

Lab Exercises	WD2.73
Matching	WD2.73
Multiple Choice	WD2.73
True/False	WD2.75
Fill-In	WD2.75
Hands-On Exercises	WD2.76
Step-by-Step	WD2.76
On Your Own	WD2.85

Lab 3 · Creating Reports and Tables — WD3.1

Objectives	WD3.1
Case Study	WD3.2
Concept Preview	WD3.4
Creating and Modifying an Outline	WD3.4
Using Outline View	WD3.5
Changing Outline Levels	WD3.7
Moving and Inserting Outline Topics	WD3.9
Collapsing and Expanding the Outline	WD3.11
Saving to a New Folder	WD3.14
Hiding Spelling and Grammar Errors	WD3.16
Formatting Documents Automatically	WD3.18
Using Click and Type	WD3.18
Applying Styles	WD3.21
Creating a Custom Style	WD3.24
Creating a Table of Contents	WD3.25
Generating a Table of Contents	WD3.26
Navigating by Headings	WD3.29
Using a Table of Contents Hyperlink	WD3.29
Using the Document Map	WD3.30
Formatting Document Sections	WD3.32
Creating a Section Break	WD3.34
Centering a Page Vertically	WD3.35
Including Source References	WD3.36
Adding Footnotes	WD3.37
Viewing Footnotes	WD3.42
Inserting a Footnote in Print Layout View	WD3.43
Formatting Picture Layout	WD3.44
Wrapping Text Around Graphics	WD3.46
Referencing Figures	WD3.48
Adding a Figure Caption	WD3.49
Adding a Cross-Reference	WD3.50
Using a Cross-Reference Hyperlink	WD3.54
Creating a Simple Table	WD3.55
Inserting a Table	WD3.55
Entering Data in a Table	WD3.57
Inserting a Row	WD3.58
Sizing a Table	WD3.59
Formatting a Table	WD3.60
Sorting a List	WD3.62
Creating Headers and Footers	WD3.65
Adding a Header	WD3.65
Adding a Footer	WD3.68
Checking the Document	WD3.69
Using Reading Layout View	WD3.70
Redisplaying Spelling and Grammar Errors	WD3.71
Checking Formatting Inconsistencies	WD3.72
Updating a Table of Contents	WD3.75
Printing Selected Pages	WD3.76
Focus on Careers	WD3.77
Concept Summary	WD3.78
Lab Review	WD3.80
Key Terms	WD3.80
MOS Skills	WD3.80
Command Summary	WD3.81
Lab Exercises	WD3.82
Matching	WD3.82
Multiple Choice	WD3.82
True/False	WD3.84
Fill-In	WD3.84
Hands-On Exercises	WD3.85
Step-by-Step	WD3.85
On Your Own	WD3.92

Working Together 1: Word 2003 and Your Web Browser — WDWT1.1

Case Study	WDWT1.1
Saving a Word Document as a Web Page	WDWT1.2
Making Text Changes	WDWT1.5
Changing the Picture Layout	WDWT1.6
Applying a Theme	WDWT1.7
Creating a Hyperlink	WDWT1.9
Previewing the Page	WDWT1.11
Making a Web Page Public	WDWT1.13
Lab Review	WDWT1.14
Key Terms	WDWT1.14

MOS Skills   WDWT1.14
Command Summary   WDWT1.14
Lab Exercises   WDWT1.15
  Step-by-Step   WDWT1.15
  On Your Own   WDWT1.18

Command Summary   WDCS.1
Glossary of Key Terms   WDG.1
Reference 1–Data File List   WDR1.1
Reference 2–MOS Skills   WDR2.1
Index   WDI.1

Acknowledgments

From Tim and Linda O'Leary

The new edition of The O'Leary Series has been made possible only through the enthusiasm and dedication of a great team of people. Because the team spans the country, literally from coast to coast, we have utilized every means of working together including conference calls, FAX, e-mail, and document collaboration. We have truly tested the team approach and it works!

Leading the team from McGraw-Hill are Don Hull, Sponsoring Editor, and Jennie Yates, Developmental Editor. Their renewed commitment, direction, and support have infused the team with the excitement of a new project.

The production staff is headed by James Labeots, Project Manager, whose planning and attention to detail has made it possible for us to successfully meet a very challenging schedule. Members of the production team include: Artemio Ortiz, Designer; Pat Rogondino and Cecelia Morales, Compositors; Susan Defosset, Copy Editor; Heather Burbridge, Production Supervisor; Matthew Perry, Supplement Coordinator; and Mark Christianson, Media Producer. We would particularly like to thank Pat, Cecelia, and Susan—team members for many past editions whom we can always depend on to do a great job.

Finally, we are particularly grateful to a small but very dedicated group of people who helped us develop the manuscript. Colleen Hayes, Susan Demar, and Kathy Duggan have helped on the last several editions and continue to provide excellent developmental support. To Steve Willis, Carol Cooper, and Sarah Martin who provide technical expertise, youthful perspective, and enthusiasm, our thanks for helping get the manuscripts out the door and meeting the deadlines.

Preface

Introduction

The 20th century not only brought the dawn of the Information Age, but also rapid changes in information technology. There is no indication that this rapid rate of change will be slowing— it may even be increasing. As we begin the 21st century, computer literacy will undoubtedly become prerequisite for whatever career a student chooses. The goal of the O'Leary Series is to assist students in attaining the necessary skills to efficiently use these applications. Equally important is the goal to provide a foundation for students to readily and easily learn to use future versions of this software. This series does this by providing detailed step-by-step instructions combined with careful selection and presentation of essential concepts.

About the Authors

Tim and Linda O'Leary live in the American Southwest and spend much of their time engaging instructors and students in conversation about learning. In fact, they have been talking about learning for more than 25 years. Something in those early conversations convinced them to write a book, to bring their interest in the learning process to the printed page. Today, they are as concerned as ever about learning, about technology, and about the challenges of presenting material in new ways, both in terms of content and the method of delivery.

A powerful and creative team, Tim combines his years of classroom teaching experience with Linda's background as a consultant and corporate trainer. Tim has taught courses at Stark Technical College in Canton, Ohio, Rochester Institute of Technology in upper New York state, and is currently a professor at Arizona State University in Tempe, Arizona. Tim and Linda have talked to and taught students from ages 8 to 80, all of them with a desire to learn something about computers and the applications that make their lives easier, more interesting, and more productive.

About the Book

Times are changing, technology is changing, and this text is changing, too. Do you think the students of today are different from yesterday? There is no doubt about it—they are. On the positive side, it is amazing how much effort students will put toward things they are convinced are relevant to them. Their effort directed at learning application programs and exploring the Web seems at times limitless. On the other hand, students can often be shortsighted, thinking that learning the skills to use the application is the only objective. The mission of the series is to build upon and extend this interest by not only teaching the specific application skills but by introducing the concepts that are common to all applications, providing students with the confidence, knowledge, and ability to easily learn the next generation of applications.

Same Great Features as the Office XP Edition with some new additions!

- **Introduction to Computer Essentials**—A brief introduction to the basics of computer hardware and software (appears in Office Volume I only).

 - **Office Outlook 2003**—A lab devoted to Microsoft Office Outlook 2003 basics (appears in Office Volume I only).

- **Introduction to Microsoft Office 2003**—Presents an overview to the Microsoft Office 2003 components: Office Word, Excel, Access, Power-Point, and Outlook. Includes a hands-on section that introduces the features that are common to all Office 2003 applications, including using menus, task panes, and the Office Help system.

- **Lab Organization**—The lab text is organized to include main and subtopic heads by grouping related tasks. For example, tasks such as changing fonts and applying character effects appear under the "Formatting" topic head. This results in a slightly more reference-like approach, making it easier for students to refer back to the text to review. This has been done without losing the logical and realistic development of the case.

- **Relevant Cases**—Four separate running cases demonstrate the features in each application. Topics are of interest to students—At Arizona State University, over 600 students were surveyed to find out what topics are of interest to them.

- **Focus on Concepts**—Each lab focuses on the concepts behind the application. Students learn the concepts, so they can succeed regardless of the software package they might be using. The concepts are previewed at the beginning of each lab and summarized at the end of each lab.

- All **Numbered Steps** and bullets appear in left margin space making it easy not to miss a step.

- **Clarified Marginal Notes**—Marginal notes have been enhanced by more clearly identifying the note content with box heads and the use of different colors.

  Additional Information—Brief asides with expanded discussion of features.

  Having Trouble?—Procedural tips advising students of possible problems and how to overcome them.

  Another Method—Alternative methods of performing a procedure.

• **Focus on Careers**—A new feature, appearing at the end of each lab, which provides an example of how the material covered may be applied in the "real world."

• A **MOS (Microsoft Office Specialist) Skills** table, appearing at the end of each lab, contains page references to MOS skills learned in the lab.

• **End-of-Chapter Material**

  • Screen Identification (appears in the first lab of each application)

  • Matching

  • Multiple Choice

  • Fill-In

  • True/False

  Hands-On Practice Exercises—Students apply the skills and concepts they learned to solve case-based exercises. Many cases in the practice exercises tie to a running case used in another application lab. This helps to demonstrate the use of the four applications across a common case setting. For example, the Adventure Travel Tours case used in the Word labs is continued in practice exercises in Excel, Access, and PowerPoint.

  • Step-by-Step

  • On Your Own

• **Rating System**—The 3-star rating system identifies the difficulty level of each practice exercise in the end-of-lab materials.

 • **Continuing Exercises**—A continuing exercise icon identifies exercises that build off of exercises completed in earlier labs.

• **Working Together Labs**—At the completion of the brief and introductory texts, a final lab demonstrates the integration of the MS Office applications.

• **References**

  Command Summary—Provides a able of all commands used in the labs.

  Glossary of Key Terms—Includes definitions for all bolded terms used in the labs and included in the Key Terms list at the end of each lab.

  Data File List—Helps organize all data and solution files.

  MOS (*Microsoft Office Specialist*) Certification Guide—Links all MOS objectives to text content and end-of-chapter exercises.

Instructor's Guide

We understand that, in today's teaching environment, offering a textbook alone is not sufficient to meet the needs of the many instructors who use our books. To teach effectively, instructors must have a full complement of supplemental resources to assist them in every facet of teaching from preparing for class, to conducting a lecture, to assessing students' comprehension. *The O'Leary Series* offers a fully-integrated supplements package and Web site, as described below.

Instructor's Resource Kit

The **Instructor's Resource Kit** contains a computerized Test Bank, an Instructor's Manual, and PowerPoint Presentation Slides. Features of the Instructor's Resource Kit are described below.

- **Instructor's Manual** The Instructor's Manual contains lab objectives, concepts, outlines, lecture notes, and command summaries. Also included are answers to all end-of chapter material, tips for covering difficult materials, additional exercises, and a schedule showing how much time is required to cover text material.

- **Computerized Test Bank** The test bank contains over 1,300 multiple choice, true/false, and discussion questions. Each question will be accompanied by the correct answer, the level of learning difficulty, and corresponding page references. Our flexible Diploma software allows you to easily generate custom exams.

- **PowerPoint Presentation Slides** The presentation slides will include lab objectives, concepts, outlines, text figures, and speaker's notes. Also included are bullets to illustrate key terms and FAQs.

Online Learning Center/Web Site

Found at **www.mhhe.com/oleary**, this site provides additional learning and instructional tools to enhance the comprehension of the text. The OLC/Web Site is divided into these three areas:

- **Information Center** Contains core information about the text, supplements, and the authors.

- **Instructor Center** Offers instructional materials, downloads, and other relevant links for professors.

- **Student Center** Contains data files, chapter competencies, chapter concepts, self-quizzes, flashcards, additional Web links, and more.

Skills Assessment

SimNet (Simulated Network Assessment Product) provides a way for you to test students' software skills in a simulated environment.

- Pre-testing options
- Post-testing options
- Course placement testing
- Diagnostic capabilities to reinforce skills
- Proficiency testing to measure skills
- Web or LAN delivery of tests.
- Computer-based training tutorials

For more information on skills assessment software, please contact your local sales representative, or visit us at **www.mhhe.com/it**.

Digital Solutions to Help You Manage Your Course

PageOut is our Course Web Site Development Center that offers a syllabus page, URL, McGraw-Hill Online Learning Center content, online exercises and quizzes, gradebook, discussion board, and an area for student Web pages.

Available free with any McGraw-Hill Technology Education product, PageOut requires no prior knowledge of HTML, no long hours of coding, and a way for course coordinators and professors to provide a full-course Web site. PageOut offers a series of templates—simply fill them with your course information and click on one of 16 designs. The process takes under an hour and leaves you with a professionally designed Web site. We'll even get you started with sample Web sites, or enter your syllabus for you! PageOut is so straightforward and intuitive, it's little wonder why over 12,000 college professors are using it. For more information, visit the PageOut Web site at www.pageout.net.

Online courses are also available. Online Learning Centers (OLCs) are your perfect solutions for Internet-based content. Simply put, these Centers are "digital cartridges" that contain a book's pedagogy and supplements. As students read the book, they can go online and take self-grading quizzes or work through interactive exercises. These also provide students appropriate access to lecture materials and other key supplements.

Online Learning Centers can be delivered through any of these platforms:

- Blackboard.com
- WebCT (a product of Universal Learning Technology)

McGraw-Hill has partnerships with WebCT and Blackboard to make it even easier to take your course online. Now you can have McGraw-Hill content delivered through the leading Internet-based learning tool for higher education.

Computing Concepts

Computing Essentials 2004 and *Computing Today* offer a unique, visual orientation that gives students a basic understanding of computing concepts. *Computing Essentials* and *Computing Today* are some of the few books on the market that are written by a professor who still teaches the courses every semester and loves it. The books encourage "active" learning with their exercises, explorations, visual illustrations, and inclusion of screen shots and numbered steps. While combining the "active" learning style with current topics and technology, these texts provide an accurate snapshot of computing trends. When bundled with software application lab manuals, students are given a complete representation of the fundamental issues surrounding the personal computing environment.

Select features of these texts include:

- **Using Technology**—Engaging coverage of hot, high-interest topics, such as phone calls via the Internet, using the Internet remotely with a Personal Digital Assistant (PDA), and Client and Server operating systems. These Web-related projects direct the student to explore current popular uses of technology.

- **Expanding Your Knowledge**—Geared for those who want to go into greater depth on a specific topic introduced within the chapter. These projects meet the needs of instructors wanting more technical depth of coverage.

- **Building Your Portfolio**—Develops critical thinking and writing skills while students examine security, privacy, and ethical issues in technology. By completing these exercises, students will be able to walk away from the class with something to show prospective employers.

- **Making IT Work for You**—Based on student surveys, *Computing Essentials* identified several special interest topics and devoted a two-page section on each in the corresponding chapter. Making IT Work for You sections engage students by presenting high interest topics that directly relate to the concepts presented in the chapter. Topics include downloading music from the Internet, creating personal Web sites, and using the Internet to make long-distance phone calls. Many of these are supported by short video presentations that will be available via CD and the Web.

- **On the Web Explorations**—Appear throughout the margins of the text and encourage students to go to the Web to visit several informative and established sites in order to learn more about the chapter's featured topic.

- **A Look to the Future Sections**—Provide insightful information about the future impact of technology and forecasts of how upcoming enhancements in the world of computing will play an important and powerful role in society.

- **End-of-Chapter Material**—A variety of material including objective questions (key terms, matching, multiple choice, and short answer completion) and critical thinking activities. This will help to reinforce the information just learned.

STUDENT'S GUIDE

As you begin each lab, take a few moments to read the **Case Study** and the Concept Preview. The case study introduces a real-life setting that is interwoven throughout the entire lab, providing the basis for understanding the use of the application. Also, notice the Additional Information, Having Trouble?, and Another Method boxes scattered throughout the book. These tips provide more information about related topics, help get you out of trouble if you are having problems, and offer suggestions on other ways to perform the same task. Finally, read the text between the steps. You will find the few minutes more it takes you is well worth the time when you are completing the practice exercises.

Many learning aids are built into the text to ensure your success with the material and to make the process of learning rewarding. The pages that follow call your attention to the key features in the text.

Objectives
Appear at the beginning of the lab and identify the main features you will be learning.

Case Study
Introduces a real-life setting that is interwoven throughout the lab, providing the basis for understanding the use of the application.

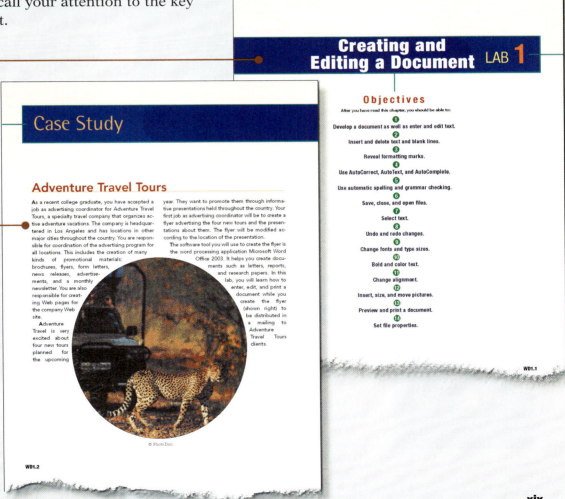

Creating and Editing a Document LAB 1

Objectives
After you have read this chapter, you should be able to:

1. Develop a document as well as enter and edit text.
2. Insert and delete text and blank lines.
3. Reveal formatting marks.
4. Use AutoCorrect, AutoText, and AutoComplete.
5. Use automatic spelling and grammar checking.
6. Save, close, and open files.
7. Select text.
8. Undo and redo changes.
9. Change fonts and type sizes.
10. Bold and color text.
11. Change alignment.
12. Insert, size, and move pictures.
13. Preview and print a document.
14. Set file properties.

WD1.1

Case Study

Adventure Travel Tours

As a recent college graduate, you have accepted a job as advertising coordinator for Adventure Travel Tours, a specialty travel company that organizes active adventure vacations. The company is headquartered in Los Angeles and has locations in other major cities throughout the country. You are responsible for coordination of the advertising program for all locations. This includes the creation of many kinds of promotional materials: brochures, flyers, form letters, news releases, advertisements, and a monthly newsletter. You are also responsible for creating Web pages for the company Web site.

Adventure Travel is very excited about four new tours planned for the upcoming year. They want to promote them through informative presentations held throughout the country. Your first job as advertising coordinator will be to create a flyer advertising the four new tours and the presentations about them. The flyer will be modified according to the location of the presentation.

The software tool you will use to create the flyer is the word processing application Microsoft Word Office 2003. It helps you create documents such as letters, reports, and research papers. In this lab, you will learn how to enter, edit, and print a document while you create the flyer (shown right) to be distributed in a mailing to Adventure Travel Tours clients.

© Photo Disc

WD1.2

xix

• Objectives, Case Study
• Concept Preview, Another Method, Having Trouble?

Concept Preview
Provides an overview to the concepts that will be presented throughout the lab.

Concept Preview
The following concepts will be introduced in this lab:

1. **Grammar Checker** The grammar checker advises you of incorrect grammar as you create and edit a document, and proposes possible corrections.
2. **AutoText and AutoComplete** The AutoText and AutoComplete features make entering text easier by providing shortcuts for entering commonly used text
3. **Spelling Checker** The spelling checker advises you of misspelled words as you create and edit a document, and proposes possible corrections.
4. **AutoCorrect** The AutoCorrect feature makes some basic assumptions about the text you are typing and, based on these assumptions, automatically corrects the entry.
5. **Word Wrap** The word wrap feature automatically decides where to end a line and wrap text to the next line based on the margin settings.
6. **Font and Font Size** A font, also commonly referred to as a typeface, is a set of characters with a specific design that has one or more font sizes.
7. **Alignment** Alignment is the positioning of text on a line between the margins or indents. There are four types of paragraph alignment: left, centered, right, and justified.
8. **Graphics** A graphic is a non-text element added to a document.

Introducing

Adventure Travel all locations acros the latest version You are very exci help you create flyers and newslet

Starting Office W

You will use the Word, to create a

Another Method
Offers additional ways to perform a procedure.

margins. The vertical ruler shows the entire page length is 11 inches with 1 inch top and bottom margins, leaving 9 inches of text space.
You will use Normal view at the standard zoom percentage of 100 percent to create the flyer about this year's new tours.

2.
- Open the Zoom drop-down menu and return the zoom percent to 100% for Print Layout view.
- Click 🔲 to switch back to Normal view.

Another Method
The voice command equivalent is "Normal view."

Your screen should be similar to Figure 1.5

Figure 1.5

2.
- Press ←Enter 2 times.
- Press Delete to remove the space at the beginning of the line.
- Press ↓.

Your screen should be similar to Figure 1.12

Figure 1.12

Having Trouble
Helps resolve potential problems as you work through each lab.

Having Trouble?
If the green underline is not displayed, choose Tools/Options, open the Spelling & Grammar tab, and select the "Check spelling as you type" and "Check Grammar as you type" options.

The insertion point is positioned at the beginning of the blank line. As you continue to create a document, the formatting marks are automatically inserted and deleted. Notice that a green wavy underline appears under the word "four." This indicates an error has been detected.

Identifying and Correcting Errors Automatically

As you enter text, Word is constantly checking the document for spelling and grammar errors. The Spelling and Grammar Status icon in the status bar displays an animated pencil icon while you are typing, indicating Word is checking for errors as you type. When you stop typing, it displays either a red

Numbered and Bulleted Steps, Additional Information

Numbered and Bulleted Steps

Provide clear Step-by-Step Instructions on how to complete a task, or series of tasks.

Additional Information

Offers brief asides with expanded coverage of content.

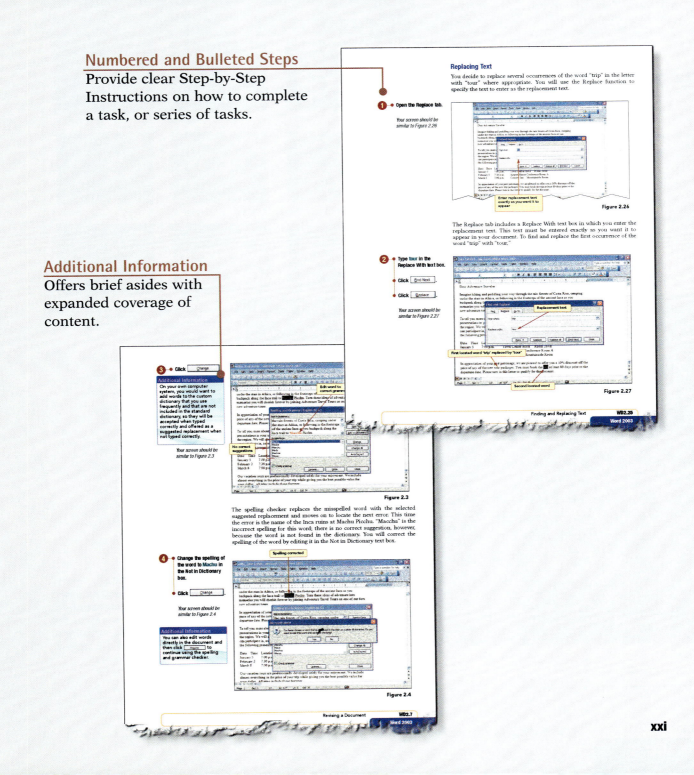

• Figures and Callouts, Tables

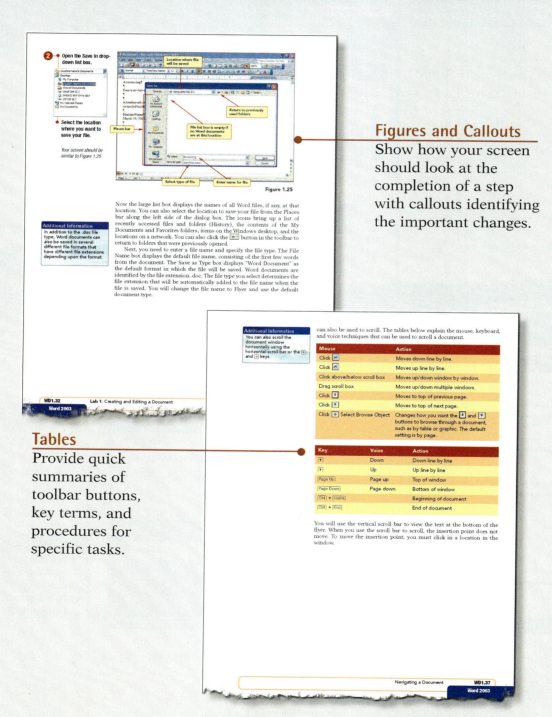

Figures and Callouts

Show how your screen should look at the completion of a step with callouts identifying the important changes.

Tables

Provide quick summaries of toolbar buttons, key terms, and procedures for specific tasks.

Focus on Careers, Concept Summary

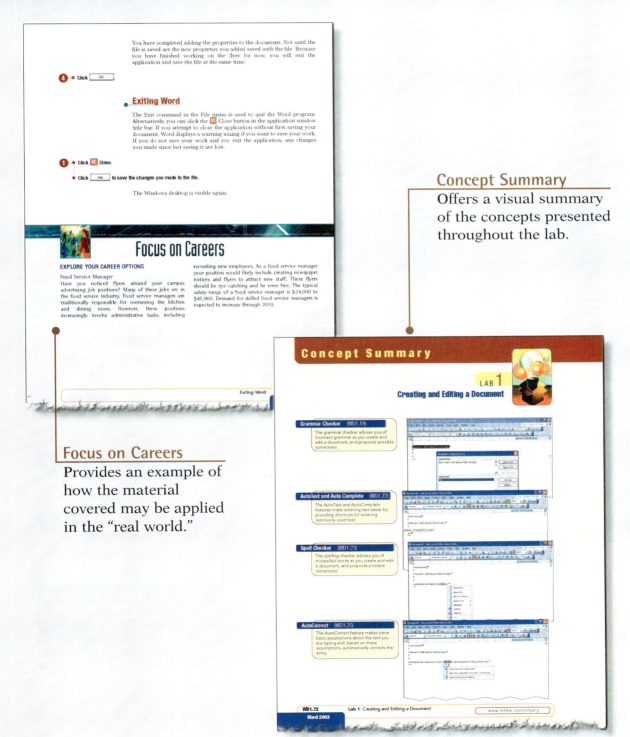

Concept Summary
Offers a visual summary of the concepts presented throughout the lab.

Focus on Careers
Provides an example of how the material covered may be applied in the "real world."

Key Terms and MOS Skills, Command Summary

Key Terms and MOS Skills

Includes a list of all bolded terms with page references and a table showing the MOS certification skills that were covered in the lab.

Command Summary

Provides a table of commands and keyboard and toolbar shortcuts for all commands used in the lab.

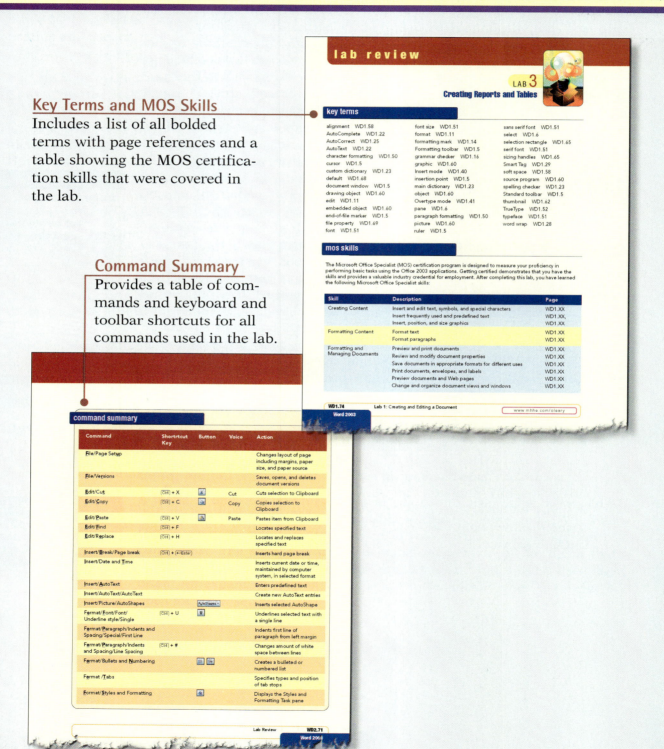

Lab Exercises: Screen Identification, Matching, Multiple Choice, True/False, Fill-in

Lab Exercises

Reinforce the terminology and concepts presented in the lab through Screen Identification, Matching, Multiple Choice, True/False, and Fill-in questions.

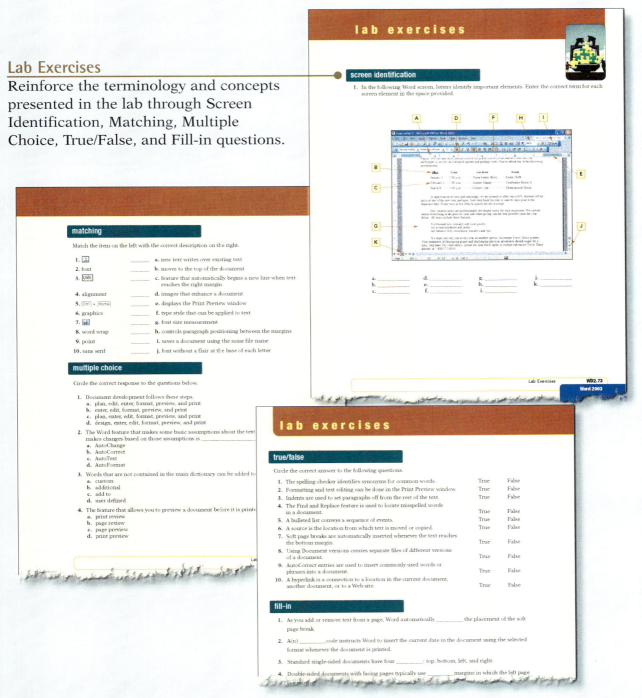

Lab Exercises: Step-by-Step, On Your Own

Lab Exercises

Provide hands-on practice and develop critical thinking skills through step-by-step and on-your-own practice exercises. These exercises have a rating system from easy to difficult and test your ability to apply the knowledge you have gained in each lab. Exercises that build off of previous exercises are noted with a ▶ Continuing Exercise icon.

On Your Own

---

lab exercises

rating system
★ Easy
★★ Moderate
★★★ Difficult

step-by-step

Writing a Memo ★

1. Adventure Travel Tours is planning to update its World Wide Web site in the near future. You have been asked to solicit suggestions from the travel agents about changes they would like to see made to the current Web site. You decide to send all the travel agents a memo asking them for their input. Your completed memo is shown here.

   a. Open a blank Word document and create the following memo in Normal view. Press [Tab] twice after you type colons (:) in the To, From, and Date lines. This will make the information following the colons line up evenly. Enter a blank line between paragraphs.

      To: Travel Agents
      From: Student Name
      Date: [Current date]

   Next month we plan to begin work on updating the current Adventure Travel Tours Web site. In preparation for this project, I would like your input about the current Web site. In the next few days as you use the Web site, pay attention to such things as the layout, colors, and content. Then send your comments back to me about both the positive and negative features of the current Web site and suggestions for changes you would like to see made in the new Web site.

   Thank you in advance for your input.

   [memo preview shown:]
   To: Travel Agents
   From: Student Name
   Date: [Current date]
   RE: Web Site Revision

   Next month we plan to begin work on updating the Adventure Travel Tours Web site. In preparation for this project, I would like your input about the Web site.

   In the next few days as you use the Web site, pay attention to the layout, colors, ease of use, and content. Then send your comments back to me about both the positive and negative features of the current Web site and suggestions for changes you would like to see made in the new Web site.

   Thank you in advance for your input.

   b. Turn on the display of formatting marks.
   c. Correct any spelling and grammar errors that are identified.
   d. Delete the word "current" from the first and second sentences. Delete the phrase "such things ... third sentence. Insert the text "ease of use," after the word "colors," in the third ... paragraph beginning with the third sentence. Include a blank line between ... t size for the entire memo to 14 pt and the alignment of the body of the memo to ... line insert the AutoText reference line "RE:".

---

p. Increase the font size of the line above "Roast Coffee" to 18 pt. Reset its line spacing to single. Insert a blank line below it.

q. Copy the remaining paragraph from the wd02_Coffee Flyer document, and insert it at the bottom of the new document. Include two blank lines between the table and the paragraph.

r. Bold and center the final paragraph. Remove the hyperlink format from the URL. Format the URL as italic, bold, and red.

s. Increase the top, left, and right margins to 1.5 inches.

t. Create the Explosion 1 AutoShape from Stars and Banners. Enter and center the word **Sale!** in red within it, and choose the gold fill color. Size the shape appropriately. Move the shape to the top left corner of the document. Delete the drawing canvas.

u. Add your name and a field with the current date several lines below the final paragraph.

v. Save the document as Coffee Flyer2. Preview and print it.

on your own

Requesting a Reference ★

1. Your first year as a biology major is going well and you are looking for a summer internship with a local research lab. You have an upcoming interview and want to come prepared with a letter of reference from your last position. Write a business letter directed to your old supervisor, Rachel McVey, at your former lab, AMT Research. Use the modified block letter style shown in the lab. Be sure to include the date, a salutation, two paragraphs, a closing, and your name as a signature. Spell-check the document, save the document as Reference Letter, and print it.

Long Distance Rates Survey ★

2. American Consumer Advocates conducted a survey in October, 2002 comparing the costs of long distance rates. Create a tabbed table using the information shown below. Bold and underline the column heads. Add style 2 tab leaders to the table entries. Above the table, write a paragraph explaining the table contents.

Company	Per Minute	Monthly Fee	Customer Service Wait
Zone LD	3.5¢	$2.00	Less than 1 minute
Pioneer Telephone	3.9¢	none	1 minute
Capsule	3.9¢	none	17 minutes
ECG	4.5¢	$1.99	5 minutes
IsTerra	4.9¢	none	10 minutes

Include your name and the date below the table. Save the document as Phone Rates and print the document.

Lab Exercises	WD2.85

Word 2003

Microsoft® Office Word 2003

Brief Edition

Introduction to Microsoft Office 2003

Objectives

After completing the Introduction to Microsoft Office 2003, you should be able to:

1 Describe Office System 2003.

2 Describe the Office 2003 applications.

3 Start an Office 2003 application.

4 Recognize the basic application window features.

5 Use menus, shortcut menus, and shortcut keys.

6 Use toolbars and task panes.

7 Use Office Help.

8 Exit an Office 2003 application.

What Is Microsoft Office System 2003?

Microsoft Office System 2003 is a comprehensive, integrated system of programs, servers and services designed to solve a wide array of business needs. Although the programs can be used individually, they are designed to work together seamlessly making it easy to connect people and organizations to information, business processes and each other. The applications include tools used to create, discuss, communicate, and manage projects. If you share a lot of documents with other people, these features facilitate access to common documents. This version has expanded and refined the communication and collaboration features and integration with the World Wide Web. In addition, several new interface features are designed to make it easier to perform tasks and help users take advantage of all the features in the applications.

The Microsoft Office System 2003 is packaged in different combinations of components. The major components and a brief description are provided in the following table.

Component	Description
Microsoft Office 2003	
Office Word 2003	Word Processor
Office Excel 2003	Spreadsheet
Office Access 2003	Database manager
Office PowerPoint 2003	Presentation graphics
Office Outlook 2003	Desktop information manager
Office FrontPage 2003	Web site creation and management
Office InfoPath 2003	Creates XML forms and documents
Office OneNote 2003	Note-taking
Office Publisher 2003	Desktop publishing
Office Visio 2003	Drawing and diagramming
Office SharePoint Portal Server v2.0 and Services	

The five components of Microsoft Office 2003—Word, Excel, Access, PowerPoint, and Outlook—are the applications you will learn about in this series of labs. They are described in more detail in the following sections.

Office Word 2003

Office Word 2003 is a word processing software application whose purpose is to help you create text-based documents. Word processors are one of the most flexible and widely used application software programs. A word processor can be used to manipulate text data to produce a letter, a report, a memo, an e-mail message, or any other type of correspondence.

Two documents you will produce in the first two Word labs, a letter and flyer, are shown here.

A letter containing a tabbed table, indented paragraphs, and text enhancements is quickly created using basic Word features.

March 25, 2005

Dear Adventure Traveler:

Imagine hiking and paddling your way through the rain forests of Costa Rica, camping under the stars in Africa, or following in the footsteps of the ancient Inca as you backpack along the Inca trail to Machu Picchu. Turn these dreams of adventure into memories you will cherish forever by joining Adventure Travel Tours on one of our four new adventure tours.

To tell you more about these exciting new adventures, we are offering several presentations in your area. These presentations will focus on the features and cultures of the region. We will also show you pictures of the places you will visit and activities you can participate in, as well as a detailed agenda and package costs. Plan to attend one of the following presentations:

Date	Time
January 5	7:00 p.m.
February 3	7:30 p.m.
March 8	7:00 p.m.

In appreciation of your past patr[...]
price of any of the new tour packages. [...]
departure date. Please turn in this letter t[...]

Our vacation tours are profession[...]
almost everything in the price of your t[...]
dollar. All tours include these features:

- **Professional tour manager and** [...]
- **All accommodations and meal**[...]
- **All entrance fees, excursions, t**[...]

We hope you will join us this ye[...]
Your memories of fascinating places an[...]
long, long time. For reservations, please[...]
directly at 1-800-777-0004.

A flyer incorporating many visual enhancements such as colored text, varied text styles, and graphic elements is both eye-catching and informative.

Announcing

New Adventure Travel Tours

Attention adventure travelers! Attend an Adventure Travel presentation to learn about some of the earth's greatest unspoiled habitats and find out how you can experience the adventure of a lifetime. This year we are introducing four new tours and offering you a unique opportunity to combine many different outdoor activities while exploring the world.

India Wildlife Adventure
Inca Trail to Machu Picchu
Safari in Tanzania
Costa Rica Rivers and Rain Forests

Presentation dates and times are January 5 at 7:00 p.m., February 3 at 7:30 p.m., and March 8 at 7:00 p.m. All presentations are held at convenient hotel locations. The hotels are located in downtown Los Angeles, in Santa Clara, and at the airport.

Call 1-800-777-0004 for presentation locations, a full color brochure, and itinerary information, costs, and trip dates.

Visit our Web site at www.AdventureTravelTours.com

The beauty of a word processor is that you can make changes or corrections as you are typing. Want to change a report from single spacing to double spacing? Alter the width of the margins? Delete some paragraphs and add others from yet another document? A word processor allows you to do all these things with ease.

Word 2003 includes many group collaboration features to help streamline how documents are developed and changed by group members. You can also create and send e-mail messages directly from within Word using all its features to create and edit the message. In addition, you can send an entire document as your e-mail message, allowing the recipient to edit the document directly without having to open or save an attachment.

Word 2003 is closely integrated with the World Wide Web, detecting when you type a Web address and automatically converting it to a hyperlink. You can also create your own hyperlinks to locations within documents, or to other documents, including those at external locations such as a Web site or file server. Its many Web-editing features, including a Web Page Wizard that guides you step by step, help you quickly create a Web page.

Office Excel 2003

Office Excel 2003 is an electronic worksheet that is used to organize, manipulate, and graph numeric data. Once used almost exclusively by accountants, worksheets are now widely used by nearly every profession. Marketing professionals record and evaluate sales trends. Teachers record grades and calculate final grades. Personal trainers record the progress of their clients.

Excel includes many features that not only help you create a well-designed worksheet, but one that produces accurate results. Formatting features include visual enhancements such as varied text styles, colors, and graphics. Other features help you enter complex formulas and identify and correct formula errors. You can also produce a visual display of data in the form of graphs or charts. As the values in the worksheet change, charts referencing those values automatically adjust to reflect the changes.

Excel also includes many advanced features and tools that help you perform what-if analysis and create different scenarios. And like all Office 2003 applications, it is easy to incorporate data created in one application into another. Two worksheets you will produce in Labs 2 and 3 of Excel are shown on the next page.

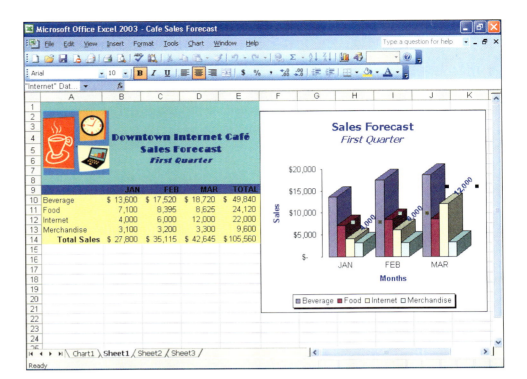

A worksheet showing the quarterly sales forecast containing a graphic, text enhancements, and a chart of the data is quickly created using basic Excel features.

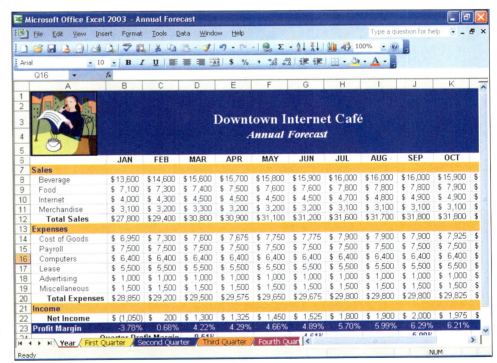

A large worksheet incorporating more complex formulas, visual enhancements such as colored text, varied text styles, and graphic elements is both informative and attractive.

You will see how easy it is to analyze data and make projections using what-if analysis and what-if graphing in Lab 3 and to incorporate Excel data in a Word document as shown in the following figures.

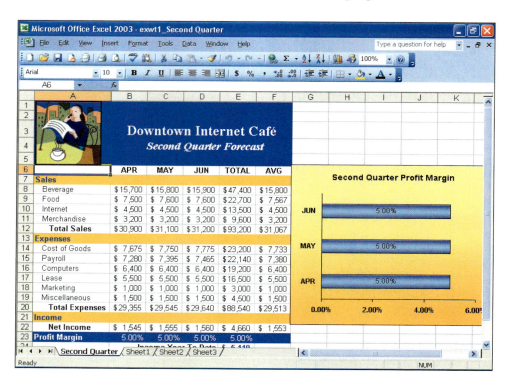

Changes you make in worksheet data while performing what-if analysis are automatically reflected in charts that reference that data.

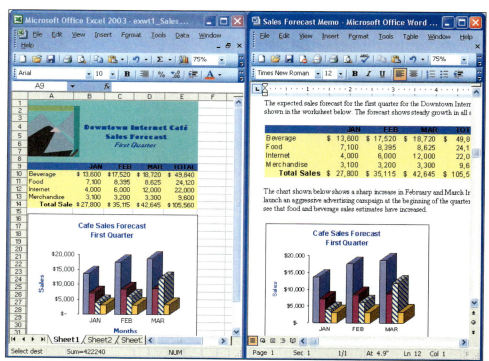

Worksheet data and charts can be copied and linked to other Office documents such as a Word document.

www.mhhe.com/oleary

Office Access 2003

Office Access 2003 is a relational database management application that is used to create and analyze a database. A database is a collection of related data. In a relational database, the most widely used database structure, data is organized in linked tables. Tables consist of columns (called fields) and rows (called records). The tables are related or linked to one another by a common field. Relational databases allow you to create smaller and more manageable database tables, since you can combine and extract data between tables.

The program provides tools to enter, edit, and retrieve data from the database as well as to analyze the database and produce reports of the output. One of the main advantages of a computerized database is the ability to quickly add, delete, and locate specific records. Records can also be easily rearranged or sorted according to different fields of data, resulting in multiple table arrangements that provide more meaningful information for different purposes. Creation of forms makes it easier to enter and edit data as well. In the Access labs you will create and organize the database table shown below.

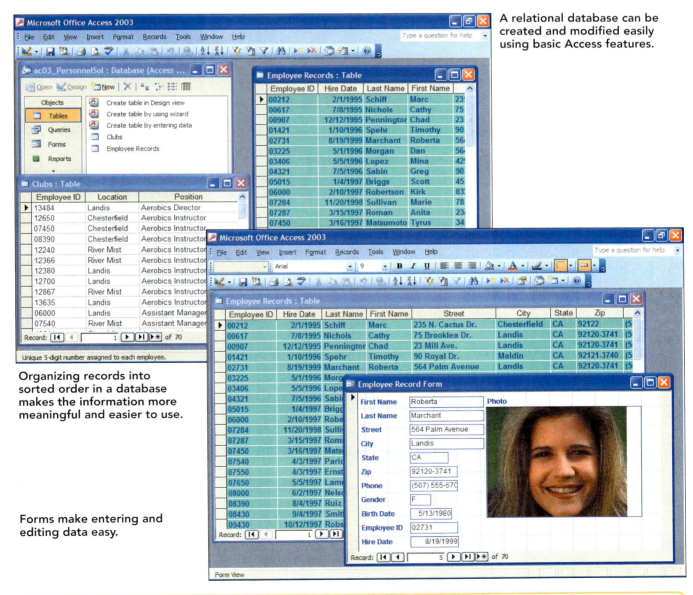

A relational database can be created and modified easily using basic Access features.

Organizing records into sorted order in a database makes the information more meaningful and easier to use.

Forms make entering and editing data easy.

Another feature is the ability to analyze the data in a table and perform calculations on different fields of data. Additionally, you can ask questions or query the table to find only certain records that meet specific conditions to be used in the analysis. Information that was once costly and time-consuming to get is now quickly and readily available. This information can then be quickly printed out in the form of reports ranging from simple listings to complex, professional-looking reports in different layout styles, or with titles, headings, subtotals, or totals.

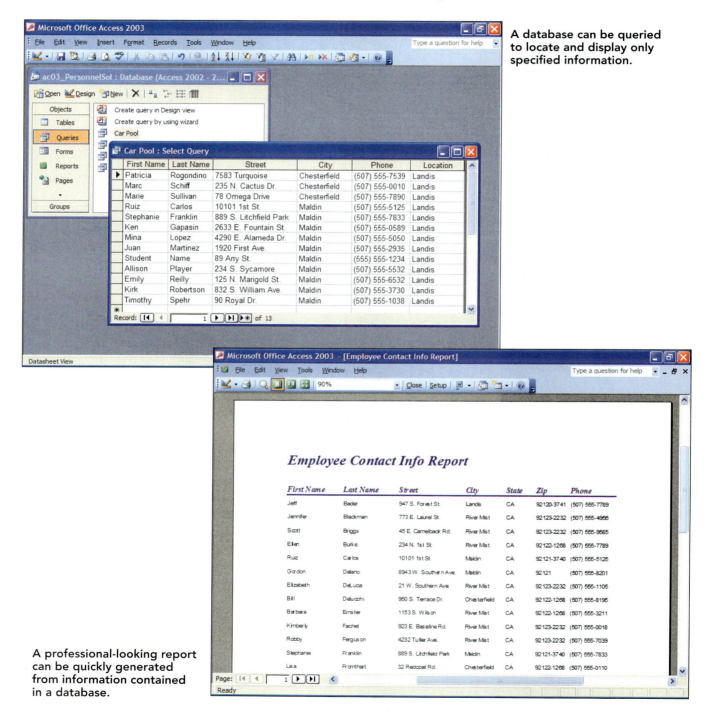

A database can be queried to locate and display only specified information.

A professional-looking report can be quickly generated from information contained in a database.

Office PowerPoint 2003

Office PowerPoint 2003 is a graphics presentation program designed to help you produce a high-quality presentation that is both interesting to the audience and effective in its ability to convey your message. A presentation can be as simple as overhead transparencies or as sophisticated as an on-screen electronic display. In the first two PowerPoint labs you will create and organize the presentation shown on the next page.

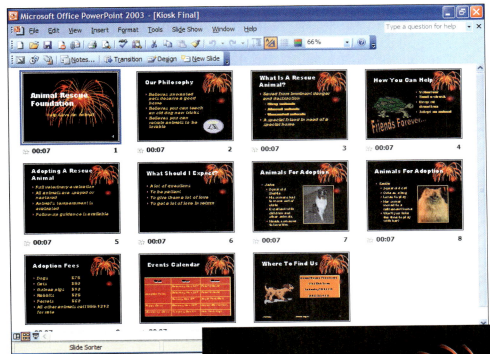

A presentation consists of a series of pages or "slides" presenting the information you want to convey in an organized and attractive manner.

When running an onscreen presentation, each slide of the presentation is displayed full-screen on your computer monitor or projected onto a screen.

Office Outlook 2003

Office Outlook 2003 is a personal information manager (PIM) program that is designed to get you organized and keep you organized. PIMs, also known as desktop managers, are designed to maximize your personal productivity by making it efficient and easy to perform everyday tasks such as scheduling meetings, recording contact information, and communicating with others, to name a few. Outlook 2003 includes an integrated e-mail program, a calendar, and contact and task management features.

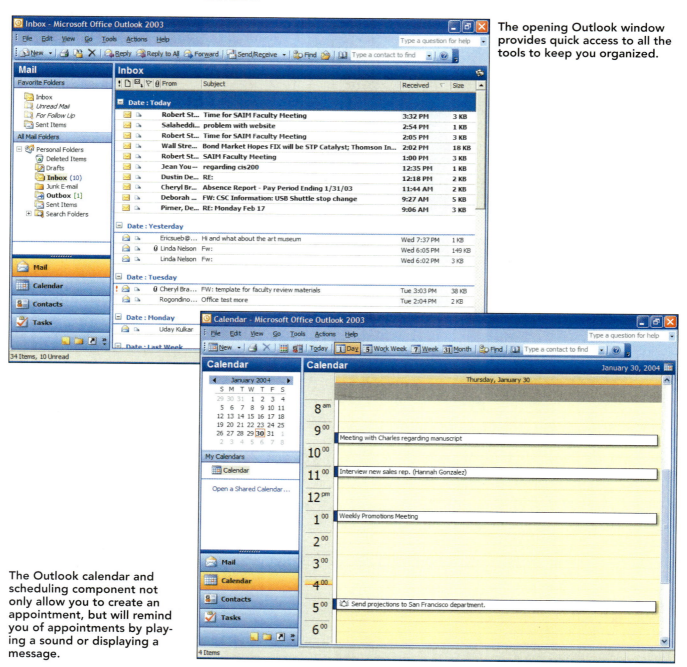

The opening Outlook window provides quick access to all the tools to keep you organized.

The Outlook calendar and scheduling component not only allow you to create an appointment, but will remind you of appointments by playing a sound or displaying a message.

Common Office 2003 Features

Additional Information

Please read the Before You Begin and Instructional Conventions sections in the Overview to Office Word 2003 (WDO.1) before starting this section.

Additional Information

It is assumed that you are already familiar with basic Windows operating system features. To review these features, refer to your Windows text or if available, the O'Leary Series *Introduction to Windows* text.

Now that you know a little about each of the applications in Microsoft Office 2003, we will take a look at some of the features that are common to all Office 2003 applications. This is a hands-on section that will introduce you to the features and allow you to get a feel for how Office 2003 works. Although Word 2003 will be used to demonstrate how the features work, only common features will be addressed. These features include using menus, Office Help, task panes, toolbars, and starting and exiting an application. The features that are specific to each application will be introduced individually in each application text.

Starting an Office 2003 Application

There are several ways to start an Office 2003 application. The two most common methods are by using the Start menu or by clicking a desktop shortcut for the program if it is available. If you use the Start menu, the steps will vary slightly depending on the version of Windows you are using.

1 ● Click **start** to display the Start menu.

● Select All Programs.

Having Trouble?

If you are using Windows 2002 or earlier, select Programs.

● Select
  Microsoft Office ▶.

● Choose
  Microsoft Office Word 2003 .

OR

1 ● Double-click the shortcut on the desktop.

2 ● If necessary, click ▢ Maximize in the title bar to maximize the window.

Additional Information

Your window may appear with olive green or silver colors, depending upon the Windows settings on your computer.

Your screen should be similar to Figure 1

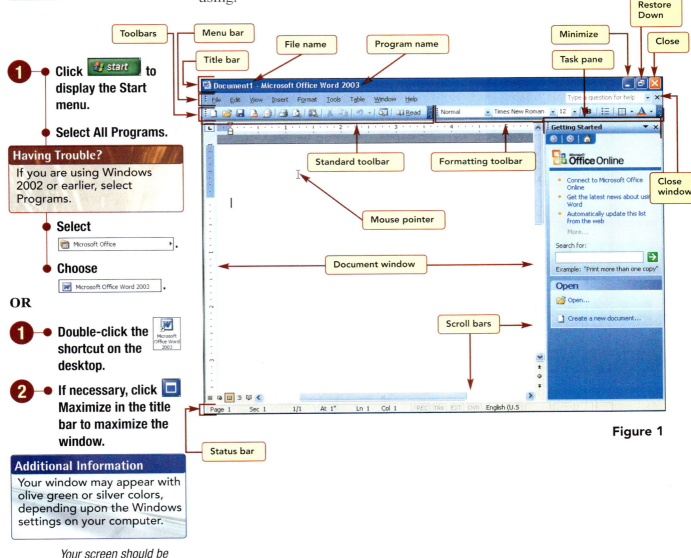

Figure 1

The Word program is started and displayed in a window on the desktop. The left end of the application window title bar displays the file name followed by the program name, Microsoft Office Word 2003. The right end of the title bar displays the ▬ Minimize, ▣ Restore Down, and ✖ Close buttons. They perform the same functions and operate in the same way as all Windows versions.

The **menu bar** below the title bar displays the application's program menu. The right end displays the document window's ✖ Close Window button. As you use the Office applications, you will see that the menu bar contains many of the same menus, such as File, Edit, and Help. You will also see several menus that are specific to each application.

The **toolbars** located below the menu bar contain buttons that are mouse shortcuts for many of the menu items. Commonly, the Office applications will display two toolbars when the application is first opened: Standard and Formatting. They may appear together on one row (as in Figure 1), or on separate rows.

The large center area of the program window is the **document window** where open application files are displayed. Currently, there is a blank Word document open. In Word, the mouse pointer appears as I when positioned in the document window and as a ⫽ when it can be used to select items. The **task pane** is displayed on the right side of the document window. Task panes provide quick access to features as you are using the application. As you perform certain actions, different task panes automatically open. In this case, since you just started an application, the Getting Started task pane is automatically displayed, providing different ways to create a new document or open an existing document.

The **status bar** at the bottom of the window displays location information and the status of different settings as they are used. Different information is displayed in the status bar for different applications.

On the right and bottom of the document window, are vertical and horizontal scroll bars. A **scroll bar** is used with a mouse to bring additional lines of information into view in a window. The vertical scroll bar is used to move up or down, and the horizontal scroll bar moves side to side in the window.

As you can see, many of the features in the Word window are the same as in other Windows applications. The common user interface makes learning and using new applications much easier.

Using Menus

A menu is one of many methods you can use to accomplish a task in a program. When opened, a menu displays a list of commands. When an Office program menu is first opened, it may display a short version of commands. The short menu is a personalized version of the menu that displays basic and frequently used commands and hides those used less often. An expanded version will display automatically after the menu is open for a few seconds.

1 **Click File to open the File menu.**

Point to each menu in the menu bar to see the full menu for each.

Point to the View menu.

Your screen should be similar to Figure 2

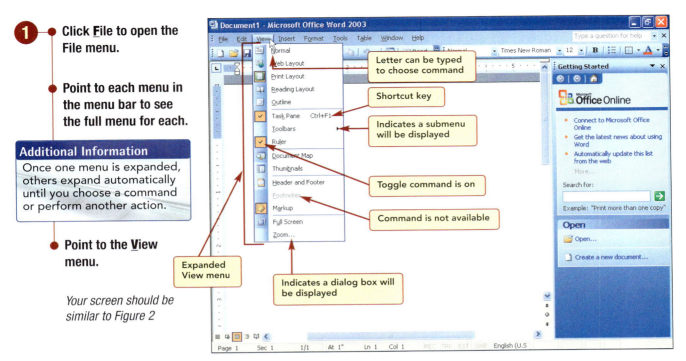

Figure 2

Many commands have images next to them so you can quickly associate the command with the image. The same image appears on the toolbar button for that feature. Menus may include the following features (not all menus include all features):

Feature	Meaning
Ellipsis (…)	Indicates a dialog box will be displayed.
▶	Indicates a submenu will be displayed.
Dimmed	Indicates the command is not available for selection until certain other conditions are met.
Shortcut key	A key or key combination that can be used to execute a command without using the menu.
Checkmark	Indicates a toggle type of command. Selecting it turns the feature on or off. A checkmark indicates the feature is on.
Underlined letter	Indicates the letter you can type to choose the command.

On the View menu, two options, Task Pane and Ruler, are checked, indicating these features are on. The Task Pane option also displays the shortcut key combination, Ctrl + F1, after the option. This indicates the command can be chosen by pressing the keys instead of using the menu. The Footnotes option is dimmed because it is not currently available. The Toolbars option will display a submenu when selected, and the Zoom command a dialog box of additional options.

Once a menu is open, you can select a command from the menu by pointing to it. A colored highlight bar, called the **selection cursor**, appears over the selected command.

2 ● **Point to the Toolbars command to select it and display the submenu.**

Your screen should be similar to Figure 3

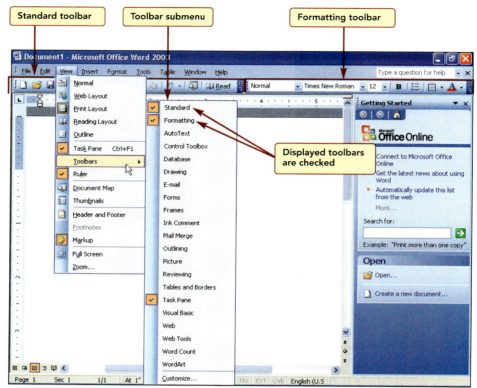

Figure 3

Currently there are three selected (checked) Toolbar options: Standard, Formatting, and although not technically a toolbar, the Task Pane. If other toolbars are selected in your menu, this is because once a toolbar has been turned on, it remains on until turned off.

To choose a command, you click on it. When the command is chosen, the associated action is performed. You will close the task pane and any other open toolbars and display the Drawing toolbar.

3 ● Click on Task Pane to turn off this feature.

● Open the View menu again, select Toolbars, and if it is not already selected, click on the Drawing toolbar option to turn it on.

● If necessary, choose View/Toolbars again and deselect any other toolbar options (there should be 3 selected toolbar options).

Your screen should be similar to Figure 4

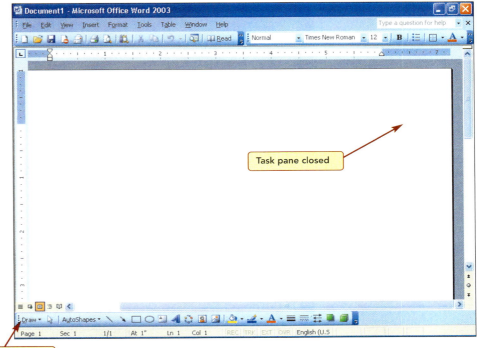

Figure 4

Drawing toolbar displayed

Additional Information

If you have a microphone and have installed and trained the Speech Recognition feature, you can speak the command sequences to open menus and choose commands. For example, to open a toolbar, you would say "View Toolbars."

Additional Information

Using voice commands, saying "Right click" will open the shortcut menu for the selected item.

The task pane is closed and the Drawing toolbar is displayed above the status bar. Any other toolbars that were open which you deselected are closed.

Using Shortcut Menus

Another way to access menu options is to use the **shortcut menu**. The shortcut menu is opened by right-clicking on an item on the screen. This menu displays only those options associated with the item. For example, right-clicking on any toolbar will display the toolbar menu options only. You will use this method to hide the Drawing toolbar again.

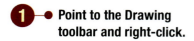

1 ● **Point to the Drawing toolbar and right-click.**

Your screen should be similar to Figure 5

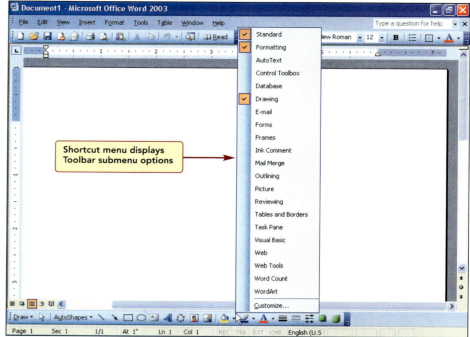

Shortcut menu displays Toolbar submenu options

Figure 5

The shortcut menu displays only the Toolbar submenu options on the View menu. Using a shortcut menu saves time over selecting the main menu command sequence.

2 ● **Choose Drawing to turn off this feature.**

Your screen should be similar to Figure 6

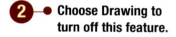

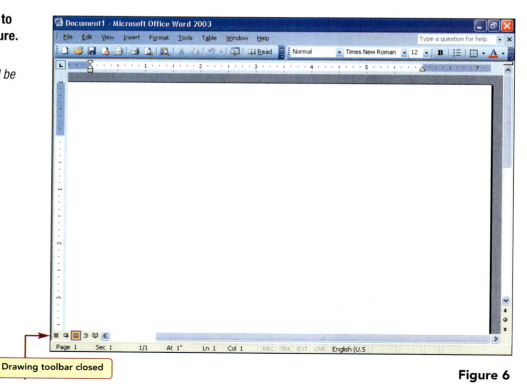

Drawing toolbar closed

Figure 6

The Drawing toolbar is no longer displayed.

Using Shortcut Keys

A third way to perform a command is to use the shortcut key or key combination associated with a particular command. If you will recall, the shortcut key associated with the **V**iew/Tas**k** Pane command is $\boxed{\text{Ctrl}} + \boxed{\text{F1}}$. To use the key combination, you hold down the first key while pressing the second.

Additional Information

Not all commands have shortcut keys.

1 ● Hold down $\boxed{\text{Ctrl}}$ and press the $\boxed{\text{F1}}$ function key.

Having Trouble?

Function keys are located above the numeric keys on the keyboard.

Your screen should be similar to Figure 7

Additional Information

Using the Speech Recognition feature, you can also use voice shortcuts for many commands. For example, to show the task pane, you would say "show task pane." Many voice commands also have several different words you can say to initiate the command. You could also say "task pane" or "view task pane."

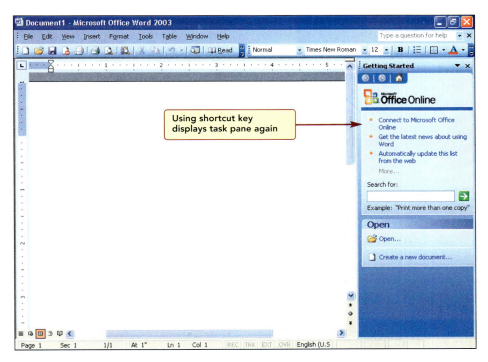

Using shortcut key displays task pane again

Figure 7

The task pane is displayed again. Using shortcut keys is the quickest way to perform many actions; however, you need to remember the key combination in order to use it.

Using Toolbars

Initially, Word displays two toolbars, Standard and Formatting, below the menu bar (see Figure 3). The **Standard toolbar** contains buttons that are used to complete the most frequently used menu commands. The **Formatting toolbar** contains buttons that are used to change the appearance or format of the document. There are many features that can be used to make working with toolbars easier.

Displaying Toolbars on Separate Rows

The default toolbar arrangement is to display both toolbars on one row. Because there is not enough space to display all the buttons on both toolbars on a single row, many buttons are hidden. The Toolbar Options button located at the end of a toolbar displays a drop-down button list of those buttons that are not displayed. Toolbars initially display the basic buttons. Like menus, they are personalized automatically, displaying those buttons you use frequently and hiding others. When you use a button from this list, it then is moved to the toolbar, and a button that has not been used recently is moved to the Toolbar Options list. It also contains an option to display the toolbars on separate rows. You will use this option to quickly see all the toolbar buttons.

1 ● Click 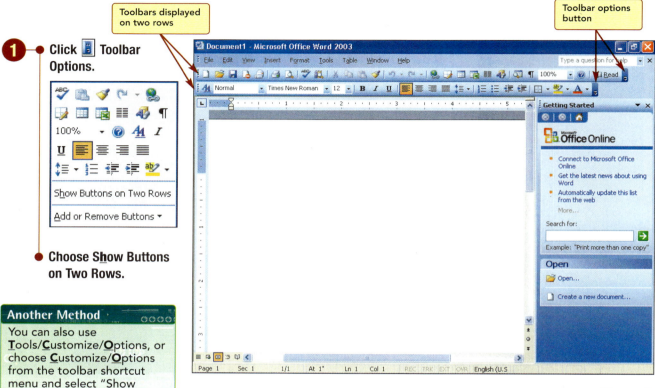 **Toolbar Options.**

● **Choose Show Buttons on Two Rows.**

Another Method

You can also use **T**ools/**C**ustomize/**O**ptions, or choose **C**ustomize/**O**ptions from the toolbar shortcut menu and select "Show Standard and Formatting toolbars on two rows."

Your screen should be similar to Figure 8

Additional Information

The Add or Remove Buttons option allows you to customize existing toolbars by selecting those buttons you want to display and by creating your own customized toolbars.

Toolbars displayed on two rows

Toolbar options button

Figure 8

The two toolbars now occupy separate rows, providing enough space for all the buttons to be displayed. Now using 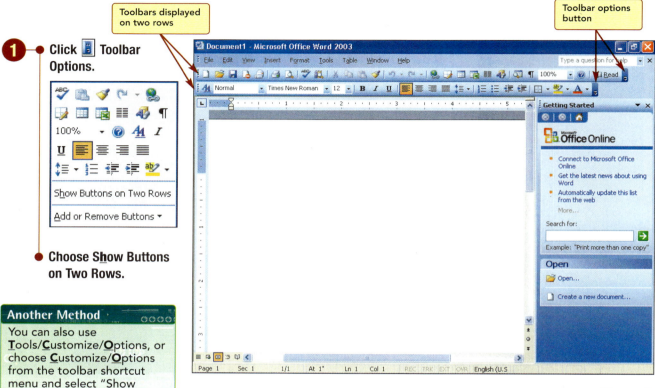 Toolbar Options is no longer necessary, and when selected only displays the options to return the toolbars display to one row and the Add or Remove Buttons option.

When a toolbar is open, it may appear docked or floating. A **docked toolbar** is fixed to an edge of the window and displays a vertical bar, called the move handle, on the left edge of the toolbar. Dragging this bar up or down allows you to move the toolbar. If multiple toolbars share the same row, dragging the bar left or right adjusts the size of the toolbar. If docked, a toolbar can occupy a row by itself, or several can be on a row together. A **floating toolbar** appears in a separate window and can be moved anywhere on the desktop.

2 Point to the move handle of the Standard toolbar and, when the mouse pointer appears as ✛, drag the toolbar into the document window.

Your screen should be similar to Figure 9

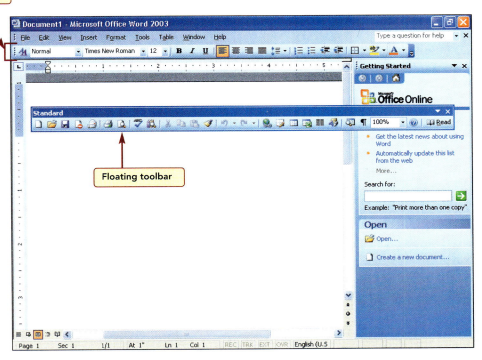

Floating toolbar

Figure 9

The Standard toolbar is now a floating toolbar and can be moved to any location in the window by dragging the title bar. If you move a floating toolbar to the edge of the window, it will attach to that location and become a docked toolbar. A floating toolbar can also be sized by dragging the edge of toolbar.

3 Drag the title bar of the floating toolbar (the mouse pointer appears as ✛) to move the toolbar to the row below the Formatting toolbar.

Move the Formatting toolbar below the Standard toolbar.

Align both toolbars with the left edge of the window by dragging the move handle horizontally.

Your screen should be similar to Figure 10

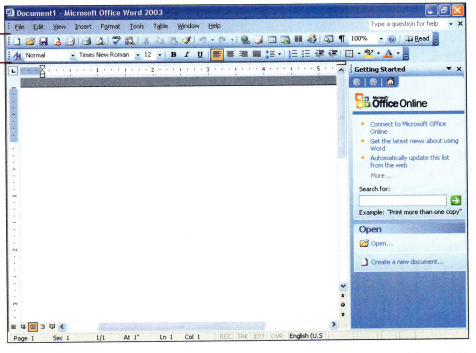

Figure 10

The two toolbars again occupy two rows. To quickly identify the toolbar buttons, you can display the button name by pointing to the button.

4 ● **Point to any button on the Standard toolbar.**

Your screen should be similar to Figure 11

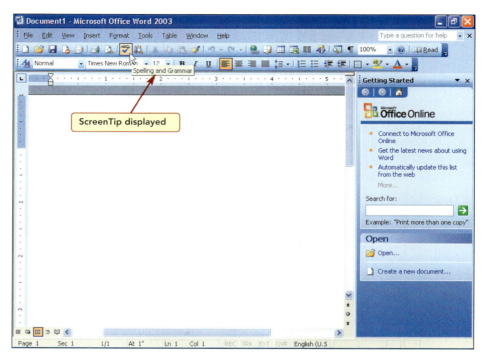

ScreenTip displayed

Figure 11

A ScreenTip containing the button name appears next to the mouse pointer. Clicking on a button will perform the associated action. You will use the 🔘 Help button to access Microsoft Word Help.

5 ● **Click** 🔘 **Microsoft Office Word Help.**

Another Method

You can also choose **H**elp/ Microsoft Office Word **H**elp, or press F1 to access Help.

Your screen should be similar to Figure 12

Accesses Word Help

Click title bar to open task pane menu

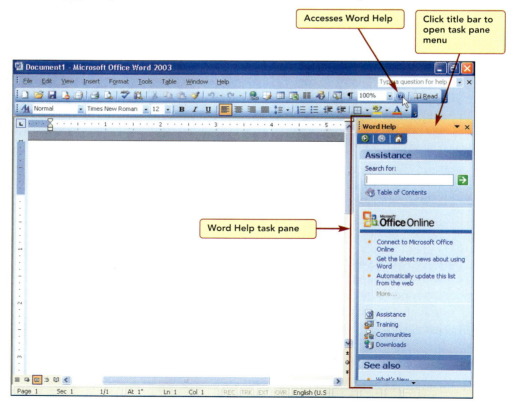

Word Help task pane

Figure 12

The Getting Started task pane is replaced by the Microsoft Word Help task pane. The name of the task pane appears in the task pane title bar.

Using Task Panes

Task panes appear automatically when certain features are used. They can also be opened manually from the task pane menu. Clicking the task pane title bar displays a drop-down menu of other task panes you can select. In Word there are 14 different task panes. You will redisplay the Getting Started task pane. Then you will quickly return to the previously displayed task pane using the 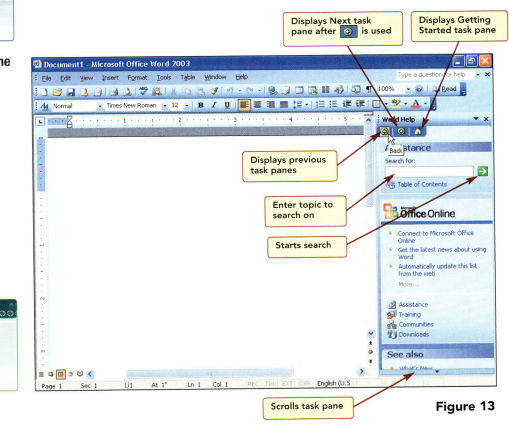 Back toolbar button in the task pane.

1 • **Click on the task pane title bar.**

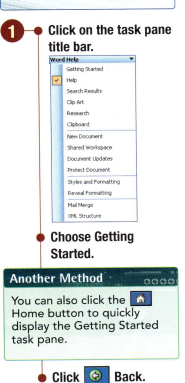

• **Choose Getting Started.**

• **Click** ⬅ **Back.**

Your screen should be similar to Figure 13

Displays Next task pane after ⬅ is used

Displays Getting Started task pane

Displays previous task panes

Enter topic to search on

Starts search

Scrolls task pane

Figure 13

The Help task pane is displayed again. Likewise, clicking the ➡ Forward button will display the task pane that was viewed before using ⬅ Back.

Using Office Help

There are several ways you can get help. One method is to conduct a search of the available help information by entering a sentence or question you want help on in the Search text box of the Help task pane. Notice the insertion point is positioned in the Search text box. This indicates it is ready for you to type an entry. You will use this method to learn about getting Help while you work.

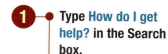

1 ● Type **How do I get help?** in the Search box.

Having Trouble?
If the insertion point is not displayed in the Search box, simply click in the box to activate it.

● Click ⟶ **Start Searching.**

Your screen should be similar to Figure 14

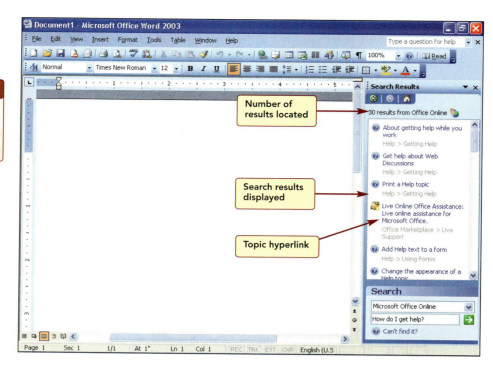

Number of results located

Search results displayed

Topic hyperlink

Figure 14

Additional Information
In addition to being connected to the Internet, the Online Content settings must be selected. Click Online Content Settings in the Help task pane and select all the options to turn on these features.

Additional Information
The number of results located and where they were found is displayed at the top of the list.

If you are connected to the Internet, the Microsoft Office Online Web site is searched and the results are displayed in the Search Results task pane. If you are not connected, the offline help information that is provided with the application and stored on your computer is searched. Generally the search results are similar, but fewer in number.

The Search Results pane displays a list of located results. The results are shown in order of relevance, with the most likely matches at the top of the list. Each result is a **hyperlink** or connection to the information located on the Online site or in Help on your computer. Clicking the hyperlink accesses and displays the information associated with the hyperlink.

You want to read the information in the topic "About getting help while you work."

2 **From the Search Results list click the "About getting help while you work" hyperlink.**

Additional Information

When you point to the hyperlink, it appears underlined and the mouse pointer appears as 🖑.

Your screen should be similar to Figure 15

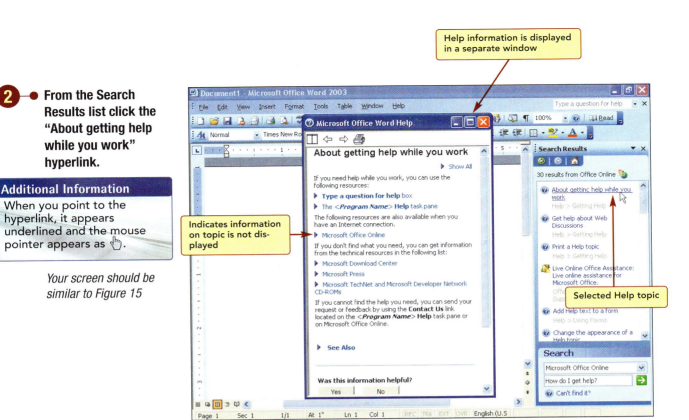

Help information is displayed in a separate window

Indicates information on topic is not displayed

Selected Help topic

Figure 15

The information on the selected topic is displayed in a separate Help window. The Help window on your screen will probably be a different size and arrangement than in Figure 15. Depending on the size of your Help window, you may need to scroll the window to see all the Help information provided. As you are reading the help topic, you will see many subtopics preceded with ▶. This indicates the information in the subtopic is not displayed. Clicking on the subtopic heading displays the information about the topic.

3 • If necessary, use the scroll bar to scroll the Help window to see the information on this topic.

• Scroll back up to the top of the window.

Additional Information

Clicking the scroll arrows scrolls the text in the window line by line, and dragging the scroll bar up or down moves to a general location within the window area.

• Click the "Type a question for help box" subtopic.

• Click the "The <Program name> Help task pane" subtopic.

• Read the information on both subtopics.

Your screen should be similar to Figure 16

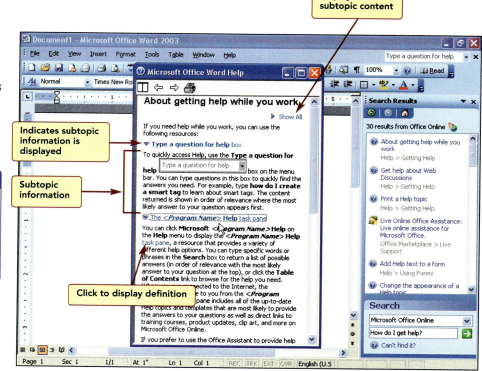

Figure 16

The ▶ preceding the subtopic has changed to ▼ indicating the subtopic content is displayed. The selected subtopics provide information about accessing Help using the "Type a question for help" box and the Help task pane. Notice the blue words "task pane" within the subtopic content. This indicates that clicking on the text will display a definition of the term. You can continue to click on the subtopic headings to display the information about each topic individually, or you can click Show All to display all the available topic information.

4 Click "task pane" to see the definition.

● Click Show All at the top of the Help window.

● Scroll the window to see the Microsoft Office Online subtopic.

● Read the information on this subtopic.

Your screen should be similar to Figure 17

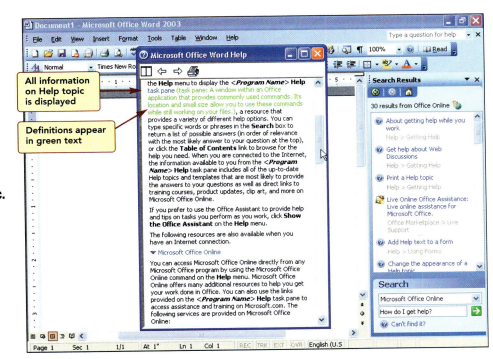

Figure 17

The information under all the subtopics is fully displayed, including definitions.

Using the Help Table of Contents

Another source of help is to use the Help table of contents. Using this method allows you to browse the Help topics to locate topics of interest to you.

1 Click ✕ Close in the Help window title bar to close the Help window.

● Click ⬅ Back in the task pane.

● Click Table of Contents (below the Search box).

Your screen should be similar to Figure 18

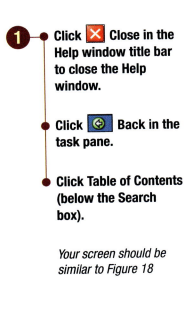

Figure 18

The entire Word Help Table of Contents is displayed in the Help task pane. Clicking on an item preceded with a 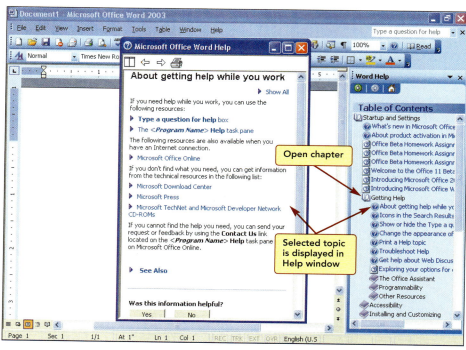 Closed Book icon opens a chapter, which expands to display additional chapters or topics. The Open Book icon identifies those chapters that are open. Clicking on an item preceded with displays the specific Help information.

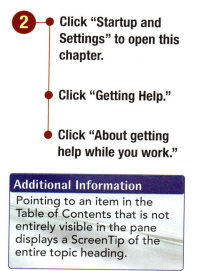

2 ● Click "Startup and Settings" to open this chapter.

● Click "Getting Help."

● Click "About getting help while you work."

Additional Information

Pointing to an item in the Table of Contents that is not entirely visible in the pane displays a ScreenTip of the entire topic heading.

Your screen should be similar to Figure 19

Figure 19

The Help window opens again and displays the information on the selected topic. To close a chapter, click the icon.

Exiting an Office 2003 Application

Now you are ready to close the Help window and exit the Word program. The Exit command on the File menu can be used to quit most Windows programs. Alternatively, you can click the ☒ Close button in the program window title bar.

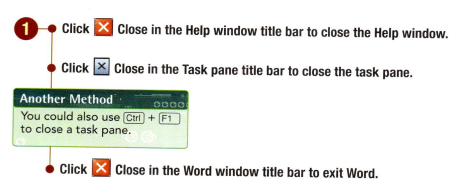

1 ● Click ☒ Close in the Help window title bar to close the Help window.

● Click ☒ Close in the Task pane title bar to close the task pane.

Another Method

You could also use Ctrl + F1 to close a task pane.

● Click ☒ Close in the Word window title bar to exit Word.

The program window is closed and the desktop is visible again.

lab review

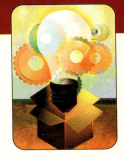

Introduction to Microsoft Office 2003

key terms

docked toolbar   I.18
document window   I.12
floating toolbar   I.18
Formatting toolbar   I.17
hyperlink   I.22
menu bar   I.12
scroll bar   I.12

selection cursor   I.14
shortcut menu   I.15
Standard toolbar   I.17
status bar   I.12
task pane   I.12
toolbar   I.12

command summary

Command	Shortcut Key	Button	Voice	Action
start/All Programs				Opens program menu
File/E**x**it	Alt + F4	✕		Exits Office program
View/**T**oolbars			View toolbars	Hides or displays toolbars
View/Tas**k** Pane	Ctrl + F1		Task pane Show task pane View task pane Hide task pane	Hides or displays task pane
Tools/**C**ustomize/**O**ptions				Changes settings associated with toolbars and menus
Help/Microsoft Word **H**elp	F1	?		Opens Help window

lab exercises

step-by-step

Using an Office Application ★

1. All Office 2003 applications have a common user interface. You will explore the Excel 2003 application and use many of the same features you learned about while using Word 2003 in this lab.

   a. Use the Start menu or a shortcut icon on your desktop to start Ofice Excel 2003. Close the Getting Started Task Pane.

   b. What shape is the mouse pointer when positioned in the document window area? _____

   c. Excel also has nine menus. Which menu is not the same as in Word? _____ Open the Tools Menu. How many commands in the Tools menu will display a submenu when selected? _____ How many commands are listed in the Formula Auditing submenu? _____

   d. Click on a blank space near the Formatting toolbar to open the toolbar shortcut menu. How many toolbars are available in Excel? _____

   e. Display the Chart toolbar. Dock the Chart toolbar above the Status bar. Change it to a floating toolbar. Close the Chart toolbar.

   f. Use the shortcut key combination to display the Task Pane. How many Task Panes are available? _____

   g. Display the Help Task Pane and search for help information on "worksheet." How many search results were returned? _____ Read the "About viewing workbooks and worksheets" topic. What is the definition of a worksheet? _____
   _____

   h. Close the Help window. Close the Excel window to exit the program.

on your own

Exploring Microsoft Help ★

1. In addition to the Help information you used in this lab, Office 2003 Online Help also includes many interactive tutorials. Selecting a Help topic that starts a tutorial will open the browser program on your computer. Both audio and written instructions are provided. You will use one of these tutorials to learn more about using Office 2003. Start Word 2003 and search for Help on "shortcut keys." Then select the "Work with the Keyboard in Office" topic. Follow the directions in the tutorial to learn about this feature. When you are done, close the browser window and the Word window.

Overview of Microsoft Office Word 2003

What Is Word Processing?

Office Word 2003 is a word processing software application whose purpose is to help you create any type of written communication. A word processor can be used to manipulate text data to produce a letter, a report, a memo, an e-mail message, or any other type of correspondence. Text data is any letter, number, or symbol that you can type on a keyboard. The grouping of the text data to form words, sentences, paragraphs, and pages of text results in the creation of a document. Through a word processor you can create, modify, store, retrieve, and print part or all of a document.

Word processors are one of the most widely used applications software programs. Putting your thoughts in writing, from the simplest note to the most complex book, is a time-consuming process. Even more time-consuming is the task of editing and retyping the document to make it better. Word processors make errors nearly nonexistent—not because they are not made, but because they are easy to correct. Word processors let you throw away the correction fluid, scissors, paste, and erasers. Now, with a few keystrokes, you can easily correct errors, move paragraphs, and reprint your document.

Word 2003 Features

Word 2003 excels in its ability to change or edit a document. Editing involves correcting spelling, grammar, and sentence-structure errors. In addition, you can easily revise or update existing text by inserting or deleting text. For example, a document that lists prices can easily be updated to reflect new prices. A document that details procedures can be revised by deleting old procedures and inserting new ones. This is especially helpful when a document is used repeatedly. Rather than recreating the whole document, you change only the parts that need to be revised.

Revision also includes the rearrangement of selected areas of text. For example, while writing a report, you may decide to change the location of a single word or several paragraphs or pages of text. You can do it easily by cutting or removing selected text from one location, then pasting or placing the selected text in another location. The selection can also be copied from one document to another.

Another time saver is word wrap. As you enter text you do not need to decide where to end each line, as you do on a typewriter. When a line is full, the program automatically wraps the text down to the next line.

To help you produce a perfect document, Word 2003 includes many additional support features. The AutoCorrect feature checks the spelling and grammar in a document as text is entered. Many common errors are corrected automatically for you. Others are identified and a correction suggested. While you enter text, the AutoComplete feature may suggest entire phrases that can be quickly inserted based on the first few characters you type. The words and phrases are included in a list of AutoText entries provided with Word 2003, or they may be ones you have included yourself. A thesaurus can be used to display alternative words that have a meaning similar or opposite to a word you entered. A Find and Replace feature can be used to quickly locate specified text and replace it with other text throughout a document.

A variety of Wizards are included in Word 2003 that provide step-by-step assistance while you produce many common types of documents, such as business letters, faxes, resumes, or reports. Templates also can be used to produce many of these documents without the step-by-step guidance provided by the Wizard.

You can also easily control the appearance or format of the document. Formatting includes such operations as changing the line spacing and margin widths, adding page numbers, and displaying page headers and footers. You can also quickly change how your text is aligned with the left or right margin. For example, text can be centered between the margins, or justified—evenly aligned on both the left and right margins. Perhaps the most noticeable formatting feature is the ability to apply different fonts (type styles and sizes) and text appearance changes such as bold, italics, and color to all or selected portions of the document. Additionally, you can add color shading behind individual pieces of text or entire paragraphs and pages to add emphasis. Automatic formatting can be turned on to automatically format text as you type by detecting when to apply selected formats to text as it is entered. In addition, Word 2003 includes a variety of tools that automate the process of many common tasks, such as creating tables, form letters, and columns.

Group collaboration on projects is common in industry today. Word 2003 includes many features to help streamline how documents are developed and changed by group members. A discussion feature allows multiple people to insert remarks in the same document without having to route the document to each person or reconcile multiple reviewers' comments. A feature called versioning allows you to save multiple versions of the same document so that you can see exactly who did what on a document and when. You can easily consolidate all changes and comments from different reviewers in one simple step and accept or reject changes as needed.

To further enhance your documents, you can insert many different types of graphic elements. You can select from over 150 border styles that can be applied to areas of text such as headings, or around graphics or entire pages. The drawing tools supplied with Word 2003 can be used to create your own drawings, or you can select from over 100 adjustable AutoShapes and modify them to your needs. All drawings can be further enhanced with 3-D effects, shadows, colors, and textures. Additionally, you can produce fancy text effects using the WordArt tool. More complex pictures can be inserted in documents by scanning your own, using supplied or purchased clip art, or downloading images from the World Wide Web.

Word 2003 is closely integrated with the World Wide Web. It detects when you are typing a Web address and converts it to a hyperlink automatically for you. You can also create your own hyperlinks to locations within documents, or to other documents, including those at external locations such as a Web site or file server. Word's many Web-editing features help you quickly create a Web page. Among these is a Web Page Wizard that guides you step by step through the process of creating a Web page. Themes can be used to quickly apply unified design elements and color schemes to your Web pages. Frames can be created to make your Web site easier for users to navigate. Pictures, graphic elements, animated graphics, sound, and movies can all be used to increase the impact of your Web pages.

You can also create and send e-mail messages directly from within Word 2003, using all its features to create and edit the message. You can also send an entire document directly by e-mail. The document becomes the message. This makes collaboration easy because you can edit the document directly without having to open or save an attachment.

Case Study for Office Word 2003 Labs

As a recent college graduate, you have accepted a job as advertising coordinator for Adventure Travel Tours, a specialty travel company that organizes active adventure vacations. The company is headquartered in Los Angeles and has locations in other major cities throughout the country. Your duties include the creation of brochures, flyers, form letters, news releases, advertisements, and a monthly newsletter, all of which promote Adventure Travel's programs. You are also responsible for working on the company Web site.

Brief Version

Lab 1: Adventure Travel has developed four new tours for the upcoming year and needs to promote them, partly through informative presentations held throughout the country. Your first job as advertising coordinator is to create a flyer advertising the four new tours and the presentations about them.

Lab 2: Your next project is to create a letter to be sent to past clients along with your flyer. The letter briefly describes Adventure Travel's four new tours and invites clients to attend an informational presentation.

Lab 3: Part of your responsibility as advertising coordinator is to gather background information about the various tour locations. You will write a report providing information about Tanzania and Peru for two of the new tours.

Working Together: Adventure Travel has a company Web site. You will convert the flyer you developed to promote the new tours and presentations to be used on the Web site.

Before You Begin

To the Student

The following assumptions have been made:

- Microsoft Office Word 2003 has been properly installed on your computer system.

- You have the data files needed to complete the series of Word 2003 labs and practice exercises. These may be supplied by your instructor and are also available at the online learning center Web site found at www.mhhe.com/oleary.

- You are already familiar with how to use Microsoft Windows and a mouse.

To the Instructor

A complete installation of Microsoft Office 2003 is required in which all components are available to students while completing the labs.

Please be aware that the following settings are assumed to be in effect for the Office Word 2003 program. These assumptions are necessary so that the screens and directions in the labs are accurate.

- The Getting Started task pane is displayed when Word is started. (Use Tools/Options/View/Startup Task Pane.)

- The ScreenTips feature is active. (Use Tools/Options/View/ScreenTips.)

- The status bar is displayed. (Use Tools/Options/View/Status bar.)

- The horizontal and vertical scroll bars are displayed. (Use Tools/Options/View/Horizontal scroll bar/Vertical scroll bar.)

- The Wrap to Window setting is off. (Use Tools/Options/View/Wrap to Window.)

- The Smart Tags feature is active. (Use Tools/Options/View/Smart tags.)

- The Mark Formatting Inconsistencies option is off. (Use Tools/Options/Edit/Mark formatting inconsistencies.)

- The Paste Options buttons are displayed. (Use Tools/Options/Edit/Show Paste Options buttons.)

- Background repagination is on. (Use Tools/Options/General/Background repagination.)

- The feature to check spelling and grammar as you type is on. (Use Tools/Options/Spelling & Grammar/Check spelling as you type/Check grammar as you type.)

- All AutoCorrect features are on. (Use Tools/AutoCorrect Options/Auto-Correct and select all options.)

- In the Introduction to Microsoft Office 2003 lab, the Standard and Formatting toolbars are displayed on one row. In all other labs they are displayed on two rows. (Use Tools/Customize/Options/Show Standard and Formatting toolbars on two rows.)
- Full menus are displayed after a short delay. (Use Tools/Customize/Options/Show full menus after a short delay.)
- Language is set to English (US). (Use Tools/Language/Set Language.)
- AutoComplete Suggestions are displayed. (Use Insert/AutoText/AutoText/ Show AutoComplete Suggestions.)
- The feature to access Online Help is on. (Choose Online Content Settings from the Help task pane and select the Show content and links from Microsoft Office Online option.)
- The Research tools include the Encarta World Dictionary, Thesaurus, MSN Search and Encyclopedia.
- The Office Assistant feature is off. (Right-click on the Assistant character, choose Options, and clear the Use the Office Assistant option.)
- All default settings for the Normal document template are in effect.

In addition, all figures in the manual reflect the use of a standard VGA display monitor set at 800 by 600. If another monitor setting is used, there may be more or fewer lines of text displayed in the windows than in the figures. This setting can be changed using Windows setup.

Microsoft Office Language Bar

The Microsoft Office Language Bar may also be displayed when you start the application. Commonly, it will appear on the title bar, however, it may appear in other locations depending upon your setup. The Language bar provides buttons to access and use the Speech Recognition and Handwriting recognition features.

Instructional Conventions

Hands-on instructions you are to perform appear as a sequence of numbered steps. Within each step, a series of bullets identifies the specific actions that must be performed. Step numbering begins over within each topic heading throughout the lab.

Command sequences you are to issue appear following the word "Choose." Each menu command selection is separated by a /. If the menu command can be selected by typing a letter of the command, the letter will appear underlined and bold. Items that need to be selected will follow the word "Select" and will appear in black text. You can select items with the mouse or directional keys. (See Example A.)

Example A

Commands that can be initiated using a button and the mouse appear following the word "Click." The icon (and the icon name if the icon does not include text) is displayed following "Click." The menu equivalent, keyboard shortcut, and/or voice command appear in an Another Method margin note when the action is first introduced. (See Example B.)

Example B

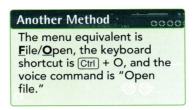

Plain blue text identifies file names you need to select or enter. Information you are asked to type appears in blue and bold. (See Example C.)

Example C

Creating and Editing a Document   LAB 1

Objectives

After completing this lab, you will know how to:

1
Develop a document as well as enter and edit text.

2
Insert and delete text and blank lines.

3
Reveal formatting marks.

4
Use AutoCorrect, AutoText, and AutoComplete.

5
Use automatic spelling and grammar checking.

6
Save, close, and open files.

7
Select text.

8
Undo and redo changes.

9
Change fonts and type sizes.

10
Bold and color text.

11
Change alignment.

12
Insert, size, and move pictures.

13
Preview and print a document.

14
Set file properties.

Case Study

Adventure Travel Tours

As a recent college graduate, you have accepted a job as advertising coordinator for Adventure Travel Tours, a specialty travel company that organizes active adventure vacations. The company is headquartered in Los Angeles and has locations in other major cities throughout the country. You are responsible for coordination of the advertising program for all locations. This includes the creation of many kinds of promotional materials: brochures, flyers, form letters, news releases, advertisements, and a monthly newsletter. You are also responsible for creating Web pages for the company Web site.

Adventure Travel is very excited about four new tours planned for the upcoming year.

They want to promote them through informative presentations held throughout the country. Your first job as advertising coordinator will be to create a flyer advertising the four new tours and the presentations about them. The flyer will be modified according to the location of the presentation.

The software tool you will use to create the flyer is the word processing application Microsoft Office Word 2003. It helps you create documents such as letters, reports, and research papers. In this lab, you will learn how to enter, edit, and print a document while you create the flyer (shown right) to be distributed in a mailing to Adventure Travel Tours clients.

© PhotoDisc

Entering and editing text is simplified with many of Word's AutoCorrect features

Formatting enhances the appearance of a document

Pictures add visual interest to a document

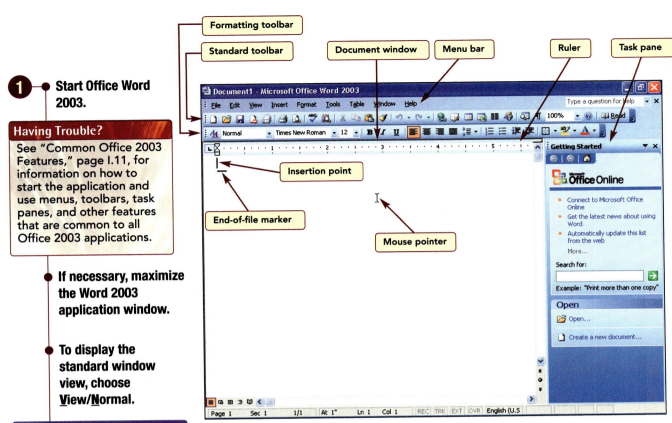

Formatting toolbar

Standard toolbar

Document window

Menu bar

Ruler

Task pane

Insertion point

End-of-file marker

Mouse pointer

Figure 1.1

See "Common Office 2003 Features," page I.11, for

1 ● Start Office Word 2003.

Having Trouble?
See "Common Office 2003 Features," page I.11, for information on how to start the application and use menus, toolbars, task panes, and other features that are common to all Office 2003 applications.

● If necessary, maximize the Word 2003 application window.

● To display the standard window view, choose **View/Normal**.

Additional Information
You will learn about the different document views shortly.

● If necessary, display the Standard and Formatting toolbars on 2 rows.

Having Trouble?
Choose **Tools/Customize/Options/Show Standard and Formatting toolbars on two rows**, to make this change.

Your screen should be similar to Figure 1.1

Exploring the Word 2003 Window

The menu bar below the title bar displays the Word program menu. It consists of nine menus that provide access to the commands and features you will use to create and modify a document.

The toolbars, normally located below the menu bar, contain buttons that are mouse shortcuts for many of the menu items. The **Standard toolbar** contains buttons for the most frequently used menu commands. The **Formatting toolbar** contains buttons that are used to change the appearance or format of the document. Word includes 21 toolbars, many of which appear automatically as you use different features. Your screen may display other toolbars if they were on when the program was last exited.

The large area below the toolbars is the **document window**. It currently displays a blank Word document. The **ruler**, displayed at the top of the document window, shows the line length in inches and is used to set margins, tab stops, and indents. The **insertion point**, also called the **cursor**, is the blinking vertical bar that marks your location in the document. The solid horizontal line is the **end-of-file marker**. Because this document contains no text, the insertion point appears at the first character space on the first line.

The task pane is displayed on the right side of the document window. A **pane** is a separate area in a window that you can view and scroll independently. Word includes 14 task panes, which are displayed depending on the task being performed. Since you just started Word, the Getting Started task pane is automatically displayed. This task pane provides different ways to create a new document or open an existing document.

The mouse pointer may appear as an I-beam (see Figure 1.1) or a left- or right-facing arrow, depending on its location in the window. When it appears as an I-beam, it is used to move the insertion point, and when it appears as an arrow, it is used to select items.

1 ● Move the mouse pointer into the left edge of the document window to see it appear as 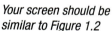.

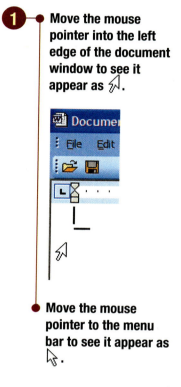

● Move the mouse pointer to the menu bar to see it appear as ⟨⟨.

Your screen should be similar to Figure 1.2

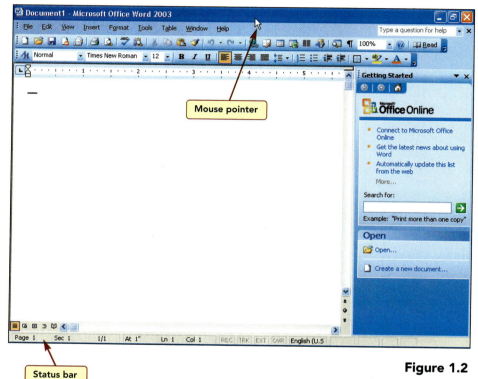

Figure 1.2

The indicators on the **status bar** show both the location of the text that is displayed in the document window as well as the location of the insertion point in a document. The numbers following the indicators specify the exact location in the document. The indicators are described in the following table.

Indicator	Meaning
Page	Indicates the page of text displayed onscreen.
Sec	Indicates the section of text displayed onscreen. A large document can be broken into sections.
1/1	Indicates the number of the page displayed onscreen, and the total number of pages in the document.
At	Indicates the vertical position in inches of the insertion point from the top of the page.
Ln	Indicates the line of text where the insertion point is located.
Col	Indicates the horizontal position of the insertion point in number of characters from the left margin.

Creating New Documents

When you first start Word, a new blank document is opened. It is like a blank piece of paper that already has many predefined settings. These settings, called default settings, are generally the most commonly used settings. You will use the blank document to create the flyer for Adventure Travel Tours. You do not need to use the task pane, so you will close it to see the entire document window.

1 ● Click ☒ **Close in the task pane title bar to close the task pane.**

Another Method

The menu equivalent is **V**iew/Tas**k** Pane and the keyboard shortcut is Ctrl + F1 . The voice command is "Task pane" to show it and "Hide task pane" to hide it.

Your screen should be similar to Figure 1.3

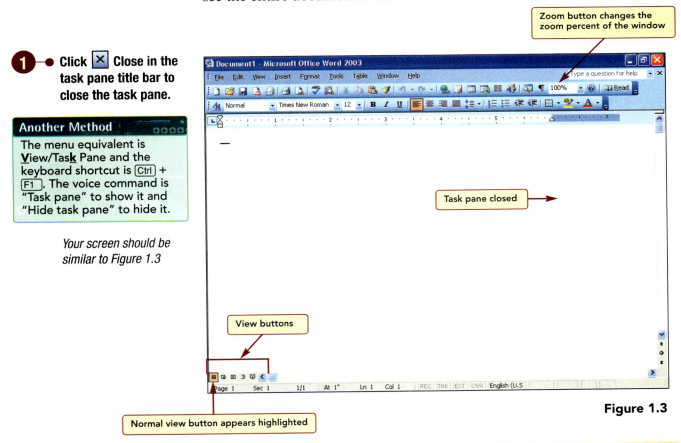

Figure 1.3

Viewing and Zooming a Document

To verify several of the default document settings more easily, you can switch to another document view. Word includes several views that are used for different purposes. You can change views using the View menu commands or the view buttons located to the left of the horizontal scroll bar. The different document views are described in the table below.

Document View	Command	Button	Effect on Text
Normal	**V**iew/**N**ormal		Shows text formatting and simple layout of the page. This is the best view to use when typing, editing, and formatting text.
Web Layout	**V**iew/**W**eb Layout		Shows the document as it will appear when viewed in a Web browser. Use this view when creating Web pages or documents that will be displayed on the screen only.
Print Layout	**V**iew/**P**rint Layout		Shows how the text and objects will appear on the printed page. This is the view to use when adjusting margins, working in columns, drawing objects, and placing graphics.
Reading Layout	**V**iew/**R**eading Layout		Automatically scales the content of the document to fit the screen so that pages are easy to read and browse. Use to review a document and add comments and highlighting.
Outline	**V**iew/**O**utline		Shows the structure of the document. This is the view to use to plan and reorganize text in a document.
Full Screen	**V**iew/**F**ull Screen		Shows the document only, without menu bar, toolbars, status bar, or any other features. Useful for viewing and reading large documents.

The view you see when first starting Word is the view that was in use when the program was last exited. Currently, your view is Normal view, as shown in Figure 1.3. You can tell which view is in use by looking at the view buttons. The button for the view that is in use appears highlighted.

In addition, you can change the amount of information displayed in the document window by "zooming in" to get a close-up view or "zooming out" to see more of the document at a reduced view. The default display, 100 percent, shows the characters the same size they will be when printed. You can increase the onscreen character size up to five times the normal display (500 percent) or reduce the character size to 10 percent. The zoom setting for each view is set independently and remains in effect until changed to another zoom setting.

You will switch to Print Layout view and "zoom out" on the document to see the entire page so you can better see the default document settings.

1 Click 📄 **Print Layout View** (located to the left of the horizontal scroll bar).

Another Method
The voice command is "Print Layout view."

Additional Information
The view buttons display the button name in a ScreenTip when you point to them.

● Choose **View/Zoom/Whole Page/** OK .

Your screen should be similar to Figure 1.4

Having Trouble?
If your zoom percentage is different, this is a function of the monitor you are using.

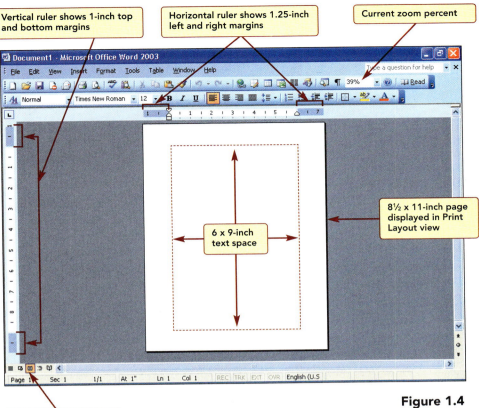

Vertical ruler shows 1-inch top and bottom margins

Horizontal ruler shows 1.25-inch left and right margins

Current zoom percent

8½ x 11-inch page displayed in Print Layout view

6 x 9-inch text space

Print Layout View button is highlighted

Figure 1.4

The zoom percentage shown in the Zoom button on the Standard toolbar has decreased to 39 percent in order to display the entire page. Print Layout view displays the current page of your document as it will appear when printed. All four edges of the paper are visible. This view also displays a vertical ruler that shows the vertical position of text.

The default document settings include a standard paper-size setting of 8.5 by 11 inches, 1-inch top and bottom margins, and 1.25-inch left and right margins. Other default settings include tab stops at every half inch and single line spacing. You can verify many of the default document settings by looking at the information displayed in the rulers. The margin boundaries on both ends of the horizontal ruler show the location of the left margin at zero and the right margin at 6-inches. The ruler shows that the distance between the left and right margins is 6 inches. Knowing that the default page size is 8.5 inches wide, this leaves 2.5 inches for margins: 1.25 inches for equal-sized left and right margins. The vertical ruler shows the entire page length is 11 inches with 1 inch top and bottom margins, leaving 9 inches of text space.

You will use Normal view at the standard zoom percentage of 100 percent to create the flyer about this year's new tours. This time you will use the 31% ▾ Zoom button on the Standard toolbar to change the Zoom percentage. The buttons on this toolbar are identified below.

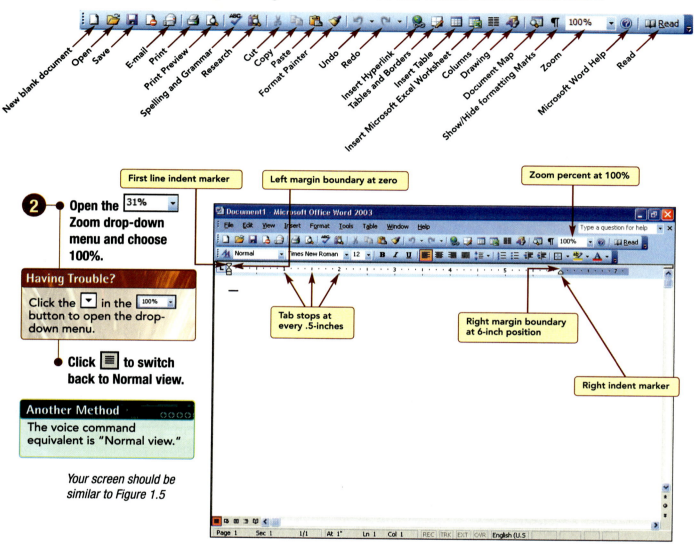

Figure 1.5

The ruler also displays other default settings. The symbol ▽ at the zero position is the first line indent marker and marks the location of the left paragraph indent. The symbol ▲ on the right end of the ruler line at the 6-inch position marks the right paragraph indent. The indent locations are the same as the left and right margin settings. The dimmed tab marks below each half-inch position show the default tab stop setting of every half inch.

Developing a Document

Your first project with Adventure Travel Tours is to create a flyer about four new tours. The development of a document follows several steps: plan, enter, edit, format, and preview and print.

Step	Description
Plan	The first step in the development of a document is to understand the purpose of the document and to plan what your document should say.
Enter	After planning the document, you enter the content of the document by typing the text using the keyboard. Text can also be entered using the handwriting and speech recognition features.
Edit	Making changes to your document is called **editing**. While typing, you probably will make typing and spelling errors that need to be corrected. This is one type of editing. Another is to revise the content that you have entered to make it clearer, or to add or delete information.
Format	Enhancing the appearance of the document to make it more readable or attractive is called **formatting**. This step is usually performed when the document is near completion, after all editing and revising have been done. It includes many features such as boldfaced text, italics, and bulleted lists.
Preview and Print	The last step is to preview and print the document. Previewing displays the document onscreen as it will appear when printed, allowing you to check the document's overall appearance and make any final changes before printing.

You will find that you will generally follow these steps in the order listed above for your first draft of a document. However, you will probably retrace steps such as editing and formatting as the final document is developed.

During the planning phase, you spoke with your manager regarding the purpose of the flyer and the content in general. The primary purpose of the flyer is to promote the new tours. A secondary purpose is to advertise the company in general.

You plan to include specific information about the new tours in the flyer as well as general information about Adventure Travel Tours. The content also needs to include information about the upcoming new tour presentations. Finally, you want to include information about the Adventure Travel Web site.

Entering Text

Now that you understand the purpose of the flyer and have a general idea of the content, you are ready to enter the text.

Text is entered using the keyboard. As you type, you will probably make simple typing errors that you want to correct. Word includes many features that make entering text and correcting errors much easier. These features include checking for spelling and grammar errors, auto correction, and word wrap. You will see how these features work while entering the title and first paragraph of the flyer.

Additional Information
You can also enter and edit text in Dictation mode using the Speech Recognition feature.

Typing Text

To enter text in a new document, simply begin typing the text. The first line of the flyer will contain the text 'Announcing four new Adventure Travel trips.' As you begin to enter this line of text, include the intentional error identified in italic.

1 ● **Type Announcing four** **new** *w*.

Your screen should be similar to Figure 1.6

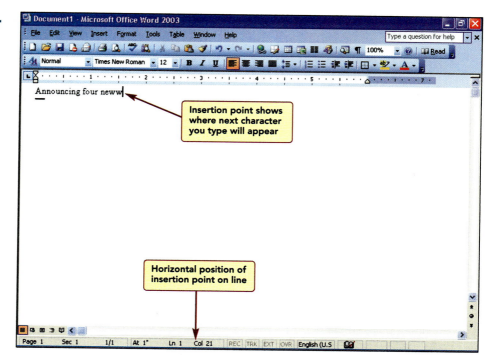

Insertion point shows where next character you type will appear

Horizontal position of insertion point on line

Figure 1.6

Notice that as you type, the insertion point moves to the right and the character appears to the left of the insertion point. The location of the insertion point shows where the next character will appear as you type. Also, the status bar reflects the new horizontal position of the insertion point on the line. As you can see from the first three indicators, page 1 of section 1 of a document consisting of only 1 page (1/1) is displayed on your screen. The next three indicators show the position of the insertion point. Currently, the insertion point is positioned at the 1-inch location from the top of the page, on line 1 from the top margin and column 21 from the left margin.

Using Backspace and Delete

You have made a typing error by typing an extra w in the word new. Removing typing entries to change or correct them is one of the basic editing tasks. Corrections may be made in many ways. Two of the most important editing keys are the Backspace key and the Delete key. The Backspace key removes a character or space to the left of the insertion point. It is particularly useful when you are moving from right to left (backward) along a line of text. The Delete key removes the character or space to the right of the insertion point and is most useful when moving from left to right along a line.

You will correct the error and continue typing the first line.

1 ● **Press** `Backspace` **to remove the extra w.**

● **Press** `Spacebar`.

● **Type Adventure Travel trips and correct any typing errors as you make them using** `Backspace` **or** `Delete`.

Another Method

Using voice dictation you would say "Backspace" and "Delete."

Your screen should be similar to Figure 1.7

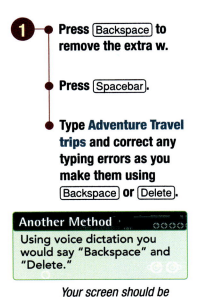

Announcing four new Adventure Travel Trips

Error deleted

Figure 1.7

Ending a Line and Inserting Blank Lines

Now you are ready to complete the first line of the announcement. To end a line and begin another line, you simply press `←Enter`. The insertion point moves to the beginning of the next line. If you press `←Enter` at the beginning of a line, a blank line is inserted into the document. If the insertion point is in the middle of a line of text and you press `←Enter`, all the text to the right of the insertion point moves to the beginning of the next line.

1 ● **Press** `←Enter` **3 times.**

Your screen should be similar to Figure 1.8

Blank lines inserted

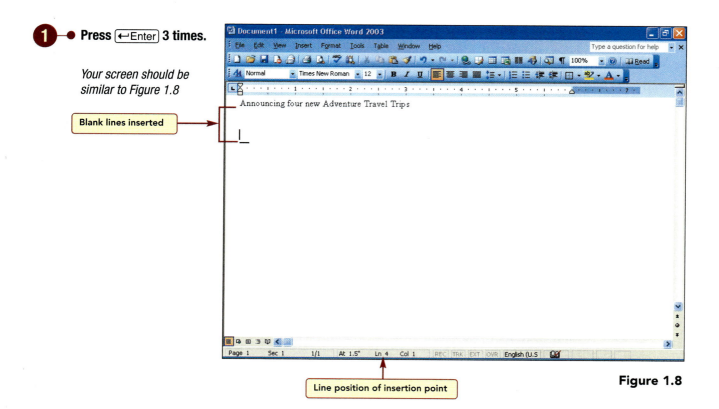

Announcing four new Adventure Travel Trips

Line position of insertion point

Figure 1.8

Another Method

Using voice dictation, you would simply say "Enter" to end a line or insert a blank line.

Pressing the first `←Enter` ended the first line of text and inserted a blank line. The next two inserted blank lines. The status bar now shows that the insertion point is positioned at the left margin (1.5 inches), on line 4, column 1 of the page.

Revealing Formatting Marks

While you are creating your document, Word automatically inserts **formatting marks** that control the appearance of your document. Word's default screen display does not show this level of detail. Sometimes, however, it is helpful to view the underlying formatting marks. Displaying these marks makes it easy to see, for example, if you have added an extra space between words or at the end of a sentence. Because you may use this feature frequently, you can access it quickly using the ¶ Show/Hide ¶ button on the Standard toolbar.

1 • Click **¶** Show/Hide ¶ (on the Standard toolbar).

Another Method

The menu equivalent is **T**ools/**O**ptions/View/A**l**, and the keyboard shortcut is Ctrl + ⇧Shift + *. The voice command is "Show formatting marks."

Your screen should be similar to Figure 1.9

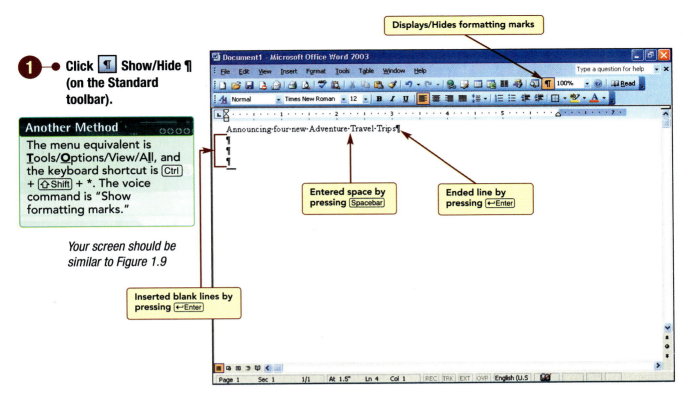

Displays/Hides formatting marks

Announcing·four·new·Adventure·Travel·Trips¶

Entered space by pressing Spacebar

Ended line by pressing ←Enter

Inserted blank lines by pressing ←Enter

Figure 1.9

The document now displays the formatting marks. The **¶** character on the line above the insertion point represents the pressing of ←Enter that created the blank line. The **¶** character at the end of the text represents the pressing of ←Enter that ended the line and moved the insertion point to the beginning of the next line. Between each word, a dot shows where the Spacebar was pressed. Formatting marks do not appear when the document is printed. You can continue to work on the document while the formatting marks are displayed, just as you did when they were hidden.

Additional Information

You can display selected formatting marks using **T**ools/**O**ptions/View and selecting the formatting marks you want to see.

Moving Through Text

After text is entered into a document, you need to know how to move around within the text to correct errors or make changes. The keyboard, mouse, or voice commands can be used to move through the text in the document window. Depending on what you are doing, one method may be more efficient than another. For example, if your hands are already on the keyboard as you are entering text, it may be quicker to use the keyboard rather than take your hands off to use the mouse.

Moving Using the Keyboard

Additional Information

Voice commands are also shown in the following table.

You use the arrow keys located on the numeric keypad or the directional keypad to move the insertion point in a document. The keyboard directional keys are described in the following table.

Key	Voice	Movement
→	Right	One character to right
←	Left	One character to left
↑	Up	One line up
↓	Down	One line down
Ctrl + →	Next word	One word to right
Ctrl + ←	Back word	One word to left
Home	Home	Left end of line
End	Go end	Right end of line

Additional Information

You can use the directional keys on the numeric keypad or the dedicated directional keypad area. If using the numeric keypad, make sure the Num Lock feature is off, otherwise numbers will be entered in the document. The Num Lock indicator light above the keypad is lit when on. Press Num Lock to turn it off.

Holding down a directional key or key combination moves quickly in the direction indicated, saving multiple presses of the key. Many of the Word insertion point movement keys can be held down to execute multiple moves. You will use many of these keys to quickly move through the text.

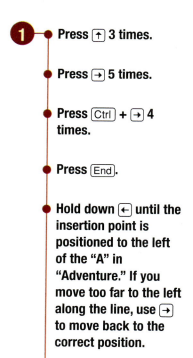

1 ● Press ↑ 3 times.

● Press → 5 times.

● Press Ctrl + → 4 times.

● Press End.

● Hold down ← until the insertion point is positioned to the left of the "A" in "Adventure." If you move too far to the left along the line, use → to move back to the correct position.

● Press Home.

Your screen should be similar to Figure 1.10

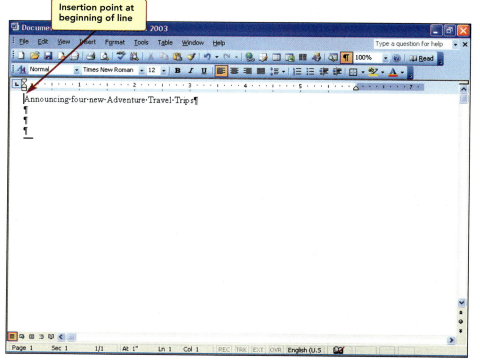

Figure 1.10

The insertion point first moved up three lines, then five character spaces to the right, four words to the right, then quickly to the end of the line. You then held down the direction key to quickly move character by character to the left, and finally to the beginning of the line.

Moving Using the Mouse

You use the mouse to move the insertion point to a specific location in a document. When you can use the mouse to move the insertion point, it is shaped as an I-beam. However, when the mouse pointer is positioned in the unmarked area to the left of a line (the left margin), it changes to an arrow. When the mouse is in this area, it can be used to highlight (select) text.

You have decided you want the flyer heading to be on two lines, with the word "Announcing" on the first line. To do this, you will insert a blank line after this word. You will move the insertion point to the location in the text where you want to insert the blank line.

1 ● Click on the right side of the "g" in "Announcing" before the dot for a space.

● Move the mouse pointer out of the way so you can see the insertion point better.

Your screen should be similar to Figure 1.11

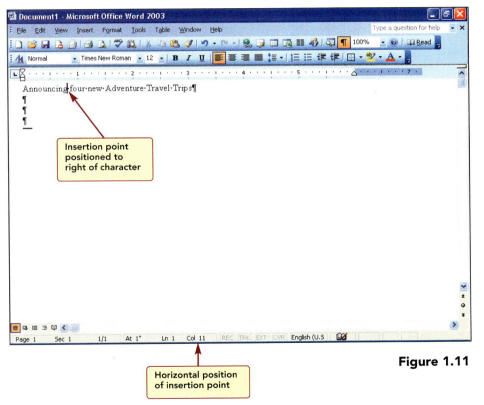

Insertion point positioned to right of character

Horizontal position of insertion point

Figure 1.11

The insertion point should now be positioned to the right of the g, and the status bar shows the column location of the insertion point as column 11. Next, you will start a new line and enter a blank line.

2 Press ⟨←Enter⟩ 2 times.

Press ⟨Delete⟩ to remove the space at the beginning of the line.

Press ⟨↓⟩.

Your screen should be similar to Figure 1.12

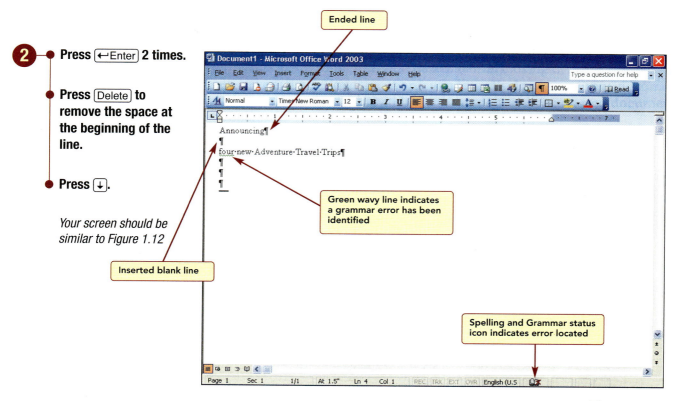

Ended line

Green wavy line indicates a grammar error has been identified

Inserted blank line

Spelling and Grammar status icon indicates error located

Figure 1.12

Having Trouble?

If the green underline is not displayed, choose **T**ools/**O**ptions, open the Spelling & Grammar tab, and select the "Check spelling as you type" and "Check Grammar as you type" options.

The insertion point is positioned at the beginning of the blank line. As you continue to create a document, the formatting marks are automatically inserted and deleted. Notice that a green wavy underline appears under the word "four." This indicates an error has been detected.

Identifying and Correcting Errors Automatically

As you enter text, Word is constantly checking the document for spelling and grammar errors. The Spelling and Grammar Status icon in the status bar displays an animated pencil icon 📝 while you are typing, indicating Word is checking for errors as you type. When you stop typing, it displays either a red checkmark 📖, indicating the program does not detect any errors, or a red X 📕, indicating the document contains an error. In many cases, Word will automatically correct errors for you. In other cases, it identifies the error by underlining it. The different colors and designs of underlines indicate the type of error that has been identified. In addition to identifying the error, Word provides suggestions as to the possible correction needed.

Checking Grammar

In addition to the green wavy line under "four," the Spelling and Grammar Status icon appears as 📕. This indicates that a spelling or grammar error has been located. The green wavy underline indicates it is a grammar error.

Concept 1
Grammar Checker

1 The **grammar checker** advises you of incorrect grammar as you create and edit a document, and proposes possible corrections. Grammar checking occurs after you enter punctuation or end a line. If grammatical errors in subject-verb agreements, verb forms, capitalization, or commonly confused words, to name a few, are detected, they are identified with a wavy green line. You can correct the grammatical error by editing it or you can open the shortcut menu for the identified error and display a suggested correction. Because not all identified grammatical errors are actual errors, you need to use discretion when correcting the errors.

1 ● **Right-click the word "four" to open the shortcut menu.**

Having Trouble?

Review shortcut menus in the "Common Office 2003 Features" section (page I.11). If the wrong shortcut menu appears, you probably did not have the I-beam positioned on the error with the green wavy line. Press [Esc] or click outside the menu to cancel it and try again.

Your screen should be similar to Figure 1.13

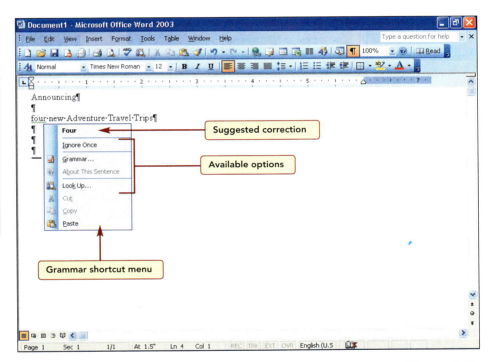

Figure 1.13

Additional Information

A dimmed menu option means it is currently unavailable.

The first item on the Grammar shortcut menu is the suggested correction, "Four." The grammar checker indicates you should capitalize the first letter of the word because it appears to be the beginning of a sentence. It also includes three available commands that are relevant to the item, described below.

Command	Effect
Ignore Once	Instructs Word to ignore the grammatical error in this sentence.
Grammar	Opens the grammar checker and displays an explanation of the error.
Look Up	Provides help about the grammatical error.

To make this correction, you could simply choose the correction from the shortcut menu and the correction would be inserted into the document. Although in this case you can readily identify the reason for the error, sometimes the reason is not so obvious. In those cases, you can open the grammar checker to find out more information.

2 ● **Choose Grammar.**

Your screen should be similar to Figure 1.14

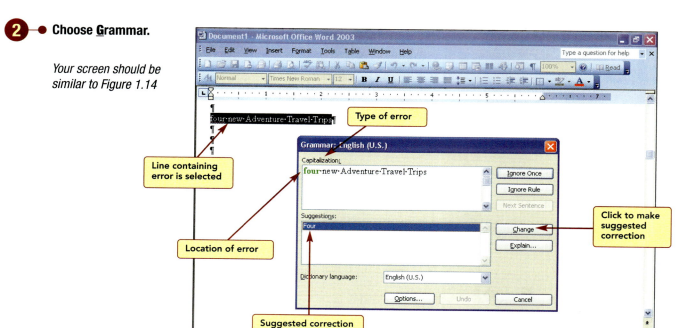

Figure 1.14

The Grammar dialog box identifies the possible grammatical error in the upper text box and the suggested correction in the Suggestions box. The line in the document containing the error is also highlighted (selected) to make it easy for you to see the location of the error. You will make the suggested change.

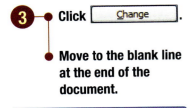

3 • Click [Change].

• **Move to the blank line at the end of the document.**

Your screen should be similar to Figure 1.15

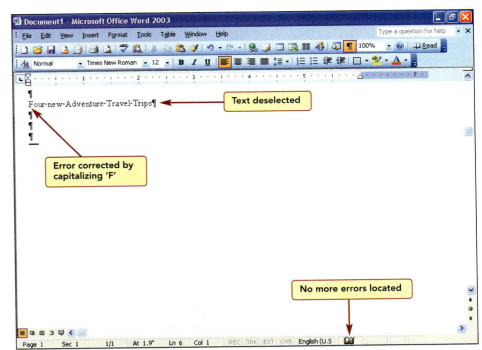

Four·new·Adventure·Travel·Trips¶

Text deselected

Error corrected by capitalizing 'F'

No more errors located

Figure 1.15

The error is corrected, the wavy green line is removed, and the Spelling and Grammar Status icon returns to .

Using AutoText and AutoComplete

Now you are ready to type the text for the first paragraph of the flyer.

1 • **Type atte.**

Your screen should be similar to Figure 1.16

Four·new·Adventure·Travel·Trips¶

Attention: (Press ENTER to Insert)

atte¶

AutoComplete ScreenTip suggests AutoText entry and how to proceed

Figure 1.16

A ScreenTip appears displaying "Attention: (Press ENTER to Insert)." This is Word's AutoText and AutoComplete feature.

2 The AutoText and AutoComplete features make entering text easier by providing shortcuts for entering commonly used text. The **AutoText** feature includes entries, such as commonly used phrases, that can be quickly inserted into a document. The AutoText entries can be selected and inserted into the document using the Insert/AutoText command. Word's standard AutoText entries include salutations and closing phrases. You can also add your own entries to the AutoText list, which can consist of text or graphics you may want to use again. Common uses are for a company name, mailing address, and a distribution list for memos.

Additionally, if the **AutoComplete** feature is on, a ScreenTip appears as you type the first few characters of an AutoText entry, suggesting the remainder of the AutoText entry you may want to use. You can choose to accept the suggestion to insert it into the document or to ignore it.

The AutoComplete ScreenTip suggests that you may be typing "Attention:." Because this is the word you are typing, you will accept the suggestion. However, you do not need the colon and will delete it. Then you will continue typing the line, including the intentional spelling error.

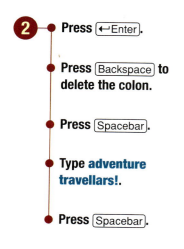

● **Press** ⏎Enter.

● **Press** Backspace **to delete the colon.**

● **Press** Spacebar.

● **Type adventure travellars!.**

● **Press** Spacebar.

Your screen should be similar to Figure 1.17

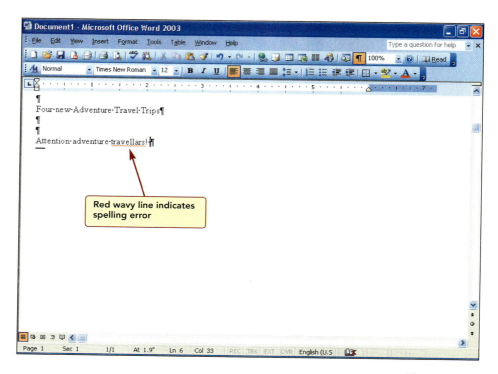

Red wavy line indicates spelling error

Figure 1.17

Checking Spelling

As soon as you complete a word by entering a space or punctuation, the program checks the word for spelling accuracy.

Concept 3

Spelling Checker

3   The **spelling checker** advises you of misspelled words as you create and edit a document, and proposes possible corrections. The spelling checker compares each word you type to a **main dictionary** of words supplied with the program. Although this dictionary includes most common words, it may not include proper names, technical terms, and so on. If the word does not appear in the main dictionary, it checks the **custom dictionary**, a dictionary that you can create to hold words you commonly use but that are not included in the main dictionary. If the word does not appear in either dictionary, the program identifies it as misspelled by displaying a red wavy line below the word. You can then correct the misspelled word by editing it. Alternatively, you can display a list of suggested spelling corrections for that word and select the correct spelling from the list to replace the misspelled word in the document.

Word automatically identified the word "travellars" as misspelled by underlining it with a wavy red line. The quickest way to correct a misspelled word is to select the correct spelling from a list of suggested spelling corrections displayed on the shortcut menu.

1 ● **Right-click on "travellars" to display the shortcut menu.**

Another Method

You can also position the insertion point on the item you want to display a shortcut menu for and press ⇧Shift + F10 to open the shortcut menu.

Your screen should be similar to Figure 1.18

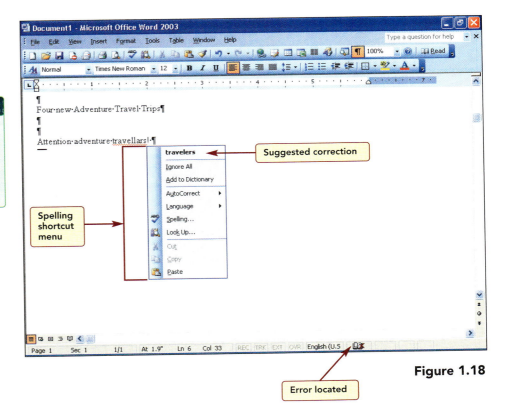

Figure 1.18

A shortcut menu of suggested correct spellings is displayed. In this case, there is only one suggested correction, which happens to be correct. The shortcut menu also includes several related menu options, described in the following table.

Option	Effect
Ignore All	Instructs Word to ignore the misspelling of this word throughout the rest of this session.
Add to Dictionary	Adds the word to the custom dictionary list. When a word is added to the custom dictionary, Word will always accept that spelling as correct.
AutoCorrect	Adds the word to the AutoCorrect list so Word can correct misspellings of it automatically as you type.
Language	Sets the language format, such as French, English, or German, to apply to the word.
Spelling	Starts the spell-checking program to check the entire document. You will learn about this feature in Lab 2.
Look Up	Searches the reference tools to locate similar words and definitions.

Sometimes there are no suggested replacements because Word cannot locate any words in its dictionary that are similar in spelling; or the suggestions are not correct. If this occurs, you need to edit the word manually. In this case the suggestion is correct.

2 ● **Choose "travelers."**

Your screen should be similar to Figure 1.19

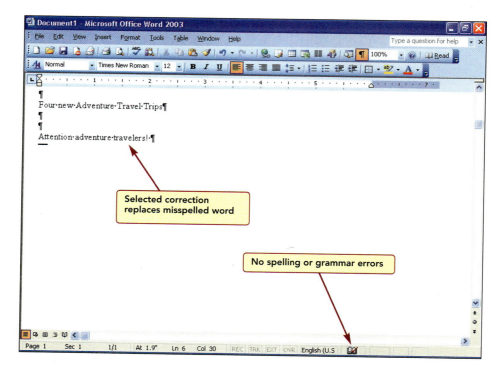

Selected correction replaces misspelled word

No spelling or grammar errors

Figure 1.19

The spelling correction you selected replaces the misspelled word in the document. The Spelling and Grammar status icon returns to ▣, indicating that as far as Word is able to detect, the document is free from errors.

Using AutoCorrect

As soon as you complete a word by entering a space or punctuation, the program checks the word for accuracy. When you complete a sentence and start another, additional checks are made. This is part of the AutoCorrect feature of Word.

Concept 4
AutoCorrect

4 The **AutoCorrect** feature makes some basic assumptions about the text you are typing and, based on these assumptions, automatically corrects the entry. The AutoCorrect feature automatically inserts proper capitalization at the beginning of sentences and in the names of days of the week. It will also change to lowercase letters any words that were incorrectly capitalized because of the accidental use of the [Caps Lock] key. In addition, it also corrects many common typing and spelling errors automatically.

One way the program automatically makes corrections is by looking for certain types of errors. For example, if two capital letters appear at the beginning of a word, Word changes the second capital letter to a lowercase letter. If a lowercase letter appears at the beginning of a sentence, Word capitalizes the first letter of the first word. If the name of a day begins with a lowercase letter, Word capitalizes the first letter. When Spelling Checker provides a single suggested spelling correction for the word, the program will automatically replace the incorrect spelling with the suggested replacement.

Another way the program makes corrections is by checking all entries against a built-in list of AutoCorrect entries. If it finds the entry on the list, the program automatically replaces the error with the correction. For example, the typing error "withthe" is automatically changed to "with the" because the error is on the AutoCorrect list. You can also add words to the AutoCorrect list that you want to be automatically corrected.

Enter the following text, including the errors (identified in italics).

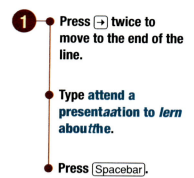

● Press → twice to move to the end of the line.

● Type **attend a presentation to *lern* about*t*he**.

● Press Spacebar.

Your screen should be similar to Figure 1.20

Having Trouble?

The "Capitalize first letter of sentences" and "Replace text as you type" AutoCorrect features must be on. Use **Tools/A**uto Correct Options and select these options if necessary.

Having Trouble?

If your screen does not display the blue box, choose **Tools/A**utoCorrect Options and select the Show AutoCorrect Options button check box.

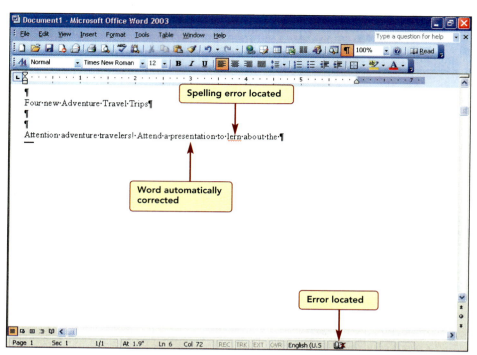

Figure 1.20

The first letter of the word "attend" was automatically capitalized because as you were typing, the program determined that it is the first word in a sentence. In a similar manner it corrected the spelling of "presentation" and separated the words "about the" with a space. The AutoCorrect feature corrected the spelling of "presentation" because it was the only suggested correction for the word supplied by the Spelling Checker. The word "lern" was not corrected because there are several suggested corrections on the Spelling shortcut menu.

When you rest the mouse pointer near text that has been corrected automatically or move the insertion point onto the word, a small blue box appears under the first character of the word. The blue box changes to the 📝▾ AutoCorrect Options button when you point directly to it.

2 Point to the word "Attend" to display the blue box.

Point to the blue box.

Click 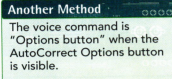 AutoCorrect Options.

Another Method ○○○○

The voice command is "Options button" when the AutoCorrect Options button is visible.

Your screen should be similar to Figure 1.21

Additional Information

If you use Backspace to delete an automatic correction and then type it again the way you want it to appear, the word will be automatically added to the exceptions list.

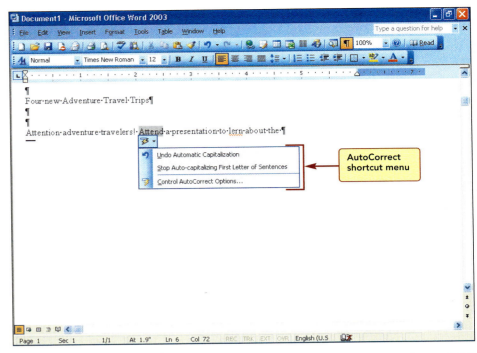

Figure 1.21

Each time Word uses the AutoCorrect feature, the AutoCorrect Options button is available. The AutoCorrect Options menu allows you to undo the AutoCorrection or to permanently disable the AutoCorrection for the remainder of your document. The Control AutoCorrect Options command can also be used to change the settings for this feature. In some cases, you may want to exclude a word from automatic correction. You can do this by manually adding the word to an exception list using **T**ools/**A**utoCorrect Options/**E**xceptions. You want to keep this AutoCorrection.

3 Click outside the menu to close it.

Open the spelling shortcut menu for "lern" and select "learn."

The spelling is corrected, and the spelling indicator in the status bar indicates that the document is free of errors.

Using Word Wrap

Now you will continue entering more of the paragraph. As you type, when the text gets close to the right margin, do not press [←Enter] to move to the next line. Word will automatically wrap words to the next line as needed.

Concept 5
Word Wrap

5 The **word wrap** feature automatically decides where to end a line and wrap text to the next line based on the margin settings. This feature saves time when entering text because you do not need to press [←Enter] at the end of a full line to begin a new line. The only time you need to press [←Enter] is to end a paragraph, to insert blank lines, or to create a short line such as a salutation. In addition, if you change the margins or insert or delete text on a line, the program automatically readjusts the text on the line to fit within the new margin settings. Word wrap is common to all word processors.

Enter the following text to complete the sentence.

1 ● **Move to the end of the line.**

● Type **earth's greatest unspoiled habitats and find out how you can experience the adventure of a lifetime.**

● **Correct any spelling or grammar errors that are identified.**

Your screen should be similar to Figure 1.22

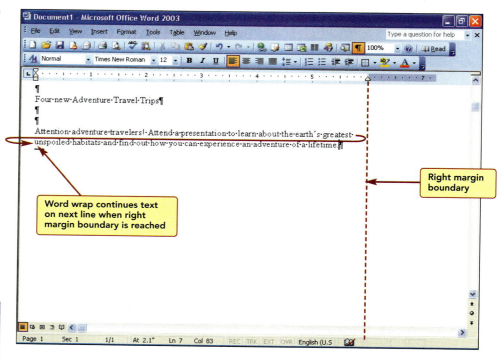

Figure 1.22

The program has wrapped the text that would overlap the right margin to the beginning of the next line.

Using Smart Tags

You have a meeting you need to attend in a few minutes, and want to continue working on the document when you get back. You decide to add your name and the current date to the document.

1 ● **Move to the end of the sentence and press** [←Enter] **twice.**

● **Type your name.**

● **Press** [←Enter].

● **Type the current date beginning with the month, and when the AutoText entry for the complete date appears, press** [←Enter] **to accept it.**

● **Press** [←Enter] **twice.**

Your screen should be similar to Figure 1.23

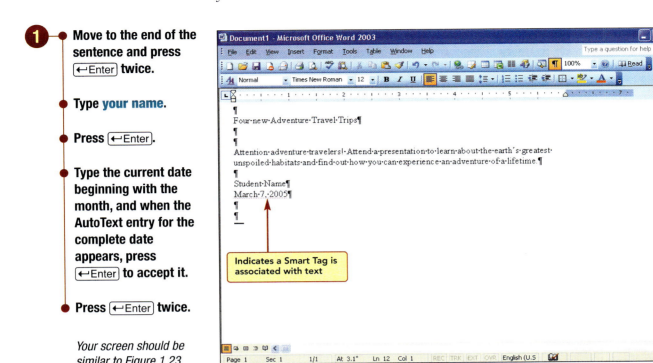

Figure 1.23

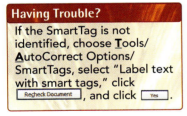

Notice that the date is underlined with a dotted purple line, which indicates that a Smart Tag is attached to the text. The **Smart Tag** feature recognizes and labels data such as names, addresses, telephone numbers, dates, times, and places as a particular type. The type of data it is recognized as determines what action can be performed with the data. For example, a name and address can be added directly from your document to the Microsoft Outlook Contacts folder. The date is recognized as a date item that can be added to the Outlook Calendar.

Because you do not need to perform any actions with the date, you will remove the Smart Tag.

2 — Point to the date to display the Smart Tag Actions button.

● Click ⓘ ▾ to open the Smart Tag Actions menu.

● Choose Remove this Smart Tag.

The purple dotted underline is removed, indicating a Smart Tag is no longer associated with the text. You will continue to see Smart Tags as you work through the labs. It is not necessary to remove them because they do not print or interfere with other actions.

Saving, Closing, and Opening Files

Before leaving to attend your meeting, you want to save your work to a file and close the file. As you enter and edit text to create a new document, the changes you make are immediately displayed onscreen and are stored in your computer's memory. However, they are not permanently stored until you save your work to a file on a disk. After a document has been saved as a file, it can be closed and opened again at a later time to be edited further.

As a backup against the accidental loss of work from power failure or other mishap, Word includes an AutoRecover feature. When this feature is on, as you work you may see a pulsing disk icon briefly appear in the status bar. This icon indicates that the program is saving your work to a temporary recovery file. The time interval between automatic saving can be set to any period you specify; the default is every 10 minutes. After a problem has occurred, when you restart the program, the recovery file is automatically opened containing all changes you made up to the last time it was saved by AutoRecover. You then need to save the recovery file. If you do not save it, it is deleted when closed. While AutoRecover is a great feature for recovering lost work, it should not be used in place of regularly saving your work.

Additional Information

Use **T**ools/**O**ptions/Save to set the AutoRecovery options.

Saving a File

You will save the work you have done so far on the flyer. You can use the Save or Save As command on the File menu to save files. The Save command or the 🖫 Save button will save the active file using the same file name by replacing the contents of the existing disk file with the document as it appears on your screen. The Save As command is used to save a file using a new file name or to a new location. This leaves the original file unchanged. When you create a new document, you can use either of the Save commands to save your work to a file on the disk. It is especially important to save a new document very soon after you create it because the AutoRecover feature does not work until a file name has been specified.

 **Click 💾 Save.**

Another Method ○○○○
The voice command is "Save."

Your screen should be similar to Figure 1.24

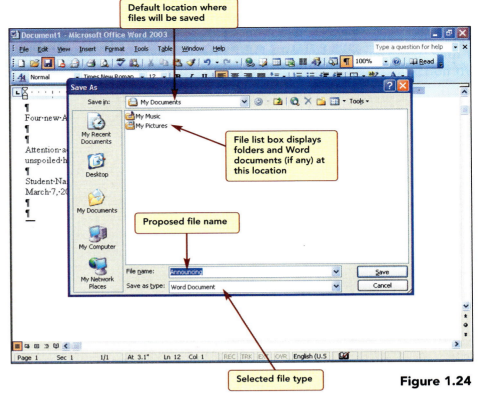

Default location where files will be saved

File list box displays folders and Word documents (if any) at this location

Proposed file name

Selected file type

Figure 1.24

Additional Information

Depending on the dialog box view, the files may be displayed differently and file details, such as the size, type, and date modified may be listed.

The Save As dialog box is used to specify the location where you will save the file and the file name. The Save In drop-down list box displays the default folder as the location where the file will be saved, and the File Name text box displays the proposed file name. The file list box displays the names of any Word documents in the default location. Only Word-type documents are listed, because Word Document is the specified file type in the Save As Type list box.

First you need to change the location where the file will be saved to the location where you save your files.

② Open the Save In drop-down list box.

Select the location where you want to save your file.

Your screen should be similar to Figure 1.25

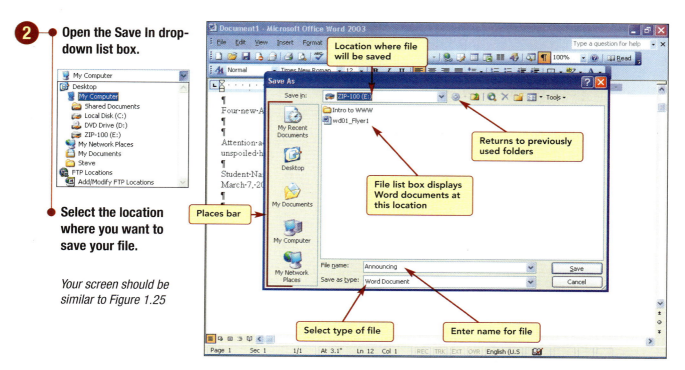

Figure 1.25

Now the large list box displays the names of all Word files, if any, at that location. You can also select the location to save your file from the Places bar along the left side of the dialog box. The icons bring up a list of recently accessed files and folders (My Recent Documents), the contents of the My Documents folder, items on the Windows desktop, and the locations on your computer or on a network. You can also click the [icon] button in the toolbar to return to folders that were previously opened.

Next, you need to enter a file name and specify the file type. The File Name box displays the default file name, consisting of the first few words from the document. The Save as Type box displays "Word Document" as the default format in which the file will be saved. Word documents are identified by the file extension .doc. The file type you select determines the file extension that will be automatically added to the file name when the file is saved. You will change the file name to Flyer and use the default document type.

3 ● **Double-click in the File Name text box.**

● **Type Flyer.**

Additional Information
The file name can be entered in either uppercase or lowercase letters and will appear exactly as you type it.

● Click [Save].

Your screen should be similar to Figure 1.26

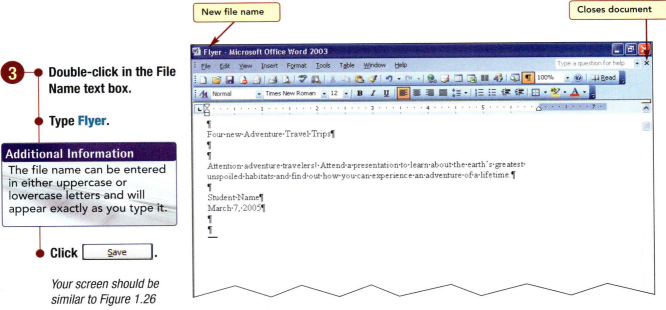

Figure 1.26

The document is saved as Flyer.doc at the location you selected, and the new file name is displayed in the Word title bar.

Closing a File

Finally, you want to close the document while you attend your meeting.

1 ● **Click ✕ Close Window in the menu bar.**

Another Method
The menu equivalent is **F**ile/**C**lose and the keyboard shortcut is Ctrl + F4. The voice command is "Close document."

Your screen should be similar to Figure 1.27

Empty document window

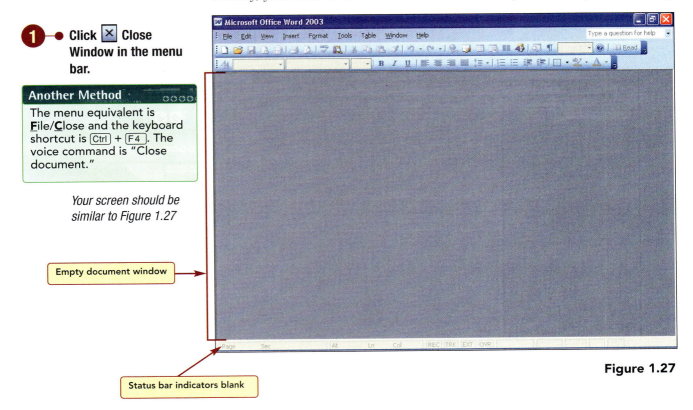

Status bar indicators blank

Figure 1.27

Because you did not make any changes to the document since saving it, the document window is closed immediately. If you had made additional changes, the program would ask whether you wanted to save the file before closing it. This prevents the accidental closing of a file that has not been saved first. Now the Word window displays an empty document window, and the status bar indicators are dimmed because no documents are open.

Opening a File

You asked your assistant to enter the remaining information in the flyer for you while you attended the meeting. Upon your return, you find a note from your assistant on your desk. The note explains that he had a little trouble entering the information and tells you that he saved the revised file as Flyer1. You want to open the file and continue working on the flyer.

Because opening a file is a very common task, there are many ways to do it. You can use the **File/O**pen command; the keyboard shortcut is Ctrl + O or 📂 Open in the Standard toolbar. Additionally, a recently used file can be opened quickly by selecting it from the list of file names displayed at the bottom of the File menu. You can also use the Getting Started task pane to open files and create new files. Like the File menu, the Getting Started task pane displays the names of recently used files.

Additional Information

The default setting is to display the last four recently used files in the File menu.

● **Choose View/Task Pane.**

● **If necessary, display the Getting Started task pane.**

● **Click More in the Open section of the task pane.**

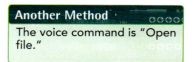

Another Method

The voice command is "Open file."

Your screen should be similar to Figure 1.28

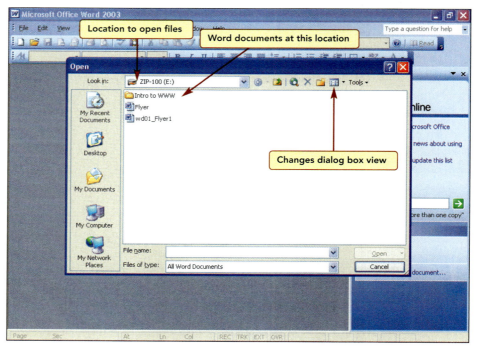

Figure 1.28

In the Open dialog box, you specify the location and name of the file you want to open. The Look In drop-down list box displays the last specified location, in this case the location where you saved the Flyer document. The large list box displays the names of all Word documents. As in the Save As dialog box, the Places bar can be used to quickly locate files.

When selecting a file to open, it is often helpful to see a preview of the file first. To do this you can change the dialog box view.

2 ● **If the Look In location is not correct, select the location containing your data files from the Look In drop-down list box.**

● **Select wd01_Flyer1.doc.**

● **Open the** 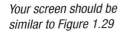 **Views drop-down list.**

● **Choose** Preview.

Your screen should be similar to Figure 1.29

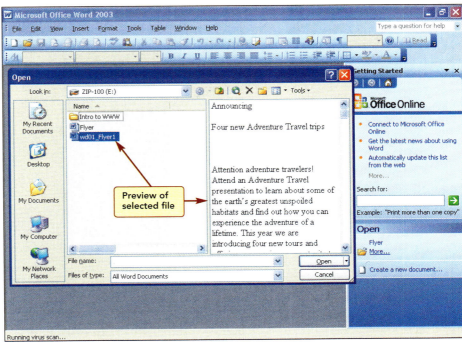

Figure 1.29

A preview of the selected file consisting of the first few lines of text in the document is displayed in the right pane of the dialog box. You will return the view to the list of file names and open this file.

3 ● **Open the** [ ] ▾ **Views drop-down list.**

● **Choose List.**

● **If necessary, select wd01_Flyer1.**

● **Click** [Open ▾].

Another Method ○○○○
You could also double-click the file name to both select and open it.

Your screen should be similar to Figure 1.30

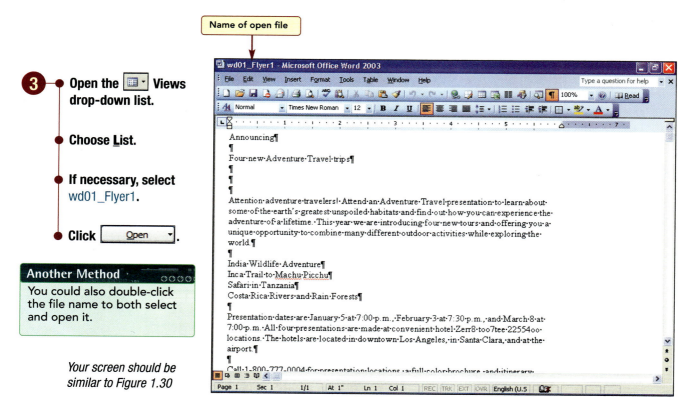

Figure 1.30

The file is opened and displayed in the document window. This file contains the text of the rest of the first draft of the flyer. The formatting marks are displayed because this feature is still on.

Navigating a Document

As documents increase in size, they cannot be easily viewed in their entirety in the document window and much time can be spent moving to different locations in the document. Word includes many features that make it easy to move around in a large document. The basic method is to scroll through a document using the scroll bar or keyboard. Another method is to move directly to a page or other identifiable item in the document, such as a table. You can also quickly return to a previous location, or browse through a document to a previous page or item.

Other features that help move through a large document include searching the document to locate specific items, and using the Document Map or a table of contents. You will learn about many of these features in later labs.

Scrolling a Document

Now that more information has been added to the document, the document window is no longer large enough to display the entire document. To bring additional text into view in the window, you can scroll the document using either the scroll bars or the keyboard. Again, both methods are useful, depending on what you are doing. Voice commands

Additional Information

If you have a mouse with a scroll wheel, you can use it to scroll a window vertically.

can also be used to scroll. The tables below explain the mouse, keyboard, and voice techniques that can be used to scroll a document.

Mouse	Action
Click ⌄	Moves down line by line.
Click ⌃	Moves up line by line.
Click above/below scroll box	Moves up/down window by window.
Drag scroll box	Moves up/down multiple windows.
Click ⤒	Moves to top of previous page.
Click ⤓	Moves to top of next page.
Click ⦿ Select Browse Object	Changes how you want the ⤓ and ⤓ buttons to browse through a document, such as by table or graphic. The default setting is by page.

Key	Voice	Action
↓	Down	Down line by line
↑	Up	Up line by line
Page Up	Page up	Top of window
Page Down	Page down	Bottom of window
Ctrl + Home		Beginning of document
Ctrl + End		End of document

Additional Information

You can also scroll the document window horizontally using the horizontal scroll bar or the ← and → keys.

You will use the vertical scroll bar to view the text at the bottom of the flyer. When you use the scroll bar to scroll, the insertion point does not move. To move the insertion point, you must click in a location in the window.

1

Click ⌄ in the vertical scroll bar 10 times.

Click anywhere in the last line to move the insertion point.

Your screen should be similar to 1.31

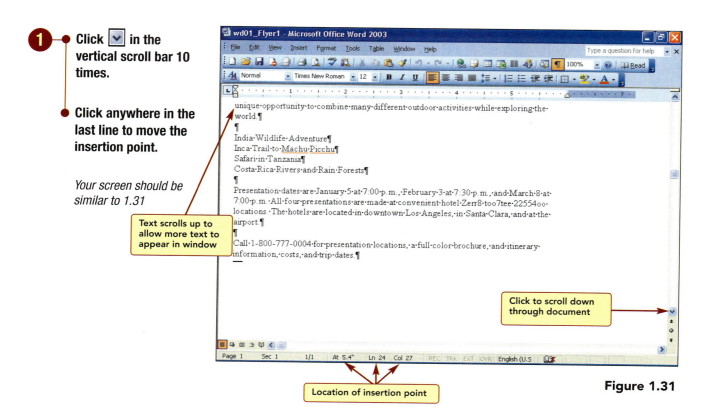

Text scrolls up to allow more text to appear in window

Click to scroll down through document

Location of insertion point

Figure 1.31

The text at the beginning of the flyer has scrolled off the top of the document window, and the text at the bottom of the flyer is now displayed.

You can also scroll the document using the keyboard. While scrolling using the keyboard, the insertion point also moves. The insertion point attempts to maintain its position in a line as you scroll up and down through the document. In a large document, scrolling line by line can take a while. You will now try out several of the mouse and keyboard scrolling features that move by larger jumps.

2

Hold down ↑ for several seconds until the insertion point is on the first line of the flyer.

Click below the scroll box in the scroll bar.

Drag the scroll box to the middle of the scroll bar.

Press Ctrl + End.

Your screen should be similar to Figure 1.32

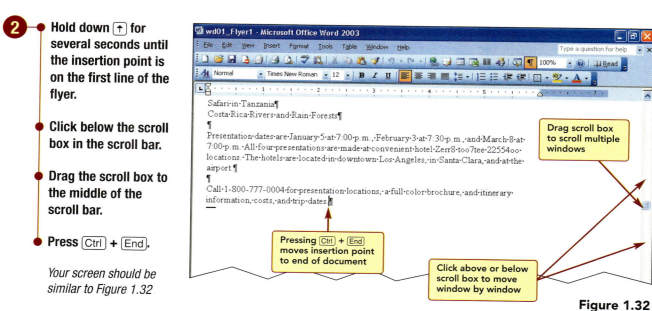

Drag scroll box to scroll multiple windows

Pressing Ctrl + End moves insertion point to end of document

Click above or below scroll box to move window by window

Figure 1.32

The insertion point is now at the end of the document. Using these features makes scrolling a large document much more efficient. Remember that when scrolling using the mouse, if you want to start working at that location, you must click at the new location to move the insertion point.

Editing Documents

While entering text and creating a document, you will find that you will want to edit or make changes and corrections to the document. Although many of the errors are identified and corrections are made automatically for you, others must be made manually. You learned how to use the [Backspace] and [Delete] keys earlier to correct errors. But deleting characters one at a time can be time consuming. Now you will learn about several additional editing features that make editing your work more efficient.

After entering the text of a document, you should proofread it for accuracy and completeness and edit the document as needed. After looking over the flyer, you have identified several errors that need to be corrected and changes you want to make to the content. The changes you want to make are shown below.

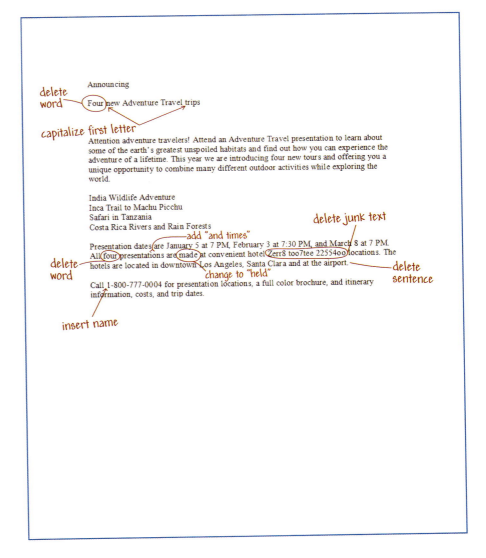

Ignoring Spelling Errors

You first notice that the spelling checker has identified the names of one of the tour locations as misspelled, though in fact it is spelled correctly. This is because it is not in the dictionary. You will instruct Word to accept the spelling of this name and all other words it encounters having the same spelling until you exit the Word application.

1 ● Scroll to the top of the document.

● Right-click on "Machu" to open the Spelling shortcut menu.

● Choose Ignore All.

● In the same manner, tell Word to ignore the spelling of Picchu.

Your screen should be similar to Figure 1.33

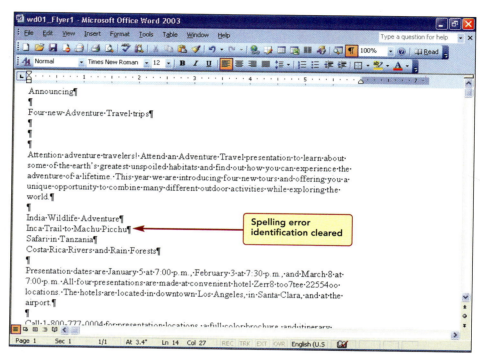

Figure 1.33

The red underlines are removed from each word. If you type any of these words again, they will not be identified as misspelled.

Inserting Text

As you continue to check the document, you see that the first sentence of the paragraph below the list of trips is incorrect. It should read: "Presentation dates and times are . . ." The sentence is missing the words "and times." In addition, you want to change the word "made" to "held" in the following sentence. These words can easily be entered into the sentence without retyping by using either Insert or Overtype mode.

In **Insert mode** new characters are inserted into the existing text by moving the existing text to the right to make space for the new characters. You will insert the words "and times" after the word "dates" in the first sentence.

Additional Information
When you exit the Word application and start it again, these words will be identified as misspelled.

Additional Information
You can ignore grammar errors using the same procedure.

Additional Information
The default setting for Word is Insert mode.

1 ● **Move to "a" in "are"**
(in the first sentence
paragraph below the
list of tours).

Additional Information

Throughout these labs, when
instructed to move to a
specific letter in the text, this
means to move the insertion
point to the left side of the
character.

● **Type and times.**

● **Press** Spacebar.

Your screen should be
similar to Figure 1.34

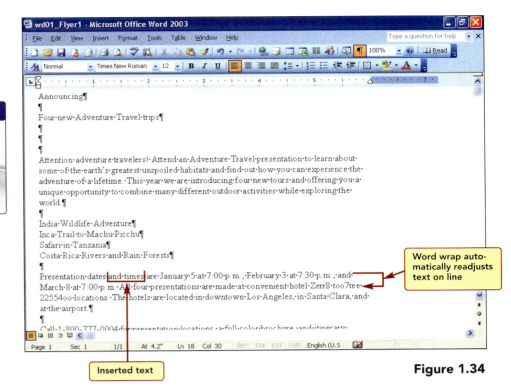

Word wrap auto-
matically readjusts
text on line

Inserted text

Figure 1.34

The inserted text pushes the existing text on the line to the right, and the
word wrap feature automatically readjusts the text on the line to fit within
the margin settings.

In the second sentence, you want to change the word "made" to "held."
You could delete this word and type in the new word, or you can use the
Overtype mode to enter text in a document. When you use **Overtype**
mode, new text replaces existing text as you type. You will switch to this
mode to change the word.

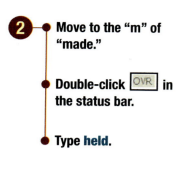

2 Move to the "m" of "made."

Double-click OVR in the status bar.

Type **held**.

Your screen should be similar to Figure 1.35

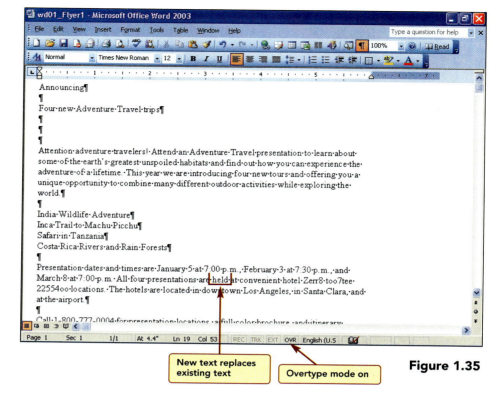

New text replaces existing text

Overtype mode on

Figure 1.35

As each character was typed, the selected character (or space) was replaced with the character being typed. Also notice that the OVR status indicator button letters are now bold, indicating the Overtype mode is on.

3 Double-click OVR.

Overtype mode is off and Insert mode is restored.

Deleting a Word

You next want to delete the word "four" from the same sentence. The Ctrl + Delete key combination deletes text to the right of the insertion point to the beginning of the next group of characters. In order to delete an entire word, you must position the insertion point at the beginning of the word.

Another Method

You can also turn Overtype mode on and off by pressing Insert or by choosing **T**ools/**O**ptions/Edit/Overtype mode.

Additional Information

The Ctrl + Backspace key combination deletes text to the left of the insertion point to the beginning of the next group of characters.

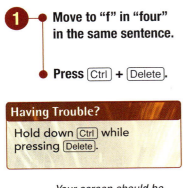

1 • Move to "f" in "four" in the same sentence.

• Press Ctrl + Delete.

Having Trouble?

Hold down Ctrl while pressing Delete.

Your screen should be similar to Figure 1.36

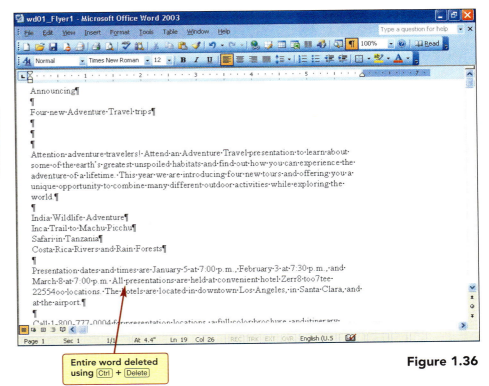

Entire word deleted using Ctrl + Delete

Figure 1.36

Selecting and Deleting Text

As you continue proofreading the flyer, you see that the end of this sentence contains a section of junk characters. To remove these characters, you could use Delete and Backspace to delete each character individually, or Ctrl + Delete or Ctrl + Backspace to delete each word or group of characters. This is very slow, however. Several characters, words, or lines of text can be deleted at once by first selecting the text and then pressing Delete. Text that is selected is highlighted.

To select text using the mouse, first move the insertion point to the beginning or end of the text to be selected, and then drag to highlight the text you want selected. You can select as little as a single letter or as much as the entire document. You can quickly select a standard block of text. Standard blocks include a sentence, paragraph, page, tabular column, rectangular portion of text, or the entire document. The following table summarizes the mouse techniques used to select standard blocks.

To Select	Procedure
Word	Double-click in the word.
Sentence	Press Ctrl and click within the sentence.
Line	Click to the left of a line when the mouse pointer is ◁.
Multiple lines	Drag up or down to the left of a line when the mouse pointer is ◁.
Paragraph	Triple-click on the paragraph or double-click to the left of the paragraph when the mouse pointer is a ◁.
Multiple paragraphs	Drag to the left of the paragraphs when the mouse pointer is ◁.
Document	Triple-click or press Ctrl and click to the left of the text when the mouse pointer is ◁.

You can also select text with the keyboard or voice commands as shown in the following table.

To Select	Keyboard	Voice
Next space or character.	⇧Shift + →	
Previous space or character.	⇧Shift + ←	
Next word.	Ctrl + ⇧Shift + →	Select next word
Previous word.	Ctrl + ⇧Shift + ←	Select last word
Text going backward to beginning of paragraph.	Ctrl + ⇧Shift + ↑	Select last line
Text going forward to end of paragraph.	Ctrl + ⇧Shift + ↓	Select next line
Entire current paragraph.		Select paragraph
Entire document.	Ctrl + A	Select all

To remove highlighting to deselect text, simply click anywhere in the document or press any directional key.

The section of characters you want to remove follow the word "hotel" in the second line of the paragraph below the list of trips.

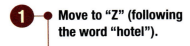

Move to "Z" (following the word "hotel").

Drag to the right until all the text including the space before the word "locations" is highlighted.

Your screen should be similar to Figure 1.37

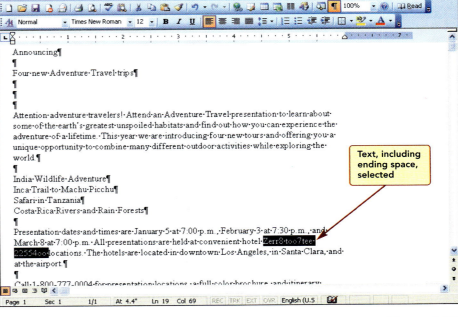

Figure 1.37

The characters you do not want are selected. Text that is selected can then be modified using many different Word features. In this case, you want to remove the selected text.

Press Delete.

Your screen should be similar to Figure 1.38

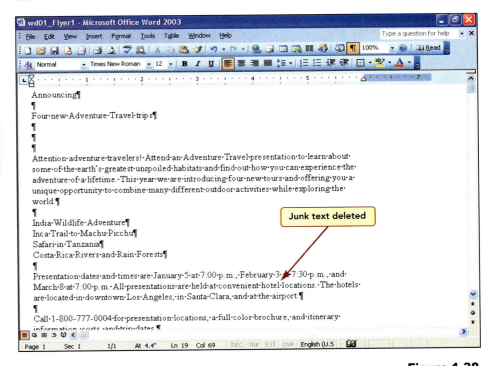

Figure 1.38

You also decide to delete the entire last sentence of the paragraph.

3 Hold down ⌈Ctrl⌉ and click anywhere in the third sentence of the paragraph below the list of trips.

● Press ⌈Delete⌉.

Your screen should be similar to Figure 1.39

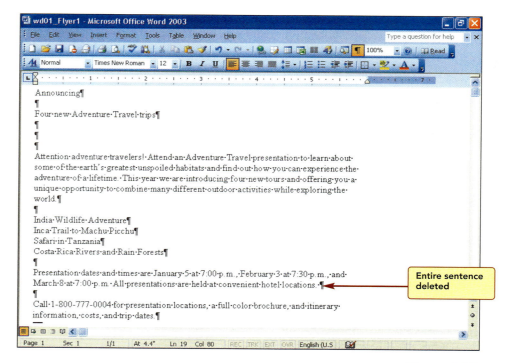

Figure 1.39

Undoing Editing Changes

After removing the sentence, you decide it may be necessary after all. To quickly restore this sentence, you can use  Undo to reverse your last action or command.

1 Click 🔄 Undo.

Another Method

The menu equivalent is **E**dit/**U**ndo (The action to be undone follows the command.) The keyboard shortcut is ⌈Ctrl⌉ + Z and the voice command is "Undo."

Your screen should be similar to Figure 1.40

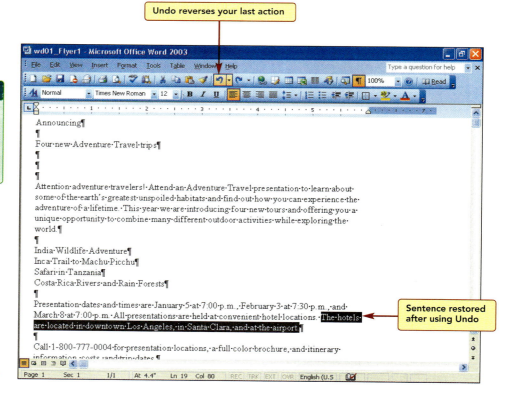

Figure 1.40

Undo returns your last deletion and restores it to its original location in the text, regardless of the current insertion point location. Notice that the Undo button includes a drop-down list button. Clicking this button displays a list of the most recent actions that can be reversed, with the most recent action at the top of the list. When you select an action from the drop-down list, you also undo all actions above it in the list.

2 • Open the Undo drop-down list.

Most recent actions that can be reversed

• **Choose Delete Word.**

Your screen should be similar to Figure 1.41

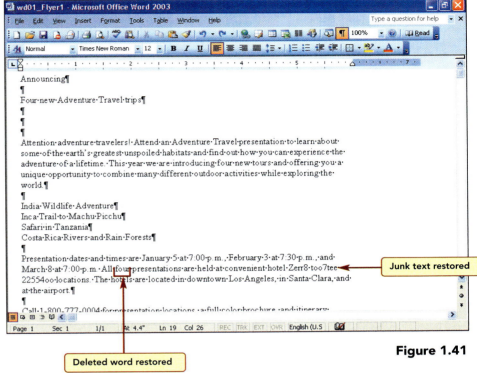

Junk text restored

Deleted word restored

Figure 1.41

The junk characters and the word "four" are restored. Immediately after you undo an action, the Redo button is available so you can restore the action you just undid. You will restore your corrections and then save the changes you have made to the document to a new file.

Another Method

The menu equivalent is **E**dit/**R**edo, the keyboard shortcut is Ctrl + Y, and the voice command is "Redo."

● Choose **F**ile/Save **A**s and save the document as Flyer1 to your data file location.

Your screen should be similar to Figure 1.42

Name of new file

Redo reverses action of using Undo

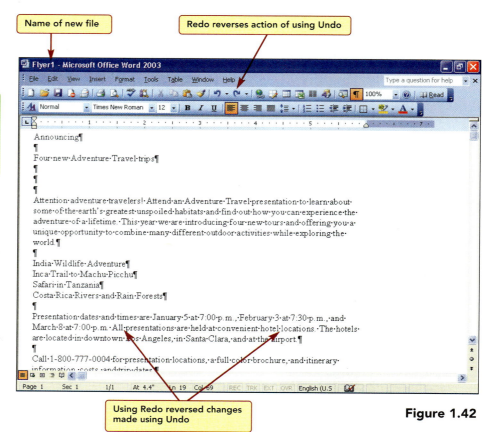

Using Redo reversed changes made using Undo

Figure 1.42

The new file name, Flyer1, is displayed in the window title bar. The original document file, wd01_Flyer1, is unchanged.

Repeatedly using the Undo or Redo buttons performs the actions in the list one by one. So that you can see what action will be performed, these button's ScreenTips identify the action.

Changing Case

You also want to delete the word "Four" from the second line of the flyer title and capitalize the first letter of each word. Although you could change the case individually for the words, you can quickly change both using the Change Case command on the Format menu.

1 • Press Ctrl + Home to move to the beginning of the document.

• Move to "F" in "Four."

• Press Ctrl + Delete.

• Click in the left margin to select the entire title line.

• Choose Format/Change Case.

Your screen should be similar to Figure 1.43

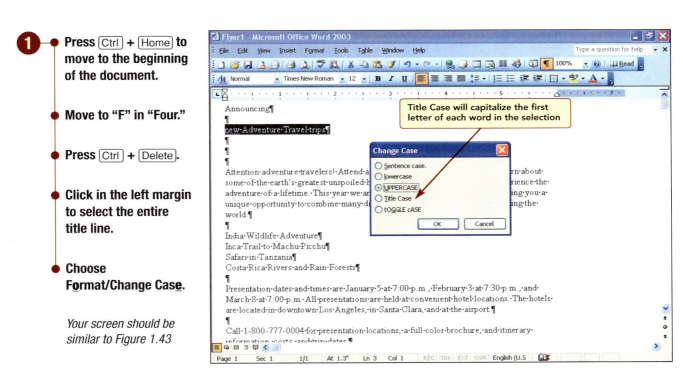

Figure 1.43

The Change Case dialog box allows you to change the case of selected words and sentences to the desired case without having to make the change manually. You want the title to appear in Title Case. In addition, since you have finished editing the flyer for now, you will also turn off the display of formatting marks.

2 • Select Title Case.

• Click OK.

• Click anywhere to deselect the title line.

• Click ¶ Show/Hide ¶.

Your screen should be similar to Figure 1.44

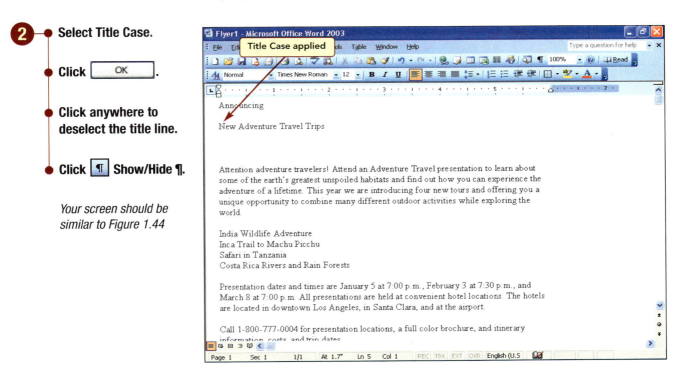

Figure 1.44

The first letter of each word in the title is now capitalized and the highlight is removed from the text. The document returns to normal display. As you have seen, in many editing situations it is helpful to display the formatting marks. However, for normal entry of text, you will probably not need the marks displayed. Now that you know how to turn this feature on and off, you can use it whenever you want when entering and editing text.

Formatting a Document

Because this document is a flyer, you want it to be easy to read and interesting to look at. Applying different formatting to characters and paragraphs can greatly enhance the appearance of the document. **Character formatting** consists of formatting features that affect the selected characters only. This includes changing the character style and size, applying effects such as bold and italics to characters, changing the character spacing and adding animated text effects. **Paragraph formatting** features affect an entire paragraph. A paragraph consists of all text up to and including the paragraph mark. Paragraph formatting features include how the paragraph is positioned or aligned between the margins, paragraph indentation, spacing above and below a paragraph, and line spacing within a paragraph.

Revealing Document Formatting

Word allows you to quickly check the formatting in a document using the Reveal Formatting task pane.

 Choose **Format/Reveal Formatting.**

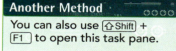 **Move to the top of the document.**

Your screen should be similar to Figure 1.45

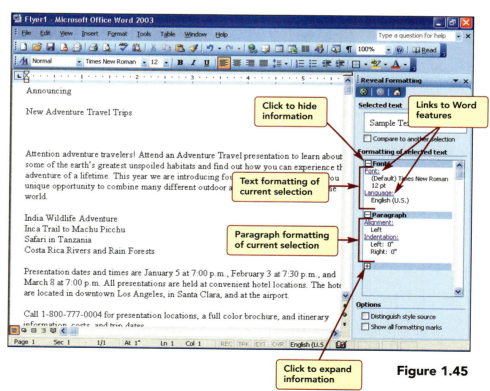

Figure 1.45

The Reveal Formatting task pane displays information about the formatting for the currently selected text and paragraph. Because you have not changed any of these settings, it displays the default document settings. It can also be used to modify these settings. The blue underlined text in the task pane indicates items that are links to Word features, providing faster access to the feature when this pane is displayed than using the menu.

Changing Fonts and Font Sizes

The first formatting change you want to make is to use different fonts and font sizes in the flyer.

Concept 6
Font and Font Size

6   A **font**, also commonly referred to as a **typeface**, is a set of characters with a specific design. The designs have names such as Times New Roman and Courier. Using fonts as a design element can add interest to your document and give readers visual cues to help them find information quickly.

Two basic types of fonts are serif and sans serif. **Serif fonts** have a flair at the base of each letter that visually leads the reader to the next letter. Two common serif fonts are Roman and Times New Roman. Serif fonts generally are used for text in paragraphs. **Sans serif fonts** do not have a flair at the base of each letter. Arial and Helvetica are two common sans serif fonts. Because sans serif fonts have a clean look, they are often used for headings in documents. A good practice is to use only two types of fonts in a document, one for text and one for headings. Too many styles can make your document look cluttered and unprofessional.

Each font has one or more sizes. **Font size** is the height and width of the character and is commonly measured in points, abbreviated "pt." One point equals about 1/72 inch, and text in most documents is 10 pt or 12 pt.

Several common fonts in different sizes are shown in the table below.

Font Name	Font Type	Font Size
Arial	Sans serif	This is 10 pt This is 16 pt.
Courier New	Serif	This is 10 pt. This is 16 pt.
Times New Roman	Serif	This is 10 pt. This is 16 pt.

To change the font before typing the text, use the command and then type. All text will appear in the specified setting until another font setting is selected. To change a font setting for existing text, select the text you want to change and then use the command. If you want to apply font formatting to a word, simply move the insertion point to the word and the formatting is automatically applied to the entire word.

First you want to increase the font size of all the text in the flyer to make it easier to read.

1 ● Triple-click to the left of the text when the mouse pointer is ⤢ to select the entire document.

Another Method

The menu equivalent is **Edit/Select All** and the keyboard shortcut is Ctrl + A.

● **Click Font:** in the task pane.

● **If necessary, click the Font tab to open it.**

Another Method

The menu equivalent is **Format/Font**.

Your screen should be similar to Figure 1.46

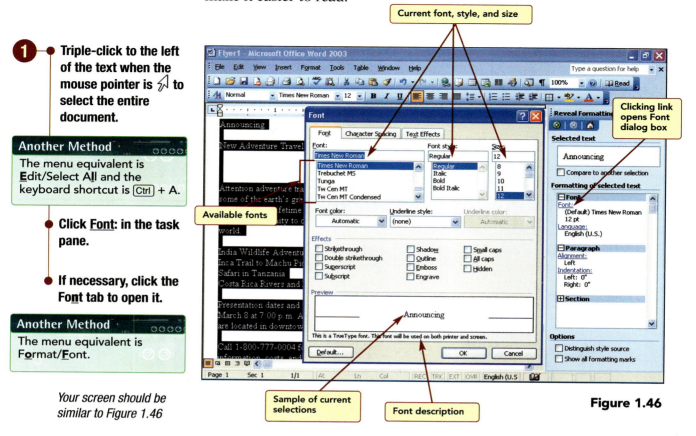

Figure 1.46

The current font settings are displayed, reflecting the default document setting of Times New Roman with a font size of 12 points. The Preview box displays an example of the currently selected font setting.

Notice the description of the font below the Preview box. It states that the selected font is a TrueType font. **TrueType** fonts are fonts that are automatically installed when you install Windows. They appear onscreen exactly as they will appear when printed. Some fonts are printer fonts, which are available only on your printer and may look different onscreen than when printed. Courier is an example of a printer font.

You will increase the font size to 14 points. As you select the option, the Preview box displays how it will appear.

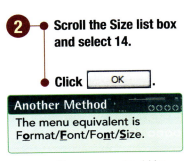

2 Scroll the Size list box and select 14.

● Click [OK].

Your screen should be similar to Figure 1.47

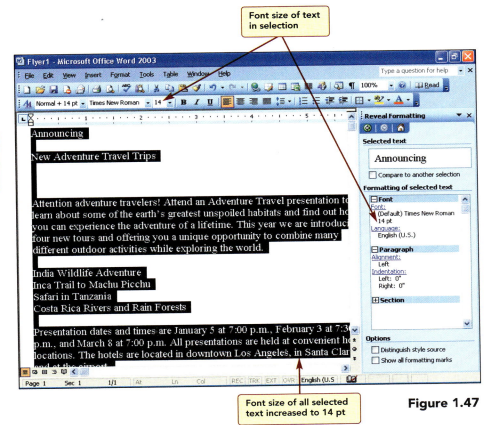

Figure 1.47

The font size of all text in the document has increased to 14 points, making the text much easier to read. The Font Size button in the Formatting toolbar and in the task pane displays the new point size setting for the text at the location of the insertion point.

Next you will change the font and size of the two title lines. Another way to change the font and size is to use the buttons on the Formatting toolbar. The Formatting toolbar buttons are identified below.

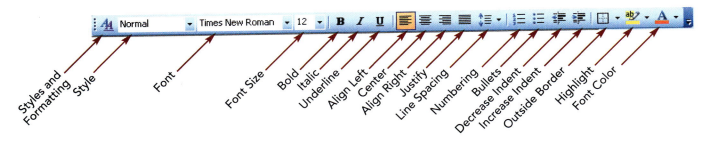

③ **Click anywhere on the word "Announcing."**

• **Open the** Times New Roman **Font drop-down list.**

• **Scroll the list and choose Comic Sans MS.**

• **Open the** 14 **Font Size drop-down list.**

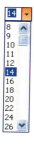

• **Scroll the list and choose 36.**

Your screen should be similar to Figure 1.48

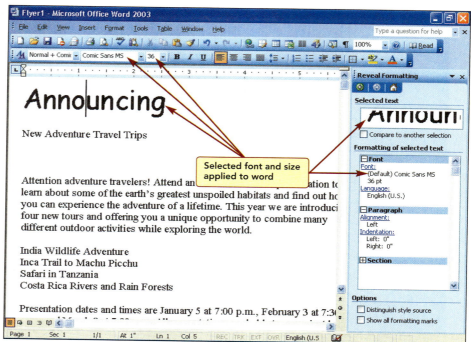

Figure 1.48

The selected font and size have been applied to the word, making the title line much more interesting and eye-catching. The Font and Font Size buttons as well as the information displayed in the Reveal Formatting task pane reflect the settings in use at the location of the insertion point.

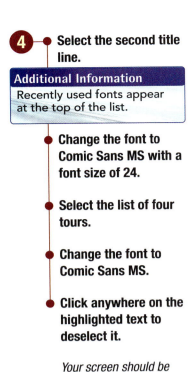

4 Select the second title line.

Additional Information
Recently used fonts appear at the top of the list.

- Change the font to Comic Sans MS with a font size of 24.

- Select the list of four tours.

- Change the font to Comic Sans MS.

- Click anywhere on the highlighted text to deselect it.

Your screen should be similar to Figure 1.49

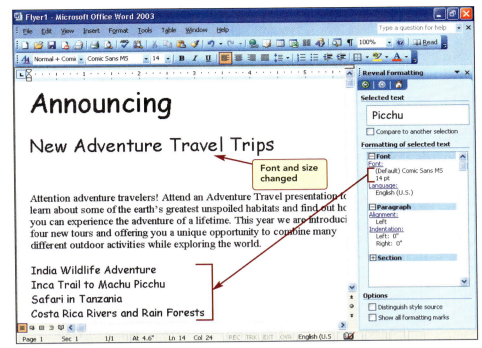

Figure 1.49

Applying Character Effects

Next you want to liven up the flyer by adding character effects such as color and bold to selected areas. The table below describes some of the effects and their uses.

Format	Example	Use
Bold, italic	**Bold** *Italic*	Adds emphasis.
Underline	<u>Underline</u>	Adds emphasis.
Strikethrough	~~Strikethrough~~	Indicates words to be deleted.
Double strikethrough	~~Double Strikethrough~~	Indicates words to be deleted.
Superscript	"To be or not to be."[1]	Used in footnotes and formulas.
Subscript	H_2O	Used in formulas.
Shadow	Shadow	Adds distinction to titles and headings.
Outline	Outline	Adds distinction to titles and headings.
Small caps	SMALL CAPS	Adds emphasis when case is not important.
All caps	ALL CAPS	Adds emphasis when case is not important.
Hidden		Prevents selected text from displaying or printing. Hidden text can be viewed by displaying formatting marks.
Color	Color Color Color	Adds interest

First you will add color and bold to the top title line. The default font color setting is Automatic. This setting automatically determines when to use black or white text. Black text is used on a light background and white text on a dark background.

1 Click anywhere on the word "Announcing."

Open the  Font Color drop-down list.

Click Green.

Click B Bold.

Your screen should be similar to Figure 1.50

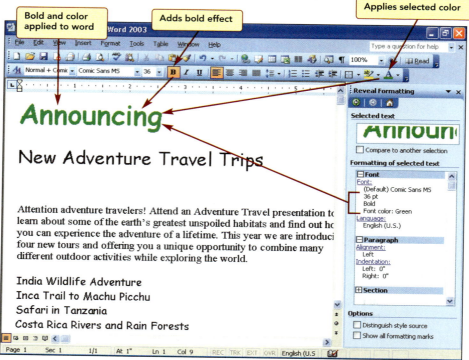

Figure 1.50

The selected color and bold effect have been applied to the entire word. The buttons and task pane information reflect the settings associated with the text at the insertion point. The Font Color button appears in the last selected color. This color can be quickly applied to other selections now simply by clicking the button.

Next you will add color and bold to several other areas of the flyer.

2

- Select the entire second title line.

- Change the font color to orange and add bold.

- Select the list of four trips.

- Click [A] Font Color to change the color to orange.

- Click [B] Bold.

- Bold the last sentence of the flyer.

- Click in the document to deselect the text.

Your screen should be similar to Figure 1.51

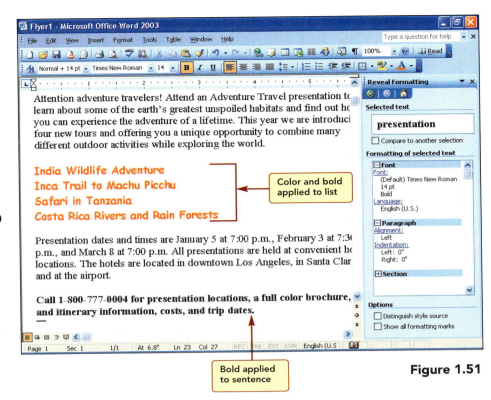

Figure 1.51

Setting Paragraph Alignment

The final formatting change you want to make is to change the paragraph alignment.

Concept 7

Alignment

7   **Alignment** is the positioning of text on a line between the margins or indents. There are four types of paragraph alignment: left, centered, right, and justified. The alignment settings affect entire paragraphs and are described in the table below.

Alignment		Effect on Text Alignment
	Left	Aligns text against the left margin of the page, leaving the right margin ragged or uneven. This is the most commonly used paragraph alignment type and therefore the default setting in all word processing software packages.
	Centered	Centers each line of text between the left and right margins. Center alignment is used mostly for headings or centering graphics on a page.
	Right	Aligns text against the right margin, leaving the left margin ragged. Use right alignment when you want text to line up on the outside of a page, such as a chapter title or a header.
	Justified	Aligns text against the right and left margins and evenly spaces out the words by inserting extra spaces, called **soft spaces**, that adjust automatically whenever additions or deletions are made to the text. Newspapers commonly use justified alignment so the columns of text are even.

The commands to change paragraph alignment are under the **F**ormat/**P**aragraph/**I**ndents and Spacing/Ali**g**nment menu. However, it is much faster to use the keyboard shortcuts, toolbar buttons, or voice commands shown below.

Alignment	Keyboard Shortcut	Button	Voice
Left	Ctrl + L		Left justify
Centered	Ctrl + E		Centered
Right	Ctrl + R		Right justify
Justified	Ctrl + J		

You want to change the alignment of all paragraphs in the flyer from the default of left-aligned to centered.

1

Press ⌈Ctrl⌉ + A to select the entire document.

Click ☰ Center (on the Formatting toolbar).

Press ⌈Ctrl⌉ + ⌈Home⌉.

Your screen should be similar to Figure 1.52

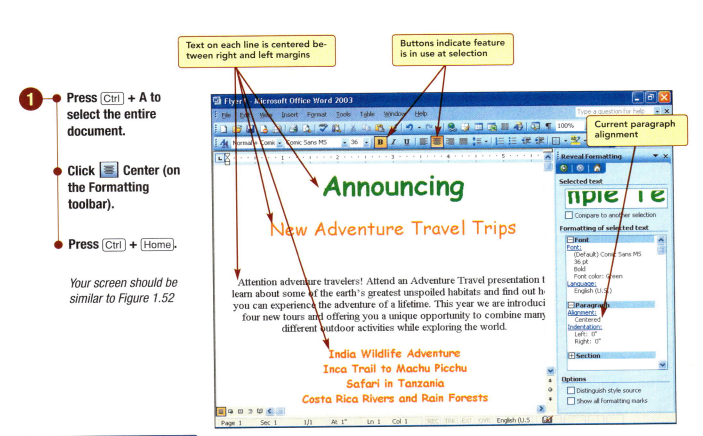

Text on each line is centered between right and left margins

Buttons indicate feature is in use at selection

Current paragraph alignment

Announcing

New Adventure Travel Trips

Attention adventure travelers! Attend an Adventure Travel presentation t learn about some of the earth's greatest unspoiled habitats and find out h you can experience the adventure of a lifetime. This year we are introduci four new tours and offering you a unique opportunity to combine many different outdoor activities while exploring the world.

India Wildlife Adventure
Inca Trail to Machu Picchu
Safari in Tanzania
Costa Rica Rivers and Rain Forests

Figure 1.52

Additional Information

The alignment settings can also be specified before typing in new text. As you type, the text is aligned according to your selection until the alignment setting is changed to another setting.

Each line of text is centered evenly between the left and right page margins. The Reveal Formatting task pane paragraph alignment setting shows the new alignment is centered. Now that you have finished formatting the document, you will close the task pane and save the flyer again using the same file name.

2

Click ☒ Close in the task pane title bar.

Click 🖫 Save to save the file using the same file name.

Additional Information

Saving a file frequently while you are making changes protects you from losing work from a power outage or other mishap.

Working with Graphics

Finally, you want to add a graphic to the flyer to add interest.

Concept 8
Graphics

8   A **graphic** is a non-text element or object, such as a drawing or picture, that can be added to a document. An **object** is an item that can be sized, moved, and manipulated.

     A graphic can be a simple **drawing object** consisting of shapes such as lines and boxes. A drawing object is part of your Word document. A **picture** is an illustration such as a graphic illustration or a scanned photograph. Pictures are graphics that were created using another program and are inserted in your Word document as embedded objects. An **embedded object** becomes part of the Word document and can be opened and edited from within the Word document using the **source program**, the program in which it was created. Any changes made to the embedded object are not made to the original picture file because they are independent. Several examples of drawing objects and pictures are shown below.

drawing object

graphic illustration

photograph

     Add graphics to your documents to help the reader understand concepts, to add interest, and to make your document stand out from others.

Inserting a Picture

Picture files can be obtained from a variety of sources. Many simple drawings called clip art are available in the Clip Organizer that comes with Microsoft Office 2003. You can also create picture files using a scanner to convert any printed document, including photographs, to an electronic format. Most images that are scanned and inserted into documents are stored as Windows bitmap files (.bmp). All types of pictures, including clip art, photographs, and other types of images, can be found on the Internet. These files are commonly stored as .jpg or .pcx files. Keep in mind that any images you locate on the Internet may be copyrighted and should only be used with permission. You can also purchase CDs containing graphics for your use.

     You want to add a picture to the flyer below the two title lines. You will move to the location in the document where you want to insert the graphic and then open the Clip Art task pane to locate a graphic.

Additional Information

You can also scan a picture and insert it directly into a Word document without saving it as a file first.

1

- Click **¶** Show/Hide to display formatting marks.

- Move to the middle blank line below the second title line.

- Choose **Insert/Picture/Clip Art**.

Your screen should be similar to Figure 1.53

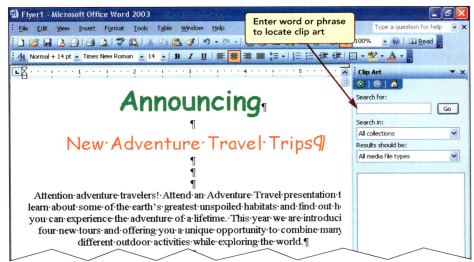

Figure 1.53

The Clip Art task pane appears in which you can enter a word or phrase that is representative of the type of picture you want to locate. You can also specify the locations to search and the type of media files, such as clip art, movies, photographs, or sound, to display in the results. You want to find clip art and photographs of nature.

2

- If necessary, select any existing text in the Search For text box.

- Type **nature**.

- If All Collections is not displayed in the Search In text box, select Everywhere from the drop-down list.

- Open the Results Should Be drop-down list, select Clip Art and Photographs and deselect all other options.

- Click **Cancel**.

Your screen should be similar to Figure 1.54

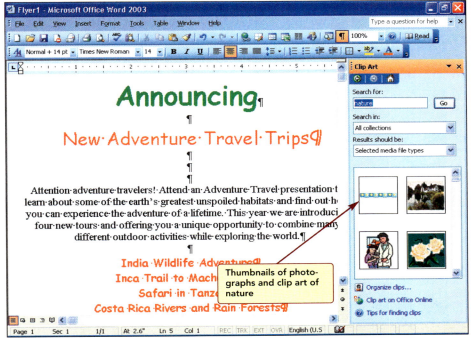

Figure 1.54

The program searches all locations on your computer and, if you have an Internet connection established, Microsoft's Clip Art and Media Web site for clip art and graphics that match your search term. The Results area displays **thumbnails**, miniature representations of pictures, of all located graphics. Pointing to a thumbnail displays a ScreenTip containing the keywords associated with the picture and information about the picture properties. It also displays a drop-down list bar that accesses the item's shortcut menu.

3 ● **Point to any thumbnail to see a ScreenTip.**

● **Scroll the list to view additional images.**

Your screen should be similar to Figure 1.55

Figure 1.55

Because so many pictures were located, you decide to narrow your search to display pictures of animals only. Additionally, because it is sometimes difficult to see the graphic, you can preview it in a larger size.

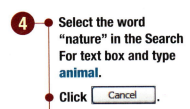

4 ● Select the word "nature" in the Search For text box and type **animal**.

● Click [Cancel].

● If necessary, expand and scroll the results area to see the graphic of a tiger.

● Point to the tiger graphic and click next to the graphic to open the shortcut menu.

● Choose **Preview/Properties**.

Your screen should be similar to Figure 1.56

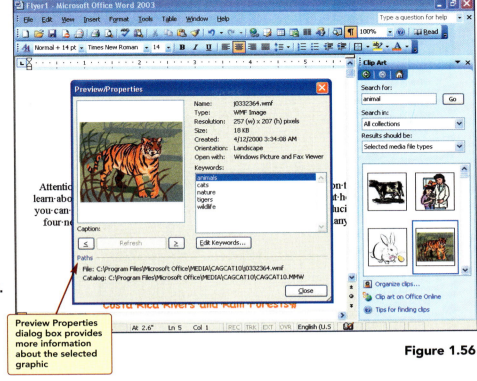

Figure 1.56

Because the search term is more specific, fewer results are displayed. The Preview/Properties dialog box displays the selected graphic larger so it is easier to see. It also displays more information about the properties associated with the graphic. You think this looks like a good choice and will insert it into the document.

5 ● Click [Close] to close the dialog box.

● Click on the graphic to insert it in the document.

Another Method
You could also choose **Insert** from the thumbnail's shortcut menu.

● Click ☒ in the task pane title bar to close it.

Your screen should be similar to Figure 1.57

Figure 1.57

The picture is inserted in the document at the insertion point. It is centered because the paragraph in which it was placed is centered. Although you think this graphic looks good, you want to see how a photograph of a lion you recently received from a client would look instead. The photograph has been saved as a picture image.

6 ● **Choose**
Insert/Picture/From File.

Another Method

You could also click 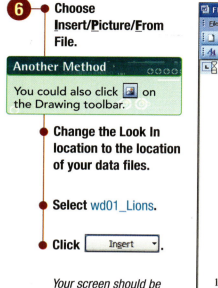 on the Drawing toolbar.

● **Change the Look In location to the location of your data files.**

● **Select** wd01_Lions.

● **Click** [Insert ▾].

Your screen should be similar to Figure 1.58

Second graphic inserted in document

Figure 1.58

The lion picture is inserted next to the clip art.

Deleting a Graphic

There are now two graphics in the flyer. You decide to use the lion picture and need to remove the graphic of the tiger. To do this, you select the graphic and delete it.

1 ● **Click on the tiger clip art graphic.**

Your screen should be similar to Figure 1.59

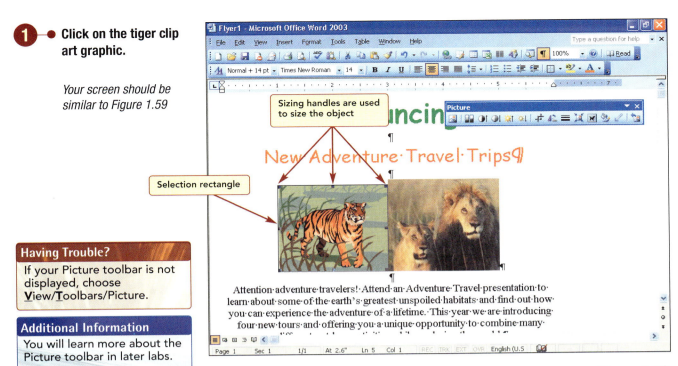

Figure 1.59

The picture is surrounded by a **selection rectangle** and eight boxes, called **sizing handles**, indicating it is a selected object and can now be deleted, sized, moved, or modified. The Picture toolbar automatically appears and is used to modify the selected picture object.

2 ● **Press** Delete.

Your screen should be similar to Figure 1.60

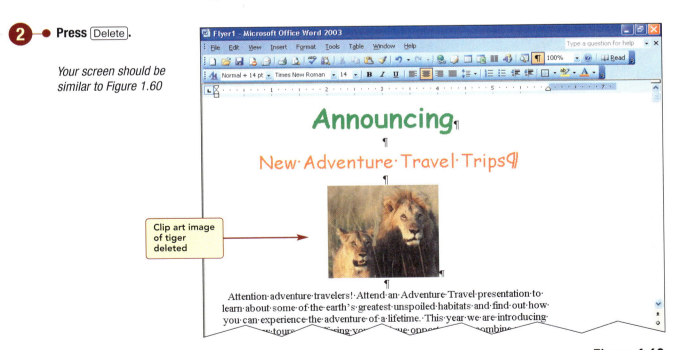

Figure 1.60

The tiger graphic is removed.

Sizing a Graphic

Usually, when a graphic is inserted, its size will need to be adjusted. A graphic object can be manipulated in many ways. You can change its size, add captions, borders, or shading, or move it to another location. A graphic object can be moved anywhere on the page, including in the margins or on top of or below other objects, including text. The only places you cannot place a graphic object are into a footnote, endnote, or caption. In this case, you want to increase the picture's size. To size a graphic, you select it and drag the sizing handles to increase or decrease the size of the object. The mouse pointer changes to ↔ when pointing to a handle. The direction of the arrow indicates the direction in which you can drag to size the graphic. You want to increase the image to approximately 3 inches wide by 2.5 inches high.

1

- **Click on the Lions graphic to select it.**

- **Point to the lower right corner handle.**

- **With the pointer as a ↖, drag outward from the picture to increase the size to approximately 3 by 2.5 inches (use the ruler as a guide and refer to Figure 1.61).**

- **Click anywhere in the document to deselect the graphic.**

- **Turn off the display of formatting marks.**

- **Click 💾 Save.**

Your screen should be similar to Figure 1.61

Figure 1.61

Previewing and Printing a Document

Although you still plan to make several formatting changes to the document, you want to give a copy of the flyer to the manager to get feedback regarding the content and layout. To save time and unnecessary printing and paper waste, it is always a good idea to first preview your document onscreen to see how it will appear when printed.

Previewing the Document

Previewing your document before printing it allows you to look over each page and make necessary adjustments before printing it.

1 Click 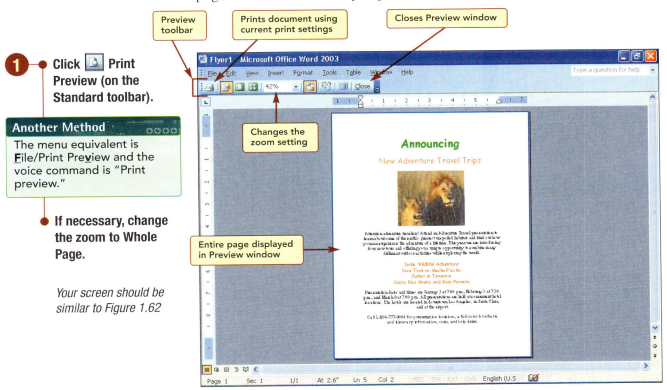 Print Preview (on the Standard toolbar).

Another Method

The menu equivalent is **F**ile/Print Pre**v**iew and the voice command is "Print preview."

If necessary, change the zoom to Whole Page.

Your screen should be similar to Figure 1.62

Figure 1.62

The Print Preview window displays a reduced view of how the current page will appear when printed. This view allows you to check your page layout before printing. The flyer looks good and does not appear to need any further modifications immediately.

The Preview window also includes its own toolbar. You can print the flyer directly from the Preview window using the Print button; however, you do not want to send the document directly to the printer just yet.

Printing the Document

First you need to add your name to the flyer and check the print settings.

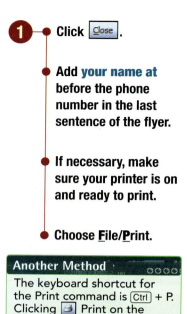

1 ● **Click** Close .

● **Add your name at** before the phone number in the last sentence of the flyer.

● **If necessary, make sure your printer is on and ready to print.**

● **Choose File/Print.**

 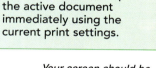
Your screen should be similar to Figure 1.63

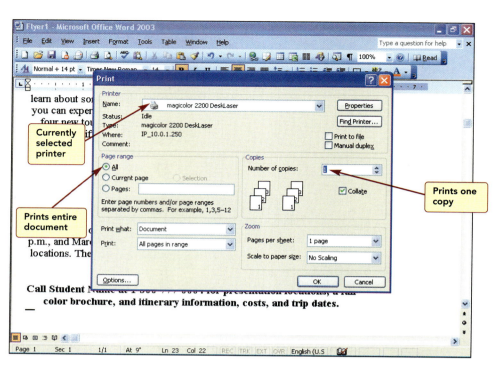

Figure 1.63

Note: Please consult your instructor for printing procedures that may differ from the following directions.

From the Print dialog box, you need to specify the printer you will be using and the document settings. The printer that is currently selected is displayed in the Name drop-down list box in the Printer section of the dialog box.

The Page Range area of the Print dialog box lets you specify how much of the document you want printed. The range options are described in the following table:

Option	Action
All	Prints entire document.
Current page	Prints selected page or page the insertion point is on.
Pages	Prints pages you specify by typing page numbers in the dialog box.
Selection	Prints selected text only.

The **default** range setting, All, is the correct setting. In the Copies section, the default setting of one copy of the document is acceptable. You will print using the default print settings.

2 If you need to change the selected printer to another printer, open the **N**ame drop-down list box and select the appropriate printer (your instructor will tell you which printer to select).

Click [OK].

Your printer should be printing the document. The printed copy of the flyer should be similar to the document shown in the Case Study at the beginning of the lab.

Setting File Properties

You have finished working on the flyer for now and want to save the changes you have made to the file. Along with the content of the file, each file can include additional **file properties** or settings that are associated with the file. Some of these properties are automatically generated. These include statistics, such as the number of words in the file, and general information, such as the date the document was created and last modified. Others, such as the author of the file, are properties that you can add to the file.

Documenting a File

You will look at the file properties and add documentation to identify you as the author and a title for the document.

1 Choose **F**ile/Proper**t**ies

Open the General tab.

Your screen should be similar to Figure 1.64

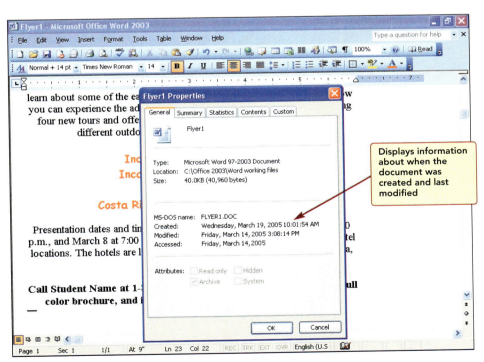

Figure 1.64

The General tab displays information about the type, location, and size of the document as well as information about when the document was created and modified. Next you will look at the document statistics.

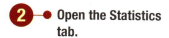

2 ● **Open the Statistics tab.**

Your screen should be similar to Figure 1.65

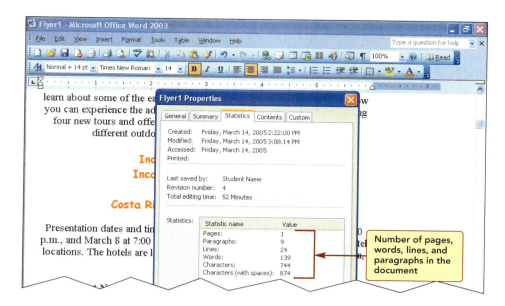

Number of pages, words, lines, and paragraphs in the document

Figure 1.65

This tab identifies who last saved the document, the revision number, and the total editing time in minutes. The table identifies the number of pages, words, lines, paragraphs, and so forth that are included in the document.

Now you want to add your own documentation to the file. Along with the documentation, you can save a picture of the first page of the file for previewing in the Open dialog box. Unlike the preview you saw when you opened the file earlier, which displayed the text of the first few lines of the document, saving a preview picture displays a graphic representation of the entire first page of the document.

3 ● **Open the Summary tab.**

● **Enter New Tour Flyer as the title and your name as the author.**

● **Select the "Save preview picture" option.**

Your screen should be similar to Figure 1.66

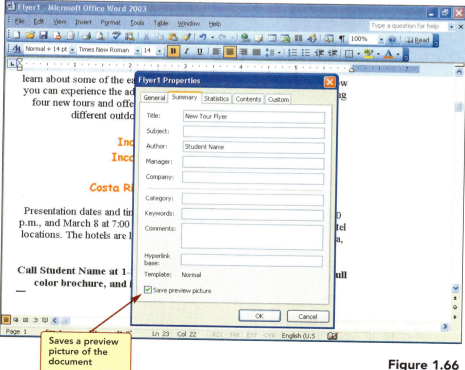

Saves a preview picture of the document

Figure 1.66

You have completed adding the properties to the document. Not until the file is saved are the new properties you added saved with the file. Because you have finished working on the flyer for now, you will exit the application and save the file at the same time.

 **4** ● Click `OK`.

Exiting Word

The Exit command in the File menu is used to quit the Word program. Alternatively, you can click the ❌ Close button in the application window title bar. If you attempt to close the application without first saving your document, Word displays a warning asking if you want to save your work. If you do not save your work and you exit the application, any changes you made since last saving it are lost.

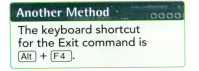 **1** ● Click ❌ Close.

● Click `Yes` to save the changes you made to the file.

Another Method
The keyboard shortcut for the Exit command is Alt + F4.

The Windows desktop is visible again.

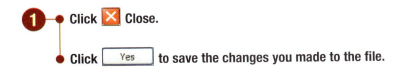

Focus on Careers

EXPLORE YOUR CAREER OPTIONS

Food Service Manager

Have you noticed flyers around your campus advertising job positions? Many of these jobs are in the food service industry. Food service managers are traditionally responsible for overseeing the kitchen and dining room. However, these positions increasingly involve administrative tasks, including recruiting new employees. As a food service manager your position would likely include creating newspaper notices and flyers to attract new staff. These flyers should be eye-catching and error-free. The typical salary range of a food service manager is $24,000 to $41,000. Demand for skilled food service managers is expected to increase through 2010.

LAB 1
Creating and Editing a Document

Grammar Checker   (WD1.19)

The grammar checker advises you of incorrect grammar as you create and edit a document, and proposes possible corrections.

AutoText and AutoComplete   (WD1.22)

The AutoText and AutoComplete features make entering text easier by providing shortcuts for entering commonly used text.

Spelling Checker   (WD1.23)

The spelling checker advises you of misspelled words as you create and edit a document, and proposes possible corrections.

AutoCorrect   (WD1.25)

The AutoCorrect feature makes some basic assumptions about the text you are typing and, based on these assumptions, automatically corrects the entry.

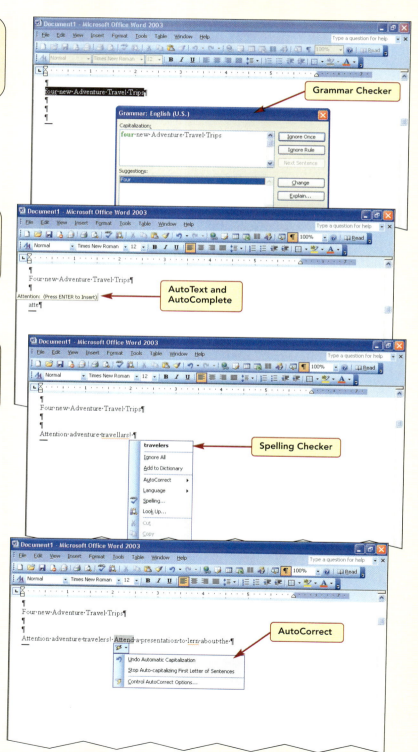

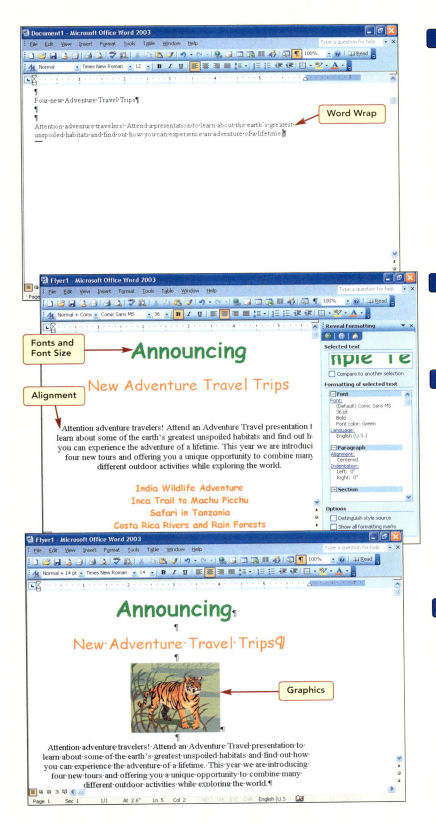

Word Wrap (WD1.28)

The word wrap feature automatically decides where to end a line and wraps text to the next line based on the margin settings.

Fonts and Font Size (WD1.51)

A font, also commonly referred to as a typeface, is a set of characters with a specific design that has one or more font sizes.

Alignment (WD1.58)

Alignment is the positioning of text on a line between the margins or indents. There are four types of paragraph alignment: left, centered, right, and justified.

Graphics (WD1.60)

A graphic is a non-text element or object, such as a drawing or picture that can be added to a document.

lab review

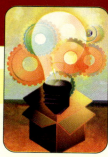

LAB 1

Creating and Editing a Document

key terms

alignment   WD1.58
AutoComplete   WD1.22
AutoCorrect   WD1.25
AutoText   WD1.22
character formatting   WD1.50
cursor   WD1.5
custom dictionary   WD1.23
default   WD1.68
document window   WD1.5
drawing object   WD1.60
edit   WD1.11
embedded object   WD1.60
end-of-file marker   WD1.5
file property   WD1.69
font   WD1.51

font size   WD1.51
format   WD1.11
formatting mark   WD1.14
Formatting toolbar   WD1.5
grammar checker   WD1.19
graphic   WD1.60
Insert mode   WD1.40
insertion point   WD1.5
main dictionary   WD1.23
object   WD1.60
Overtype mode   WD1.41
pane   WD1.6
paragraph formatting   WD1.50
picture   WD1.60
ruler   WD1.5

sans serif font   WD1.51
select   WD1.6
selection rectangle   WD1.65
serif font   WD1.51
sizing handles   WD1.65
Smart Tag   WD1.29
soft space   WD1.58
source program   WD1.60
spelling checker   WD1.23
Standard toolbar   WD1.5
thumbnail   WD1.62
TrueType   WD1.52
typeface   WD1.51
word wrap   WD1.28

mos skills

The Microsoft Office Specialist (MOS) certification program is designed to measure your proficiency in performing basic tasks using the Office 2003 applications. Getting certified demonstrates that you have the skills and provides a valuable industry credential for employment. After completing this lab, you have learned the following Microsoft Office Word Specialist skills:

Skill	Description	Page
Creating Content	Insert and edit text, symbols, and special characters	WD1.11
	Insert frequently used and predefined text	WD1.21
	Insert, position, and size graphics	WD1.60
Formatting Content	Format text	WD1.50
	Format paragraphs	WD1.57
Formatting and Managing Documents	Preview and print documents	WD1.67
	Review and modify document properties	WD1.69
	Print documents, envelopes, and labels	WD1.67
	Preview documents and Web pages	WD1.67
	Change and organize document views and windows	WD1.8

command summary

Command	Shortcut Key	Button	Voice	Action
File/**N**ew	Ctrl + N		New file	Opens new document
File/**O**pen	Ctrl + O		Open	Opens existing document file
File/**C**lose	Ctrl + F4		Close Document	Closes document
File/**S**ave	Ctrl + S		Save	Saves document using same file name
File/Save **A**s				Saves document using a new file name, type, and/or location
File/Print Pre**v**iew			Print Preview	Displays document as it will appear when printed
File/**P**rint	Ctrl + P		Print	Prints document using selected print settings
File/Proper**t**ies				Displays file statistics, summary, and property settings
File/E**x**it	Alt + F4			Exits Word program
Edit/**U**ndo	Ctrl + Z		Undo	Restores last editing change
Edit/**R**edo	Ctrl + Y		Redo	Restores last Undo or repeats last command or action
Edit/Cle**a**r/**C**ontents	Delete			Deletes characters you do not want
Edit/Select A**l**l	Ctrl + A			Selects all text in document
View/**N**ormal			Normal View	Shows text formatting and simple layout of page
View/**W**eb Layout			Web Layout View	Shows document as it will appear when viewed in a Web browser
View/**P**rint Layout			Print Layout View	Shows how text and objects will appear on printed page
View/**R**eading Layout				Scales document to fit screen as pages in a book
View/**O**utline				Shows structure of document

command summary (continued)

Command	Shortcut Key	Button	Voice	Action
View/F**u**ll Screen			View full screen	Displays document only, without application features such as menu bars or toolbars
View/**R**uler				Displays/hides horizontal ruler bar
View/**Z**oom/**W**hole Page				Fits entire page on screen
Insert/**A**utoText/AutoTe**x**t/**S**how/AutoComplete suggestions				Turns on AutoComplete feature
Insert/**P**icture/**C**lip Art		🖼		Accesses Clip Organizer and inserts selected clip
Insert/**P**icture/**F**rom File		🖼		Inserts selected picture
F**o**rmat/**F**ont/Fo**n**t/**F**ont		Times New Roman ▾		Changes typeface
F**o**rmat/**F**ont/Fo**n**t/**F**ont Style/Bold	Ctrl + B	**B**	On bold	Makes selected text bold
F**o**rmat/**F**ont/Fo**n**t/**S**ize		12 ▾		Changes font size
F**o**rmat/**F**ont/Fo**n**t/**C**olor		A ▾		Changes text to selected color
F**o**rmat/**P**aragraph/**I**ndents and Spacing/Ali**g**nment/Center	Ctrl + E	▤	Centered	Centers text between left and right margins
F**o**rmat/**P**aragraph/**I**ndents and Spacing/Ali**g**nment/Justified	Ctrl + J	▤		Aligns text equally between left and right margins
F**o**rmat/**P**aragraph/**I**ndents and Spacing/Ali**g**nment/Left	Ctrl + L	▤	Left justify	Aligns text to left margin
F**o**rmat/**P**aragraph/**I**ndents and Spacing/Ali**g**nment/Right	Ctrl + R	▤	Right justify	Aligns text to right margin
F**o**rmat/Change Cas**e**				Changes case of selected text
F**o**rmat/Re**v**eal Formatting	⇧Shift + F1			Opens Reveal Formatting task pane

Command	Shortcut Key	Button	Voice	Action
F**o**rmat/**Pi**cture				Changes format settings associated with selected picture
Tools/**W**ord Count				Reviews document statistics
Tools/**A**utoCorrect Options/**E**xceptions			Options button	Displays or hides AutoCorrect option buttons
Tools/**A**utoCorrect Options/ **Sh**ow AutoCorrect Options buttons			Options button	Displays or hides AutoCorrect option buttons
Tools/**C**ustomize/ **O**ptions/**S**howStandard and Formatting toolbars				Displays Standard and Formatting toolbars on two rows
Tools/**O**ptions/Edit/ O**v**ertype Mode	Insert	OVR		Switches between Insert and Overtype modes
Tools/**O**ptions/Spelling and Grammar				Changes settings associated with Spelling and Grammar checking
Tools/**O**ptions/View/A**ll**	Ctrl + ⇧Shift + *	¶		Displays or hides formatting marks
Tools/**O**ptions/Save				Changes settings associated with saving files

screen identification

1. In the following Word screen, letters identify important elements. Enter the correct term for each screen element in the space provided.

Possible answers for the screen identification are:

Scrolls down	Show/Hide	A. _____	L. _____
Normal view	Zoom	B. _____	M. _____
tab mark	Center	C. _____	N. _____
Formatting toolbar	Spelling and grammar	D. _____	O. _____
Save	status icon	E. _____	P. _____
Print layout view	Redo	F. _____	Q. _____
Overtype	Bold	G. _____	R. _____
Font color	Status bar	H. _____	S. _____
Print Preview	Scroll bar	I. _____	T. _____
Standard toolbar	Graphic	J. _____	U. _____
Font	Paragraph mark	K. _____	V. _____
Undo	tab stop		

matching

Match the item on the left with the correct description on the right.

1. 🔍 _____ a. new text writes over existing text

2. font _____ b. moves to the top of the document

3. OVR _____ c. feature that automatically begins a new line when text reaches the right margin

4. alignment _____ d. images that enhance a document

5. Ctrl + Home _____ e. displays the Print Preview window

6. graphics _____ f. type style that can be applied to text

7. 💾 _____ g. font size measurement

8. word wrap _____ h. controls paragraph positioning between the margins

9. point _____ i. saves a document using the same file name

10. sans serif _____ j. font without a flair at the base of each letter

11. 🅰️▾

multiple choice

Circle the correct response to the questions below.

1. Document development follows these steps.
   a. plan, edit, enter, format, preview, and print
   b. enter, edit, format, preview, and print
   c. plan, enter, edit, format, preview, and print
   d. design, enter, edit, format, preview, and print

2. The Word feature that makes some basic assumptions about the text entered and automatically makes changes based on those assumptions is _____.
   a. AutoChange
   b. AutoCorrect
   c. AutoText
   d. AutoFormat

3. Words that are not contained in the main dictionary can be added to the _____ dictionary.
   a. custom
   b. additional
   c. add to
   d. user defined

4. The feature that allows you to preview a document before it is printed is _____.
   a. print review
   b. page review
   c. page preview
   d. print preview

5. When text is evenly aligned on both margins it is _____.
   a. center aligned
   b. justified
   c. left aligned
   d. right aligned

6. Words that may be spelled incorrectly in a document are indicated by a _____.
   a. green wavy line
   b. red wavy line
   c. blue wavy line
   d. purple dotted underline

7. Font sizes are measured in _____.
   a. inches
   b. points
   c. bits
   d. pieces

8. The _____ feature automatically decides where to end a line and where the next line of text begins based on the margin settings.
   a. line wrap
   b. word wrap
   c. wrap around
   d. end wrap

9. A set of characters with a specific design is called a(n) _____.
   a. style
   b. font
   c. AutoFormat
   d. design

true/false

Circle the correct answer to the following questions.

1. A wavy red line indicates a potential grammar error.	True	False
2. The first three steps in developing a document are: plan, enter, and edit.	True	False
3. Text can be entered in a document in either the Insert or Overtype mode.	True	False
4. The Delete key erases the character to the right of the insertion point.	True	False
5. The automatic word wrap feature checks for typing errors.	True	False
6. The Word document file name extension is .wrd.	True	False
7. Font sizes are measured in inches.	True	False
8. Word inserts hidden marks into a document to control the display of text.	True	False
9. The AutoCorrect feature automatically identifies and corrects certain types of errors.	True	False

fill-in

1. A small blue box appearing under a word or character indicates that the _____ feature was applied.

2. If a word is underlined with purple dots, this indicates a(n) _____.

3. The _____ feature displays each page of your document in a reduced size so you can see the page layout.

4. To size a graphic evenly, click and drag the _____ in one corner of the graphic.

5. It is good practice to use only _____ types of fonts in a document.

6. When you use _____, new text replaces existing text as you type.

7. The _____ sits on the right side of the window and contains buttons and icons to help you perform common tasks, such as opening a blank document.

8. Use _____ when you want to keep your existing document with the original name and make a copy with a new name.

9. The _____ window displays a reduced view of how the current page will appear when printed.

10. The _____ feature includes entries, such as commonly used phrases, that can be quickly inserted into a document.

Hands-On Exercises

step-by-step

Writing a Memo ★

1. Adventure Travel Tours is planning to update its World Wide Web site in the near future. You have been asked to solicit suggestions from the travel agents about changes they would like to see made to the current Web site. You decide to send all the travel agents a memo asking them for their input. Your completed memo is shown here.

   a. Open a blank Word document and create the following memo in Normal view. Press `Tab ⇥` twice after you type colons (:) in the To, From, and Date lines. This will make the information following the colons line up evenly. Enter a blank line between paragraphs.

To:	Travel Agents
From:	Student Name
Date:	[Current date]

   Next month we plan to begin work on updating the current Adventure Travel Tours Web site. In preparation for this project, I would like your input about the current Web site. In the next few days as you use the Web site, pay attention to such things as the layout, colors, and content. Then send your comments back to me about both the positive and negative features of the current Web site and suggestions for changes you would like to see made in the new Web site.

   Thank you in advance for your input.

   To: Travel Agents
   From: Student Name
   Date: [Current date]
   RE: Web Site Revision

   Next month we plan to begin work on updating the Adventure Travel Tours Web site. In preparation for this project, I would like your input about the Web site.

   In the next few days as you use the Web site, pay attention to the layout, colors, ease of use, and content. Then send your comments back to me about both the positive and negative features of the current Web site and suggestions for changes you would like to see made in the new Web site.

   Thank you in advance for your input.

   b. Turn on the display of formatting marks.

   c. Correct any spelling and grammar errors that are identified.

   d. Delete the word "current" from the first and second sentences. Delete the phrase "such things as" from the third sentence. Insert the text "ease of use," after the word "colors," in the third sentence.

   e. Start a new paragraph beginning with the third sentence. Include a blank line between paragraphs.

   f. Change the font size for the entire memo to 14 pt and the alignment of the body of the memo to justified.

   g. Under the Date line insert the AutoText reference line "RE:".

h. Press [Tab⇆] twice and type **Web Site Revision**. Insert a blank line below the reference line.

i. Save the document as Web Site Memo in your data file location.

j. Include your name in the file properties as author and the file name as the title.

k. Preview and print the document.

Writing a Newspaper Article ★★

2. You work for the Animal Rescue Foundation, a nonprofit organization that rescues and finds homes for unwanted animals. In next week's newspaper, you plan to run an article to try to encourage people from the community to support the Foundation by joining the Animal Angels volunteer group. Your completed article is shown here.

a. Enter the following information in a new Word document in Normal view, pressing [←Enter] where indicated.

Volunteers Needed! [←Enter] (4 times)

The Animal Rescue Foundation is in need of your help. Over the past 6 months, we have seen a 20 percent increase in the number of rescued animals. With the increase in animals, we need more people to join Animal Angels, our volunteer group. [←Enter] (2 times)

Our volunteer program is both diverse and flexible; no matter how hectic your schedule, we can find a place for you. Quite simply, it is our goal to have volunteers actively involved in many areas of our organization–from providing direct care for the animals to contributing to the every day functioning of our shelter and programs to furthering animal welfare and our mission of finding a loving home for each animal. Here are just some of the opportunities that await you. [←Enter] (2 times)

Foster parent [←Enter]
Work at adoption fairs [←Enter]
Provide obedience training [←Enter]
Pet grooming specialists [←Enter]
Repair, organize, and distribute donations [←Enter]
Greeters and matchmakers [←Enter]
Adoption counselor [←Enter]
Follow-up on adoptions [←Enter]
Kennel and animal care assistants [←Enter]
Special event volunteers [←Enter]
Grounds maintenance keepers [←Enter]

Volunteers Needed!

The Animal Rescue Foundation is in need of your help. Over the past six months, we have seen a *20 percent* increase in the number of rescued animals. With the increase in animals, we need more people to join Animal Angels, our volunteer group.

Our volunteer program is both diverse and flexible; no matter how hectic your schedule, we can find a place for you. It is our goal to have volunteers actively involved in many areas of our organization--from providing direct care for the animals to contributing to the every day functioning of our shelter and programs to furthering animal welfare and our mission of finding a loving home for each animal. Here are just some of the opportunities that await you.

Foster parent
Work at adoption fairs
Socialize the cats
Provide obedience training
Pet grooming specialists
Repair, organize, and distribute donations
Greeters and matchmakers
Adoption counselor
Kennel and animal care assistants
Special event volunteers
Grounds maintenance keepers
Humane educators

Thank you for your interest in giving your time and energy to the abused, homeless, and neglected animals that come to us each year. It is our desire that the time you spend here will be as rewarding for you as it is for the animals. We are proud of our organization and would like for you to become a part of the team.

Please call us at 603-555-1313 to join us!

Student Name
[Current Date]

Communication specialists [←Enter]

Humane educators [←Enter] (2 times)

Thank you for your interest in giving your time and energy to the abused, homeless, and neglected animals that come to us each year. It is our desire that the time you spend here will be as rewarding for you as it is for the animals. We are proud of our organization and would like for you to become a part of the team. [←Enter] (2 times)

Please call us at 603-555-1313 to join us! [←Enter]

b. Correct any spelling or grammar errors. Save the document as Volunteers Needed.

c. Turn on the display of formatting marks. Check the document and remove any extra blank spaces between words or at the end of lines.

d. Switch to Print Layout view and center the title. Change the title font to Broadway (or a font of your choice), 16 pt.

e. In the first paragraph, change the number 6 to the word "six." Add italics and bold to the text "20 percent." Delete the phrase "Quite simply," from the second paragraph. Capitalize the following word, "It."

f. Justify the three main paragraphs. Center and bold the list of ways they can help.

g. Delete the "Communication specialists" and "Follow-up on adoptions" items from the list. Add "Socialize the cats" as the third item in the list.

h. Center, bold, and increase the font size to 14 pt of the last sentence.

i. Below the title insert the clip art graphic of the veterinarian and child holding a cat by searching on the keyword "animal." Center it and reduce the size of the graphic.

j. Add your name and the current date on separate lines several lines below the last line. Left-align both lines. Turn off the display of formatting marks.

k. Preview the document and if necessary reduce the graphic some more to fit the document on a single page.

l. Include your name in the file properties as author and the file name as the title.

m. Save the document again. Print the document.

Creating a Grand Opening Flyer ★ ★

3. The Downtown Internet Cafe is planning a grand opening celebration. The cafe combines the relaxed atmosphere of a coffee house with the fun of using the Internet. You want to create a flyer about the celebration that you can give to customers and also post in the window of other local businesses about the celebration. Your completed flyer is shown here.

a. Open a new Word document and enter the following text in Normal view, pressing [←Enter] where indicated.

Grand Opening Celebration [←Enter] (2 times)

Downtown Internet Cafe [←Enter] (2 times)

Your neighborhood coffee shop [←Enter] (4 times)

Stop on by and enjoy an excellent dark Italian Roast coffee, premium loose teas, blended drinks and quality light fare of sandwiches, pitas and salads. [←Enter] (2 times)

Starting Monday, July 1st and continuing all week through Sunday, July 7th we will take 20% off all espresso, cappuccino and latte drinks. Plus take $1.00 off any sandwich order. With any specialty coffee drink order, you will also receive 15 FREE minutes of high-speed Internet access. [←Enter] (2 times)

So enjoy a drink and then get online with the fastest connection in the neighborhood! [←Enter] (6 times)

2314 Telegraph Avenue [←Enter]

Cafe Hours: Sunday - Thursday 8:00 A.M. to 9:00 P.M. Friday and Saturday 8:00 A.M. to 12:00 A.M. [←Enter]

Grand Opening Celebration

Downtown Internet Cafe

Your neighborhood coffee shop

Stop on by and enjoy an excellent dark Italian Roast coffee, premium loose teas, blended drinks and quality light fare of sandwiches, pitas and salads.

Starting Monday, July 1st and continuing all week through Sunday, July 7th we will take 20% off all espresso, cappuccino and latte drinks. Plus take $1.00 off any sandwich order. With any specialty coffee drink order, you will also receive 15 FREE minutes of high-speed Internet access.

So enjoy a drink and then get online with the fastest connection in the neighborhood!

2314 Telegraph Avenue
Cafe Hours: Sunday - Thursday 8:00 A.M. – 9:00 P.M. Friday - Saturday 8:00 A.M. - 12:00 P.M.

Student Name
[Current Date]

b. Correct any spelling and grammar errors that are identified.

c. Save the document as Grand Opening.

d. Type **Join Us for Live Entertainment!** after the location and hours. Use the Undo Typing feature to remove this sentence.

e. Turn on the display of formatting marks. Center the entire document.

f. Switch to Print Layout view. Change the first line to a font color of red, font type of Arial Rounded MT Bold or a font of your choice, and size of 24 pt.

g. Change the second line to a font color of blue, font type of Arial Rounded MT Bold or a font of your choice, and size of 36 pt.

h. Change the third line to a font color of red and a font size of 16 pt.

i. Increase the font size of the three paragraphs to 14 points.

j. Insert the graphic file wd01_coffee (from your data files) on the middle blank line below the third title line.

k. Size the graphic to be approximately 2 by 3 inches using the ruler as a guide.

l. Add your name and the current date, left-aligned, on separate lines two lines below the last line. Turn off the display of formatting marks.

m. Preview the document. If necessary, reduce the size of the pictures so the entire flyer fits on one page.

n. Include your name in the file properties as author and the file name as the title. Save and print the flyer.

Preparing a Lecture on Note-Taking Skills ★ ★ ★

4. You teach a college survival skills class and have recently read about the results of a survey conducted by the Pilot Pen Company of America about note-taking skills. The survey of 500 teenagers found that students typically begin taking classroom notes by sixth grade and that only half had been taught how to take classroom notes. It also found that those students trained in note-taking earned better grades. Note taking becomes increasingly important in high school and is essential in college. Lecture notes are a key component for mastering material. In response to the survey, the pen manufacturer came up with 10 tips for better note-taking. You started a document of these tips that you plan to use to supplement your lecture on this topic. You will continue to revise and format the document. The revised document is shown here.

a. Open the Word document wd01_Note Taking Skills.

b. Turn on the display of formatting marks.

c. Correct any spelling and grammar errors that are identified. Save the document as **Note Taking Skills**.

d. Switch to Print Layout view. Change the font of the title line to a font of your choice, 18 pt. Center and add color of your choice to the title line.

e. In the Write Legibly tip, delete the word "cursive" and add the word "an erasable" before the word "pen." Change the tip heading "Use Margins" to "Use Wide Margins."

Tips for Taking Better Classroom Notes

Be Ready
Review your assigned reading and previous notes you've taken before class. Bring plenty lots of paper and a sharpened pencil, an erasable pen or a pen that won't skip or smudge. Write the class name, date and that day's topic at the top the page.

Write Legibly
Print if your handwriting is poor. Use a pencil or an erasable pen if you cross out material a lot so that your notes are easier to read. Take notes in one-liners rather than paragraph form. Skip a line between ideas to make it easier to find information when you're studying for a test.

Use Wide Margins
Leave a wide margin on one side of your paper so you'll have space to write your own thoughts and call attention to key material. Draw arrows or stars beside important information like dates, names and events. If you miss getting a date, name, number or other fact, make a mark in the margin so you'll remember to come back to it.

Fill in Gaps
Check with a classmate or your teacher after class to get any missing names, dates, facts or other information you couldn't write down.

Mark Questionable Material
Jot down a "?" in the margin beside something you disagree with or do not think you recorded correctly. When appropriate, ask your teacher, classmate, or refer to your textbook, for clarification.

Student Name
[Current Date]

f. Above the Mark Questionable Material tip, insert the following tip:

Fill in Gaps

Check with a classmate or your teacher after class to get any missing names, dates, facts or other information you couldn't write down.

g. Increase the font size of the tip heading lines to 14 pt, bold, and a color of your choice.

h. Change the alignment of the paragraphs to justified. Use Undo Changes to return the alignment to left. Use Redo Changes to return the paragraphs to justified again.

i. Insert a clip art graphic of your choice (search on "pen") below the title. Size it appropriately and center it.

j. Add your name and the current date, centered, on separate lines two lines below the last line.

k. Include your name in the file properties as author and the file name as the title. Save the document. Preview and print the document.

Writing an Article on Water Conservation ★ ★ ★

5. Each month the town newsletter is included with the utility bill. This month the main article is about conserving water. You started the column a few days ago and just need to continue the article by adding a few more suggestions. Then you need to edit and format the text and include a graphic to enhance the appearance of the article. Your completed article is shown here.

a. Open the file named wd01_Conserve Water and enter the following suggestions in the category indicated. Be sure to leave a blank line above each category heading.

Personal Use Tips

Turn the water off when brushing your teeth or shaving

Keep a jug of cold water in the refrigerator instead of letting the tap run until cool

Repair Tips

Repair dripping faucets by replacing washers

Outdoor Tips

When washing the car, use soap and water from a bucket. Use a hose with a shut-off nozzle for the final rinse

b. Use Undo Changes to remove the last sentence. Use Redo Changes to return the last sentence to the document.

How Can I Conserve Water?

Nearly 75% of water used indoors is in the bathroom with baths, showers and toilet flushing account for most of this. If you have a lawn, chances are that this is your biggest water use. Typically, at least 50% of water consumed by households is used outdoors. The City's Water Conservation Program has many publications that offer suggestions to help you conserve water. Some of these suggestions include:

Personal Use Tips
Take short showers instead of baths
Run dishwashers and clothes washers with full loads only, or adjust water level to load size
Turn the water off when brushing your teeth or shaving
Keep a jug of cold water in the refrigerator instead of letting the tap run until cool

Repair Tips
Install low-flow showerheads or flow restrictors
Check your toilet for leaks by placing a few drops of food coloring in the tank. If it shows up in the bowl, replace the flapper
Replace older toilets with new low-flow toilets or place a plastic jug filled with water in the tank to displace some of the water
Repair dripping faucets by replacing washers

Outdoor Tips
When washing the car, use soap and water from a bucket. Use a hose with a shut-off nozzle for the final rinse

Student Name
[Current Date]

c. Turn on the display of formatting marks.

d. Correct any spelling and grammar errors. Save the document as Water Conservation.

e. Switch to Print Layout view. Center the title. Change the font to Impact with a point size of 24. Add a color of your choice to the title.

f. Change the three category heads to bold with a type size of 14 pt. Center the heads. Use the same color as in the title for the heads.

g. Change the alignment of the introductory paragraph to justified.

h. Insert the picture wd01_water hose (from your data files) below the main title of the article.

i. Size the picture to be 2 inches wide (use the ruler as a guide). Center it below the title.

j. Add your name and the current date two lines below the last line.

k. Include your name in the file properties as author and the file name as the title. Save the document again. Preview and print the document.

on your own

Creating a Cruise Flyer ★

1. Adventure Travel Tours is offering a great deal on a cruise to Hawaii. Using the features of Word you have learned so far, create a flyer that will advertise this tour. Be sure to use at least two colors of text, two sizes of text, and two kinds of paragraph alignment. Include a graphic from the Clip Organizer. Include your name at the bottom of the flyer. Include your name in the file properties as author and the file name as the title. Save the document as Hawaii Cruise Flyer.

Creating a Computer Lab Rules Flyer ★

2. You work in the computer lab of your school and have been asked to create a flyer to post that identifies the rules students should follow when using the computer workstations. Create a flyer that explains the five most important rules to follow while working in the computer lab. Use a piece of clip art to liven up your flyer. Include different font sizes, paragraph alignments, and other formatting features to make the flyer attractive. Apply different font colors for each rule. Include your name at the bottom of the flyer. Include your name in the file properties as author and the file name as the title. Save the document as Lab Rules.

CPR Training Memo ★ ★

3. Lifestyle Fitness Club has decided to require that all employees know how to perform CPR and has organized two classes to teach the procedure. You want to notify all employees about the classes by including a memo with their pay check. Using Hands-On Exercise 1 as a model, provide information about when and where the classes will be held. Include information about how people sign up for the class. Also, advise them that they will be paid for their time while attending the class. Include your name in the file properties as author and the file name as the title. Save the memo as CPR Classes.

Keeping Your Computer Clean ★★★

4. Wherever you work, in a bakery, repair shop, retail store, or your own home office, all types of environmental factors from dust to cat hair can cause havoc with your computer. It is important to keep your personal computers clean to prevent such problems as an overheated monitor, malfunctioning keyboard, or even a crashed hard drive. Using the Web as a resource, research how to clean your computer. Then write a one-page report on your findings that includes information on cleaning three areas: monitor, keyboard, and CPU. Include a title at the top of the document and your name and the current date below the title. Center the title lines. Use at least two colors of text, two sizes of text, and two kinds of paragraph alignment. Include a graphic from the Clip Organizer. At the end of the document, include references to the sources you used. Include your name in the file properties as author and the file name as the title. Save the document as Computer Cleaning.

Writing a Career Report ★★★

5. Using the library or the Web, research information about your chosen career. Write a one-page report about your findings that includes information on three areas: Career Description; Educational Requirements; Salary and Employment projections. Include a title at the top of the document and your name and the current date below the title. Center the title lines. Justify the paragraphs. At the end of the document, include references to the sources you used. Include your name in the file properties as author and the file name as the title. Save the document as Career Report.

Revising and Refining a Document

Objectives

After completing this lab, you will know how to:

1 Use the Spelling and Grammar tool and the Thesaurus.

2 Move, cut, and copy text and formats.

3 Control document paging.

4 Find and replace text.

5 Insert the current date.

6 Change margins, line spacing, and indents.

7 Create a tabbed table.

8 Add color highlighting and underlines to text.

9 Create numbered and bulleted lists.

10 Use an AutoText entry.

11 Insert and Modify an AutoShape.

12 Edit in Print Preview.

13 Create document versions.

Case Study

Adventure Travel Tours

After creating the rough draft of the new tours flyer, you showed the printed copy to your manager at Adventure Travel Tours. Your manager then made several suggestions for improving the flyer's style and appearance. In addition, you created a letter to be sent to clients along with your flyer. The letter briefly describes Adventure Travel's four new tours and invites clients to attend an informational presentation. Your manager likes the idea, but also wants the letter to include information about the new Adventure Travel Tours Web site and a 10 percent discount for early booking.

In this lab, you will learn more about editing documents so you can reorganize and refine both your flyer and a rough draft of the letter to clients. You will also learn to use many more of the formatting features included in Office Word 2003 so you can add style and interest to your documents. Formatting features can greatly improve the appearance and design of any document you produce, so that it communicates its message more clearly. The completed letter and revised flyer are shown here.

© Corbis

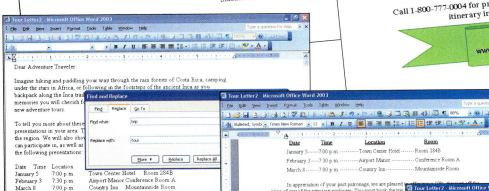

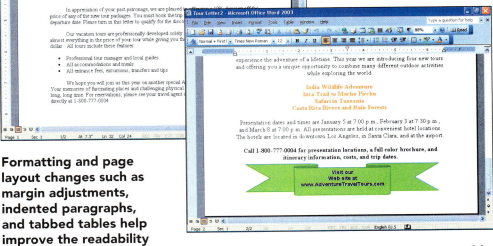

Features such as the Spelling Checker, Thesaurus, Move and Copy, and Find and Replace make it easy to revise and refine your document.

Formatting and page layout changes such as margin adjustments, indented paragraphs, and tabbed tables help improve the readability and style of the document.

Graphic enhancements such as AutoShapes add interest to a document.

Concept Preview

The following concepts will be introduced in this lab:

1 **Thesaurus**   Word's Thesaurus is a reference tool that provides synonyms, antonyms, and related words for a selected word or phrase.

2 **Move and Copy**   Text and graphic selections can be moved or copied to new locations in a document or between documents, saving you time by not having to retype the same information.

3 **Page Break**   A page break marks the point at which one page ends and another begins. Two types of page breaks can be used in a document: soft page breaks and hard page breaks.

4 **Find and Replace**   To make editing easier, you can use the Find and Replace feature to find text in a document and replace it with other text as directed.

5 **Field**   A field is a placeholder that instructs Word to insert information into a document.

6 **Page Margin**   The page margin is the blank space around the edge of the page. Standard single-sided documents have four margins: top, bottom, left, and right.

7 **Indents**   To help your reader find information quickly, you can indent paragraphs from the margins. Indenting paragraphs sets them off from the rest of the document.

8 **Line Spacing**   Adjusting the line spacing, or the vertical space between lines of text, helps set off areas of text from others and when increased makes it easier to read and edit text.

9 **Bulleted and Numbered Lists**   Whenever possible, add bullets or numbers before items in a list to organize information and make your writing clear and easy to read.

Revising a Document

After speaking with the manager about the letter's content, you planned the basic topics that need to be included in the letter: to advertise the new tours, invite clients to the presentations, describe the early-booking discount, and promote the new Web site. You quickly entered the text for the letter, saved it as Tour Letter, and printed out a hard copy. As you are reading the document again, you mark up the printout with the changes and corrections you want to make. The marked-up copy is shown here.

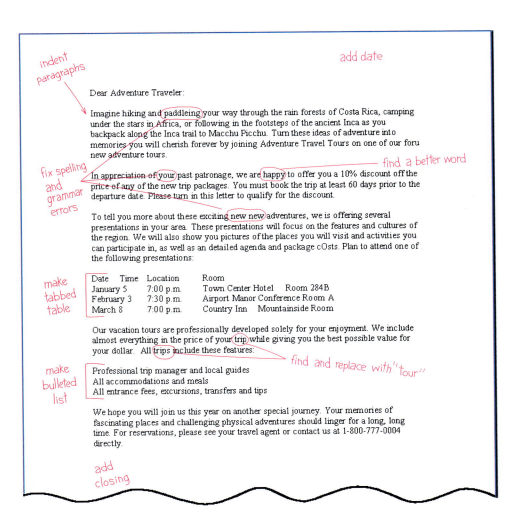

Spell-Checking the Entire Document

The first correction you want to make is to clean up the spelling and grammar errors that Word has identified.

1 **Start Office Word 2003 and open the file wd02_Tour Letter.**

If necessary, switch to Normal view with a zoom of 100%.

Your screen should be similar to Figure 2.1

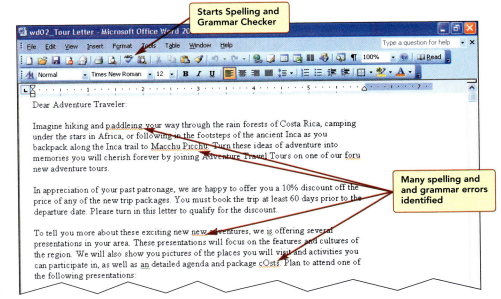

Figure 2.1

To correct the misspelled words and grammatical errors, you can use the shortcut menu to correct each individual word or error, as you learned in Lab 1. However, in many cases you may find it more efficient to wait until you are finished writing before you correct errors. Rather than continually breaking your train of thought to correct errors as you type, you can manually turn on the spelling and grammar checker to locate and correct all the errors in the document at once.

2 ● Click  **Spelling and Grammar.**

Another Method

The menu equivalent is **T**ools/**S**pelling and Grammar and the keyboard shortcut is F7.

● If necessary, select the Chec**k** grammar option to turn on grammar checking.

Your screen should be similar to Figure 2.2

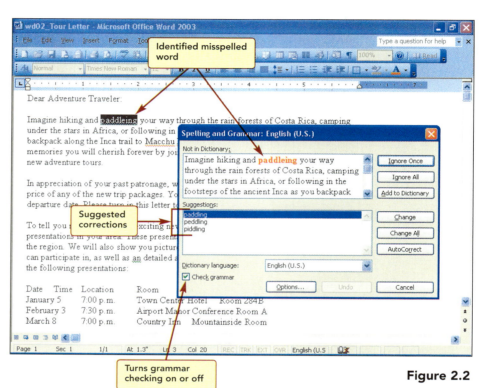

Figure 2.2

Additional Information

You can also double-click the Spelling and Grammar status icon 🕮 to move to the next spelling or grammar error and open the spelling shortcut menu.

Additional Information

Because the contents of the list are determined only by spelling, any instances of terms that seem inappropriate in context are completely coincidental.

Additional Information

The [Change All] option replaces the same word throughout the document with the word you select in the Suggestions box.

The Spelling and Grammar dialog box is displayed, and the spelling and grammar checker has immediately located the first word that may be misspelled, "paddleing." The sentence with the misspelled word in red is displayed in the Not in Dictionary text box, and the word is highlighted in the document.

The Suggestions list box displays the words the spelling checker has located in the dictionary that most closely match the misspelled word. The most likely match is highlighted. Sometimes the spelling checker does not display any suggested replacements. This occurs when it cannot locate any words in the dictionaries that are similar in spelling. If no suggestions are provided, the Not in Dictionary text box simply displays the word that is highlighted in the text.

To change the spelling of the word to one of the suggested spellings, highlight the correct word in the list and then click [Change]. If there were no suggested replacements, and you did not want to use any of the option buttons, you could edit the word yourself by typing the correction in the Not in Dictionary box. In this case, the correct replacement, "paddling," is already highlighted.

3 ● Click [Change].

Additional Information

On your own computer system, you would want to add words to the custom dictionary that you use frequently and that are not included in the standard dictionary, so they will be accepted when typed correctly and offered as a suggested replacement when not typed correctly.

Your screen should be similar to Figure 2.3

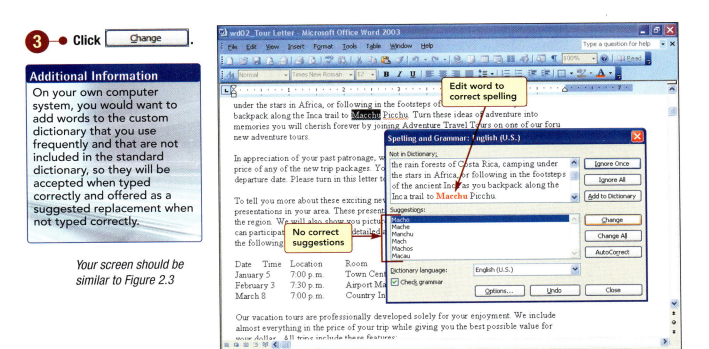

Figure 2.3

The spelling checker replaces the misspelled word with the selected suggested replacement and moves on to locate the next error. This time the error is the name of the Inca ruins at Machu Picchu. "Macchu" is the incorrect spelling for this word; there is no correct suggestion, however, because the word is not found in the dictionary. You will correct the spelling of the word by editing it in the Not in Dictionary text box.

4 ● Change the spelling of the word to **Machu** in the Not in Dictionary box.

● Click [Change].

Your screen should be similar to Figure 2.4

Additional Information

You can also edit words directly in the document and then click [Resume] to continue using the Spelling and Grammar Checker.

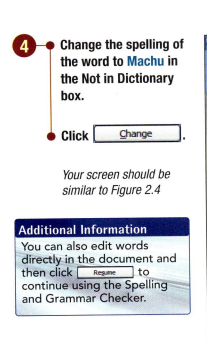
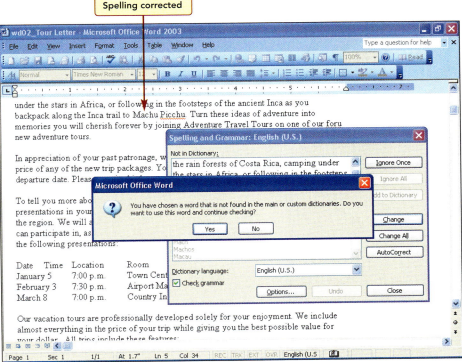

Figure 2.4

Word displays a question dialog box advising you that the correction to the word is not found in its dictionaries and asking you to confirm that you want to continue.

Click Yes .

Click Ignore All **for the next located word, Picchu.**

Your screen should be similar to Figure 2.5

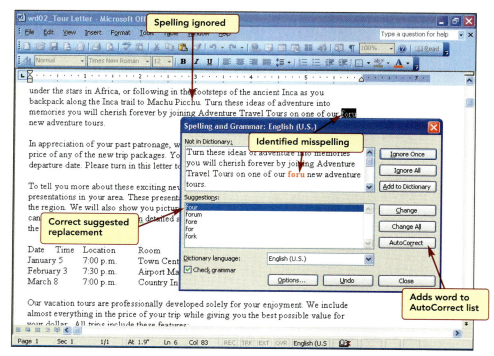

Figure 2.5

Additional Information

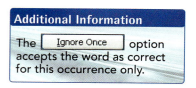

The Ignore Once option accepts the word as correct for this occurrence only.

The spelling of the word "Picchu" is ignored, and the word is no longer identified as misspelled. If this word is used in other locations in this document, the spelling will be accepted.

The next located error, "foru," is a typing error that you make frequently when typing the word four. The correct spelling is selected in the Suggestions list box. You want to change it to the suggested word and add it to the list of words that are automatically corrected.

Click AutoCorrect .

Having Trouble?

If a dialog box appears telling you an AutoCorrect entry already exists for this word, simply click Yes to continue.

Your screen should be similar to Figure 2.6

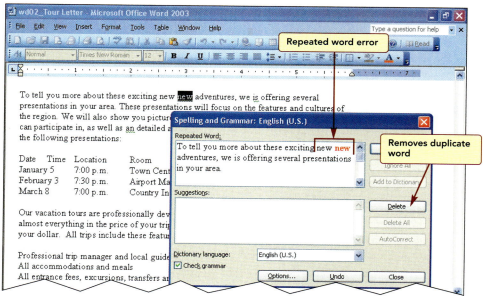

Figure 2.6

The word is corrected in the document. Because you also added it to the AutoCorrect list, in the future whenever you type this word incorrectly as "foru," it will automatically be changed to "four." The next five errors that will be identified and their causes are shown in the following table

Identified Error	Cause	Action	Result
new	Repeated word	Delete	Duplicate word "new" is deleted
we is	Subject-verb disagreement	Change	we are
cOsts	Inconsistent capitalization	Change	costs
an detailed	Grammatical error	Change	a

7 • **Click** [Delete] **to delete the repeated word "new."**

• **Continue to respond to the spelling and grammar checker by clicking** [Change] **for the next three identified errors.**

• **Click** [OK] **in response to the message telling you that the spelling and grammar check is complete.**

• **Move to the top of the document and save the revised document as** Tour Letter2 **to the appropriate data file location.**

Your screen should be similar to Figure 2.7

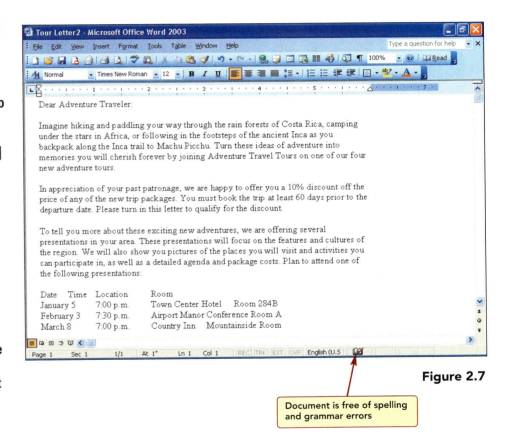

Document is free of spelling and grammar errors

Figure 2.7

Using the Thesaurus

The next text change you want to make is to find a better word for "ideas" in the first paragraph and "happy" in the second paragraph. To help find a similar word, you will use the thesaurus tool.

<table>
<tr><td colspan="2">

Concept 1

Thesaurus

</td></tr>
<tr><td>

1

</td><td>

Word's **thesaurus** is a reference tool that provides synonyms, antonyms, and related words for a selected word or phrase. **Synonyms** are words with a similar meaning, such as "cheerful" and "happy." **Antonyms** are words with an opposite meaning, such as "cheerful" and "sad." Related words are words that are variations of the same word, such as "cheerful" and "cheer." The Thesaurus can help to liven up your documents by adding interest and variety to your text.

</td></tr>
</table>

First you need to identify the word you want looked up by moving the insertion point onto the word. Then you use the thesaurus to suggest alternative words. The quickest way to get synonyms is to use the shortcut menu for the word you want to replace.

1 ● **Right-click on the word "ideas" (first paragraph, third sentence).**

● **Select Synonyms.**

Your screen should be similar to Figure 2.8

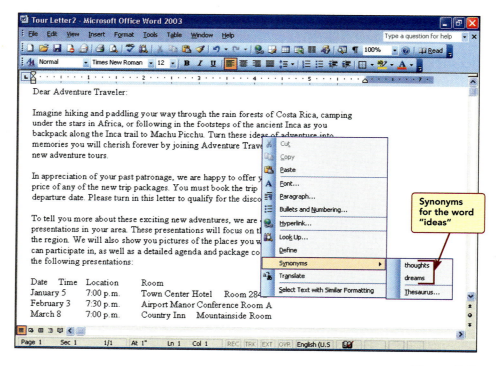

Figure 2.8

The Synonyms shortcut menu lists two words with similar meanings. You decide to replace "ideas" with "dreams." Then you will look for a synonym for "happy." You will use the Research pane to locate synonyms this time.

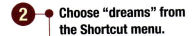

2 **Choose "dreams" from the Shortcut menu.**

• **With the insertion point in the word "happy" (first sentence, second paragraph), hold down ⇧Shift and press F7 .**

Another Method

The menu equivalent is **T**ools/**L**anguage/**T**hesaurus. You can also use **T**ools/**R**esearch or use 📖 Research to open the Research task pane and enter the word in the Search For box.

• **If necessary, select Thesaurus: English from the search scope list box.**

Your screen should be similar to Figure 2.9

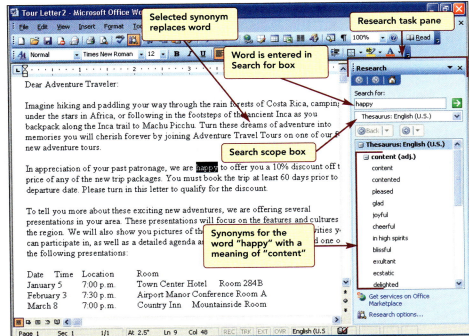

Figure 2.9

The Research task pane opens and the word the insertion point is on is displayed in the Search For text box. The list box displays words that have similar meanings for the word "happy" with a meaning of "content (adj)." The best choice from this list is "pleased." To see whether any other words are closer in meaning, you will look up synonyms for the word "pleased."

3 **Choose "pleased."**

Additional Information

You can also choose Look Up from the word's drop-down menu to look up synonyms for the word.

Your screen should be similar to Figure 2.10

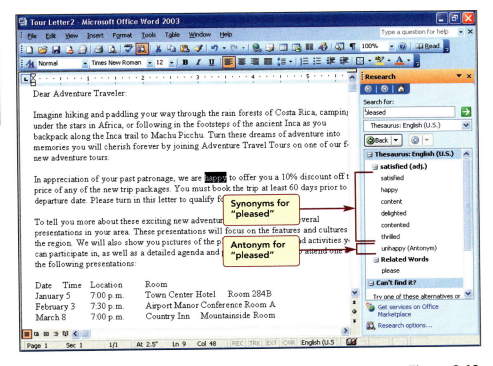

Figure 2.10

The word "pleased" is the new search term, and the list displays synonyms, as well as an antonym, for this word. You decide to use "pleased" and will return to the previous list and insert the word into the document.

4 • Click 🔄 to display the list for the word "happy."

• Open the "pleased" synonym drop-down menu.

• Choose Insert.

• Close the Research task pane.

Your screen should be similar to Figure 2.11

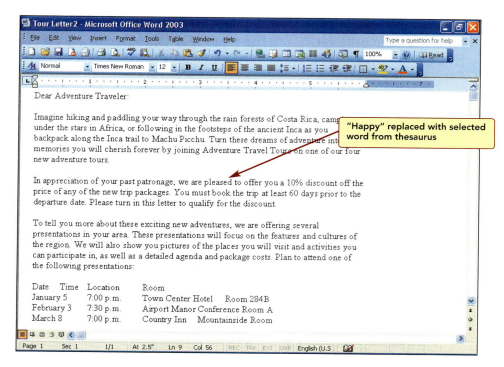

Figure 2.11

The word "happy" is replaced with the selected word from the thesaurus.

Moving and Copying Selections

After looking over the letter, you decide to add the company name in several other locations and to change the order of paragraphs. To make these changes quickly, you can move and copy selections.

Concept 2

Move and Copy

2   Text and graphic selections can be moved or copied to new locations in a document or between documents, saving you time by not having to recreate the same information. A selection that is moved is cut from its original location, called the **source**, and inserted at a new location, called the **destination**. A selection that is copied leaves the original in the source and inserts a duplicate at the destination.

When a selection is cut or copied, the selection is stored in the **system Clipboard**, a temporary Windows storage area in memory. It is also stored in the **Office Clipboard**. The system Clipboard holds only the last cut or copied item, whereas the Office Clipboard can store up to 24 items that have been cut or copied. This feature allows you to insert multiple items from various Office documents and paste all or part of the collection of items into another document.

Using Copy and Paste

You want to include the company name in the last paragraph of the letter in two places. Because the name has already been entered in the first paragraph, you will copy it instead of typing the name again.

1 ● Select "Adventure Travel Tours" (first paragraph, last sentence).

● Click [ ] Copy.

● Move to the beginning of the word "journey" (last paragraph, first sentence).

● Click [ ] Paste.

Another Method

The menu equivalent to copy is **E**dit/**C**opy, the keyboard shortcut is Ctrl + C, and the voice command is "Copy." The menu equivalent to paste is **E**dit/**P**aste, the keyboard shortcut is Ctrl + V, and the voice command is "Paste."

Your screen should be similar to Figure 2.12

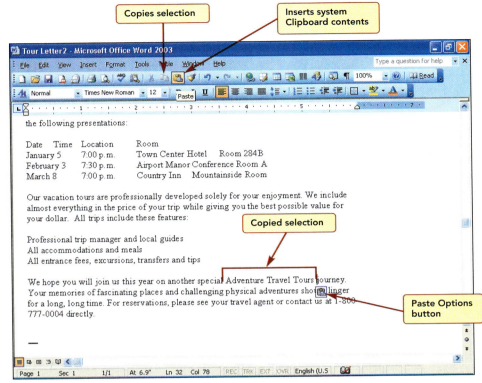

Figure 2.12

The copied selection is inserted at the location you specified. The [ ] Paste Options button appears automatically whenever a selection is pasted. It is used to control the format of the pasted item.

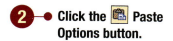

2 ● Click the 🔳 **Paste Options button.**

Your screen should be similar to Figure 2.13

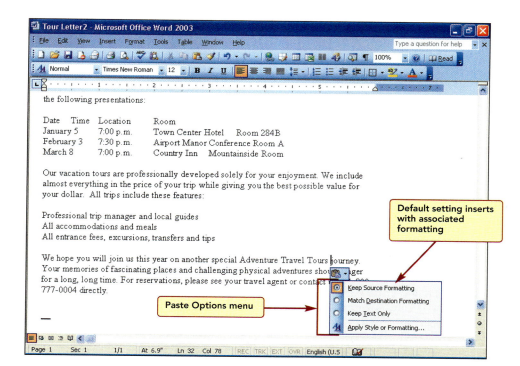

Default setting inserts with associated formatting

Paste Options menu

Figure 2.13

The options are used to specify whether to insert the item with the same formatting that it had in the source, to change it to the formatting of the surrounding destination text, or to insert text only (from a selection that is a combination of text and graphics). You can also apply new formatting to the selection. The default, to keep the formatting from the source, is appropriate. Next, you want to insert the company name in place of the word "us" in the last sentence of the letter.

3 ● **Click outside the menu to close it.**

● **Select "us" (last sentence).**

● **Right-click on the selection and choose Paste from the shortcut menu.**

Your screen should be similar to Figure 2.14

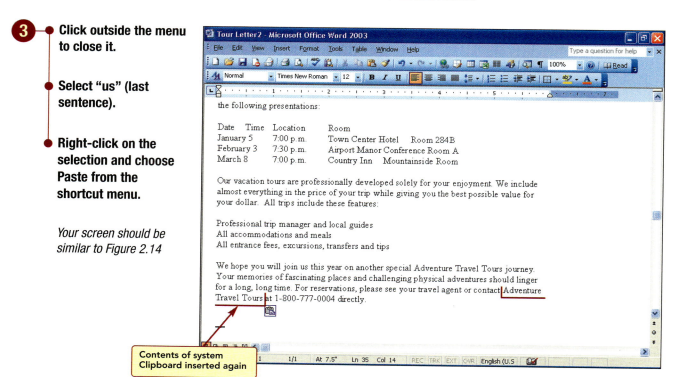

Contents of system Clipboard inserted again

Figure 2.14

The selected text was deleted and replaced with the contents of the system Clipboard. The system Clipboard contents remain in the Clipboard until another item is copied or cut, allowing you to paste the same item multiple times.

Using Cut and Paste

You want the paragraph about the 10 percent discount (second paragraph) to follow the list of presentation dates. To do this, you will move the paragraph from its current location to the new location. The Cut and Paste commands on the Edit menu are used to move selections. You will use the shortcut menu to select the Cut command.

 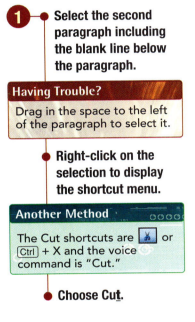
1 ● Select the second paragraph including the blank line below the paragraph.

Having Trouble?

Drag in the space to the left of the paragraph to select it.

● Right-click on the selection to display the shortcut menu.

Another Method

The Cut shortcuts are ✖ or Ctrl + X and the voice command is "Cut."

● Choose Cu**t**.

Your screen should be similar to Figure 2.15

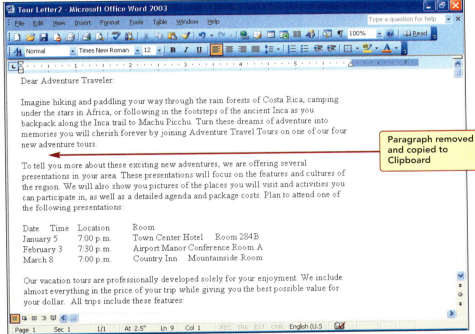

Figure 2.15

The selected paragraph is removed from the source and copied to the Clipboard. Next, you need to move the insertion point to the location where the text will be inserted and paste the text into the document from the Clipboard.

2

- Move to the beginning of the paragraph below the list of presentation dates.

- Click 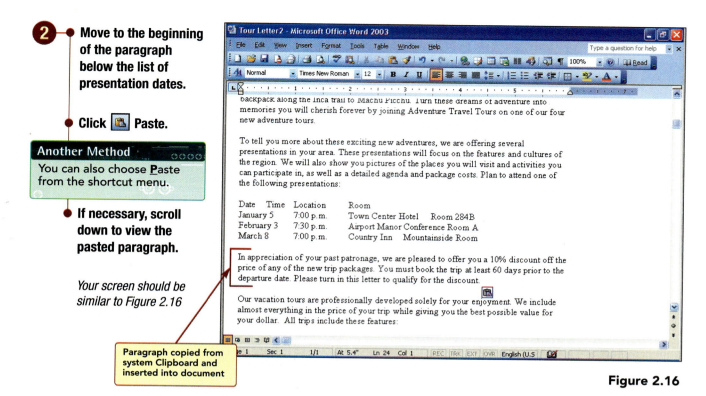 Paste.

Another Method ○○○○

You can also choose **P**aste from the shortcut menu.

- If necessary, scroll down to view the pasted paragraph.

Your screen should be similar to Figure 2.16

Paragraph copied from system Clipboard and inserted into document

Figure 2.16

The cut paragraph is reentered into the document at the insertion point location. That was much quicker than retyping the whole paragraph!

Using Drag and Drop

Finally, you also decide to move the word "directly" in the last paragraph so that the sentence reads ". . . contact Adventure Travel Tours directly at 1-888-777-0004." Rather than use Cut and Paste to move this text, you will use the **drag and drop** editing feature. This feature is most useful for copying or moving short distances in a document.

To use drag and drop to move a selection, point to the selection and drag it to the location where you want the selection inserted. The mouse pointer appears as ⇖ as you drag, and a temporary insertion point shows you where the text will be placed when you release the mouse button.

Additional Information

You can also use drag and drop to copy a selection by holding down Ctrl while dragging. The mouse pointer shape is ⇖.

1 ● Select "directly" (last word in last paragraph).

● Drag the selection to before "at" in the same sentence.

Additional Information

You can also move or copy a selection by holding down the right mouse button while dragging. When you release the mouse button, a shortcut menu appears with the available move and copy options.

Your screen should be similar to Figure 2.17

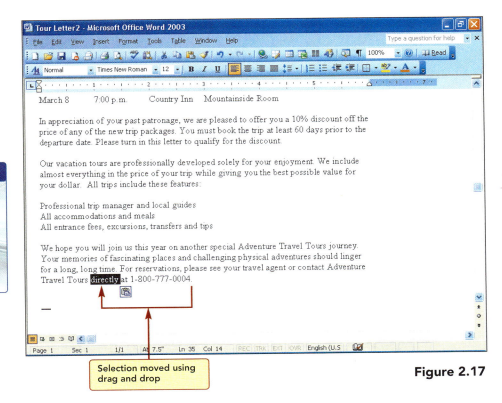

Selection moved using drag and drop

Figure 2.17

The selection is moved to the new location.

Copying Between Documents

You plan to include the flyer with the letter to be mailed to clients. To do this, you will open the flyer document and copy it into the letter document file. Because all Office 2003 applications allow you to open and use multiple files at the same time, this is a very simple procedure.

1 ● Move to the top of the document.

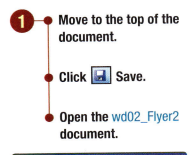

● Click ■ Save.

● Open the wd02_Flyer2 document.

Additional Information

Sometimes you may want to open several files at once. To do this you can select multiple files from the Open dialog box by holding down [Ctrl] while clicking on each file name. If the files are adjacent, you can click the first file name, hold down [⇧Shift] and click on the name of the last file.

Your screen should be similar to Figure 2.18

Each document is open in its own window

Figure 2.18

The flyer document is opened and displayed in a separate window. It contains the insertion point, which indicates that it is the **active window**, or the window in which you can work. The taskbar displays a button for each open document window; it can be used to switch quickly from one window to the other.

You can also display both open documents on the screen at once to make it easy to compare documents or to move information between documents.

2 ● **Choose Window/Compare Side by Side with Tour Letter2.**

Your screen should be similar to Figure 2.19

Additional Information
The Arrange All command divides the screen horizontally.

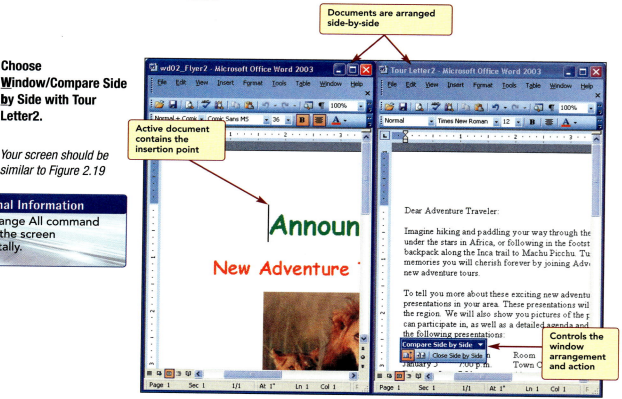

> Documents are arranged side-by-side

> Active document contains the insertion point

> Controls the window arrangement and action

Figure 2.19

The two document windows are arranged side-by-side on the screen. The active window displays the insertion point and is the document you can work in. Simply clicking on the other document makes it active. When you use this feature, the documents in both windows will scroll together so you can compare text easily. If you are not comparing text, this feature can be turned off so that they scroll independently. The Compare Side by Side toolbar automatically appears and is used to control the window arrangement and action.

> Synchronous scrolling

> Reset window position

You will copy the entire flyer to the bottom of the letter document using drag and drop. To copy between documents using drag and drop, hold down the right mouse button while dragging. When you release the button, a shortcut menu appears where you specify the action you want to perform. If you drag using the left mouse button, the selection is moved by default.

- Click ▼ 3 times in the wd02_Flyer2 window scrollbar to see both windows scroll.

- Click 🗐 Synchronous Scrolling in the Compare Side by Side toolbar to turn off this feature.

- Click ▼ 3 times in the wd02_Flyer2 window scrollbar to scroll the active window only.

- Select the entire flyer.

Having Trouble?

Triple-click in the left margin to quickly select the entire document.

- Right-drag the selection to the blank line immediately below the last paragraph of the letter.

- Release the mouse button and choose **C**opy Here from the shortcut menu.

- Click Close Side by Side to return the display to a single document window.

Your screen should be similar to Figure 2.20

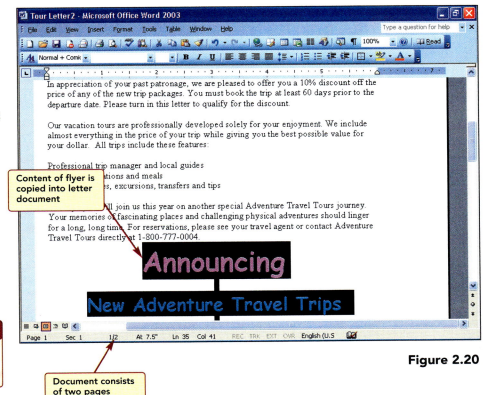

Content of flyer is copied into letter document

Document consists of two pages

Figure 2.20

Another Method

If you did not want to arrange windows, you could just copy the selection in the active window, click on the taskbar button of the other open window to make it active, and then paste the selection in the document.

The letter now consists of two pages. Notice the status bar shows the insertion point location is on page 1/2.

Controlling Document Paging

As text and graphics are added to a document, Word automatically starts a new page when text extends beyond the bottom margin setting. The beginning of a new page is identified by a page break.

Concept 3
Page Break

3 A **page break** marks the point at which one page ends and another begins. Two types of page breaks can be used in a document: soft page breaks and hard page breaks. As you fill a page with text or graphics, Word inserts a **soft page break** automatically when the bottom margin is reached and starts a new page. As you add or remove text from a page, Word automatically readjusts the placement of the soft page break.

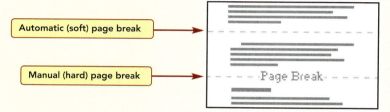

Many times, however, you may want to force a page break to occur at a specific location. To do this you can manually insert a **hard page break**. This action instructs Word to begin a new page regardless of the amount of text on the previous page. When a hard page break is used, its location is never moved regardless of the changes that are made to the amount of text on the preceding page. All soft page breaks that precede or follow a hard page break continue to adjust automatically. Sometimes you may find that you have to remove the hard page break and reenter it at another location as you edit the document.

You will switch back to Normal view to see the soft page break that was entered in the document.

1 ● **Click in the document to deselect the flyer text.**

● **Switch to Normal view.**

● **If necessary, scroll the document to see the dotted page break line.**

Additional Information

As you drag the scroll box, a ScreenTip displays the number of the page that is displayed in the window.

Your screen should be similar to Figure 2.21

Figure 2.21

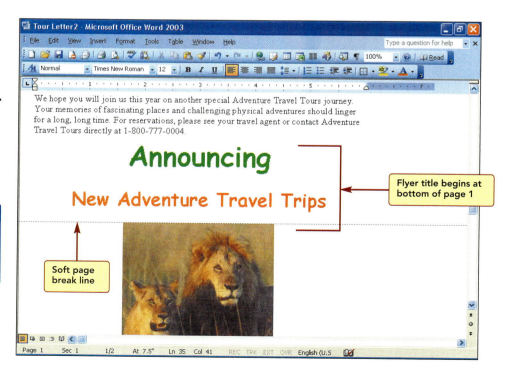

To show where one page ends and another begins, Word displays a dotted line across the page to mark the soft page break.

Inserting a Hard Page Break

Many times the location of the soft page break is not appropriate. In this case, the location of the soft page break displays the flyer title on the bottom of page 1 and the remaining portion of the flyer on page 2. Because you want the entire flyer to print on a page by itself, you will manually insert a hard page break above the flyer title.

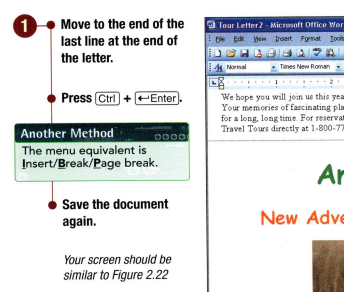

1 ● Move to the end of the last line at the end of the letter.

● Press ⌈Ctrl⌋ + ⌈←Enter⌋.

Another Method
The menu equivalent is Insert/**B**reak/**P**age break.

● Save the document again.

Your screen should be similar to Figure 2.22

Figure 2.22

Additional Information
To remove a hard page break, simply select the hard page break line and press ⌈Delete⌋.

A dotted line and the words "Page Break" appear across the page above the flyer title, indicating that a hard page break was entered at that position.

Finding and Replacing Text

As you continue proofing the letter, you notice that the word "trip" is used frequently. You think that the letter would read better if the word "tour" was used in place of "trip" in some instances. To do this, you will use the Find and Replace feature.

4 To make editing easier, you can use the Find and Replace feature to find text in a document and replace it with other text as directed. For example, suppose you created a lengthy document describing the type of clothing and equipment needed to set up a world-class home gym, and then you decided to change "sneakers" to "athletic shoes." Instead of deleting every occurrence of "sneakers" and typing "athletic shoes," you can use the Find and Replace feature to perform the task automatically.

You can also find and replace occurrences of special formatting, such as replacing bold text with italicized text, as well as find and replace formatting marks. Additionally, special characters and symbols, such as an arrow or copyright symbol, can be easily located or replaced. This feature is fast and accurate; however, use care when replacing so that you do not replace unintended matches.

Finding Text

First, you will use the Find command to locate all occurrences of the word "trip" in the document.

1 Move the insertion point to the top of the document.

Another Method

Reminder: Use Ctrl + Home to quickly move to the top of the document.

● **Choose Edit/Find.**

Another Method

The keyboard shortcut is Ctrl + F. You can also open the Find and Replace dialog box by clicking the 🔘 Select Browse Object button in the vertical scroll bar and selecting 🔍 Find from the menu.

Your screen should be similar to Figure 2.23

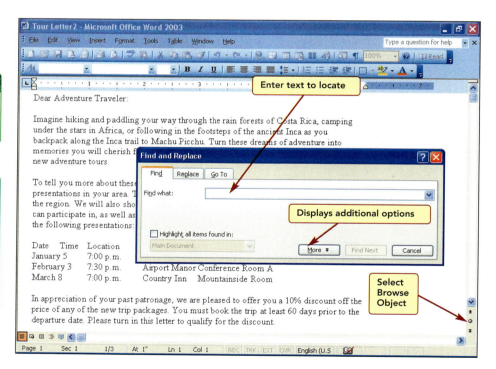

Figure 2.23

The Find and Replace dialog box is used to define the information you want to locate and replace. In the Find What text box, you enter the text you want to locate. In addition, you can use the search options to refine the search.

2 ● Click [More ▼].

Your screen should be similar to Figure 2.24

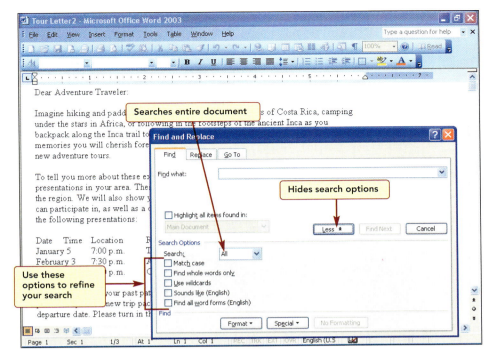

Figure 2.24

The additional options can be combined in many ways to help you find and replace text in documents. They are described in the table below.

Option	Effect on Text
Match case	Finds only those words in which the capitalization matches the text you typed.
Find whole words only	Finds matches that are whole words and not part of a larger word. For example, finds "cat" only and not "catastrophe" too.
Use wildcards	Fine-tunes a search; for example, c?t finds "cat" and "cot" (one-character matches), while c*t finds "cat" and "court" (searches for one or more characters).
Sounds like (English)	Finds words that sound like the word you type; very helpful if you do not know the correct spelling of the word you want to find.
Find all word forms (English)	Finds and replaces all forms of a word; for example, "buy" will replace "purchase," and "bought" will replace "purchased."
Format ▾	Finds text with formatting characteristics specified and/or replaces text with specified formatting. If no Find text is specified, locates all occurrences of specified formatting.
Special ▾	Finds/replaces all occurrences of special characters.

When you enter the text to find, you can type everything lowercase, because the Match Case option is not selected. If Match Case is not selected, the search will not be **case sensitive**. This means that lowercase letters will match both upper- and lowercase letters in the text.

Also notice that the Search option default setting is All, which means Word will search the entire document, including headers and footers. You can also choose to search Up or Down the document. These options search in the direction specified but exclude the headers, footers, footnotes, and comments from the area to search. Because you want to search the entire document, All is the appropriate setting. You will hide the search options again and begin the search.

Additional Information

You will learn about headers, footers, footnotes, and comments in later labs.

3 ● Click [Less ±] to close the advanced search options.

● Type **trip** in the Find What text box.

● Click [Find Next].

Your screen should be similar to Figure 2.25

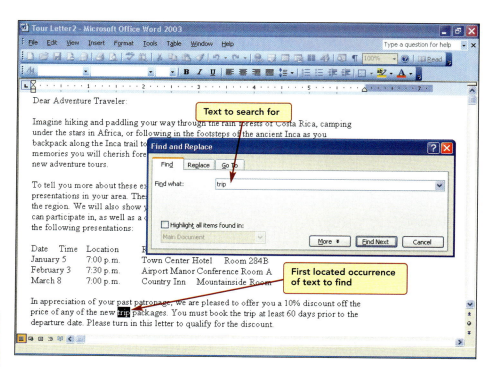

Figure 2.25

Additional Information

If the search does not begin at the top of the document, when Word reaches the end of the document it asks if you want to continue searching from the beginning of the document. You can also highlight text to restrict the search to a selection.

Word searches for all occurrences of the text to find beginning at the insertion point, locates the first occurrence of the word "trip," and highlights it in the document.

4 ● Continue to click [Find Next] to locate all occurrences of the word.

● Click [OK] when Word indicates the entire document has been searched.

The word "trip" is used seven times in the document.

Replacing Text

You decide to replace several occurrences of the word "trip" in the letter with "tour" where appropriate. You will use the Replace feature to specify the text to enter as the replacement text.

1 ● **Open the Replace tab.**

Your screen should be similar to Figure 2.26

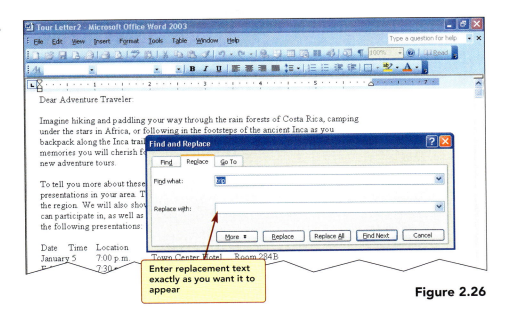

Enter replacement text exactly as you want it to appear

Figure 2.26

The Replace tab includes a Replace With text box in which you enter the replacement text. This text must be entered exactly as you want it to appear in your document. To find and replace the first occurrence of the word "trip" with "tour,"

2 ● **Type tour in the Replace With text box.**

● **Click** Find Next .

● **Click** Replace .

Your screen should be similar to Figure 2.27

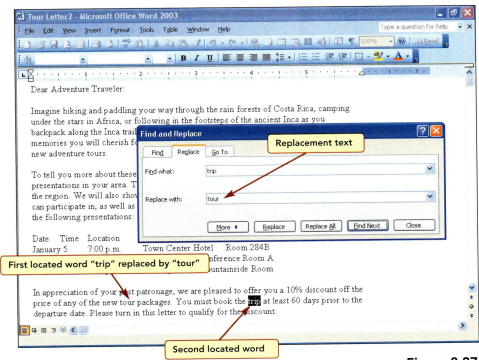

Replacement text

First located word "trip" replaced by "tour"

Second located word

Figure 2.27

Word replaced the first located word with "tour" and has highlighted the second occurrence of the word "trip." You do not want to replace this occurrence of the word. You will continue the search without replacing the highlighted text.

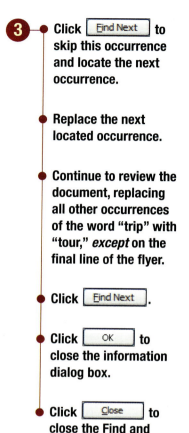

3 • Click [Find Next] to skip this occurrence and locate the next occurrence.

• Replace the next located occurrence.

• Continue to review the document, replacing all other occurrences of the word "trip" with "tour," *except* on the final line of the flyer.

• Click [Find Next].

• Click [OK] to close the information dialog box.

• Click [Close] to close the Find and Replace dialog box.

Your screen should be similar to Figure 2.28

Tour Letter2 - Microsoft Office Word 2003

File   Edit   View   Insert   Format   Tools   Table   Window   Help

Type a question for help

Normal   Times New Roman   12   B   I   U   100%

Dear Adventure Traveler:

Imagine hiking and paddling your way through the rain forests of Costa Rica, camping under the stars in Africa, or following in the footsteps of the ancient Inca as you backpack along the Inca trail to Machu Picchu. Turn these dreams of adventure into memories you will cherish forever by joining Adventure Travel Tours on one of our four new adventure tours.

To tell you more about these exciting new adventures, we are offering several presentations in your area. These presentations will focus on the features and cultures of the region. We will also show you pictures of the places you will visit and activities you can participate in, as well as a detailed agenda and package costs. Plan to attend one of the following presentations:

Date	Time	Location	Room
January 5	7:00 p.m.	Town Center Hotel	Room 284B
February 3	7:30 p.m.	Airport Manor Conference Room A	
March 8	7:00 p.m.	Country Inn	Mountainside Room

In appreciation of your past patronage, we are pleased to offer you a 10% discount off the price of any of the new tour packages. You must book the trip at least 60 days prior to the departure date. Please turn in this letter to qualify for the discount.

Page 1   Sec 1   1/3   At 1"   Ln 1   Col 1   REC   TRK   EXT   OVR   English (U.S

Figure 2.28

When using the Find and Replace feature, if you wanted to change all the occurrences of the located text, it is much faster to use [Replace All]. Exercise care when using this option, however, because the search text you specify might be part of another word and you may accidentally replace text you want to keep. If this happens, you could use Undo to reverse the action.

Inserting the Current Date

The last text change you need to make is to add the date to the letter. The Date and Time command on the Insert menu inserts the current date as maintained by your computer system into your document at the location of the insertion point. You want to enter the date on the first line of the letter, five lines above the salutation.

1

If necessary, move to the "D" in "Dear" at the top of the letter.

Press ⟨←Enter⟩ **4 times to insert four blank lines.**

Move to the first blank line.

Choose Insert/Date and Time.

Your screen should be similar to Figure 2.29

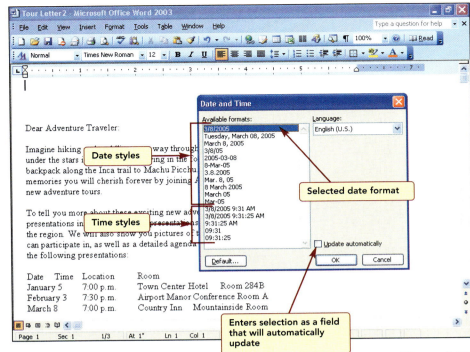

Figure 2.29

Additional Information

The current time can also be inserted into a document using the same procedure.

From the Date and Time dialog box, you select the style in which you want the date displayed in your document. The Available Formats list box displays the format styles for the current date and time. You want to display the date in the format Month XX, 2XXX, the third format setting in the list.

You also want the date to be updated automatically whenever the letter is sent to new Adventure Tours travelers. You use the Update Automatically option to do this, which enters the date as a field.

Concept 5

Field

5

A **field** is a placeholder that instructs Word to insert information into a document. The **field code** contains the directions as to the type of information to insert or action to perform. Field codes appear between curly brackets {}, also called braces. The information that is displayed as a result of the field code is called the **field result**. Many field codes are automatically inserted when you use certain commands; others you can create and insert yourself. Many fields update automatically when the document changes. Using fields makes it easier and faster to perform many common or repetitive tasks.

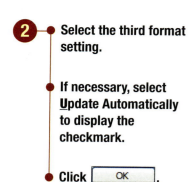

2 ● Select the third format setting.

● If necessary, select **U**pdate Automatically to display the checkmark.

● Click [OK].

Additional Information

You can use [Alt] + [⇧Shift] + D to insert the current date as a field in the format MM/DD/YY.

Your screen should be similar to Figure 2.30

Having Trouble?

The date in Figure 2.30 will be different from the date that appears on your screen.

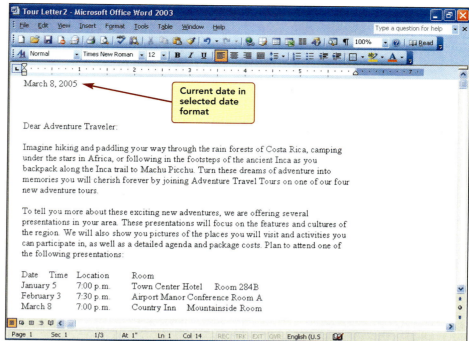

Figure 2.30

The current date is entered in the document in the format you selected. The date is the field result. You will display the field code to see the underlying instructions.

3 ● Right-click on the date and choose **T**oggle Field Codes from the shortcut menu.

Another Method

The keyboard shortcut is [⇧Shift] + [F9].

Your screen should be similar to Figure 2.31

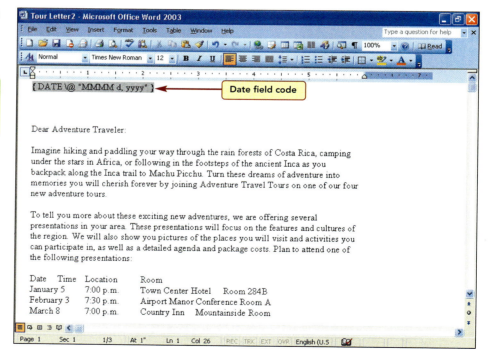

Figure 2.31

The field code includes the field name (DATE) followed by the field properties, in this case the date format instructions. Whenever this document is printed, Word will print the current system date using this format. The field result and code may appear with a shaded background depending upon the setting selected in your program. To show or remove field shading choose Tools/Options/View and then select Never, Always, or When Selected from the field shading box. The shading does not print.

4 ● Press [⇧ Shift] + [F9] to display the field result again.

● Save the document.

Modifying Page Layout

Next the manager has suggested that you make several formatting changes to improve the appearance of the letter and flyer. Many formatting features that can be used in a document affect the layout of an entire page. These formatting features include page margin settings, vertical alignment of text on a page, headers and footers, and orientation of text on a page.

Changing Margin Settings

One of the first changes you will make is to change the page margin settings.

6 The **page margin** is the blank space around the edge of a page. Generally, the text you enter appears in the printable area inside the margins. However, some items can be positioned in the margin space. You can set different page margin widths to alter the appearance of the document.

Standard single-sided documents have four margins: top, bottom, left, and right. Double-sided documents with facing pages, such as books and magazines, also have four margins: top, bottom, inside, and outside. These documents typically use mirror margins in which the left page is a mirror image of the right page. This means that the inside margins are the same width and the outside margins are the same width. (See the illustrations below.)

You can also set a "gutter" margin that reserves space on the left side of single-sided documents, or on the inside margin of double-sided documents, to accommodate binding. There are also special margin settings for headers and footers. (You will learn about these features in Lab 3.)

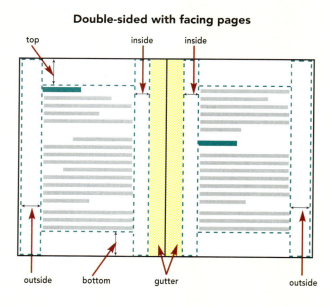

Single-sided with gutter

left   top

gutter   bottom   right

Double-sided with facing pages

top   inside   inside

outside   bottom   gutter   outside

To see how the changes you make to margin settings will look on the page, you will first change the document view to Print Layout view and Page Width zoom.

1 • Click 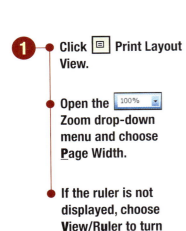 **Print Layout View.**

• **Open the** `100%` **Zoom drop-down menu and choose Page Width.**

• **If the ruler is not displayed, choose View/Ruler to turn it on.**

Your screen should be similar to Figure 2.32

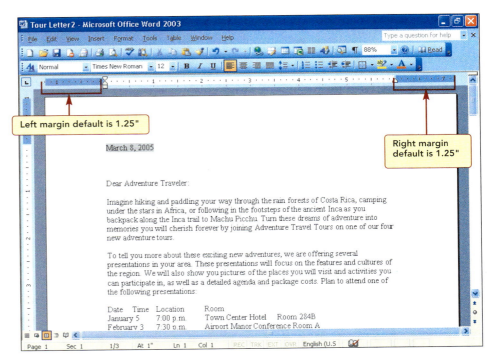

Figure 2.32

The default left and right margin settings of 1.25 inches are now easy to see. As you make changes to the margin settings next, you will be able to easily see the change in the layout of the document on the page.

You would like to see how the letter would look if you changed the right and left margin widths to 1 inch. The Page Setup command on the File menu is used to change settings associated with the layout of the entire document.

2 • **Choose File/Page Setup.**

• **If necessary, open the Margins tab.**

Another Method

You can also double-click on the ruler to display the Page Setup dialog box.

Your screen should be similar to Figure 2.33

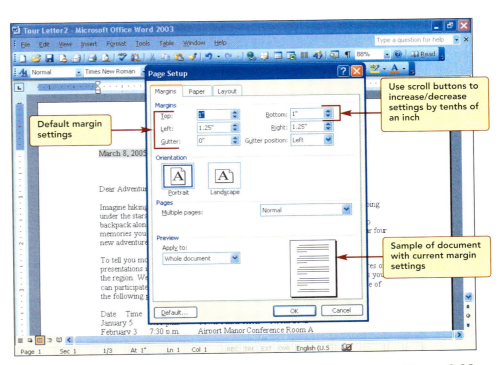

Figure 2.33

The Margins tab of the Page Setup dialog box displays the default margin settings for a single-sided document. The Preview box shows how the current margin settings will appear on a page. New margin settings can be entered by typing the value in the text box, or by clicking the ▲ and ▼ scroll buttons or pressing the ↑ or ↓ keys to increase or decrease the settings by tenths of an inch.

● **3** ● **Using any of these methods, set the left and right margins to 1 inch.**

● **Click** OK .

Your screen should be similar to Figure 2.34

Letter is reformatted to new margin settings

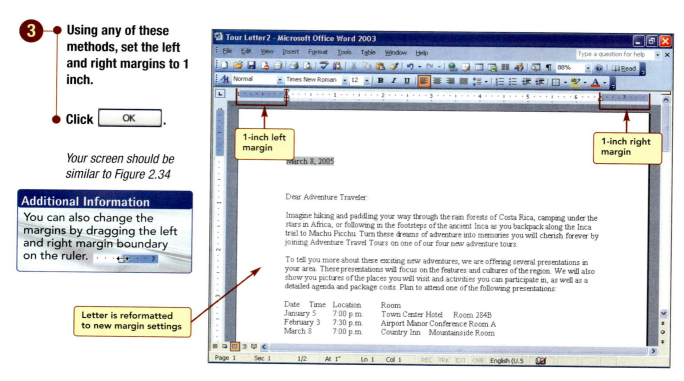

Figure 2.34

You can see that the letter has been reformatted to fit within the new margin settings. You would like to see what both pages look like at the same time.

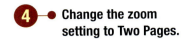

4 **Change the zoom setting to Two Pages.**

Your screen should be similar to Figure 2.35

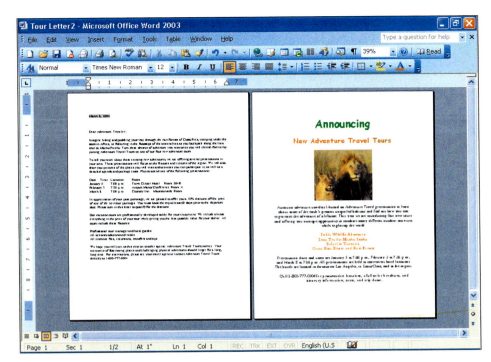

Figure 2.35

Both pages are displayed in the document window. Although the text is difficult to read, you can easily see the layout of the pages and that the margin settings have been changed for both pages.

More Paragraph Formatting

To give the document more interest, you can indent paragraphs, use tabs to create tabular columns of data, and change the line spacing. These formatting features are all paragraph formats that affect the entire selected paragraph.

Indenting Paragraphs

Business letters typically are either created using a block layout style or a modified block style with indented paragraphs. In a block style, all parts of the letter, including the date, inside address, all paragraphs in the body, and closing lines, are evenly aligned with the left margin. The block layout style has a very formal appearance. The modified block style, on the other hand, has a more casual appearance. In this style, certain elements such as the date, all paragraphs in the body, and the closing lines are indented from the left margin.

7 To help your reader find information quickly, you can **indent** paragraphs from the margins. Indenting paragraphs sets them off from the rest of the document. There are four types of indents, and their effects are described below.

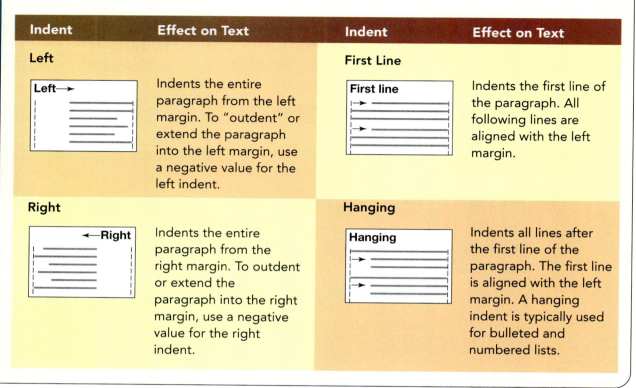

Indent	Effect on Text	Indent	Effect on Text
Left	Indents the entire paragraph from the left margin. To "outdent" or extend the paragraph into the left margin, use a negative value for the left indent.	**First Line**	Indents the first line of the paragraph. All following lines are aligned with the left margin.
Right	Indents the entire paragraph from the right margin. To outdent or extend the paragraph into the right margin, use a negative value for the right indent.	**Hanging**	Indents all lines after the first line of the paragraph. The first line is aligned with the left margin. A hanging indent is typically used for bulleted and numbered lists.

You want to change the letter style from the block paragraph style to the modified block style. You will begin by indenting the first line of the first paragraph.

1 ● **Return the zoom to Page Width.**

● **Right-click anywhere in the first paragraph.**

● **Choose Paragraph from the shortcut menu.**

● **If necessary, open the Indents and Spacing tab.**

Another Method

The menu equivalent is **F**ormat/**P**aragraph.

Your screen should be similar to Figure 2.36

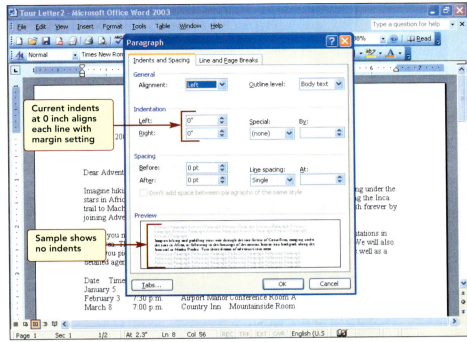

Figure 2.36

The Indents and Spacing tab shows that the left and right indentation settings for the current paragraph are 0. This setting aligns each line of the paragraph with the margin setting. Specifying an indent value would indent each line of the selected paragraph the specified amount from the margin. However, you only want to indent the first line of the paragraph.

2 ● **From the Special drop-down list box, select First line.**

Your screen should be similar to Figure 2.37

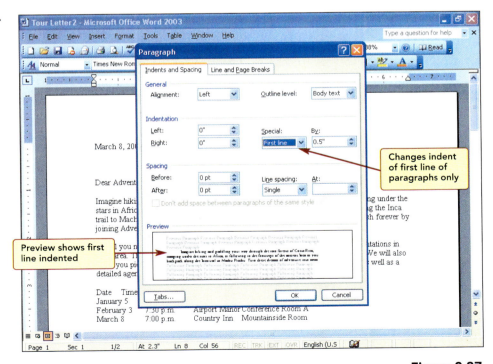

Figure 2.37

The default first line indent setting of 0.5 inch displayed in the By text box is acceptable. The Preview area shows how this setting will affect a paragraph.

3 ● Click [OK].

Your screen should be similar to Figure 2.38

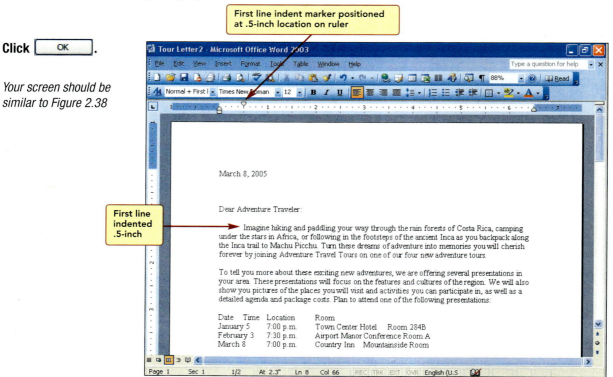

First line indent marker positioned at .5-inch location on ruler

First line indented .5-inch

March 8, 2005

Dear Adventure Traveler:

Imagine hiking and paddling your way through the rain forests of Costa Rica, camping under the stars in Africa, or following in the footsteps of the ancient Inca as you backpack along the Inca trail to Machu Picchu. Turn these dreams of adventure into memories you will cherish forever by joining Adventure Travel Tours on one of our four new adventure tours.

To tell you more about these exciting new adventures, we are offering several presentations in your area. These presentations will focus on the features and cultures of the region. We will also show you pictures of the places you will visit and activities you can participate in, as well as a detailed agenda and package costs. Plan to attend one of the following presentations:

Date   Time   Location   Room
January 5   7:00 p.m.   Town Center Hotel   Room 284B
February 3 7:30 p.m.   Airport Manor Conference Room A
March 8   7:00 p.m.   Country Inn   Mountainside Room

Figure 2.38

The first line of the paragraph indents a half inch from the left margin. The text in the paragraph wraps as needed, and the text on the following line begins at the left margin. Notice that the First Line Indent marker on the ruler moved to the 0.5-inch position. This marker controls the location of the first line of text in the paragraph.

A much quicker way to indent the first line of a paragraph is to press [Tab ⇥] at the beginning of the paragraph. When the insertion point is positioned at the beginning of a line, pressing [Tab ⇥] indents the first line of the paragraph to the first tab stop from the left margin. A **tab stop** is a marked location on the horizontal ruler that indicates how far to indent text when the [Tab ⇥] key is pressed. The default tab stops are every .5 inch.

4 • Move to the beginning of the second paragraph.

• Press Tab ⇥.

Your screen should be similar to Figure 2.39

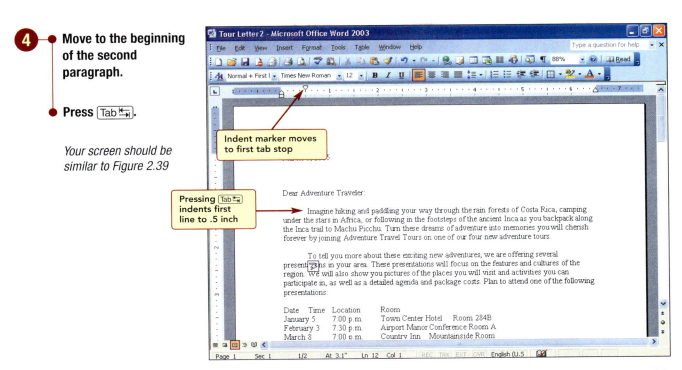

Indent marker moves to first tab stop

Pressing Tab ⇥ indents first line to .5 inch

Dear Adventure Traveler:

Imagine hiking and paddling your way through the rain forests of Costa Rica, camping under the stars in Africa, or following in the footsteps of the ancient Inca as you backpack along the Inca trail to Machu Picchu. Turn these dreams of adventure into memories you will cherish forever by joining Adventure Travel Tours on one of our four new adventure tours.

To tell you more about these exciting new adventures, we are offering several presentations in your area. These presentations will focus on the features and cultures of the region. We will also show you pictures of the places you will visit and activities you can participate in, as well as a detailed agenda and package costs. Plan to attend one of the following presentations:

Date	Time	Location	Room
January 5	7:00 p.m.	Town Center Hotel	Room 284B
February 3	7:30 p.m.	Airport Manor	Conference Room A
March 8	7:00 p.m.	Country Inn	Mountainside Room

Figure 2.39

Indenting the line using Tab ⇥ moves the first line to the first tab stop and also moves the indent marker to that position on the ruler. If the insertion point was positioned anywhere else within the line of text, pressing Tab ⇥ would move the text to the right of the insertion point to the next tab stop and the indent marker would not move.

You can indent the remaining paragraphs individually, or you can select the paragraphs and indent them simultaneously by either using the Format menu or dragging the upper indent marker on the ruler.

Additional Information

To indent an entire paragraph, click in front of any line except the first line and press Tab ⇥.

5 • Select the remaining text on page 1.

• Drag the First Line Indent marker on the ruler to the 0.5-inch position.

Additional Information

A ScreenTip identifies the First Line Indent marker when you point to it.

• If necessary, scroll the window to display the entire selection.

Your screen should be similar to Figure 2.40

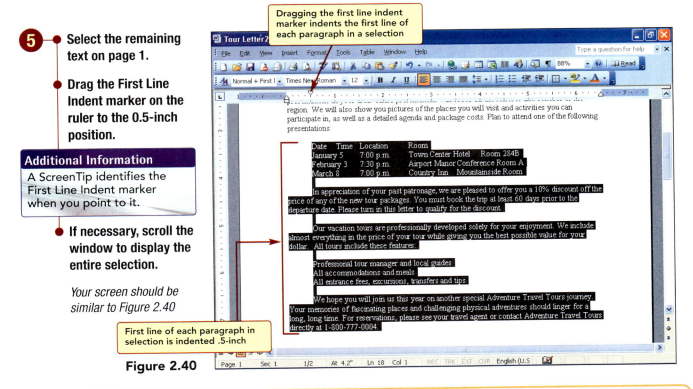

Dragging the first line indent marker indents the first line of each paragraph in a selection

region. We will also show you pictures of the places you will visit and activities you can participate in, as well as a detailed agenda and package costs. Plan to attend one of the following presentations:

Date	Time	Location	Room
January 5	7:00 p.m.	Town Center Hotel	Room 284B
February 3	7:30 p.m.	Airport Manor	Conference Room A
March 8	7:00 p.m.	Country Inn	Mountainside Room

In appreciation of your past patronage, we are pleased to offer you a 10% discount off the price of any of the new tour packages. You must book the trip at least 60 days prior to the departure date. Please turn in this letter to qualify for the discount.

Our vacation tours are professionally developed solely for your enjoyment. We include almost everything in the price of your tour while giving you the best possible value for your dollar. All tours include these features:

Professional tour manager and local guides
All accommodations and meals
All entrance fees, excursions, transfers and tips

We hope you will join us this year on another special Adventure Travel Tours journey. Your memories of fascinating places and challenging physical adventures should linger for a long, long time. For reservations, please see your travel agent or contact Adventure Travel Tours directly at 1-800-777-0004.

First line of each paragraph in selection is indented .5-inch

Figure 2.40

The first line of each paragraph in the selection is indented. Notice that each line of the date and time information is also indented. This is because each line ends with a paragraph mark. Word considers each line a separate paragraph.

Setting Tab Stops

Next you want to improve the appearance of the list of presentation times and dates. The date and time information was entered using tabs to separate the different columns of information. However, because the default tab stops are set at every 0.5 inch, the columns are not evenly spaced. You want to reformat this information to appear as a tabbed table of information so that it is easier to read as shown below.

Date	Time	Location	Room
January 5 ----- 7:00 pm -----------Town Center Hotel -------Room 284B
February 3 ---- 7:30 pm ----------Airport Manor ------------Conference Room A
March 8 ------- 7:00 pm -----------Country Inn----------------Mountainside Room

To improve the appearance of the data, you will create custom tab stops that will align the data in evenly spaced columns. The default tab stops of every 0.5 inch are visible on the ruler as light vertical lines below the numbers. As with other default settings, you can change the location of tab stops in the document.

You can also select from five different types of tab stops that control how characters are positioned or aligned with the tab stop. The following table explains the five tab types, the tab marks that appear in the tab alignment selector box (on the left end of the horizontal ruler), and the effects on the text.

Tab Type	Tab Mark	Effects on Text	Example
Left	⌊	Extends text to right from tab stop	left
Center	⊥	Aligns text centered on tab stop	center
Right	⌋	Extends text to left from tab stop	right
Decimal	⊥	Aligns text with decimal point	35.78
Bar	∣	Draws a vertical line through text at tab stop	∣

To align the data, you will place three left tab stops at the 1.5-inch, 2.75-inch, and 4.5-inch positions. You can quickly specify custom tab stop locations and types using the ruler. To select a type of tab stop, click the tab alignment selector box to cycle through the types. Then, to specify where to place the selected tab stop type, click on the location in the ruler. As you specify the new tab stop settings, the table data will align to the new settings.

1 Select the line of table headings and the three lines of data.

● If necessary, click the tab alignment selector box until the left tab icon 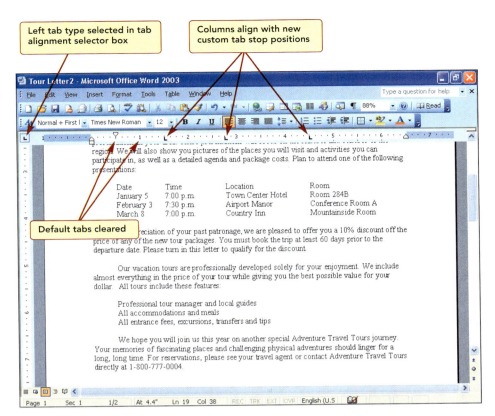 appears.

● Click on the 1.5-inch position on the ruler.

● Click on the 2.75-inch and the 4.5-inch positions on the ruler.

● Click anywhere in the table to deselect it.

Your screen should be similar to Figure 2.41

Left tab type selected in tab alignment selector box

Columns align with new custom tab stop positions

Default tabs cleared

Date	Time	Location	Room
January 5	7:00 p.m.	Town Center Hotel	Room 284B
February 3	7:30 p.m.	Airport Manor	Conference Room A
March 8	7:00 p.m.	Country Inn	Mountainside Room

Figure 2.41

The three tabbed columns appropriately align with the new tab stops. All default tabs to the left of the custom tab stops are cleared. After looking at the columns, you decide the column headings would look better centered over the columns of data. To make this change, you will remove the three custom tabs for the heading line by dragging them off the ruler and then add three center tab stops.

2 • Move to anywhere in the heading line.

• Drag the three left tab stop marks off the ruler.

• Click the tab alignment selector box until the center tab icon 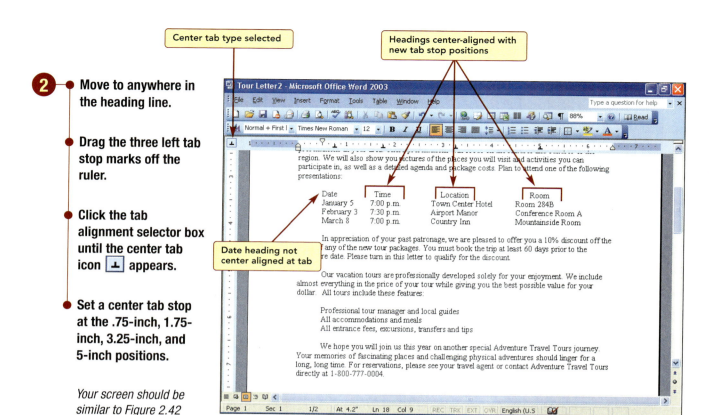 appears.

• Set a center tab stop at the .75-inch, 1.75-inch, 3.25-inch, and 5-inch positions.

Your screen should be similar to Figure 2.42

Headings center-aligned with new tab stop positions

Date heading not center aligned at tab

Figure 2.42

The Time, Location, and Room headings are appropriately centered on the tab stops. However, the Date heading still needs to be indented to the .75 tab stop position by pressing [Tab ⇥].

Heading center-aligned at .75-inch position

3 • If necessary, move to the "D" in "Date."

• Press [Tab ⇥].

Your screen should be similar to Figure 2.43

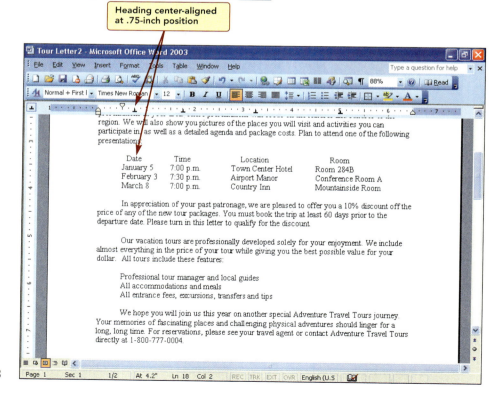

Figure 2.43

The Date heading is now centered at the .75-inch tab stop. As you can see, setting different types of tab stops is helpful for aligning text or numeric data vertically in columns. Using tab stops ensures that the text will indent to the same set location. Setting custom tab stops instead of pressing Tab↹ or Spacebar repeatedly is a more professional way to format a document, as well as faster and more accurate. It also makes editing easier because you can change the tab stop settings for several paragraphs at once.

Adding Tab Leaders

To make the presentation times and location data even easier to read, you will add tab leaders to the table. **Leader characters** are solid, dotted, or dashed lines that fill the blank space between tab stops. They help the reader's eye move across the blank space between the information aligned at the tab stops.

1 • **Select the three lines of presentation information, excluding the heading line.**

• **Choose Format/Tabs.**

Your screen should be similar to Figure 2.44

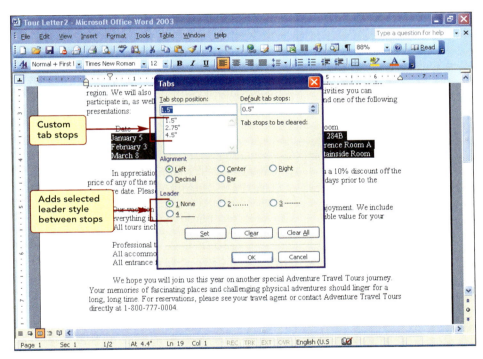

Figure 2.44

Notice that the Tabs dialog box displays the custom tabs you set on the ruler. You can set tab positions in the dialog box by entering the tab positions in the text box. The current tab leader setting is set to None for the 1.5-inch tab stop. You can select from three styles of tab leaders. You will use the third tab leader style, a series of dashed lines. The tab leader fills the empty space to the left of the tab stop. Each tab stop must have the leader individually set.

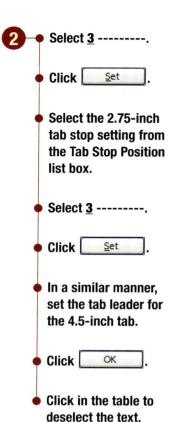

2 ● Select **3** ----------.

● Click [Set].

● Select the 2.75-inch tab stop setting from the Tab Stop Position list box.

● Select **3** ----------.

● Click [Set].

● In a similar manner, set the tab leader for the 4.5-inch tab.

● Click [OK].

● Click in the table to deselect the text.

Your screen should be similar to Figure 2.45

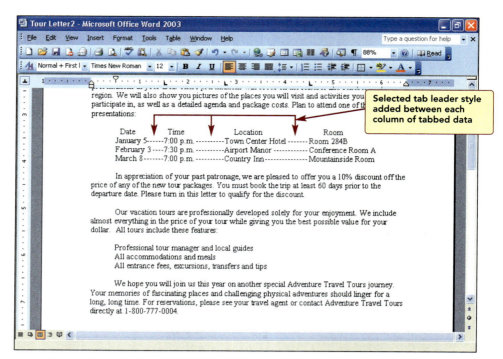

> Selected tab leader style added between each column of tabbed data

Figure 2.45

The selected leader style has been added to the blank space between each column of tabbed text.

Changing Line Spacing

You also want to increase the spacing between the lines in the table to make the presentation data even easier to read.

Concept 8

8   Adjusting the **line spacing**, or the vertical space between lines of text, helps set off areas of text from others and when increased makes it easier to read and edit text. The default setting of single line spacing accommodates the largest font in that line, plus a small amount of extra space. If a line contains a character or object, such as a graphic, that is larger than the surrounding text, the spacing for that line is automatically adjusted. Additional line spacing settings are described in the table below.

Spacing	Effect
1.5 lines	Spacing is one and a half times that of single line spacing.
Double (2.0)	Spacing is twice that of single line spacing.
At least	Uses a value specified in points as the minimum line spacing that is needed to fit the largest font or graphic on the line.
Exactly	Uses a value specified in points as a fixed line spacing amount that is not adjusted, making all lines evenly spaced. Graphics or text that is too large will appear clipped.
Multiple	Uses a percentage value to increase or decrease the spacing. For example, 1.3 will increase the spacing by 33 percent.

In addition to changing line spacing within paragraphs, you can also change the spacing before or after paragraphs. For example, the line spacing of text within paragraphs could be set to single and the spacing between paragraphs to double.

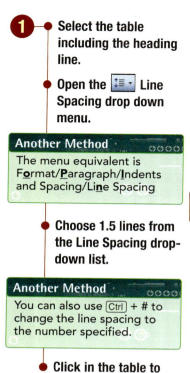

1 Select the table including the heading line.

● Open the ⌷≣⌷▾ Line Spacing drop down menu.

Another Method

The menu equivalent is F**o**rmat/**P**aragraph/**I**ndents and Spacing/Li**n**e Spacing

● Choose 1.5 lines from the Line Spacing drop-down list.

Another Method

You can also use Ctrl + # to change the line spacing to the number specified.

● Click in the table to deselect the text.

Your screen should be similar to Figure 2.46

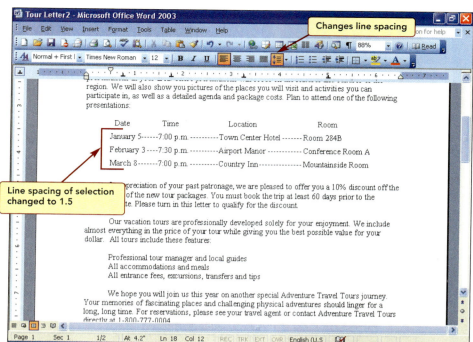

Figure 2.46

The line spacing within the selection has increased to 1.5 lines.

More Character Formatting

As you look at the letter, you still feel that the table of presentation dates and times does not stand out enough. You can add emphasis to information in your documents by formatting specific characters or words. Applying color shading behind text is commonly used to identify areas of text that you want to stand out. It is frequently used to mark text that you want to locate easily as you are revising a document. Italics, underlines, and bold are other character formats that add emphasis and draw the reader's attention to important items. Word applies character formatting to the entire selection or to the entire word at the insertion point. You can apply formatting to a portion of a word by selecting the area to be formatted first.

Adding Color Highlighting

First, you want to see how a color highlight behind the tabbed table of presentation times and locations would look.

1 ● **Open the** 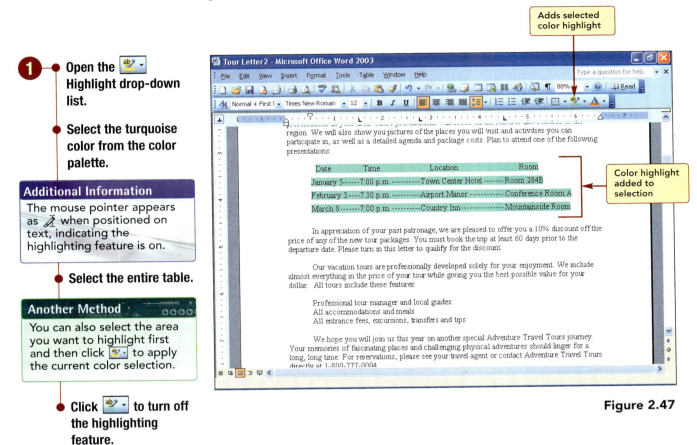 **Highlight drop-down list.**

● **Select the turquoise color from the color palette.**

Additional Information
The mouse pointer appears as ✎ when positioned on text, indicating the highlighting feature is on.

● **Select the entire table.**

Another Method
You can also select the area you want to highlight first and then click to apply the current color selection.

● **Click to turn off the highlighting feature.**

Your screen should be similar to Figure 2.47

Another Method
You can also press Esc to turn off highlighting.

Additional Information
When you use highlights in a document you plan to print in black and white, select a light color so the text is visible.

Figure 2.47

Although the highlight makes the table stand out, it does not look good.

Underlining Text

Instead, you decide to bold and underline the headings. The default underline style is a single black line. In addition, Word includes 15 other types of underlines.

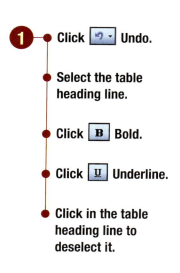

- Click 🔄 ▾ **Undo.**

- **Select the table heading line.**

- Click **B** **Bold.**

- Click **U** **Underline.**

- **Click in the table heading line to deselect it.**

Your screen should be similar to Figure 2.48

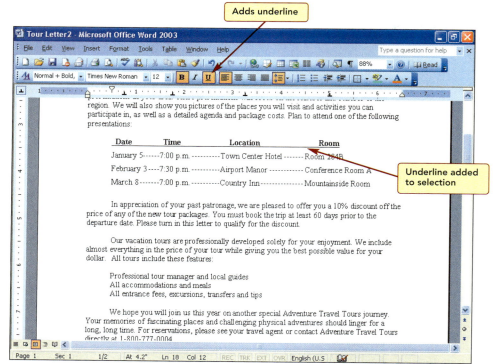

Figure 2.48

All the words are bold, and a single black underline has been added below the entire selection. You decide you want the underline to appear under each word only and to stand out more. To do this, you will select another underline style and apply the underline to the word individually. When the insertion point is positioned on a word, the selected underline style is applied to the entire word.

2 • Click 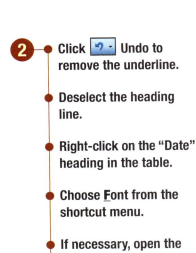 Undo to remove the underline.

• Deselect the heading line.

• Right-click on the "Date" heading in the table.

• Choose **F**ont from the shortcut menu.

• If necessary, open the Font tab.

• Open the **U**nderline style drop-down list box.

Your screen should be similar to Figure 2.49

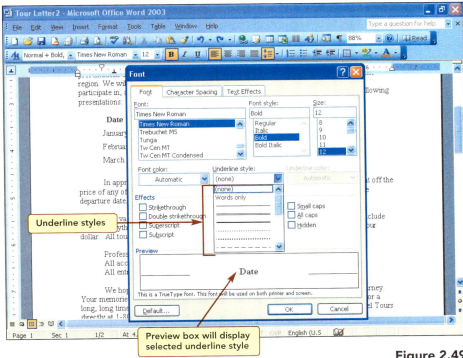

Figure 2.49

The None option removes underlining from a selection, and the Words Only option displays underlines under words in the selection only, not under the spaces between words. The Words Only option uses the default single underline style. You will add a double underline below the word.

3 • Select several underline styles and see how they appear in the Preview box.

• Select the double underline style.

• Click 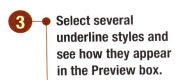.

Additional Information

Using **U** Underline or the keyboard shortcut Ctrl + U adds the default single underline style.

Your screen should be similar to Figure 2.50

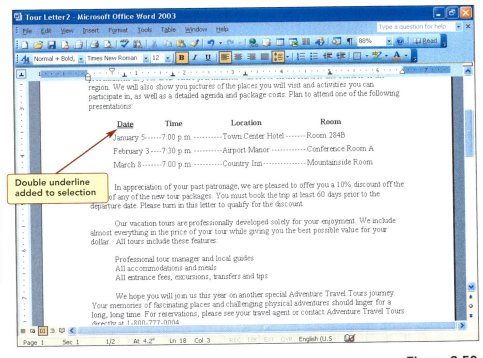

Figure 2.50

The selected word is underlined using the double underline style.

Copying Formats with Format Painter

You want to quickly apply the same formats to the other headings. To do this you can use the **Format Painter**. This feature applies the formats associated with the current selection to new selections. If the selection is a paragraph (including the paragraph mark), the formatting is applied to the entire paragraph. If the selection is a character, the format is applied to a character, word, or selection you specify. To turn on the feature, move the insertion point to the text whose formats you want to copy and click the 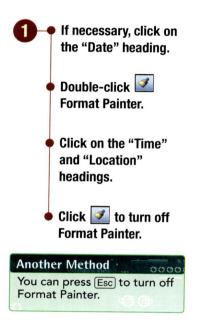 Format Painter button. Then select the text to which you want the formats applied. The format is automatically applied to an entire word simply by clicking on the word. To apply the format to more or less text, you must select the area. If you double-click the 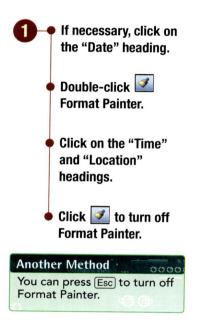 Format Painter button, you can apply the format multiple times.

1 If necessary, click on the "Date" heading.

Double-click 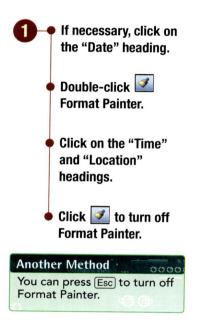 Format Painter.

Click on the "Time" and "Location" headings.

Click 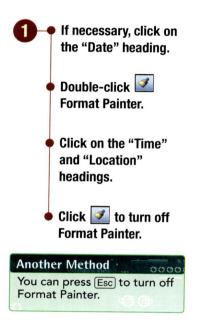 to turn off Format Painter.

Your screen should be similar to Figure 2.51

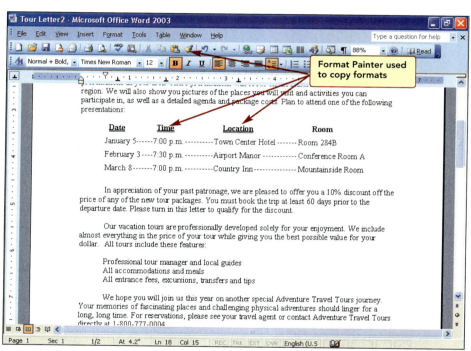

Figure 2.51

Applying Formats Using the Styles and Formatting Task Pane

The last heading to format is Room. Another way to apply existing formatting is to use the Styles and Formatting task pane.

Displays and hides Styles and
Formatting task pane

Task pane

1 **Click** 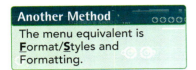 **Styles and Formatting on the Formatting toolbar.**

Another Method

The menu equivalent is **F**ormat/**S**tyles and Formatting.

Your screen should be similar to Figure 2.52

Formatting associated with selected text

All formats used in document

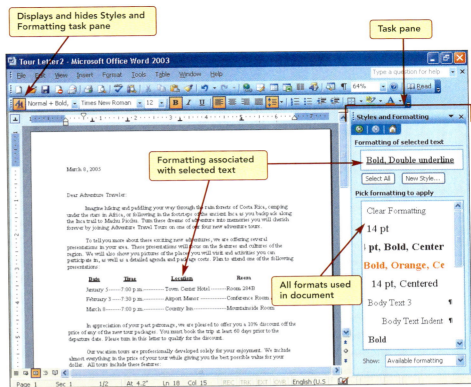

Figure 2.52

Using the Styles and Formatting task pane, you can apply styles, create new styles, and modify existing styles. The formatting associated with the selected text appears in the Formatting of Selected text box at the top of the pane. The names of all other formats available are listed in the Pick Formatting to Apply list box. The names are in alphabetical order and are displayed using the associated formatting. To apply an existing format to a selection, you can pick the format from this list.

2 **Click on the "Room" table heading.**

● **Scroll the list box and click** Bold, Double underline **.**

Your screen should be similar to Figure 2.53

Selected format applied to word

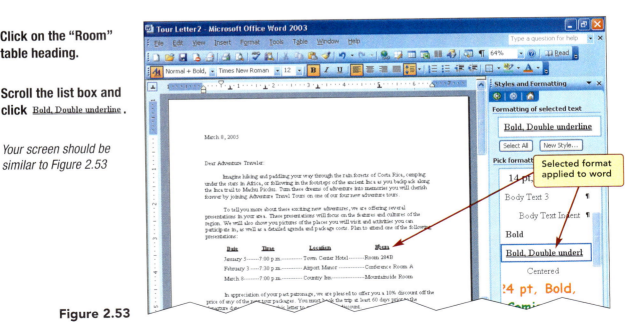

Figure 2.53

The selected formatting is applied to the word.

3 ● Click ⊞ **Styles and Formatting to hide the task pane.**

● **Save the document again.**

Creating Lists

Additional Information

A list can be used whenever you present three or more related pieces of information.

The next change you want to make is to display the three lines of information about tour features as an itemized list so that they stand out better from the surrounding text.

Concept 9
Bulleted and Numbered Lists

9   Whenever possible, add bullets or numbers before items in a list to organize information and to make your writing clear and easy to read. Word includes many basic bullet, a dot or other symbol, and number formats from which you can select. Additionally, there are many picture bullets available. If none of the predesigned bullet or number formats suits your needs, you can also create your own customized designs.

Use a **bulleted list** when you have several items in a paragraph that logically make a list. A bulleted list displays one of several styles of bullets before each item in the list. You can select from several types of symbols to use as bullets and you can change the color, size, and position of the bullet.

Use a **numbered list** when you want to convey a sequence of events, such as a procedure that has steps to follow in a certain order. A numbered list displays numbers or letters before the text. Word automatically increments the number or letter as you start a new paragraph. You can select from several different numbering schemes to create your numbered lists.

Use an **outline numbered list** to display multiple outline levels that show a hierarchical structure of the items in the list. There can be up to nine levels.

Numbering a List

Because both bullet and number formats will indent the items automatically when applied, you first need to remove the indent from the three tour features. Then you will try a numbered list format to see how it looks.

1 • Select the three tour features.

• Drag the First Line Indent marker on the ruler back to the margin boundary.

• Right-click on the selection and choose **Bullets and Numbering.**

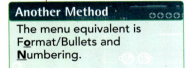

Another Method

The menu equivalent is F**o**rmat/Bullets and **N**umbering.

• Open the **N**umbered tab.

Your screen should be similar to Figure 2.54

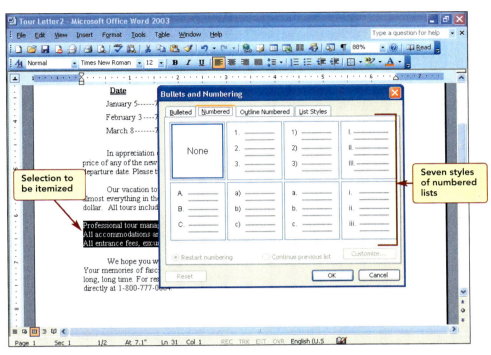

Figure 2.54

Additional Information

The None option is used to remove an existing numbering format.

The Bullets and Numbering dialog box displays examples of seven built-in numbered list formats. You can also change the appearance of the built-in formats using the Customize option. For example, you could change the color of the number for the entire list. You will use the second number format.

2 ● Select the second numbered list format option.

● Click [OK].

Your screen should be similar to Figure 2.55

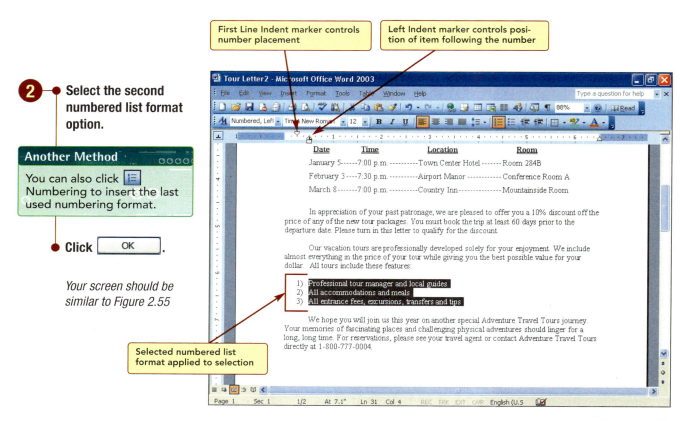

Selected numbered list format applied to selection

Figure 2.55

A number is inserted at the 0.25-inch position before each line, and the text following the number is indented to the 0.5-inch position. In an itemized list, the First Line Indent marker on the ruler controls the position of the number or bullet, and the Left Indent marker controls the position of the item following the number or bullet. The Left Indent marker creates a hanging indent. If the text following each bullet were longer than a line, the text on the following lines would also be indented to the 0.5-inch position.

Bulleting a List

After looking at the list, you decide it really would be more appropriate if it were a bulleted list instead of a numbered list.

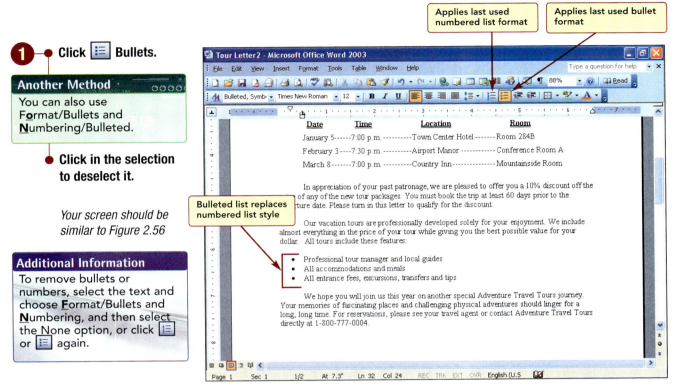

1 • Click 📇 Bullets.

• Click in the selection to deselect it.

Your screen should be similar to Figure 2.56

Figure 2.56

The bullet format that was last used in Word replaces the number. Therefore your document may display a different bullet design than shown in Figure 2.56.

Using AutoText Entries

While looking at the letter, you realize that the closing lines have not been added to the document. You can quickly insert text and graphics that you use frequently using the AutoText feature. As you learned in Lab 1, Word includes a list of standard AutoText entries that consists of standard phrases such as salutations and closings. In addition to the standard list, you can create your own AutoText entries.

Inserting an AutoText Entry

You will use the AutoText feature to add a standard closing to the letter.

1 ● **Move to the blank line at the end of the letter.**

● **If needed, insert another blank line to separate the closing from the last paragraph.**

● **Choose Insert/AutoText/ Closing.**

● **Choose Best regards.**

● **Press** ←Enter **4 times.**

● **Type your name followed by a comma and a space.**

Your screen should be similar to Figure 2.57

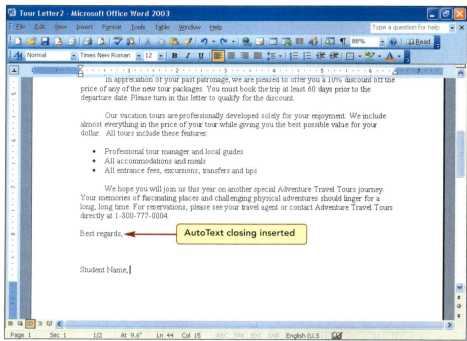

Figure 2.57

Creating an AutoText Entry

Following your name you want to include your job title. Since this is an item you frequently add to correspondence, you will create an AutoText entry for it.

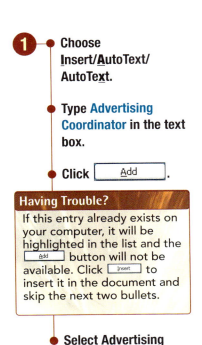

1 ● Choose Insert/AutoText/AutoText.

● Type **Advertising Coordinator** in the text box.

● Click [Add].

Having Trouble?

If this entry already exists on your computer, it will be highlighted in the list and the [Add] button will not be available. Click [Insert] to insert it in the document and skip the next two bullets.

● Select Advertising Coordinator from the list.

● Click [Insert].

● Finally, indent both closing lines to the 3.5-inch position.

● Save the document again.

Your screen should be similar to Figure 2.58

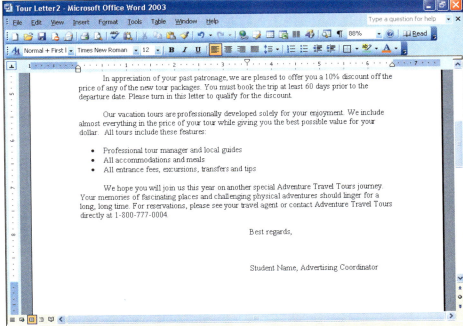

In appreciation of your past patronage, we are pleased to offer you a 10% discount off the price of any of the new tour packages. You must book the trip at least 60 days prior to the departure date. Please turn in this letter to qualify for the discount.

Our vacation tours are professionally developed solely for your enjoyment. We include almost everything in the price of your tour while giving you the best possible value for your dollar. All tours include these features:

- Professional tour manager and local guides
- All accommodations and meals
- All entrance fees, excursions, transfers and tips

We hope you will join us this year on another special Adventure Travel Tours journey. Your memories of fascinating places and challenging physical adventures should linger for a long, long time. For reservations, please see your travel agent or contact Adventure Travel Tours directly at 1-800-777-0004.

Best regards,

Student Name, Advertising Coordinator

Figure 2.58

Using AutoText entries saves you time when entering commonly used words and phrases. The entries you create are listed in the Normal category of the AutoText menu.

Adding and Modifying an AutoShape

You also want to add a special graphic to the flyer containing information about the company Web site to catch the reader's attention. To quickly add a shape, you will use one of the ready-made shapes called **AutoShapes** that are supplied with Word. These include basic shapes such as rectangles and circles, a variety of lines, block arrows, flowchart symbols, stars and banners, and callouts. Additional shapes are available in the Clip Organizer. You can also combine AutoShapes to create more complex designs. To see and create AutoShapes, the view needs to be Print Layout view. In Normal view, AutoShapes are not displayed. If you are using Normal view when you begin to create an AutoShape, the view will change automatically to Print Layout view.

Inserting an AutoShape

You want to add a graphic of a banner to the bottom of the flyer. The Drawing toolbar is used to create AutoShapes. The buttons on the Drawing toolbar, identified below, are used to create and enhance drawing objects.

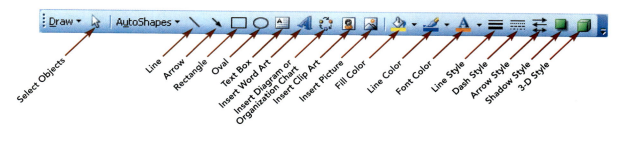

1. **Press Ctrl + End to move to the bottom of the flyer.**

   Click [ ] Drawing to display the Drawing toolbar.

   Another Method
   The menu equivalent is **V**iew/**T**oolbars/Drawing.

   Click AutoShapes ▾.

   Select Stars and Banners.

   Click [ ] Down Ribbon.

   Your screen should be similar to Figure 2.59

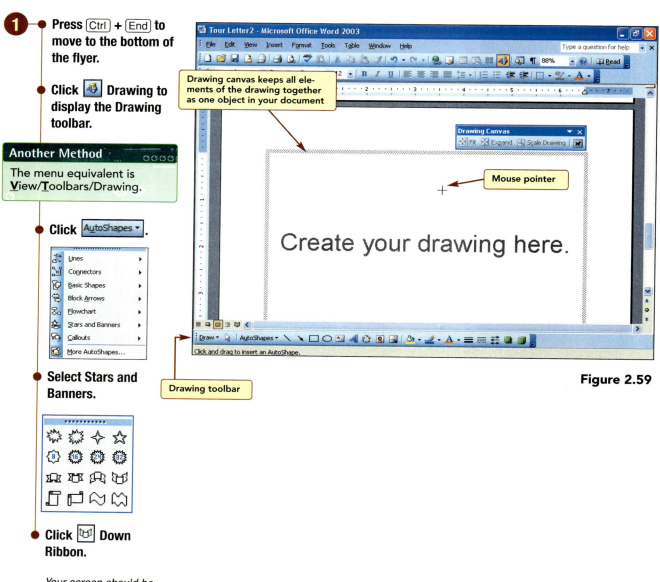

Figure 2.59

A drawing canvas in which you can draw a picture is inserted as an object in the document. All items drawn in the drawing canvas stay as a complete picture within your document and can be moved and resized as a unit. The Drawing Canvas toolbar is used to control features associated with the drawing canvas.

2 ● **Click in the drawing canvas to insert the AutoShape.**

● **Drag the sizing handles to increase length and width of the AutoShape size to that shown in Figure 2.60.**

Additional Information

To maintain the height and width proportions of the AutoShape, hold down ⬆Shift while you drag.

Your screen should be similar to Figure 2.60

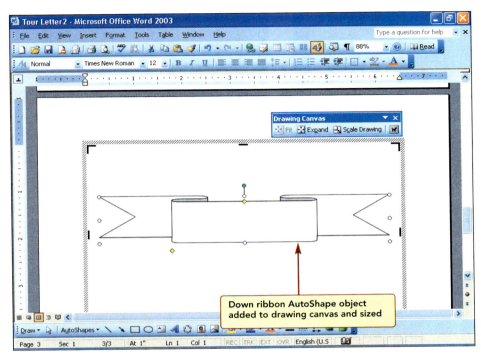

Figure 2.60

Filling the AutoShape with Color

The AutoShape can also be enhanced using many of the features on the Drawing toolbar, such as adding a background fill color and line color.

1 Open the  Fill Color drop-down menu in the Drawing toolbar.

● Select the lime fill color.

● In the same manner, open the Line Color menu in the Drawing toolbar and select green.

Your screen should be similar to Figure 2.61

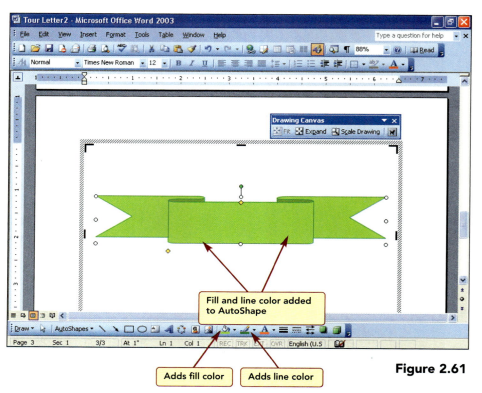

Figure 2.61

Adding Text to an AutoShape

Next you will add text to the AutoShape. The manager has also asked you to add information about the company's Web site to the flyer. You will include the Web site's address, called a **URL** (Uniform Resource Locator), in the AutoShape. Word automatically recognizes URLs you enter and creates a hyperlink of the entry. A **hyperlink** is a connection to a location in the current document, another document, or to a Web site. It allows the reader to jump to the referenced location by clicking on the hyperlink text when reading the document on the screen.

1 Right-click on the shape to open the shortcut menu.

Choose Add Te**x**t.

Using the Formatting toolbar buttons, change the font to Arial, size 12, bold, and centered.

Type Visit our.

Press ⏎Enter.

Type Web site at.

Press ⏎Enter.

Type www.Adventure TravelTours.com and press Spacebar.

If necessary, adjust the AutoShape size to fully display the text.

Your screen should be similar to Figure 2.62

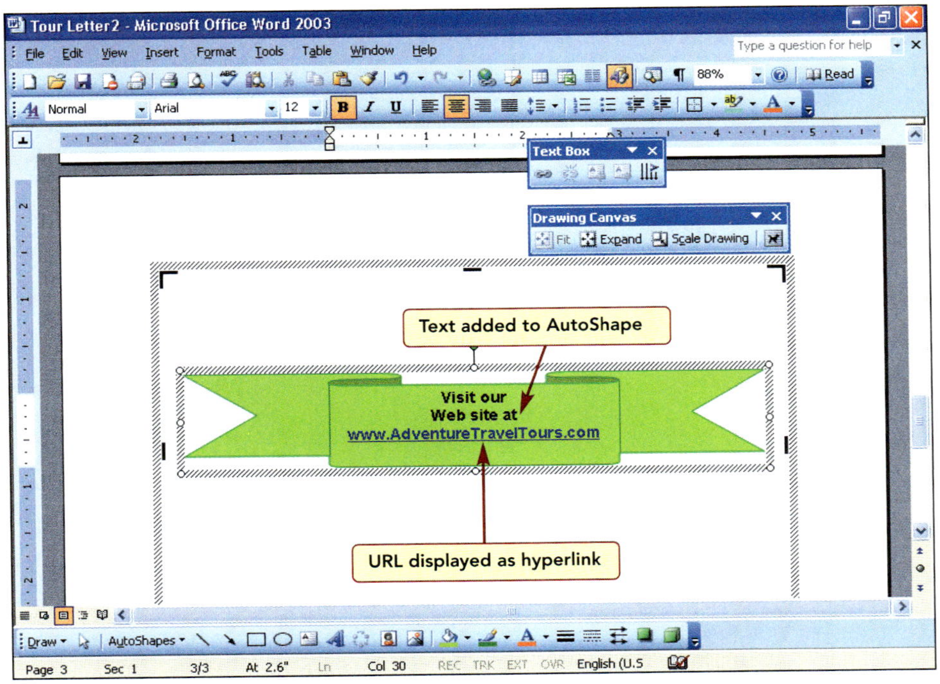

Figure 2.62

Additional Information

The text box toolbar appears automatically. It is used to work with text entered in objects.

Additional Information

You can turn off the AutoFormat feature so the hyperlinks are not created automatically using **S**top Automatically Creating Hyperlinks on the AutoCorrect Options button menu.

The text appears in the selected font settings. The text color is black because the default font color setting is Automatic. This setting will make the text color black if the background fill color is light and white if the fill color is dark.

The Web address is automatically formatted in blue and underlined, indicating the entry is a hyperlink. The **AutoFormat** feature makes certain formatting changes automatically to your document. These formats include formatting a Web address, replacing ordinals (1st) with superscript (1st), fractions (1/2) with fraction characters (½), and applying a bulleted list format to a list if you type an asterisk (*) followed by a space at the beginning of a paragraph. These AutoFormat features can be turned off if the corrections are not needed in your document.

Because this is a document you plan to print, you do not want the text displayed as a link. Since the hyperlink was created using the AutoFormat feature, you can undo the correction or turn it off using the AutoCorrect Options button.

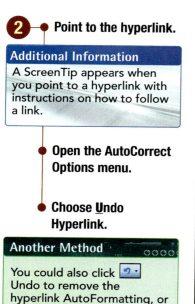

2 ● **Point to the hyperlink.**

● **Open the AutoCorrect Options menu.**

● **Choose Undo Hyperlink.**

Your screen should be similar to Figure 2.63

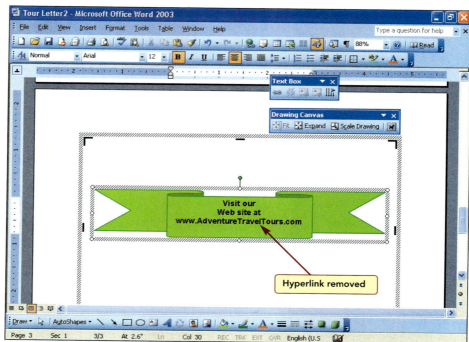

Figure 2.63

The Web address now appears as normal text.

Moving an AutoShape

Next, you need to move the AutoShape to the bottom of the flyer. In order for the object to fit in this space, you can either make the drawing canvas smaller by sizing it to fit the AutoShape, or you can delete the drawing canvas object. Since the Autoshape is a single object, it is not necessary to use the drawing canvas (which is designed to keep multiple objects together). To remove the drawing canvas, you first need to drag the AutoShape off of it, then select the drawing canvas and delete it.

1 ● Zoom to Whole Page and scroll the window to see the bottom of the flyer.

● Drag the AutoShape object to move and center it between the margins in the space at the bottom of the flyer.

● Click on page 3 to select the drawing canvas and press Delete.

● Click 🖉 Drawing to close the Drawing toolbar.

Your screen should be similar to Figure 2.64

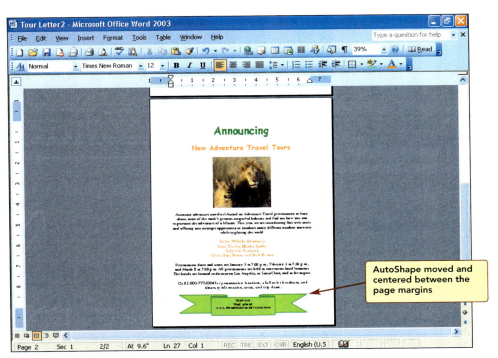

Figure 2.64

The banner complements the colors used in the flyer and adds the needed information about the Web site.

Editing While Previewing

Next you will preview and make any final changes to the letter before printing it. When previewing a large document, it is often useful to see multiple pages at the same time to check formatting and other items. Additionally, you can quickly edit while previewing, to make final changes to your document.

Previewing Multiple Pages

First, you want to display both pages of your document in the preview window. You can view up to six pages at the same time in the Preview window.

1 ● **Return the zoom to Page Width.**

● **Press** Ctrl + Home **to move to the top of the document.**

● **Click** 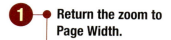 **Print Preview.**

● **Click** ▦ **Multiple pages and select 1x2 pages.**

1 x 2 Pages

Having Trouble?

Point to the icons on the Multiple Pages drop-down menu to highlight the number of pages and click while selected.

Your screen should be similar to Figure 2.65

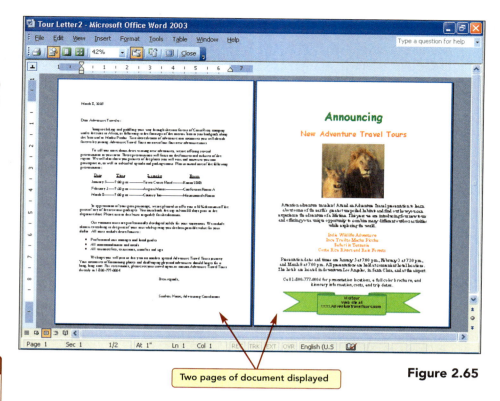

Two pages of document displayed

Figure 2.65

Editing in Print Preview

Now that you can see the entire letter, you see that the date needs to be indented to the 3.5-inch tab position. While in Print Preview, you can also edit and format text. The mouse pointer can be a magnifying glass 🔍 or an I-beam when it is positioned on text in the document. The 🔍 indicates that when you click on a document, the screen will toggle between the Whole Page view you currently see and 100 percent magnification. The I-beam means you can edit the document.

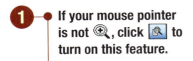

1 • **If your mouse pointer is not 🔍, click 🔍 to turn on this feature.**

• **Click near the date in the letter.**

Your screen should be similar to Figure 2.66

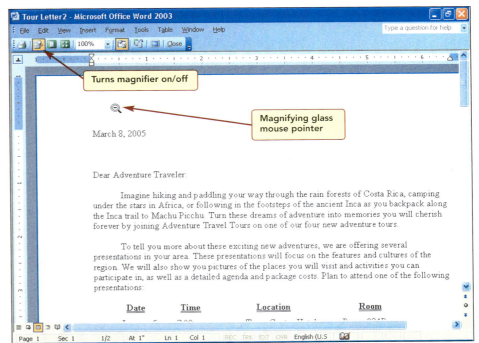

Figure 2.66

A single page is displayed in the size it will appear when printed (100 percent zoom). Now that the document is large enough to work in, you will switch from zooming the document to editing it. When in editing mode, the mouse pointer changes to an I-beam and the insertion point is displayed. Then you can edit the document as in Normal view.

2 • **Click 🔍 Magnifier to change to editing.**

• **If necessary, click 📄 View Ruler to display the ruler.**

Additional Information

Pointing to the top of left edge of the window will temporarily display the ruler if the ruler display is off.

• **Move to the beginning of the date.**

• **Indent the date to the 3.5-inch position.**

Your screen should be similar to Figure 2.67

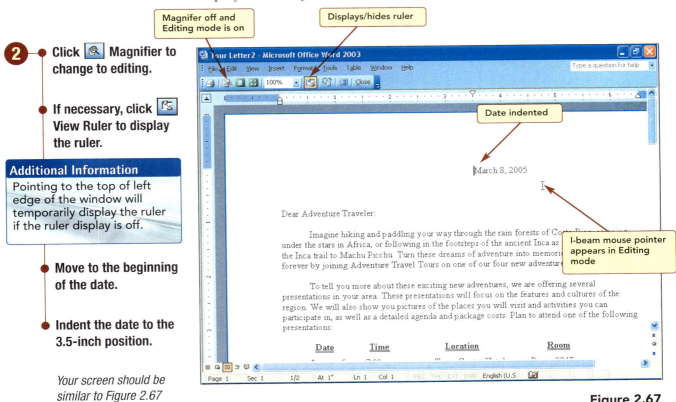

Figure 2.67

While looking at the document, you decide to emphasize some of the text by adding bold. Because you are using Print Preview, the Standard and Formatting toolbars are not displayed. You could display the Formatting toolbar or you could use the Format menu to change the text. Another quick way, however, is to use the keyboard shortcut.

3 • Select the three bulleted items.

• Press Ctrl + B to add bold.

• Click 🔍 Magnifier to turn off editing.

Another Method

The [43%] Zoom button can also be used to specify the magnification.

• Click the document to see both pages again.

Your screen should be similar to Figure 2.68

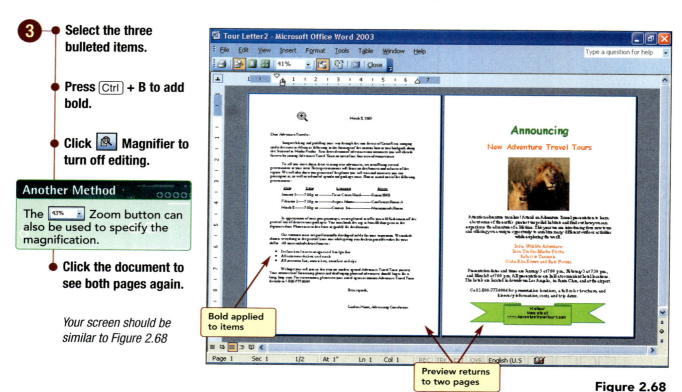

Figure 2.68

Now that the document has been edited and formatted the way you want, you will print a copy of the letter from the Print Preview window using the default print settings.

Note: If you need to specify a different printer, you will need to use the Print command on the File menu.

4 • Click 🖨 Print.

• Close the Print Preview window.

The printed output should be similar to text shown in the Case Study at the beginning of the lab.

Using Document Versions

You want to save the current version of the flyer without the banner and another version with the banner. In addition to saving documents as individual files, you can save multiple versions of the same document within the same file. Each **version** is a "snapshot" of a document at a specific time. This is helpful if you want to have a record of changes you have made to a document. It can also be used to save a variation of a document that you may want to use for another purpose. Saving versions also saves disk space because Word saves only the differences between versions, not an entire copy of each version. This is especially effective when a document contains many graphics. After you have saved several versions of the document, you can go back and review, open, print, and delete earlier versions.

Creating Versions

You can have Word automatically save a version of your document each time the document is closed. This method is used when you need a record of who made changes and when. Alternatively, you can manually specify when to create a version. This method creates a version showing the document as you want it at a specific time. You will manually create the two versions of the flyer document. First you will create a version of the flyer without the banner.

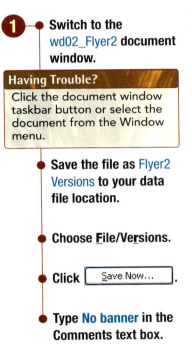

1 ● **Switch to the** wd02_Flyer2 **document window.**

Having Trouble?
Click the document window taskbar button or select the document from the Window menu.

● **Save the file as** Flyer2 Versions **to your data file location.**

● **Choose** F̲ile/Ve̲rsions.

● **Click** [S̲ave Now...] **.**

● **Type** No banner **in the Comments text box.**

Your screen should be similar to Figure 2.69

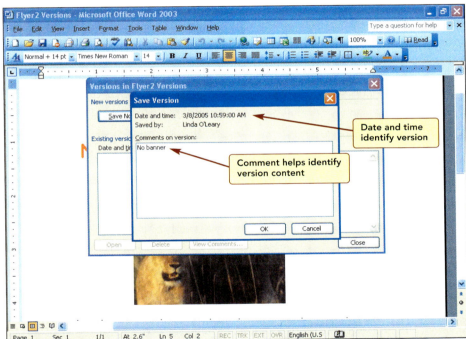

Figure 2.69

When a version is saved, the date and time are used to identify the version. By including a comment, you will be able to more easily identify the version content. Next, you will copy the banner from the letter to the Flyer2 document and save the revised flyer as second version.

2 ● Click [OK] to complete the command.

● Switch to the Tour Letter2 document.

● Click on the AutoShape (not the text) to select it.

● Click [⎙] Copy.

● Switch back to the flyer and paste the banner at the bottom of the flyer.

● Position the banner appropriately.

● Choose File/Versions

● Click [Save Now...].

● Type Banner in the Comments text box.

Your screen should be similar to Figure 2.70

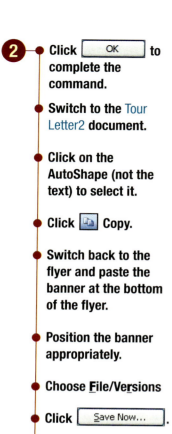

Figure 2.70

The first version you created is displayed in the Versions dialog box. The version information includes the date and time the version was saved, the name of the person who saved each version, and the comment. The second version will be added to this list when you complete the command. The most recent version always appears at the top of the list.

Opening a Version

Once a version has been created, you can go back and open, print, and delete earlier versions. You will open the "No banner" version.

1 • Click [OK] to complete the command.

• Choose **F**ile/**V**ersions.

• Select the "No banner" version from the list box.

• Click [Open].

• Scroll the windows to see the bottom of each document.

Your screen should be similar to Figure 2.71

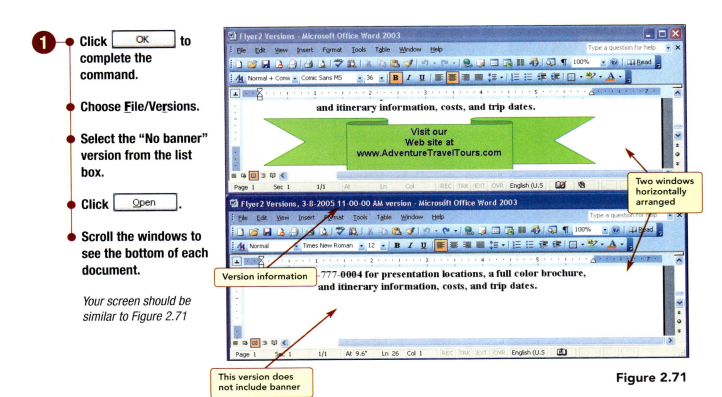

Two windows horizontally arranged

Version information

This version does not include banner

Figure 2.71

The "No banner" version is open in another window and the two windows are horizontally arranged on the screen. The version information appears in the title bar. You can view and print the version document. If you edit a document version, the revision needs to be saved as a new document file.

2 • Close the "No banner" version window.

• Maximize and then close the Flyer2 Versions window.

• Close and save the Tour Letter2 document.

• Exit Word.

• If a question dialog box appears about a picture in the Clipboard, click [No].

Focus on Careers

EXPLORE YOUR CAREER OPTIONS

Assistant Broadcast Producer

Have you wondered who does the background research for a film or television broadcast? Or who is responsible for making sure a film production runs on schedule? Assistant producers are responsible for background research and the daily operations of a shooting schedule. They may also produce written materials for broadcast. These written materials are often compiled from multiple documents and sources. The typical salary range for an assistant broadcast producer is $27,000 to $38,000. Demand for those with relevant training and experience is expected to continue in this competitive job market.

LAB 2
Revising and Refining a Document

Thesaurus (WD2.10)

Word's Thesaurus is a reference tool that provides synonyms, antonyms, and related words for a selected word or phrase.

Move and Copy (WD2.12)

Text and graphic selections can be moved or copied to new locations in a document or between documents, saving you time by not having to retype the same information.

Page Break (WD2.20)

A page break marks the point at which one page ends and another begins. Two types of page breaks can be used in a document: soft page breaks and hard page breaks.

Find and Replace (WD2.22)

To make editing easier, you can use the Find and Replace feature to find text in a document and replace it with other text as directed.

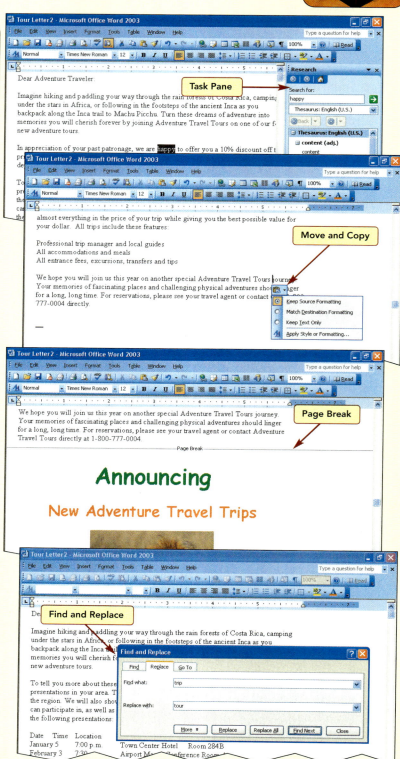

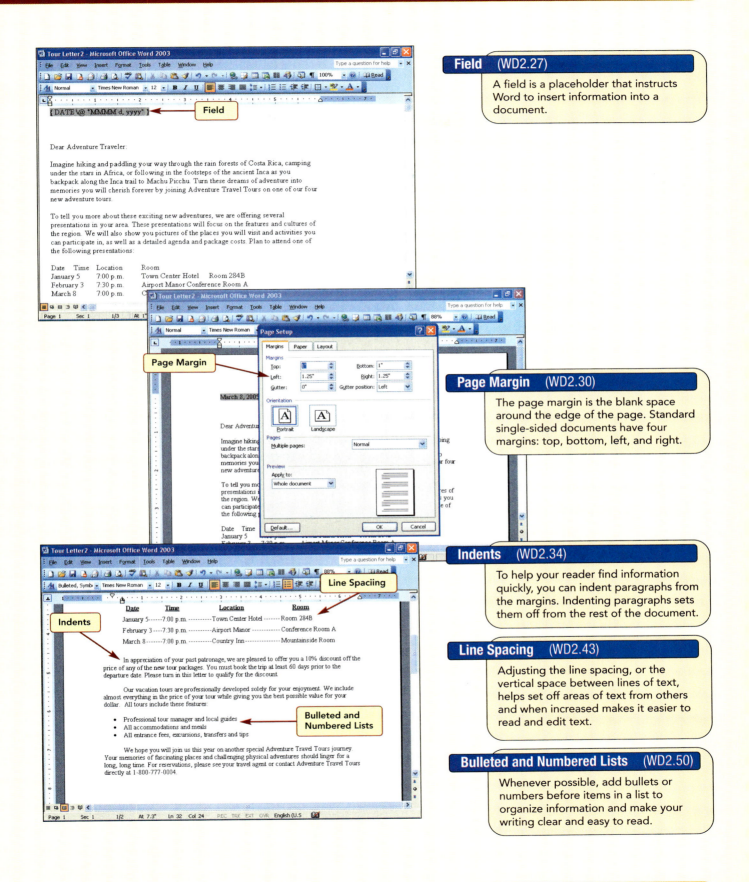

Field (WD2.27)

A field is a placeholder that instructs Word to insert information into a document.

Page Margin (WD2.30)

The page margin is the blank space around the edge of the page. Standard single-sided documents have four margins: top, bottom, left, and right.

Indents (WD2.34)

To help your reader find information quickly, you can indent paragraphs from the margins. Indenting paragraphs sets them off from the rest of the document.

Line Spacing (WD2.43)

Adjusting the line spacing, or the vertical space between lines of text, helps set off areas of text from others and when increased makes it easier to read and edit text.

Bulleted and Numbered Lists (WD2.50)

Whenever possible, add bullets or numbers before items in a list to organize information and make your writing clear and easy to read.

lab review

LAB 2
Revising and Refining a Document

mos skills

The Microsoft Office Specialist (MOS) certification program is designed to measure your proficiency in performing basic tasks using the Office 2003 applications. Getting certified demonstrates that you have the skills and provides a valuable industry credential for employment. After completing this lab, you have learned the following Microsoft Office Word Specialist skills:

Skill	Description	Page
Creating Content	Insert and edit text, symbols, and special characters	WD2.12
	Insert frequently used and predefined text	WD2.53
	Insert, position, and size graphics	WD2.55
	Navigate to specific content	WD2.22
Organizing Content	Create bulleted and numbered lists and outlines	WD2.50
	Insert and modify hyperlinks	WD2.58
Formatting Content	Format text	WD2.45
	Format paragraphs	WD2.33
	Modify document layout and page setup	WD2.29
Formatting and Managing Documents	Print documents, envelopes, and labels	WD2.64
	Preview documents and Web pages	WD2.61
	Change and organize document views and windows	WD2.18

Command	Shortcut Key	Button	Voice	Action
File/Page Set**u**p				Changes layout of page including margins, paper size, and paper source
File/Ve**r**sions				Saves, opens, and deletes document versions
Edit/Cu**t**	Ctrl + X	✂	Cut	Cuts selection to Clipboard
Edit/**C**opy	Ctrl + C	📋	Copy	Copies selection to Clipboard
Edit/**P**aste	Ctrl + V	📋	Paste	Pastes item from Clipboard
Edit/**F**ind	Ctrl + F			Locates specified text
Edit/R**e**place	Ctrl + H			Locates and replaces specified text
Insert/**B**reak/**P**age break	Ctrl + ↵Enter			Inserts hard page break
Insert/Date and **T**ime				Inserts current date or time, maintained by computer system, in selected format
Insert/**A**utoText				Enters predefined text
Insert/**A**utoText/AutoTe**x**t				Creates new AutoText entries
Insert/**P**icture/**A**utoShapes		AutoShapes ▾		Inserts selected AutoShape
F**o**rmat/**F**ont/Fo**n**t/ **U**nderline style/Single	Ctrl + U	U		Underlines selected text with a single line
F**o**rmat/**P**aragraph/**I**ndents and Spacing/Special/First Line	Tab			Indents first line of paragraph from left margin
F**o**rmat/**P**aragraph/**I**ndents and Spacing/Line Spacing	Ctrl + #	‡≡ ▾		Changes amount of white space between lines
F**o**rmat/Bullets and **N**umbering		≔ ≔		Creates a bulleted or numbered list
Form**a**t /**T**abs				Specifies types and positions of tab stops
Format/**S**tyles and Formatting		🄐🄐		Displays the Styles and Formatting task pane

command summary (continued)

Command	Shortcut Key	Button	Voice	Action
Tools/**S**pelling and Grammar	F7	[ABC]		Starts Spelling and Grammar Checker
Tools/**L**anguage/Thesaurus	⇧Shift + F7			Starts Thesaurus tool
Window/Compare Side **b**y Side				Displays two document windows side by side to make it easy to compare content

lab exercises

matching

Match the item on the left with the correct description on the right.

1. field   _____   **a.** indents first line of paragraph

2. Tab   _____   **b.** mouse procedure that moves or copies a selection to a new location

3. synonyms   _____   **c.** placeholder that instructs Word to insert information into a document

4. destination   _____   **d.** automatically inserted by Word to start a new page when a previous page is filled with text

5. drag and drop   _____   **e.** location of copied text

6. active window   _____   **f.** saved "snapshot" of a document

7. soft page break _____   **g.** words with similar meaning

8. version   _____   **h.** document window displaying the insertion point

9. leader character _____   **i.** vertical space between lines of text

10. line spacing   _____   **j.** solid, dotted, or dashed lines between tab stops

11. Ctrl + ↵Enter

multiple choice

Circle the correct response to the questions below.

1. The _____ is a reference tool that provides synonyms and antonyms.
   a. find and replace feature
   b. AutoText feature
   c. thesaurus
   d. Clipboard

2. A _____ marks the point at which one page ends and another begins.
   a. leader character
   b. selection point
   c. field code
   d. page break

3. The _____ feature makes certain formatting changes automatically to your document.
   a. AutoText
   b. AutoComplete
   c. AutoFormat
   d. AutoCorrect

4. The field _____ contains the directions that tell Word the type of information to insert.
   a. results
   b. code
   c. placeholder
   d. format

5. The blank space around the edge of the page is called the _____ .
   a. gutter
   b. indent
   c. margin
   d. white space

6. The information that is displayed as a result of a field is called _____.
   a. a field code
   b. a field result
   c. case sensitive
   d. a wildcard

7. To convey a sequence of events in a document, you should consider using a _____ .
   a. bulleted list
   b. numbered list
   c. organization list
   d. paragraph list

8. A _____ is a Web site address.
   a. URL
   b. RUL
   c. WSL
   d. ULR

9. The feature most useful for copying or moving short distances in a document is _____ .
   a. drag and drop
   b. drop and drag
   c. move and place
   d. drag and place

10. _____ is a feature that applies the formats associated with a selection to another selection.
   a. Format Painter
   b. Find and Replace
   c. AutoFormat
   d. AutoShapes

true/false

Circle the correct answer to the following questions.

1. The spelling checker identifies synonyms for common words.   True   False
2. Formatting and text editing can be done in the Print Preview window.   True   False
3. Indents are used to set paragraphs off from the rest of the text.   True   False
4. The Find and Replace feature is used to locate misspelled words in a document.   True   False
5. A bulleted list conveys a sequence of events.   True   False
6. A source is the location from which text is moved or copied.   True   False
7. Soft page breaks are automatically inserted whenever the text reaches the bottom margin.   True   False
8. Using document versions creates separate files of different versions of a document.   True   False
9. AutoCorrect entries are used to insert commonly used words or phrases into a document.   True   False
10. A hyperlink is a connection to a location in the current document, another document, or to a Web site.   True   False

fill-in

1. As you add or remove text from a page, Word automatically _____ the placement of the soft page break.

2. A(n) _____ code instructs Word to insert the current date in the document using the selected format whenever the document is printed.

3. Standard single-sided documents have four _____: top, bottom, left, and right.

4. Double-sided documents with facing pages typically use _____ margins.

5. Text and graphic selections can be _____ to new locations in a document, saving time.

6. In a _____ style letter, all parts are aligned with the left margin. _____ and _____ organize information and make your writing clear and easy to read.

7. Multiple _____ in a file provide "snapshots" of a document at specific times.

8. The _____ feature makes certain formatting changes automatically to your document.

9. Two types of page breaks that can be used in a document are: _____ and _____.

10. When a selection is moved or copied, the selection is stored in the _____ Clipboard, a temporary Windows storage area in memory.

Hands-On Exercises

step-by-step

Finalizing the Water Conservation Article ★

1. You are still working on the column for the utility company newsletter. You need to add information to the article and make several formatting changes to the document. Your completed article is shown here:

a. Open the document wd02_Conservation Tips.

b. Find and replace all occurrences of "H₂O" with "water." Spell and grammar-check the document.

c. Open the document Water Conservation you created in Step-by-Step Exercise 5 in Lab 1. Find and replace "%" with "percent." Display the document windows side-by-side. Copy the tips from the wd02_Conservation Tips document to the appropriate category in the Water Conservation article. Close the wd02_Conservation Tips document.

d. Change the line spacing of the tips to single spaced.

e. Save the document using the file name Water Conservation2.

f. Change the top and bottom margins to .75 inch. Change the right and left margins to 1 inch.

g. Apply three different bullet styles to the tips under the three categories. Indent the bulleted tips to the .75-inch position.

h. Use the thesaurus to find a better word for "biggest" in the first paragraph. Indent the first paragraph.

i. Below the last group of tips, add the text **Visit us for more water conservation tips at www.watertips.com**. Remove the hyperlink formatting. Format this line using the same format as the tip category headings. Add a color highlight to the line.

j. Replace the date in the last line with a date field.

k. Preview the document and, if necessary, reduce the size of the graphic to make the entire document fit on one page. Print the document.

l. Save the document using the same file name.

How Can I Conserve Water?

Nearly 75 percent of water used indoors is in the bathroom with baths, showers and toilet flushing account for most of this. If you have a lawn, chances are that this is your main water use. Typically, at least 50 percent of water consumed by households is used outdoors. The City's Water Conservation Program has many publications that offer suggestions to help you conserve water. Some of these suggestions include:

Personal Use Tips
- Take short showers instead of baths
- Run dishwashers and clothes washers with full loads only, or adjust water level to load size
- Turn the water off when brushing your teeth or shaving
- Keep a jug of cold water in the refrigerator instead of letting the tap run until cool

Repair Tips
- Install low-flow showerheads or flow restrictors
- Check your toilet for leaks by placing a few drops of food coloring in the tank. If it shows up in the bowl, replace the flapper
- Replace older toilets with new low-flow toilets or place a plastic jug filled with water in the tank to displace some of the water
- Repair dripping faucets by replacing washers
- Check for hidden leaks by monitoring your WATER meter
- Insulate your WATER pipes – you'll get hot WATER faster and avoid wasting WATER while it heats up

Outdoor Tips
- When washing the car, use soap and water from a bucket. Use a hose with a shut-off nozzle for the final rinse
- Plant low-WATER use and native plants instead of turf
- Clean your driveway with a broom, not a hose
- Adjust irrigation when the seasons change
- Adjust sprinkler so only the lawn is Watered, not the sidewalk or street
- Don't WATER on windy days
- When mowing, raise the blade level to its highest level. Close cut grass makes the roots work harder, requiring more WATER

Visit us for more water conservation tips at www.watertips.com

Student Name-2/3/2005

Expanding the Note-Taking Skills Handout ★

2. You are still working on the handout for your lecture on note-taking. You have several more tips you need to add to the document. You also want to rearrange the order of the tips and make several formatting changes to the document. Your completed document is shown here.

Tips for Taking Better Classroom Notes

Be Ready
- Review your assigned reading and previous notes you've taken before class.
- Bring plenty lots of paper and a sharpened pencil, an erasable pen or a pen that won't skip or smudge.
- Write the class name, date and that day's topic at the top the page.

Write Legibly
- ✓ Print if your handwriting is poor.
- ✓ Use a pencil or an erasable pen if you cross out material a lot so that your notes are easier to read.
- ✓ Take notes in one-liners rather than paragraph form.
- ✓ Skip a line between ideas to make it easier to find information when you're studying for a test.

Use Abbreviations
- ➤ Abbreviations let you write more quickly. To abbreviate, condense a wor[d] or use a symbol. For instance, use b/c for because, w/ for with; w/o for w[ithout] government.
- ➤ Always use the same abbreviations for the same words and phrases so yo[u] what they stand for.

Use Wide Margins
- o Leave a wide margin on one side of your paper so you'll have space to [write] and call attention to key material.
- o Draw arrows or stars beside important information like dates, names and
- o If you miss getting a date, name, number or other fact, make a mark remember to come back to it.

Fill in Gaps
- Check with a classmate or your teacher after class to get any missing nam[es] information you couldn't write down.

Mark Questionable Material
- o Jot down a "?" in the margin beside something you disagree with or do not think you recorded correctly. When appropriate, ask your teacher, classmate, or refer to your textbook, for clarification.

Check the Board
- When your teacher writes something on the board or projects it, that's a signal that the information is important. Copy everything down, and note that it was on the board.

Listen for Cues
- ➤ Don't try to write everything down.
- ➤ Listen for cues from your teacher about what is important. When you hear "The reasons why..." "Here is how..." or a change in tone of voice, that indicates something noteworthy is about to be said.
- ➤ Write down dates, names, definitions, and formulas, and why they are important.
- ➤ Write down the idea of any examples or stories your teacher gives when explaining a point or concept. These will help you remember the material.

Keep Organized
- Keep notes for the same class together, along with any handouts.

Review and Highlight
- ❖ Go over your notes after class or after school while the lecture is still fresh in your mind.
- ❖ Complete any partially recorded notes and clarify any unintelligible sections as quickly as possible.
- ❖ Add information that will help you comprehend the material.
- ❖ Use a highlighter or a different color of ink to highlight, underline or circle important words and phrases.

Student Name
2/3/2005

Good Notes = Better Grades

---

a. Open the file **wd02_Note Taking Tips**. Spell-check the document.

b. Use the thesaurus to find a better word for "gist" in the first tip.

c. Open the document **Note Taking Skills** you created in Step-by-Step Exercise 4 in Lab 1. Display the document windows side-by-side. Copy the tips from the wd02_Note Taking Tips document to the end of the tips in the Note Taking Skills document. Close the wd02_Note Taking Tips document.

d. Use Format Painter to change the format of the new headings to the same as the existing headings.

e. Move the Use Abbreviations tip below the Write Legibly tip. Move the Check the Board and Listen for Cues tips below the Mark Questionable Materials tip.

f. Change the left and right and top margins to.75 inch.

g. Break the tips under each topic heading into separate bulleted items using bullet styles of your choice. (A bulleted item may be more than one sentence if it contains an explanation or is a continuation of the same tip topic.)

h. Preview the document and insert a hard page break above the Mark Questionable Materials topic heading while previewing it.

i. Add the AutoShape "Wave" symbol from the Stars and Banners category to the document.

j. Add the text **Good Notes = Better Grades** to the shape. Bold, center, and size the text to 16 pt. Size the AutoShape to just large enough to display the text in a single line.

k. Add a fill color to the shape and color to the text to complement the colors you used in the document. Move the AutoShape to below your name. Delete the drawing canvas.

l. Replace the date in the last line with a date field using a format of your choice.

m. Save the document as Note Taking Skills2, preview and print it.

Promoting a Yoga Class ★ ★

3. The Lifestyle Fitness Club has just started a new series of yoga classes. You want to spread the word by creating a flyer for club members to pick up at the front desk. You have created a Word document with the basic information that you want to include in the flyer. Now you just need to make it look better. Your completed flyer is shown here:

a. Open the file wd02_Yoga Flyer.

b. Find each occurrence of "Yoga" and replace it with "yoga" wherever it is not at the beginning of a sentence or wherever it is not part of a class title. Find and replace all occurrences of "mins" with "minutes."

c. Use the spelling and grammar checker to correct the identified errors.

d. Bold, color, and center both title lines. Increase the font size of the main title line to 24 and the second title line to 18.

e. Set the right and left margins to 1 inch and the top and bottom margins to .7 inch.

f. Center the introductory paragraph. Set line spacing for the first paragraph to 1.5.

g. Bold, color, center and increase the font size to 14 of the three headings: Class Description, October Schedule, and Costs.

h. Use drag and drop to move the Yoga for Athletes class description below the Yoga for Beginners description. Adjust the line spacing as needed between descriptions. Highlight the three class names in yellow.

i. Add a bullet style of your choice to each of the three class description paragraphs.

j. Create a tabbed table of the schedule. Bold, underline, and add color to the table heads: Day, Time, Length, and Class. Use center tab styles for the Day and Class heads and center them over the columns. Add tab leaders of your choice between the Time, Length, and Class columns of data.

k. Create a tabbed table of the costs. Bold, underline, and add color to the two table heads, Series and Cost. Center tab the Series head over the column. Add a tab leader style of your choice between the Series and Cost columns of data.

Stressed? Feel short on time?
Don't worry. Yoga and meditation can help.

LifeStyle Fitness Club now offers a series of Yoga classes to learn Yoga postures linked by the breath into a graceful flow uniting mind, body, and spirit. Emphasis is placed on calming the mind and strengthening the will in addition to greatly improving strength, flexibility, and balance.

Class Description

- Gentle Yoga is a gentle, restorative Yoga class that focuses on basic stretching, gentle strengthening exercises, guided relaxation and restorative Yoga postures. If you are interested in opening your body and heart in a nurturing environment, this class is for you.

- Yoga for Beginners is a course designed to introduce the new student to the basics of Anusara Yoga and will begin the process of stretching and strengthening the entire body. This class is suitable for people of all ages and fitness levels.

- Yoga for Athletes is a total strength and flexibility workout. Warm up to sun salutation, a flowing aerobic sequence, standing postures, and floor work, meditation and final relaxation complete the series.

October Schedule

Day	Time	Length	Class
Mon/Wed/Fri	7:00am	60 minutes	Yoga for Beginners
	4:30pm	75 minutes	Gentle Yoga
	6:00pm	75 minutes	Yoga for Athletes
Tuesday/Thurs	7:30 am	60 minutes	Yoga for Beginners
	9:00am	75 minutes	Gentle Yoga
	4:30pm	75 minutes	Yoga for Athletes
	6:00pm	75 minutes	Yoga for Beginners
	7:30pm	75 minutes	Yoga for Athletes
Saturday	9:00am	90 minutes	Yoga for Beginners
	10:30am	75 minutes	Yoga for Athletes
Sunday	10:00am	90 minutes	Gentle Yoga

Costs

Series	Cost
6 class package (30 days)	$ 25
10 class package (45 days)	$ 45
20 class package (90 days)	$ 95

Student Name – February 4, 2005

l. Add the AutoShape "No" symbol from the Basic Shapes menu to the document.

m. Add the text **Stress** to the shape. Bold, center, and size the text to 18 pt. Center the text vertically in the shape by adding a blank line above it. Size the AutoShape to just large enough to display the text in a single line.

n. Add a red fill color to the shape and green color to the text. Move the AutoShape to the space to the left of the title lines. Delete the drawing canvas.

o. Add your name and the current date as a field on the last line on the page.

p. Save the document as Yoga Flyer. Print the document.

Orientation Meeting Schedule ★ ★ ★

4. The Animal Rescue Foundation is actively seeking volunteers to help support the organization. You are preparing an article to run in the newspaper promoting the organization and asking for volunteer help. In anticipation of attracting many new volunteers, the organization plans to hold extra Volunteer Orientation meetings for better convenience. You want to create a separate informational flyer about the schedule to give to volunteers. You also decide to include the orientation schedule in the article. Your completed document is shown here.

Volunteers Needed!

The Animal Rescue Foundation is in need of your help. Over the past six months, we have seen a *20 percent* increase in the number of rescued animals. With the increase in animals, we need more people to join Animal Angels, our volunteer group.

Our volunteer program is both diverse and flexible; no matter how hectic your schedule, we can find a place for you. It is our goal to have volunteers actively involved in many areas of our organization--from providing direct care for the animals to contributing to the every day functioning of our shelter and programs to furthering animal welfare and our mission of finding a loving home for each animal. Here are just some of the opportunities that await you.

Foster parent
Work at adoption fairs
Socialize the cats
Provide obedience training
Pet grooming specialists
Repair, organize, and distribute donations
Greeters and matchmakers
Adoption counselor
Kennel and animal care assistants
Special event volunteers
Grounds maintenance keepers
Humane educators

If you are interested in becoming a volunteer with the Animal Rescue Foundation in any capacity, you must attend a volunteer orientation. The orientations will be held in the Multi-Purpose Room and last approximately two hours.

Visit us at www.arf.com
for more information

CTOBER ORIENTATION SCHEDULE

ay	Date	Time
turday	October 5	10:00 a.m.
		1:00 p.m.
nday	October 7	7:00 p.m.
ursday	October 10	10:00 a.m.
		7:00 p.m.
turday	October 12	9:00 a.m.
		3:00 p.m.
esday	October 15	10:00 a.m.
		7:00 p.m.
ednesday	October 16	7:00 p.m.
turday	October 19	10:00 a.m.
nday	October 21	7:00 p.m.
turday	October 26	1:00 p.m.
esday	October 29	7:00 p.m.
ednesday	October 30	10:00 a.m.
		7:00 p.m.

ed a orientation, you will be called for a brief interview in which you and Events Coordinator can discuss your specific interests and availability. s may be necessary depending on your interest (i.e., Animal

interest in giving your time and energy to the abused, homeless, and neglected animals that come to us each year. It is our desire that the time you spend here will be as rewarding for you as it is for the animals. We are proud of our organization and would like for you to become a part of the team.

Please call us at 603-555-1313 to join us!

Student Name
February 17, 2005

a. Open a new document and set the left and right page margins to 1 inch.

b. On the first line center the title **OCTOBER ORIENTATION SCHEDULE**. Apply formats of your choice to the title line.

c. Several lines below the title, type the following paragraphs:

If you are interested in becoming a volunteer with the Animal Rescue Foundation in any capacity, you must attend a volunteer meeting. The meetings will be held in the Multi-Purpose Room and last approximately two hours.

After you have attended a meeting, you will be called for a short interview in which you and our Volunteer/Special Events Coordinator can discuss your specific interests and availability. Additional meetings may be necessary depending on your interests (i.e., Animal Care/Handling).

d. Spell-check the document. Use the thesaurus to find a better word for "short" in the second paragraph.

e. Find and replace all occurrences of "meeting" with "orientation." Correct any identified grammar errors.

f. Set the line spacing of the paragraphs to double.

g. Several lines below the last paragraph, place center tab stops at 1½, 3⅛, and 4½ inches on the ruler.

h. Enter the word **Day** at the first tab stop, **Date** at the second tab stop, and **Time** at the third tab stop.

i. Using a left tab at 1¼ and 2¾ and a right tab stop at 5, enter the schedule information shown here into the table.

Saturday	October 5	10:00 A.M.
		1:00 P.M.
Monday	October 7	7:00 P.M.
Thursday	October 10	10:00 A.M.
		7:00 P.M.
Saturday	October 12	9:00 A.M.
		3:00 P.M.
Tuesday	October 15	10:00 A.M.
		7:00 P.M.
Wednesday	October 16	7:00 P.M.
Saturday	October 19	10:00 A.M.
Monday	October 21	7:00 P.M.
Saturday	October 26	1:00 P.M.
Tuesday	October 29	7:00 P.M.
Wednesday	October 30	10:00 A.M.
		7:00 P.M.

j. Change the font size of the table headings to 14 points, bold, and the same color as the title. Add an underline style of your choice to the table headings. Bold the text in the remainder of the table.

k. Move the second paragraph below the table.

l. Add your name and the current date as a field several lines below the last paragraph.

(continued on next page)

m. Save the document as Orientation Schedule.

n. Open the Volunteers Needed document you created in Lab 1, Step-by-Step Exercise 2. Set the left and right page margins to 1 inch.

o. Save the document as Volunteers Needed2.

p. Display the document windows side-by-side. Copy the text and the table from the Orientation Schedule document to below the list of volunteer jobs. Change the spacing of the copied paragraph to single spaced. Make any adjustments to the table as needed.

q. Apply the same formatting to the table title as you used in the article title. Insert a hard page break above the table title.

r. Move the paragraph that begins "If you are interested…" to the bottom of page one.

s. Create an AutoShape of your choice and add the text **Visit us at www.arf.com for more information**. Size the AutoShape appropriately. Remove the hyperlink format from the URL. Add color to the URL. Add a fill color to the AutoShape. Center the AutoShape at the bottom of the first page. Remove the drawing canvas.

t. Highlight the last line in the Volunteers Needed2 document.

u. Change the date to a date field. Save, preview, and print the Volunteers Needed2 document.

v. Create a version in the Orientation Schedule file with the comment "No AutoShape." Copy the AutoShape from Volunteers Needed2 to the bottom of the Orientation Schedule document. Center it. Save this version as "AutoShape." Preview and print the AutoShape version of the document (shown at right).

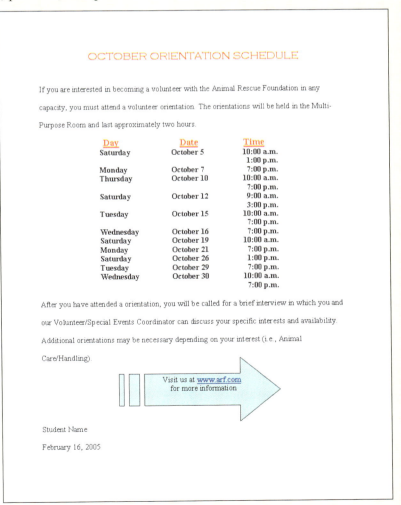

Advertising Weekly Specials ★ ★ ★

5. Now that the Downtown Internet Cafe has had its grand opening celebration, the owner wants to continue to bring in new and repeat customers by offering weekly specials. You want to create a flyer describing the roast coffee varieties and specials for the week. Your completed flyer is shown here.

a. Open a new document.

b. Enter the title **Downtown Internet Cafe** on the first line. Add three blank lines.

c. Enter **Roast Coffee** on line 4 followed by two blank lines.

d. Center the first line and change the font color to blue with a font size of 48 pt.

e. Center the second line and change it to blue with a font size of 22 pt.

f. On line 7, place a left tab stop at .5 and center tabs at 2.5 and 4.5 inches.

g. Enter the word **Coffee** at the first tab stop, **Description** at the second tab stop, and **Cost/Pound** at the third tab stop.

h. Enter the rest of the information for the table shown in the final document using left tabs at .5, 2, and 5.

i. Add tab leaders of your choice between the data in the table.

j. Increase the font of the table headings to 14 pt. Add bold, color, and an underline style of your choice to the table headings.

k. Open the file wd02_Coffee Flyer. Display the document windows side-by-side. Copy the first two paragraphs and insert them above "Roast Coffee" in the new document.

l. Spell-check the document. Use the thesaurus to find better words for "desire" and "giant" in the first paragraph.

m. Use Find and Replace to replace all occurrences of "java" with "coffee" (except the one following "high-powered").

n. Center the words "Coffee Sale" below the title. Make them bold, font size 24 pt, and a color of your choice.

o. Make the paragraph that begins with "Tired" bold, centered, and 14 pt, and set their line spacing to double. Add blue color to the URL.

Sale!

Downtown Internet Café

Coffee Sale

Tired of brewing a wimpy cup of coffee that just doesn't have the punch you crave? Then point your Web browser to *www.somecoffee.com* for our huge sale, and have our high-powered java delivered right to your front door. You'll never buy bland supermarket coffee again.

Through January, take $2 off the regular coffee prices shown below.

Roast Coffee

Coffee	Description	Cost/Pound
Colombian Blend	Classic body and aroma	$11
French Roast	Sophisticated taste	$10
Kenyan	Robust and deep flavor	$12
Arabian Blend	Strong yet subtle	$11

You can also order online at *www.somecoffee.com* today, and get coffee delivered right to your door! But hurry, our sale won't last forever.

Student Name
February 7, 2005

p. Increase the font size of the line above "Roast Coffee" to 18 pt. Center the text. Insert a blank line below it.

q. Copy the remaining paragraph from the wd02_Coffee Flyer document, and insert it at the bottom of the new document. Include two blank lines between the table and the paragraph.

r. Bold and center the final paragraph. Remove the hyperlink format from the URL. Format the URL as italic and blue.

s. Increase the top, left, and right margins to 1.5 inches.

t. Create the Explosion 1 AutoShape from Stars and Banners. Enter and center the word **Sale!** in red within it, size 22, and choose the gold fill color. Size the shape appropriately. Move the shape to the top left corner of the document. Delete the drawing canvas.

u. Add your name and a field with the current date several lines below the final paragraph. If necessary, adjust the formatting of the document so it fits on one page.

v. Save the document as Coffee Flyer2. Preview and print it.

on your own

Requesting a Reference ★

1. Your first year as a biology major is going well and you are looking for a summer internship with a local research lab. You have an upcoming interview and want to come prepared with a letter of reference from your last position. Write a business letter directed to your old supervisor, Rachel McVey, at your former lab, AMT Research. Use the modified block letter style shown in the lab. Be sure to include the date, a salutation, two paragraphs, a closing, and your name as a signature. Spell-check the document, save the document as Reference Letter, and print it.

Long Distance Rates Survey ★

2. American Consumer Advocates conducted a survey in October, 2002 comparing the costs of long distance rates. Create a tabbed table using the information shown below. Bold and underline the column heads. Add style 2 tab leaders to the table entries. Above the table, write a paragraph explaining the table contents.

Company	Per Minute	Monthly Fee	Customer Service Wait
Zone LD	3.5¢	$2.00	Less than 1 minute
Pioneer Telephone	3.9¢	none	1 minute
Capsule	3.9¢	none	17 minutes
ECG	4.5¢	$1.99	5 minutes
IsTerra	4.9¢	none	10 minutes

Include your name and the date below the table. Save the document as Phone Rates and print the document.

★ ★

3. Create a flyer to advertise something you have for sale (used car, stereo, computer, etc.). Integrate the following features into the flyer:

- Different fonts in different sizes, colors, and styles
- Bulleted or numbered list
- Indents
- An AutoShape
- A graphic
- A tabbed table with tab leaders

Include your name as the contact information. Save the document as For Sale Flyer and print it.

★ ★

4. You work for the City of New Orleans on a committee dedicated to attracting new residents. You have been asked to produce a relocation packet to aid people planning to move to the city. This packet includes information on local services, the weather, and the community at large. Use the information provided in the file wd02_New Orleans to create a one-page factsheet. Your completed project should include an introductory paragraph on relocation, graphics, table with the average weather statistics, a bulleted list of local attractions, and AutoShapes. Include your name as the contact and save the file as New Orleans2. Print the file.

★ ★ ★

5. Your political science class is studying the 2000 presidential election. Your instructor has divided the class into three groups and assigned each group a research project. Your group is to find out how Americans voted for the presidential candidates by age and sex. Use the Web to research this topic and write a one-page report on your findings. Include a table of the data you found. Use other features demonstrated in this lab, including AutoShapes, indents, bulleted lists, font colors, and so forth to make your report attractive and easy to read. Be sure to reference your sources on the Web for the data you located. Include your name and the current date below the report. Save the report as Election Results and print your report.

Creating Reports and Tables

LAB 3

Objectives

After you have completed this lab, you will know how to:

1 Create and modify an outline.

2 Hide spelling and grammar errors.

3 Use Click and Type, Document Map and Reading Layout.

4 Apply styles.

5 Create and update a table of contents.

6 Create a section break.

7 Center a page vertically.

8 Wrap text around graphics.

9 Add footnotes, captions, and cross-references.

10 Create and format a simple table.

11 Sort a list.

12 Add headers, footers, and page numbers.

13 Check formatting inconsistencies.

14 Print selected pages and save to a new folder.

Case Study

Adventure Travel Tours

Adventure Travel Tours provides information on their tours in a variety of forms. Travel brochures, for instance, contain basic tour information in a promotional format and are designed to entice potential clients to sign up for a tour. More detailed regional information packets are given to people who have already signed up for a tour, so they can prepare for their vacation. These packets include facts about each region's climate, geography, and culture. Additional informational formats include pages on Adventure Travel's Web site and scheduled group presentations.

Part of your responsibility as advertising coordinator is to gather the information that

© PhotoDisc

Adventure Travel will publicize about each regional tour. Specifically, you have been asked to provide information for two of the new tours: the Tanzania Safari and the Machu Picchu trail. Because this information is used in a variety of formats, your research needs to be easily adapted. You will therefore present your facts in the form of a general report on Tanzania and Peru.

In this lab, you will learn to use many of the features of Office Word 2003 that make it easy to create an attractive and well-organized report. A portion of the completed report is shown on the right.

A table of contents listing can be created quickly from heading styles in a document

Wrapping text around graphics, adding figure captions, footnotes, headers, and footers are among many features that can be used to enhance a report

Including tables and using table formats make the report attractive and easy to read

A list can be quickly sorted to appear in alphabetical order

Tanzania and Peru

Table of Contents

Tanzania	1
Geography and Climate	1
Ngorongoro Conservation Area	2
Serengeti Plain	2
Culture	2
Animal Life	2
Peru	3
Geography and Climate	3
La Costa	3
La Sierra	3
La Selva	4
Culture	4
Historical Culture	4
Machu Picchu	5
Current Culture	
Animal Life	
Works Cited	

Student Name
March 28, 2005

Student Name 1

Tanzania

Geography and Climate

"In the midst of a great wilderness, full of wild beasts...I fancied I saw a summit...covered with a dazzlingly white cloud (qtd. in Cole 56). This is how Johann Krapf, the first outsider to witness the splendor of Africa's highest mountain, described Kilimanjaro. The peak was real, though the white clouds he "fancied" he saw were the dense layer of snow that coats the mountain.[1]

Tanzania is primarily a plateau that slopes gently downward into the country's five hundred miles of Indian Ocean coastline. Nearly three-quarters of Tanzania is dry savannah, so much so that the Swahili word for the central plateau is *nyika*, meaning "wasteland." Winding through these flatlands is the Great Rift Valley, which forms narrow and shallow lakes in its long path. Several of these great lakes form a belt-like oasis of green vegetation. Contrasting with the severity of the plains are the coastal areas, which are lush with ample rainfall. In the north the plateau slopes dramatically into Mt. Kilimanjaro.

Figure 1 - Giraffe in Serengeti

Ngorongoro Conservation Area

Some of Tanzania's most distinguishing geographical features are found in the Ngorongoro Conservation Area.[2] The park is composed of many craters and gorges, as well as lakes, forest, and plains. Among these features is the area's namesake, the Ngorongoro Crater. The Crater is a huge expanse, covering more than one hundred square miles. On the Crater's floor, grasslands blend into swamps, lakes, rivers, and woodland. Also within the Conservation Area's perimeter is the Olduvai Gorge, commonly referred to as the "Cradle of Mankind," where in 1931 the stone tools of prehistoric man were found. This find subsequently led to the discovery of the remains of humans who lived 1.75 million years ago.

Serengeti Plain

Adjacent to the western edge of the Ngorongoro Conservation Area is the Serengeti Plain. Its area is approximately 5,700 square miles, and its central savanna supports many grazing animals with plentiful water and lush grasses. Its southern portion is dry grassland with watercourses and twenty inches of rainfall annually. The north is wooded grassland with watercourses and tributaries to larger rivers. Only two seasons occur on the Serengeti: dry and wet. The dry season occurs between June and October and the wet season between November to May.

---

[1] Mt. Kilimanjaro is 19,340 feet high, making it the fourth tallest mountain in the world.
[2] The Conservation Area is a national preserve spanning 3,196 square miles.

Created on 3/8/2005 1:00:00 PM

Student Name 3

coming from the east. Some areas in the south are considered drier than the Sahara. Conversely, there are a few areas in this region where mountain rivers meet the ocean that are green with life and do not give the impression of being in a desert at all.

La Sierra

Inland and to the east is the mountainous region called La Sierra, encompassing Peru's share of the Andes mountain range. The southern portion of this region is prone to volcanic activity, and some volcanoes are active today. La Sierra is subject to a dry season from May to September, which is winter in that part of the world. Temperatures are moderate by day, and can be freezing in some areas during the night. The weather is typically sunny, with moderate annual precipitation. The former Incan capital Cuzco is in this region, as well as the Sacred Valley of the Incas. This region also contains Lake Titicaca, the world's highest navigable lake.[3]

La Selva

La Selva, a region of tropical rainforest, is the easternmost region in Peru. This region, with its eastern foot of the Andes Mountains, forms the Amazon Basin, into which numerous rivers flow. The Amazon River begins at the meeting point of the two dominant rivers, the Ucayali and Marañon. La Selva is extremely wet, with some areas exceeding an annual precipitation of 137 inches. Its wettest season occurs from November to April. The weather here is humid and extremely hot.

Region	Annual Rainfall (Inches)	Average Temperature (Fahrenheit)
La Costa	2	68
La Sierra	35	54
La Selva	137	80

Culture

Historical Culture

Peru is where the Incas built their homes and cities. They lived in the southern portion of La Sierra until around 1300 CE[4], when they moved north to the fertile Cuzco Valley. From here they built their empire, overrunning and assimilating neighboring lands and cultures. They organized into a socialist-type theocracy under an emperor—the Inca—whom they worshipped as a deity. The Inca Empire reached its maximum size by the late fifteenth and early sixteenth centuries.

In 1532 the Spanish explorer Francisco Pizarro landed in Peru. He saw great opportunity in seizing the empire because of the rich gold deposits in the Cuzco Valley, and did so with superior armament. This opened the door for masses of gold- and adventure-seeking conquistadors to join in the pursuit, who brought with them both modern weaponry and

---

[3] Lake Titicaca is 12,507 feet above sea level.
[4] Common Era (CE) is the period dating from the birth of Christ.

Created on 3/8/2005 1:00:00 PM

Student Name 5

Works Cited

Camerapix Publishers International. *Spectrum Guide to Tanzania*. Edison: Hunter, 1992.

Cole, Tom. *Geographic Expeditions*. San Francisco: Geographic Expeditions, 1999.

Hudson, Rex A., ed. "Peru: A Country Study." *The Library of Congress—Country Studies*. 1992. <http://lcweb2.loc.gov/frd/cs/petoc.html#pe0049> (11 Jan. 2001).

"The Living Edens: Manu—Peru's Hidden Rainforest." *PBS Online*. <http://www.pbs.org/edens/manu> (11 Jan. 2001).

Valdizan, Mónica V. "Virtual Peru." 9 Jan. 1999. http://www.xs4all.nl/~govertme/visitperu/ (11 Jan. 2001).

Concept Preview

The following concepts will be introduced in this lab:

1 **Style** Applying a style, a predefined set of formatting characteristics, to a selection allows you to quickly apply a whole group of formats in one simple step.

2 **Section** To format different parts of a document differently, you can divide a document into sections.

3 **Footnote and Endnote** A footnote is a source reference or text offering additional explanation that is placed at the bottom of a page. An endnote is also a source reference or long comment that typically appears at the end of a document.

4 **Text Wrapping** You can control the appearance of text around a graphic object by specifying the text wrapping style.

5 **Captions and Cross References** A caption is a numbered label for a figure, table, picture, or graph. A cross-reference is a reference from one part of a document to related information in another part.

6 **Splitting Windows** To view different parts of the document at the same time, you can create a split window by dividing the document window into two horizontal sections.

7 **Table** A table is used to organize information into an easy-to-read format of horizontal rows and vertical columns.

8 **Sort** Word can quickly arrange or sort text, numbers, or data in lists or tables in alphabetical, numeric, or date order based on the first character in each paragraph.

9 **Header and Footer** A header is a line or several lines of text in the top margin of each page. A footer is a line or several lines of text in the margin space at the bottom of every page.

Creating and Modifying an Outline

After several days of research, you have gathered many notes from various sources including books, magazines, and the Web. However, the notes are very disorganized and you are having some difficulty getting started writing the report. Often the best way to start is by creating an outline of the main topics.

Word 2003 allows you to create and view document content easily as an outline using Outline view. Outline view shows the hierarchy of topics in a document by displaying the different heading levels indented to represent their level in the document's structure, as shown in the example at right. The arrangement of headings in a hierarchy of importance

- ◇ **Tanzania**
  - ▫ *Culture*
  - ◇ *Geography*
    - ▫ Climate
  - ▫ *Animal Life*
- ◇ **Peru**
  - ◇ *Culture*
    - ◇ Historical Culture
      - ▫ Machu Picchu
  - ▫ *Geography and Climate*
  - ▫ *Animal Life*

quickly shows the relationship between topics. You can use Outline view to help you create a new document or to view and reorganize the topics in an existing document.

Using Outline View

You will use Outline view to help you organize the main topics of the report.

1 ● **Start Office Word 2003.**

● **Close the task pane.**

● **Click** 📃 **Outline View.**

Your screen should be similar to Figure 3.1

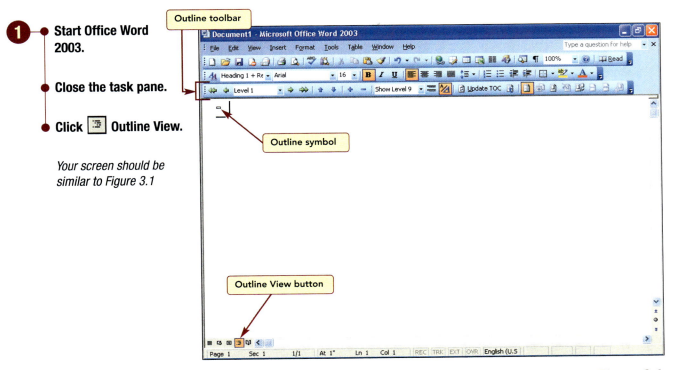

Figure 3.1

The Outline toolbar is displayed. It contains buttons that make it easy to modify the outline. The first line of the blank document displays an outline symbol. There are three outline symbols (⊟, ⊕, and ⊡) that are used to identify the levels of topics in the outline and to quickly reorganize topics. You will begin by entering the main topic headings for the report.

2 • Type the following headings, pressing ⏎Enter after each except the last:

Tanzania

Climate

Geography

Animal Life

Peru

Culture

Historical Culture

Machu Picchu

Geography and Climate

Animal Life (do not press ⏎Enter)

• Correct any misspelled words and use Ignore All for any identified proper names.

Your screen should be similar to Figure 3.2

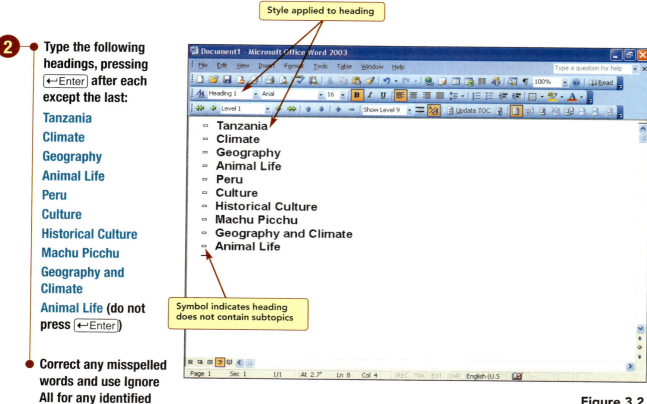

Style applied to heading

Symbol indicates heading does not contain subtopics

Figure 3.2

Each heading is preceded by the ⬚ outline symbol, which indicates that the heading does not contain subtopics. As you create a new document in Outline view, Word automatically applies styles to the text as it is entered in the outline.

Concept 1

Style

1 Applying a **style**, a predefined set of formatting characteristics, to a selection allows you to quickly apply a whole group of formats in one simple step. Word includes 75 predefined styles. Each style is assigned a name. You can also create your own custom styles. Many styles are automatically applied when certain features, such as footnotes, are used. Others must be applied manually to selected text. Styles can be applied to characters, paragraphs, tables, and lists as described below.

Type of Style	Description
Character	Affects selected text within a paragraph, such as the font and size of text, and bold and italic formats.
Paragraph	Controls all aspects of a paragraph's appearance, such as text alignment, tab stops, and line spacing. It can also include character formatting. The default paragraph style is Normal, which includes character settings of Times New Roman, 12 pt, and paragraph settings of left indent at 0, single line spacing, and left alignment. In addition, many paragraph styles are designed to affect specific text elements such as headings, captions, and footnotes.
Table	Provides a consistent look to borders, shading, alignment, and fonts in tables.
List	Applies similar alignment, numbering or bullet characters, and fonts to lists.

The Style button indicates that the text is formatted as a Heading 1 style. **Heading styles** are one of the most commonly used styles. They are designed to identify different levels of headings in a document. Heading styles include combinations of fonts, type sizes, bold, and italics. The first four heading styles and the formats associated with each are shown in the table below:

Heading Level	Appearance
Heading 1	**Arial, 16 pt, bold, left align**
Heading 2	***Arial, 14 pt, bold, italic, left align***
Heading 3	**Arial, 13 pt, bold, left align**
Heading 4	**Times New Roman, 14 pt, bold, left align**

Additional Information

All Heading styles also includes 12 pt line spacing before the heading and 3 pt spacing after.

The first-level headings in a document should be assigned a Heading 1 style. This style is the largest and most prominent. The second-level headings (subheadings) should be assigned the Heading 2 style, and so on. Headings give the reader another visual cue about how information is organized in your document.

Changing Outline Levels

Next, you need to arrange the headings by outline levels. As you rearrange the topic headings and subheadings, different heading styles are applied based upon the position or level of the topic within the outline hierarchy. Headings that are level 1 appear as the top level of the outline and appear in a Heading 1 style, level 2 headings appear indented below level 1 headings and appear in a Heading 2 style, and so on.

The outline symbols are used to select and move the heading to a new location or level within the document. Dragging the outline symbol to the right or left changes the level. To demote a heading to a lower level, drag the symbol to the right; to promote a heading to a higher level, drag the symbol to the left. As you drag the symbol, a vertical solid gray line appears at each outline level to show where the heading will be placed.

First you will make the Climate topic heading a subtopic below the main heading of Tanzania.

1 ● Drag the ⊟ symbol of the Climate heading to the right one level.

Additional Information

The mouse pointer changes to ✛, indicating that dragging it will move the heading.

Your screen should be similar to Figure 3.3

Note that I am NOT replacing screens unless otherwise indicated. cm

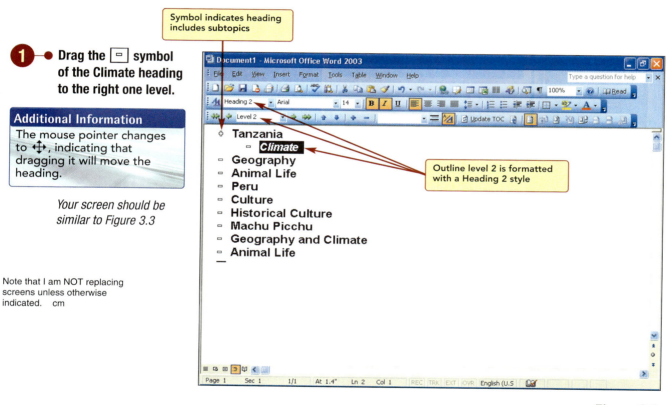

Figure 3.3

The Climate heading has changed to a Heading 2 style, and the heading is indented one level to show it is subordinate to the heading above it. The Tanzania heading now displays a ⊕ outline symbol, which indicates the topic heading includes subtopics. You can also click ✦ Promote and ➔ Demote on the Outlining toolbar to change outline levels.

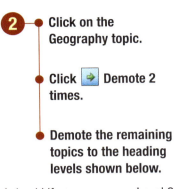

2 ● Click on the Geography topic.

● Click  Demote 2 times.

● Demote the remaining topics to the heading levels shown below.

Animal Life	Level 2
Culture	Level 2
Historical Culture	Level 3
Machu Picchu	Level 4
Geography and Climate	Level 2
Animal Life	Level 2

Your screen should be similar to Figure 3.4

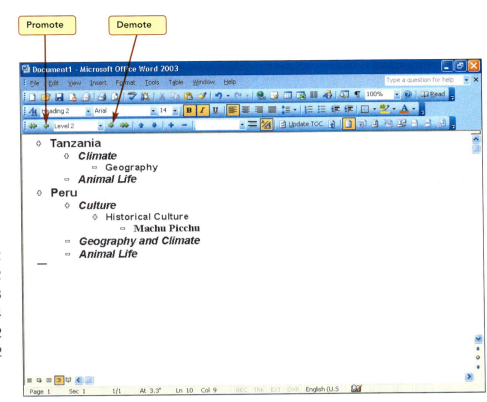

Figure 3.4

Moving and Inserting Outline Topics

Another Method

You can also click ⬆ Move Up and ⬇ Move Down to move a topic.

Next you want to change the order of topics. To move a heading to a different location, drag the outline symbol up or down. As you drag, a horizontal line shows where the heading will be placed when you release the mouse button.

1

- **Drag the Geography heading up above the Climate heading.**

- **Promote the Geography heading to a level 2.**

- **Demote the Climate heading to a level 3.**

Your screen should be similar to Figure 3.5

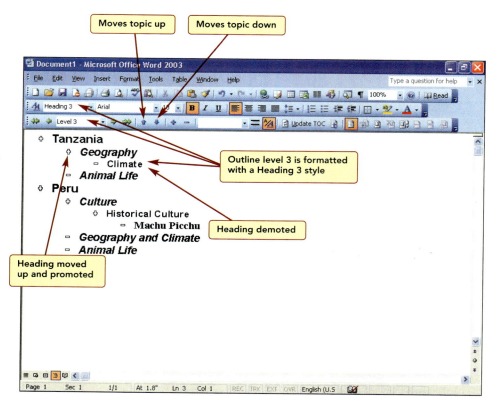

Figure 3.5

As you check the outline, you realize you forgot a heading for Culture under Tanzania.

2

- **Move to the beginning of the Geography heading for Tanzania.**

- **Press ⏎Enter to insert a blank topic heading.**

- **Type Culture on the blank heading line.**

Your screen should be similar to Figure 3.6

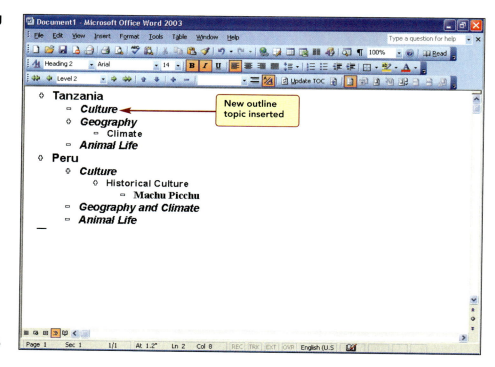

Figure 3.6

When you are satisfied with the organization, you can switch to Normal view or Print Layout view to add detailed body text and graphics.

3 ● **Switch to Normal view.**

Your screen should be similar to Figure 3.7

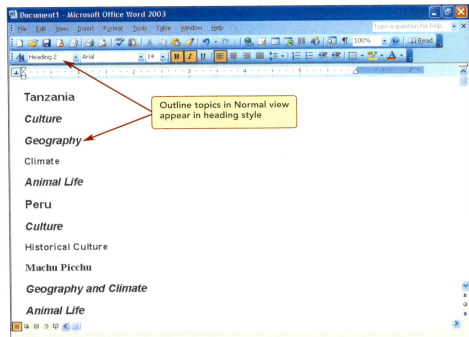

Figure 3.7

The topic headings appear left-aligned on the page in the style that was applied to the text as the outline was created.

Collapsing and Expanding the Outline

You have continued to work on the outline and report organization. Then you entered much of the information for the report and saved it. You will open the document to see the information that has been added to the report.

1 ● **Open the file wd03_Tour Research.**

● **Switch to Outline view.**

● **Scroll the window to view the entire document.**

● **Return to the top of the document.**

Your screen should be similar to Figure 3.8

Figure 3.8

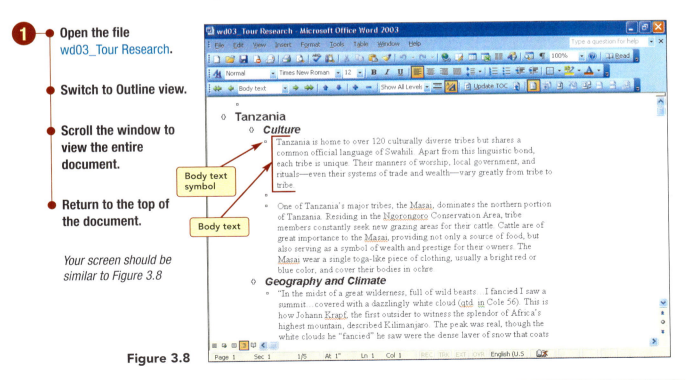

The document is displayed as an outline with the topic headings indented appropriately. The body text appears below the appropriate heading. Any text not identified with a heading style is considered body text. The small square to the left of a paragraph identifies it as body text.

In Outline view, you can display as much or as little of the document text as you want. To make it easier to view and reorganize the document's structure, you can "collapse" the document to show just the headings you want. Alternatively, you can "expand" the document to display part of the body text below each heading or the entire body text. You can then easily move the headings around until the order is logical, and the body text will follow the heading. The table below shows how you can collapse and expand the amount of text displayed in Outline view.

To Collapse	Do This
Text below a specific heading level	Select the lowest heading you want to display from the [____] Show Level drop-down menu.
All subheadings and body text under a heading	Double-click [✛] next to the heading.
Text under a heading, one level at a time	Click the heading text, and then click [−] Collapse.
All body text	Select the heading level you want to see from the [____] Show Level drop-down menu.
All body text except first line	Click [≡] Show First Line Only.

To Expand	Do This
All headings and body text	Select Show All Levels from the [____] Show Level drop-down menu.
All collapsed subheadings and body text under a heading	Double-click [✛] next to the heading.
Collapsed text under a heading, one level at a time	Click the heading text, then click [+] Expand.

To change the amount of information displayed, you will collapse the display of the text under the Geography and Climate heading first. Then you will collapse everything below a level 3 heading so you can quickly check the report organization.

2 Double-click ⊕ of the Geography and Climate heading.

Open the ⬜ Show Level drop-down list.

Choose Show Level 3.

Your screen should be similar to Figure 3.9

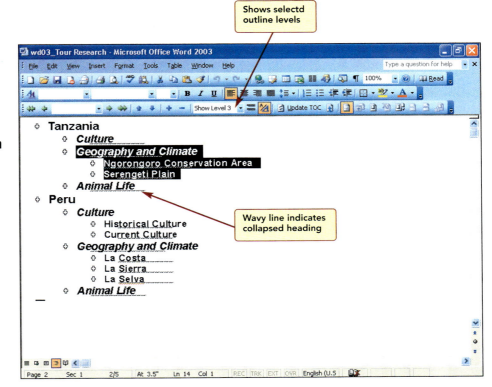

Figure 3.9

Now only the three heading levels are displayed. The wavy line below a heading means the heading includes hidden or collapsed headings or body text.

As you look at the organization of the report, you decide to move the discussion of culture to follow the Geography and Climate section. Moving headings in Outline view quickly selects and moves the entire topic, including subtopics and all body text.

3

- Drag the Culture heading in the Tanzania section down to above the Animal Life heading in the same section.

- Drag the Culture heading in the Peru section down to above the Animal Life heading in the same section.

- Choose **Show All Levels** from the Show Level 3 ▾ Show Level drop-down list.

- Scroll the report to see the top of the Peru Culture section on page 3.

- Click in the document to deselect the text.

Your screen should be similar to Figure 3.10

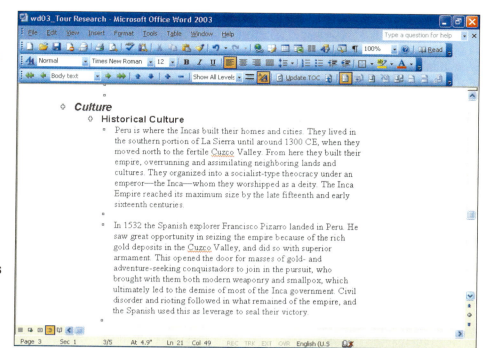

Figure 3.10

The subtopics and body text appear below the heading you moved. When you move or change the level of a heading that includes collapsed subordinate text, the collapsed text is also selected. Any changes you make to the heading, such as moving, copying, or deleting it, also affect the collapsed text.

Saving to a New Folder

Next, you will save the outline and the research document with its changes in a folder that you will use to hold files related to the report. You can create a new folder at the same time you save a file.

1 ● Choose **F**ile/Save **A**s.

● Change the Save In location to the appropriate location for your data files.

● Click 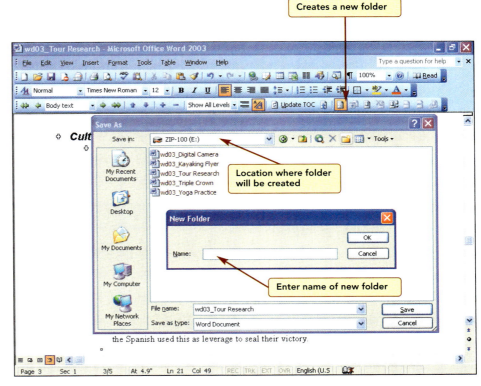 Create New Folder.

Your screen should be similar to Figure 3.11

Figure 3.11

In the New Folder dialog box, you enter the folder name. The rules for naming folders are the same as for naming files, except they typically do not include an extension.

2 ● Type **Report** in the Name text box.

● Click 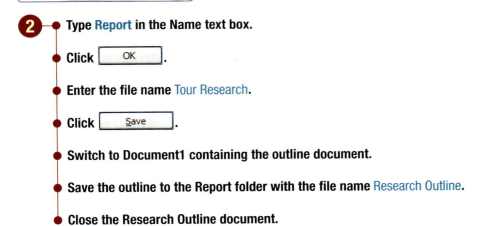 OK .

● Enter the file name Tour Research.

● Click Save .

● Switch to Document1 containing the outline document.

● Save the outline to the Report folder with the file name Research Outline.

● Close the Research Outline document.

The documents are saved in the newly created folder, Report.

Hiding Spelling and Grammar Errors

As you have been working on the report, you have noticed that many spelling and grammar errors are identified. You want to scroll the document to take a quick look at the types of errors identified. You have noticed that scrolling a larger document in Print Layout view takes more time because the view displays the extra blank (white) space on the page and the space allocated for the headers and footers. You can hide the display of this white space to make it faster to move through the document.

1 ● **Switch to Print Layout view.**

● **Click on the gray page separator space between any pages.**

> **Additional Information**
> The mouse pointer appears as ⊞ when you can hide the white space.

● **Scroll to see the bottom of page 4 and the top of page 5.**

Your screen should be similar to Figure 3.12

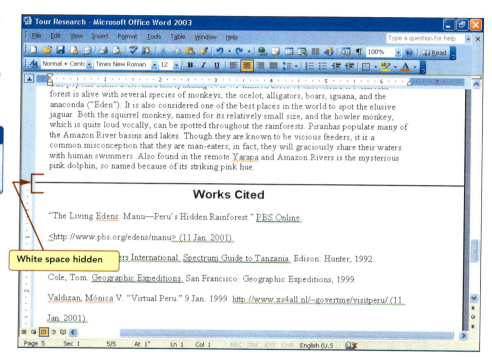

Figure 3.12

Any extra white space is eliminated, making scrolling much faster. As you scrolled the document you noticed that most of the identified errors are for proper names and words that are not in the dictionary. While working on a document, you can turn off the display of these errors so that they are not distracting.

2 ● **Choose Tools/Options.**

● **Open the Spelling & Grammar tab.**

Your screen should be similar to Figure 3.13

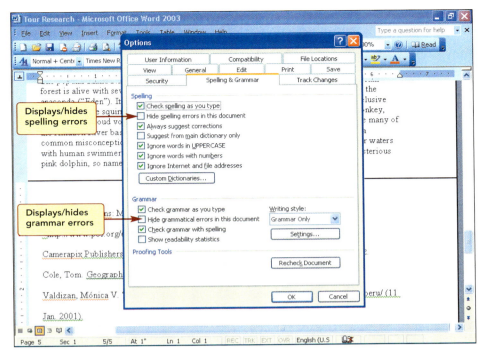

Figure 3.13

The Options dialog box is used to change the way many features in Word operate. The Spelling and Grammar tab displays options that control how these features operate. Checkmarks next to options indicate the setting is on. You want to turn off the display of spelling and grammar errors.

3 ● **Select Hide spelling errors in this document.**

● **Select Hide grammatical errors in this document.**

● **Click** [OK].

● **Click on the gray page separator line to show the white space again.**

Additional Information

The mouse pointer appears as ⊞ when you can show white space.

● **Scroll up to see the top of page 4.**

Your screen should be similar to Figure 3.14

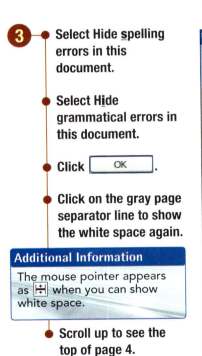

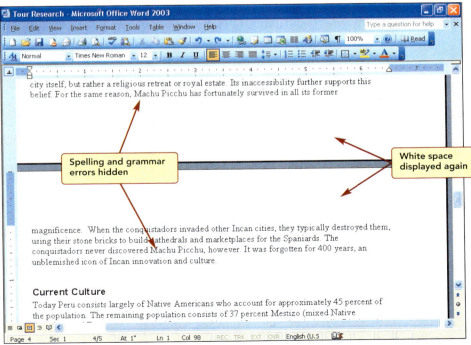

Figure 3.14

The red and green wavy lines are no longer displayed. You can still run spelling and grammar checking manually to check errors at any time. The extra blank space at the bottom of page 4 and the header and footer space are displayed again. Now that you know how to use this feature, you can turn it on and off whenever you want.

Formatting Documents Automatically

Now that you have finished reorganizing the report, you want to add a title page. Generally, this page includes information such as the report title, the name of the author, and the date. You also want this page to include a table of contents list.

When preparing research reports, two styles of report formatting are commonly used: MLA (Modern Language Association) and APA (American Psychological Association). Although they require the same basic information, they differ in how this information is presented. For example, MLA style does not include a separate title page, but APA style does. The report you will create in this lab will use many of style requirements of the MLA. However, because this report is not a formal report to be presented at a conference or other academic proceeding, some liberties have been taken with the style to demonstrate features in Word.

Using Click and Type

You will create a new page above the first report topic where you will enter the title information using the **Click and Type** feature. This feature, available in Print Layout and Web Layout views, is used to quickly insert text, graphics, and other items in a blank area of a document, avoiding the need to enter blank lines. This feature also applies the paragraph formatting needed to position an item at the location you clicked.

1 ● Press ⌈Ctrl⌉ + ⌈Home⌉ to move to the top of the document.

● Press ⌈Ctrl⌉ + ⌈←Enter⌉ to insert a hard page break and create a blank page above it.

● Move to the top of the blank new page.

● Move the mouse pointer from left to right across the page and observe the change in the mouse pointer.

Your screen should be similar to Figure 3.15

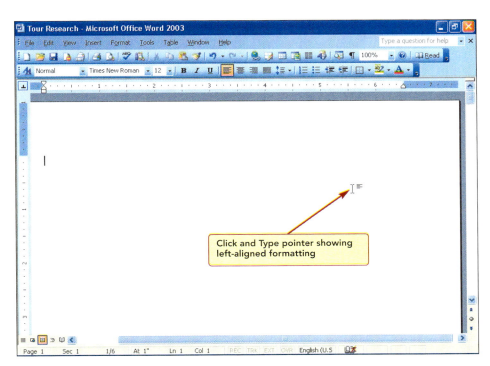

Click and Type pointer showing left-aligned formatting

Figure 3.15

Print Layout view includes formatting "zones" that control the formatting that will be applied. As you move the mouse pointer through the zones, the I-beam pointer displays an icon that indicates the formatting that will be applied when you double-click at that location. This is the Click and Type pointer. The pointer shapes and their associated formatting are described in the table below.

Pointer shape	Formatting applied
I≡	Align left
I	Align center
≡I	Align right
I≡	Left indent

To enable the Click and Type pointer, first click on a blank area, then as you move the mouse pointer, the pointer shape indicates how the item will be formatted. Double-clicking on the location in the page moves the insertion point to that location and applies the formatting to the entry. You will enter the report title centered on the page.

2
- Click on a blank area of the page to enable Click and Type.

- Double-click on the center of the page at the .5-inch vertical ruler position while the mouse pointer is a I.

- Type the report title, **Tanzania and Peru**.

Your screen should be similar to Figure 3.16

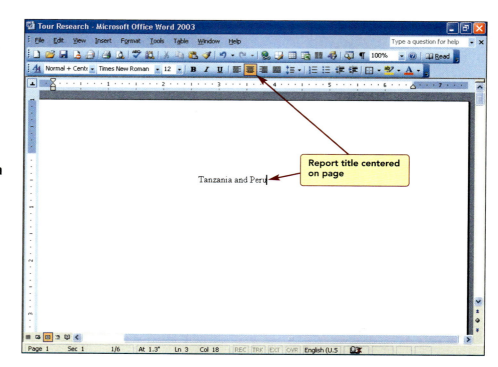

Figure 3.16

Next you will add a heading for the table of contents listing you will create. Then you will enter your name and date at the bottom of the title page.

3
- Double-click on the center of the page at the 1.5-inch vertical ruler position while the mouse pointer is a I.

- Enter the title **Table of Contents**.

- In the same manner, enter **your name** centered at the 3-inch vertical ruler position.

- Press **←Enter**.

- Enter the current date centered below your name.

Your screen should be similar to Figure 3.17

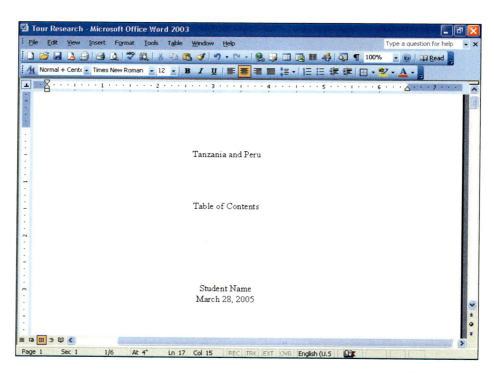

Figure 3.17

Applying Styles

Next you want to improve the appearance of the main title. You can do this quickly by applying a style to the title.

1 • **Move to anywhere in the Tanzania and Peru title.**

• **Click 🔠 Styles and Formatting.**

Your screen should be similar to Figure 3.18

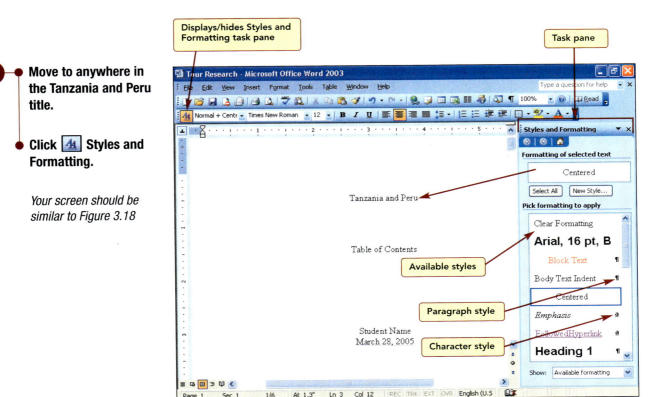

Figure 3.18

The Styles and Formatting task pane appears. The "Formatting of selected text" box shows that the text of the current selection is centered. The "Pick formatting to apply" list box displays the names of all available styles and formatting, including those that you have applied directly, in alphabetical order. The symbols to the right of the style name indicate the type of style, such as a paragraph style ¶ or a character style a . You want to display the complete list of styles and apply the Title style to the text.

2 Select All styles from the Show drop-down list box.

● Scroll to the bottom of the "Pick formatting to apply" list and choose Title.

Your screen should be similar to Figure 3.19

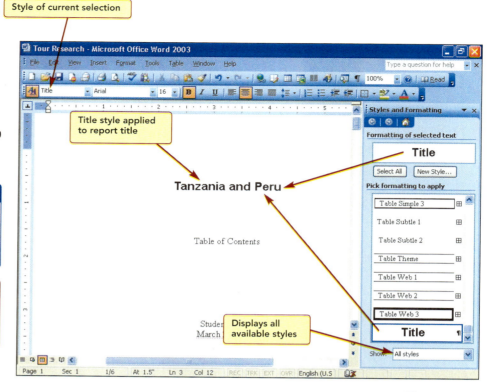

Figure 3.19

Notice that the entire title appears in the selected style. This is because a Title style is a paragraph style, affecting the entire paragraph at the insertion point. Also notice that the Style drop-down list button in the Formatting toolbar now displays "Title" as the style applied to the selection. This style includes formatting settings of Arial, 16 pt, and bold.

Next, you want to apply a Subtitle style to the Table of Contents heading. Another way to select a style is from the Style drop-down menu.

3 Move the insertion point to anywhere in the Table of Contents heading.

Open the Normal + Cente ▾ Style drop-down menu.

Your screen should be similar to Figure 3.20

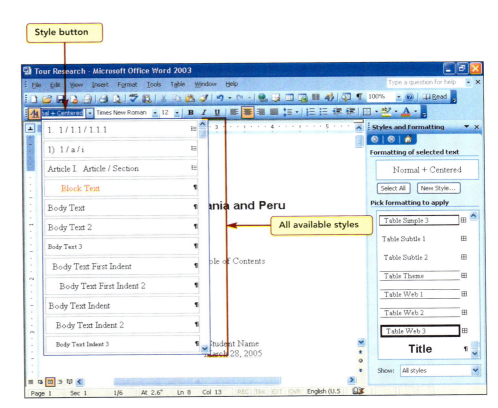

Figure 3.20

The Style drop-down menu displays all available styles. The style names are listed in alphabetical order and appear formatted in that style.

4 Scroll the Style drop-down menu and choose Subtitle.

Your screen should be similar to Figure 3.21

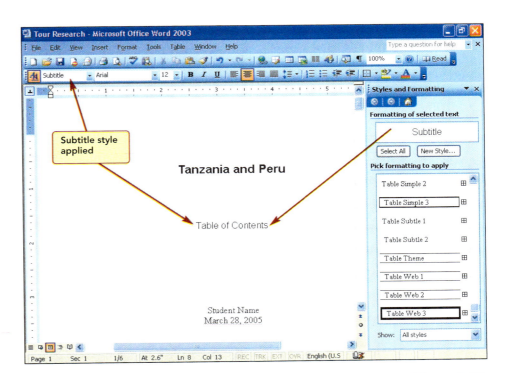

Figure 3.21

Creating a Custom Style

Although the Title style looks good, you want to enhance it further using the shadow text effect. Then you will save the formatting associated with the title as a custom style so you can quickly apply the style in the future.

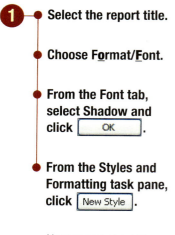

1 ● Select the report title.

● Choose **F**ormat/**F**ont.

● From the Font tab, select **Shadow** and click OK .

● From the Styles and Formatting task pane, click New Style .

Your screen should be similar to Figure 3.22

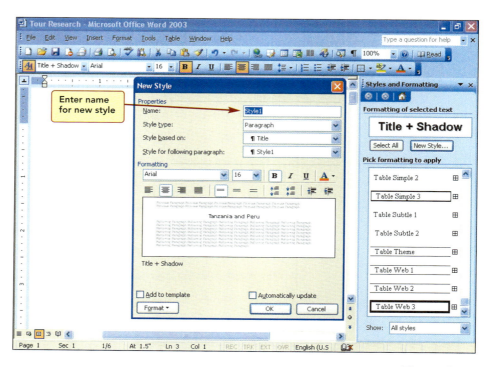

Figure 3.22

The New Style dialog box displays the settings associated with the selected text. The only action you need to take is give the style a more descriptive name.

2 ● In the Name text box, type **Shadow Title**.

● Click OK .

Having Trouble?

If this style already exists on your computer, click OK and Cancel to continue.

Your screen should be similar to Figure 3.23

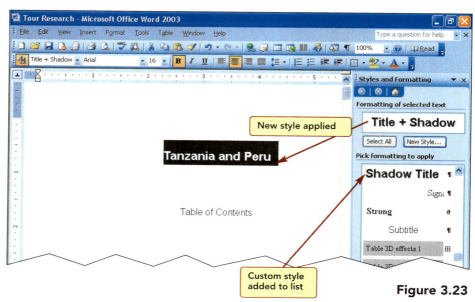

Figure 3.23

The new style name has been added to the list of available styles and can be applied like any other style. If you ever need to change a style back to the default document style, you can easily clear the style by moving to the text whose style you want removed and choosing Clear Formatting from the Style drop-down menu. You can also use **E**dit/Cle**a**r/**F**ormats to have the same effect.

Creating a Table of Contents

Now you are ready to create the table of contents. A table of contents is a listing of the topic headings that appear in a document and their associated page references (see the sample below). It shows the reader at a glance the topics that are included in the document and makes it easier for the reader to locate information. Word can generate a table of contents automatically after you have applied heading styles to the document headings.

Table of Contents

Tanzania	*2*
Geography and Climate	**2**
Ngorongoro Conservation Area	2
Serengeti Plain	2
Culture	**2**
Animal Life	**3**
Peru	*3*
Geography and Climate	**3**
La Costa	3
La Sierra	4
La Selva	4
Culture	**4**
Historical Culture	4
Current Culture	5
Animal Life	**5**

Generating a Table of Contents

You want the table of contents listing to be displayed several lines below the table of contents heading on the title page.

1 ● Close the Styles and Formatting task pane.

● Move to the second blank line below the Table of Contents heading.

Having Trouble?

If needed, use ¶ Show/Hide to help locate the position in the document.

● Choose Insert/Reference/Index and Tables.

● Open the Table of Contents tab.

Your screen should be similar to Figure 3.24

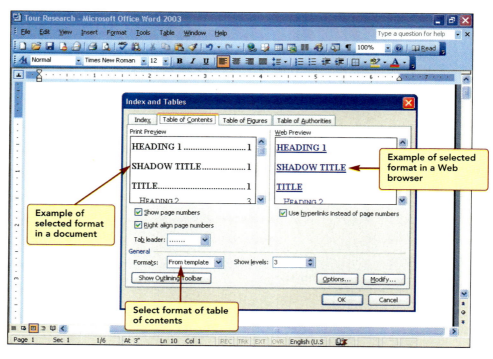

Figure 3.24

From the Table of Contents tab, you first need to select the format or design of the table of contents. There are seven predesigned table of contents formats available in the Formats drop-down list box. The default style is selected, and the Preview boxes display an example of how the selected format will look in a normal printed document or in a document when viewed in a Web browser. You will use one of the other predesigned formats.

2 • Open the Formats drop-down list box.

• Select several formats and look at the preview area to see an example of the selected format.

• Choose Distinctive.

Your screen should be similar to Figure 3.25

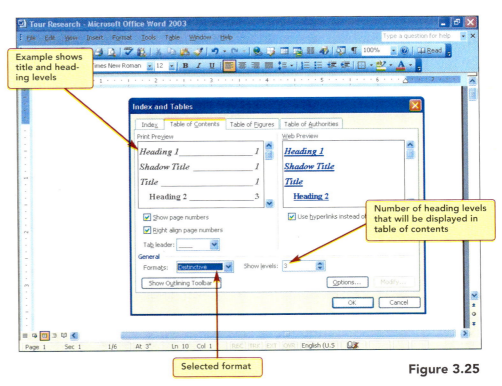

Example shows title and heading levels

Number of heading levels that will be displayed in table of contents

Selected format

Figure 3.25

The Print Preview area shows this style will display the page numbers flush with the right margin, and with a solid line tab leader between the heading entry and the page number. This format will display in the table of contents all entries in the document that are formatted with Headings 1, 2, and 3, as well as Title and Subtitle styles. You want the table of contents to include topics formatted with the Heading 4 style, but to exclude those formatted with the Title and Subtitle styles. You will modify the settings for the Distinctive format and turn off the use of these styles.

3 • Change the level number in the Show Levels text box to 4.

• Click [Options...].

Your screen should be similar to Figure 3.26

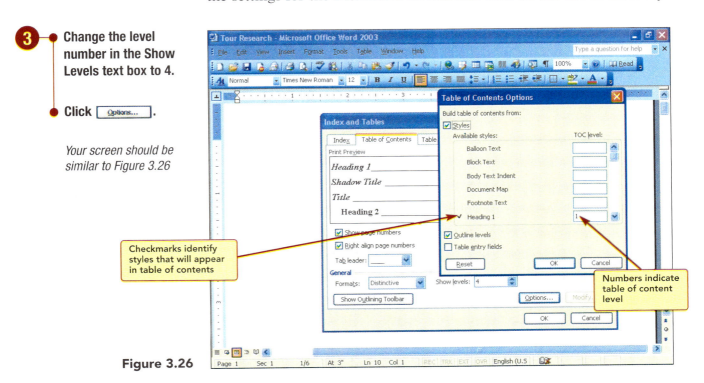

Checkmarks identify styles that will appear in table of contents

Numbers indicate table of content level

Figure 3.26

The Table of Contents Options dialog box shows the styles that are used to build the table of contents. The checkmark indicates the styles Word will look for in the document to use as items to include in the table of contents, and the number indicates the level at which they will be displayed. To clear a style selection, simply delete the number from the TOC level text box.

4 ● **Scroll to the bottom of the Available Styles list to see the Subtitle and Title selections.**

● **Delete the numbers from the Shadow Title, Subtitle, and Title text boxes to clear the checkmarks.**

● **Click [OK].**

Your screen should be similar to Figure 3.27

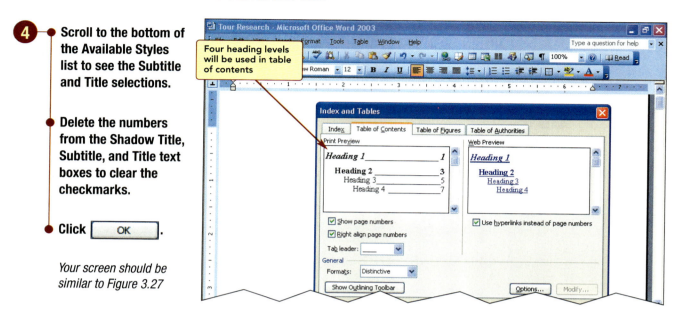

Figure 3.27

The Print Preview area now shows that four levels of headings will be used in the table of contents listing, and the title and subtitle will not be included. Now you are ready to generate the listing.

5 ● **Click [OK].**

Your screen should be similar to Figure 3.28

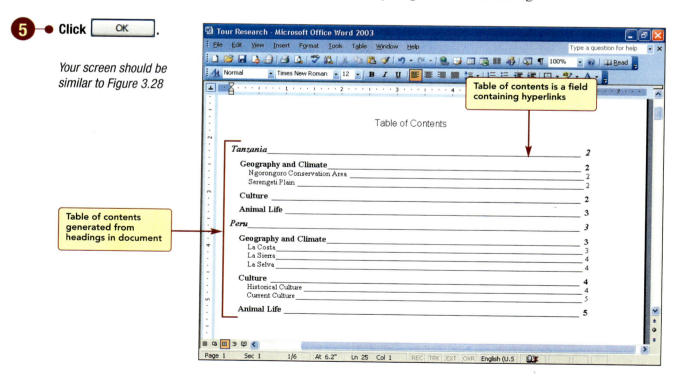

Figure 3.28

Word searches for headings with the specified styles, sorts them by heading level, references their page numbers, and displays the table of contents using the Distinctive style in the document. The headings that were assigned a Heading 1 style are aligned with the left margin, and subordinate heading levels are indented as appropriate. The title and subtitle headings are not included. The table of contents that is generated is a field. This means it can be updated to reflect changes you may make at a later time in your document.

Navigating by Headings

In a large document, locating and moving to an area of text you want to view can take a lot of time. However, after headings have been applied to different areas of a document, there are several features that can make navigation easier. As a help when scrolling by dragging the scroll box, a ScreenTip identifies the topic heading in addition to the page number that will be displayed when you stop dragging the scroll box. If you have generated a table of contents, you can use the table of contents entries to quickly move to different areas. Even more convenient, however, is to use the Document Map feature to jump to a selected location.

Using a Table of Contents Hyperlink

Not only does the table of contents display the location of information in the report, but it can also be used to quickly move to a specific area. This is because each entry in the table is a separate field that is a hyperlink to the heading in the document. Because the table of contents is a field, it will appear shaded when selected. More importantly, it means that the table of contents can be easily updated to reflect changes you may make to the document after the list is generated.

A hyperlink, as you have learned, is a connection to a location in the current document, another document, or to a Web site. In this case, the table of contents hyperlinks are connections to locations in this document. Simply holding down Ctrl while clicking on a hyperlink in a Word document will move you directly to the selected location.

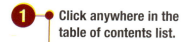

1 ● **Click anywhere in the table of contents list.**

● **Hold down** Ctrl **and click the Peru table of contents line.**

Your screen should be similar to Figure 3.29

Additional Information

Pointing to an entry in a table of contents displays a ScreenTip with directions on how to follow the hyperlink.

Additional Information

The mouse pointer shape changes to a ⟨ʰᵐ⟩ when holding down Ctrl and pointing to a hyperlink.

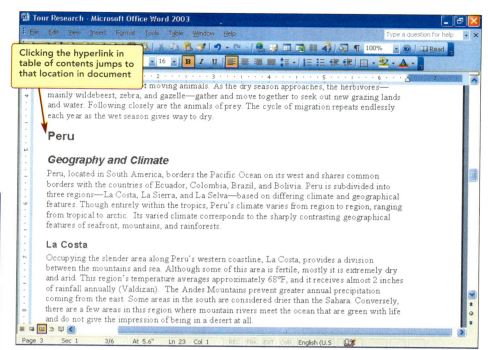

Figure 3.29

The insertion point jumps to the Peru heading in the document.

Using the Document Map

Now, however, the table of contents is no longer visible. If you wanted to move to a different topic, you would need to return to the top of the document and select another hyperlink. Another way to quickly move to different locations in the document is to use the Document Map feature. **Document Map** displays a list of the headings style in a document in a separate pane that is used to quickly navigate through the document and keep track of your location in it. When your document does not contain any headings formatted with heading styles, the program automatically searches the document for paragraphs that look like headings (for example, short lines with a larger font size) and displays them in the Document Map. If it cannot find any such headings, the Document Map is blank.

1 ● Click [icon] **Document Map.**

Another Method

The menu equivalent is **View/Document Map**.

Your screen should be similar to Figure 3.30

Document Map pane displays headings in your document

Indicates all subordinate levels are displayed

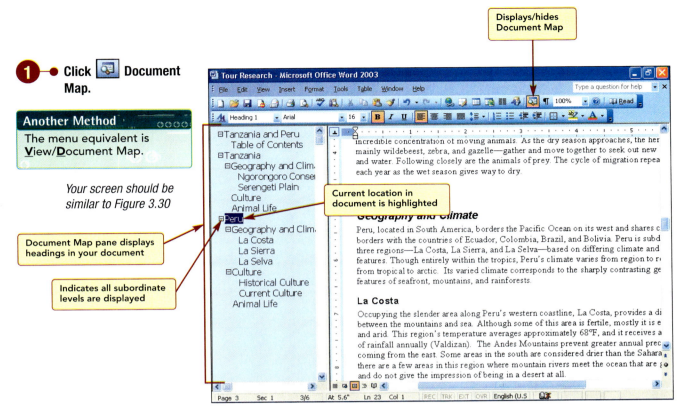

Displays/hides Document Map

Current location in document is highlighted

Figure 3.30

Additional Information

The Document Map pane can be resized by dragging the divider line between the panes.

The Document Map pane on the left edge of the window displays the headings in the document. All text that is formatted with a heading style is displayed in the Document Map pane. Notice the ⊟ symbol to the left of many of the headings in the Document Map; this symbol indicates that all subordinate headings are displayed. A ⊞ symbol would indicate that subordinate headings are not displayed. The highlighted heading shows your location in the document. Clicking on a heading in the Document Map quickly jumps to that location in the document.

2 ● **Click on Culture (under Peru) in the Document Map.**

● **Click on Table of Contents.**

Your screen should be similar to Figure 3.31

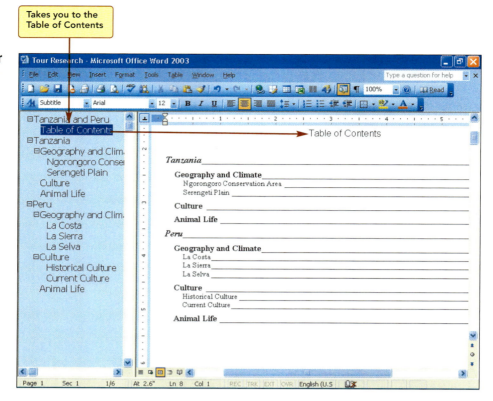

Figure 3.31

You quickly moved from one topic location in the document to another. When using the Document Map, the selected topic heading is displayed at the top of the window and is highlighted in the Document Map.

The Document Map feature is available in all views and remains displayed in the view you are using until you turn it off. It must be turned on and off in each view independently.

Formatting Document Sections

You want to change the layout of the title page so that the text on the page is centered vertically between the top and bottom page margins. Because page layout settings affect entire documents, you need to create separate sections in the document to make this change to the title page only.

Concept 2

2   To format different parts of a document differently, you can divide a document into **sections**. Initially a document is one section. To separate it into different parts, you insert section breaks. The **section break** identifies the end of a section and stores the document format settings, such as margins and page layout, associated with that section of the document.

The three types of section breaks, described in the following table, control the location where the text following a section break begins.

Type	Action
Next Page	Starts the new section on the next page.
Continuous	Starts the new section on the same page.
Odd or Even	Starts the new section on the next odd or even numbered page.

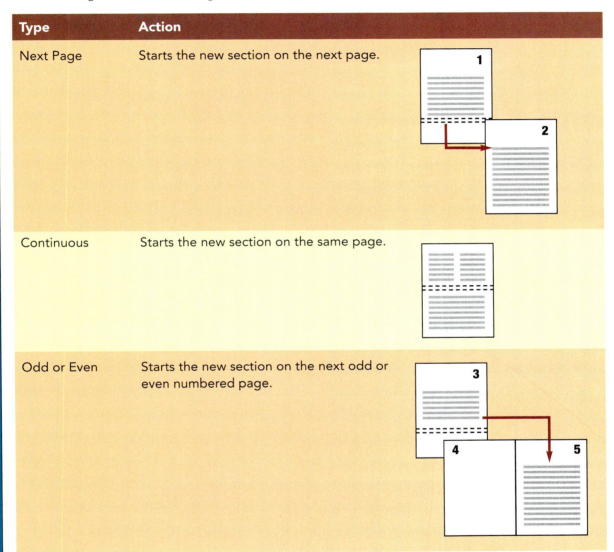

If you delete a section break, the preceding text becomes part of the following section and assumes its section formatting.

Creating a Section Break

Because the page layout you want to use on the title page is different from the rest of the document, you need to divide the document into two sections. You will delete the hard page break line you inserted and replace it with a section break.

1 ● **Switch to Normal view with 100% zoom.**

● **Scroll to see the bottom of page 1.**

● **Delete the hard page break line.**

Having Trouble?

To remove a hard page break, click on the page break line and press Delete.

● **Choose Insert/Break.**

Your screen should be similar to Figure 3.32

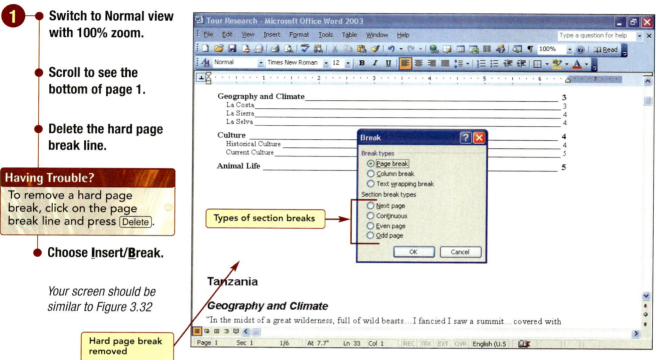

Types of section breaks

Hard page break removed

Figure 3.32

In the Break dialog box, you specify the type of section break you want to insert. In this case, you want the new section to start on the next page.

2 ● **Select Next page.**

● **Click** OK **.**

● **Delete the blank line above the Tanzania heading.**

Your screen should be similar to Figure 3.33

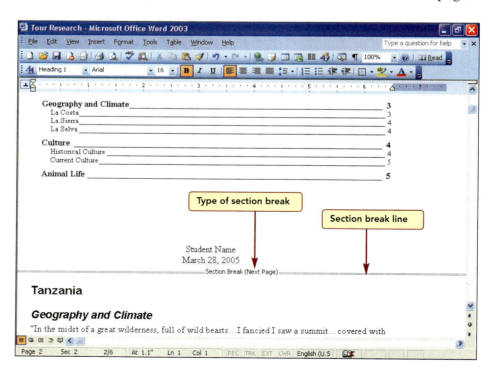

Type of section break

Section break line

Figure 3.33

A double dotted line and the words "Section Break" identify the type of document break that was inserted.

Centering a Page Vertically

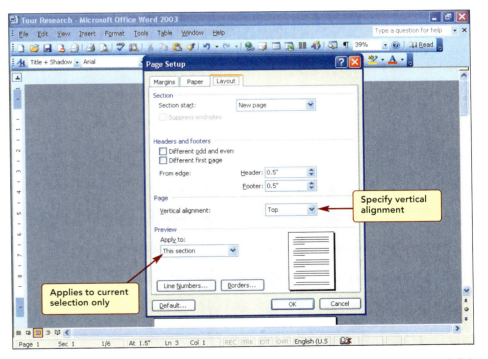

Now that the title page is in a separate section, you can format it differently from the rest of the report. You want to change the layout of the title page to centered vertically. Vertical alignment determines the position of the text on a page relative to the top and bottom margins. The four vertical alignment settings are described in the following table.

Additional Information

If you do not create a section break first, Word will automatically insert a section break for you if you change the formatting of selected text, such as inserting columns or centering selected text vertically on a page.

Vertical Alignment	Effect	Vertical Alignment	Effect
Top	Aligns first line of text on page with the top margin. This is the default setting.	Center	Centers text between top and bottom margins.
Bottom	Aligns last line of text on page with the bottom margin.	Justified	Vertically justifies text so that it is spaced evenly down the page.

1
- Switch back to Print Layout view.
- Move to anywhere in the title page.
- Click 🖼 Document Map to turn off this feature.
- Zoom to Whole Page.
- Double-click on the vertical ruler to open the Page Setup dialog box.

Another Method

The menu equivalent is File/Page Setup.

- Open the Layout tab.

Your screen should be similar to Figure 3.34

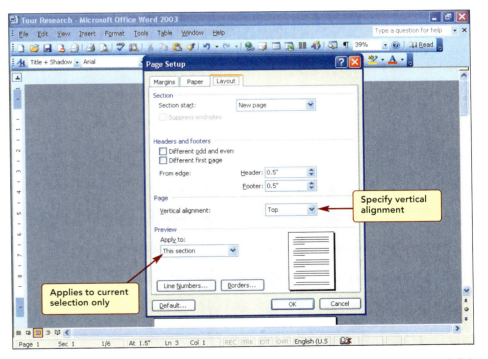

Figure 3.34

From the Vertical Alignment drop-down list box, you specify how the text is to be aligned on the page vertically. In addition, from the Apply To drop-down list box you need to specify the part of the document you want to be aligned to the new setting. Because you already divided the document into sections, this setting is already appropriately selected. You only need to specify the vertical alignment.

2 • From the **V**ertical Alignment drop-down list, select Center.

• Click [OK].

• Delete all blank lines above the title.

• Click 💾 Save to save the changes you have made to the document.

Your screen should be similar to Figure 3.35

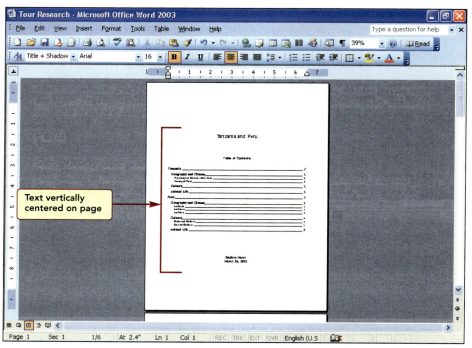

Text vertically centered on page

Figure 3.35

Now you can see that the text on the title page is centered vertically between the top and bottom margins. Word required a section break at this location because a different page format, in this case vertical alignment, was used on this page than the rest of the document.

Including Source References

This document already includes parenthetical source references entered according to the MLA style for research papers. However, you still have several reference notes you want to include in the report as footnotes to help clarify some information.

Concept 3

Footnote and Endnote

3 Including source references or notes that explain or comment on information in the text as footnotes or endnotes is an essential element of a documented research paper. A **footnote** is a source reference or text offering additional explanation that is placed at the bottom of a page. An **endnote** is also a source reference or long comment that typically appears at the end of a document. You can have both footnotes and endnotes in the same document.

Footnotes and endnotes consist of two parts, the note reference mark and the note text. The **note reference mark** is commonly a superscript number appearing in the document at the end of the material being referenced (for example, text). It can also be a character or combination of characters. The **note text** for a footnote appears at the bottom of the page on which the reference mark appears. The footnote text is separated from the document text by a horizontal line called the **note separator**. Endnote text appears as a listing at the end of the document.

Note text can be of any length and formatted just as you would any other text. You can also customize the appearance of the note separators.

Adding Footnotes

The first footnote reference you want to add is the height of Mt. Kilimanjaro. This note will follow the reference to the mountain at the end of the first paragraph in the Geography and Climate section for Tanzania. To identify the location of the footnote number in the document, you position the insertion point at the document location first.

1 • Switch to Normal view and display the Document Map.

• Click on the Tanzania heading in the Document Map pane.

• Change the zoom to Page Width.

• Move to the end of the first paragraph after the word "mountain."

• Choose **I**nsert/ Refere**n**ce/Foot**n**ote.

Another Method

The keyboard shortcut to insert a footnote using the default settings is [Alt] + [Ctrl] + F.

Your screen should be similar to Figure 3.36

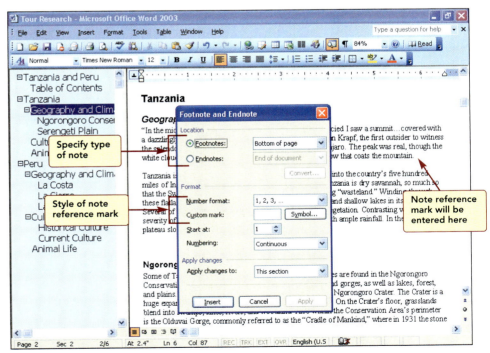

Figure 3.36

In the Footnote and Endnote dialog box, you specify whether you want to create footnotes or endnotes and the type of reference mark you want to appear in the document: a numbered mark or a custom mark. A custom mark can be any nonnumeric character, such as an asterisk, that you enter in the text box. You want to create numbered footnotes, so the default settings of Footnote and AutoNumber are acceptable.

2 • Click [Insert].

Your screen should be similar to Figure 3.37

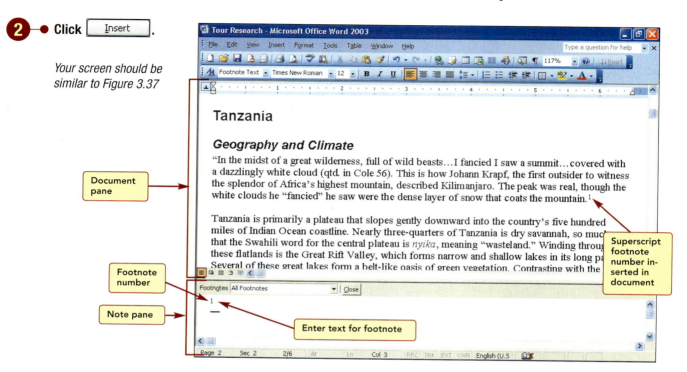

Figure 3.37

The document window is now horizontally divided into upper and lower panes. The Document Map pane is temporarily hidden while these two panes are displayed. When you close the lower pane, the Document Map pane will be displayed again.

The report is displayed in the upper pane. The footnote number, 1, appears as a superscript in the document where the insertion point was positioned when the footnote was created. The note pane displays the footnote number and the insertion point. This is where you enter the text for the footnote. When you enter a footnote, you can use the same menus, commands, and features as you would in the document window. Any commands that are not available are dimmed.

3 ● **Type Mt. Kilimanjaro is 19,340 feet high, making it the fourth tallest mountain in the world.**

Your screen should be similar to Figure 3.38

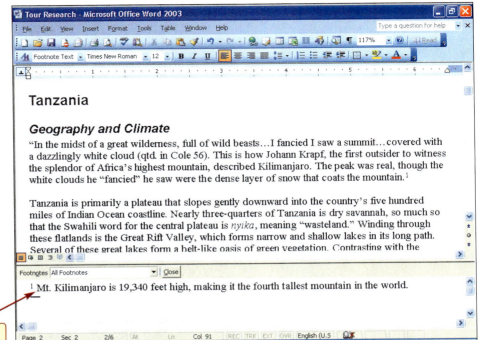

Footnote text

Figure 3.38

The second footnote you want to add is in the Geography and Climate section under Peru.

4 ● **Click Close to close the footnote pane and to redisplay the Document Map.**

● **Click on La Sierra in the Document Map.**

● **Click at the end of the paragraph following the word "lake."**

● **Choose Insert/ Reference/Footnote/ Insert .**

Your screen should be similar to Figure 3.39

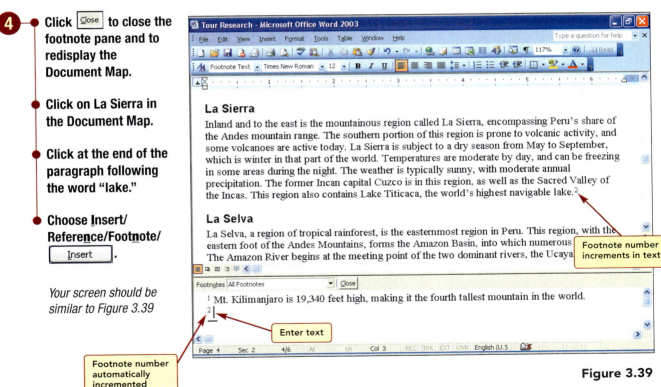

Footnote number increments in text

Enter text

Footnote number automatically incremented

Figure 3.39

The footnote number 2 is automatically entered at the insertion point location. The note pane is active again, so you can enter the text for the second footnote. You want to add a note about Lake Titicaca.

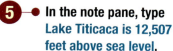

5 • In the note pane, type **Lake Titicaca is 12,507 feet above sea level.**

Your screen should be similar to Figure 3.40

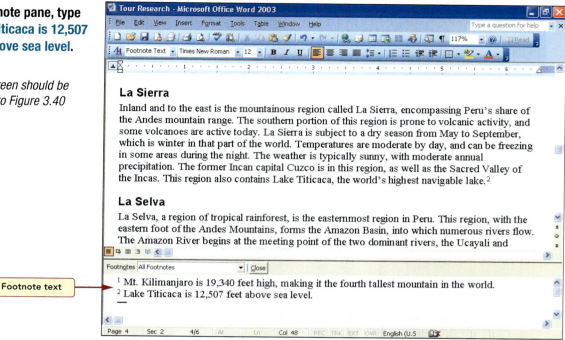

La Sierra

Inland and to the east is the mountainous region called La Sierra, encompassing Peru's share of the Andes mountain range. The southern portion of this region is prone to volcanic activity, and some volcanoes are active today. La Sierra is subject to a dry season from May to September, which is winter in that part of the world. Temperatures are moderate by day, and can be freezing in some areas during the night. The weather is typically sunny, with moderate annual precipitation. The former Incan capital Cuzco is in this region, as well as the Sacred Valley of the Incas. This region also contains Lake Titicaca, the world's highest navigable lake.[2]

La Selva

La Selva, a region of tropical rainforest, is the easternmost region in Peru. This region, with the eastern foot of the Andes Mountains, forms the Amazon Basin, into which numerous rivers flow. The Amazon River begins at the meeting point of the two dominant rivers, the Ucayali and

Footnote text →
[1] Mt. Kilimanjaro is 19,340 feet high, making it the fourth tallest mountain in the world.
[2] Lake Titicaca is 12,507 feet above sea level.

Figure 3.40

Now you realize that you forgot to enter a footnote earlier in the document, on page 2.

6 • Close the note pane.

• Click Ngorongoro Conservation Area in the Document Map.

• Move to the end of the first sentence of the first paragraph, following the word "Area."

• Insert a footnote at this location.

Your screen should be similar to Figure 3.41

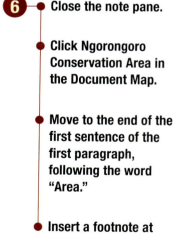

Footnote number inserted

Ngorongoro Conservation Area

Some of Tanzania's most distinguishing geographical features are found in the Ngorongoro Conservation Area.[2] The park is composed of many craters and gorges, as well as lakes, forest, and plains. Among these features is the area's namesake, the Ngorongoro Crater. The Crater is a huge expanse, covering more than one hundred square miles. On the Crater's floor, grasslands blend into swamps, lakes, rivers, and woodland. Also within the Conservation Area's perimeter is the Olduvai Gorge, commonly referred to as the "Cradle of Mankind," where in 1931 the stone tools of prehistoric man were found. This find subsequently led to the discovery of the remains of humans who lived 1.75 million years ago.

Serengeti Plain

Adjacent to the western edge of the Ngorongoro Conservation Area is the Serengeti Plain. Its area is approximately 5,700 square miles, and its central savanna supports many grazing animals

[1] Mt. Kilimanjaro is 19,340 feet high, making it the fourth tallest mountain in the world.
[2]
[3] Lake Titicaca is 12,507 feet above sea level.

Footnote number automatically adjusted for location in the text

Figure 3.41

Notice that this footnote is now number 2 in the document, and a blank footnote line has been entered in the note pane for the footnote text. Word automatically adjusted the footnote numbers when the new footnote was inserted.

 7 In the note pane, type **The Conservation Area is a national preserve spanning 3,196 square miles.**

Your screen should be similar to Figure 3.42

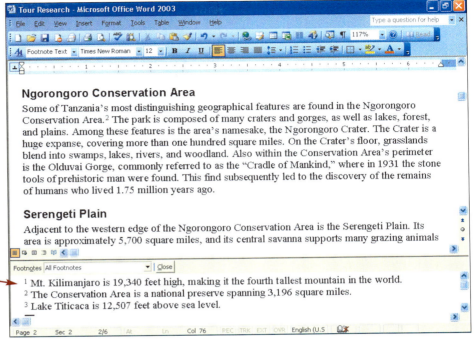

Figure 3.42

You are finished entering footnotes for now.

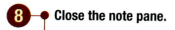

8 Close the note pane.

If necessary scroll to see the bottom of this page.

Your screen should be similar to Figure 3.43

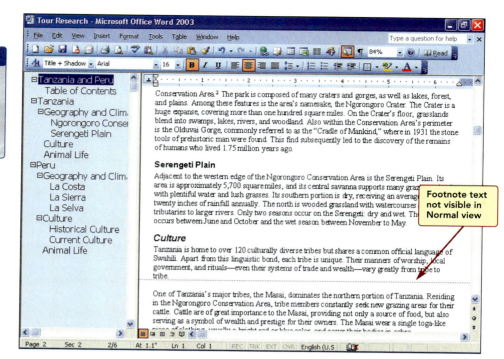

Figure 3.43

In Normal view, if the footnote pane is not open, you cannot see the footnote text.

Viewing Footnotes

To see the footnote text in Normal view, you point to the note reference mark and the footnote is displayed as a ScreenTip. Alternatively, you can switch to Print Layout view where the footnotes are displayed as they will appear when the document is printed.

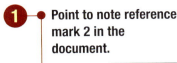

1 ● Point to note reference mark 2 in the document.

> The Conservation Area is a national preserve spanning 3,196 square miles.

Footnote appears in ScreenTip

● **Switch to Print Layout view and set the zoom to 75 percent.**

● **If necessary, scroll to the bottom of page 2 to see the footnotes.**

Your screen should be similar to Figure 3.44

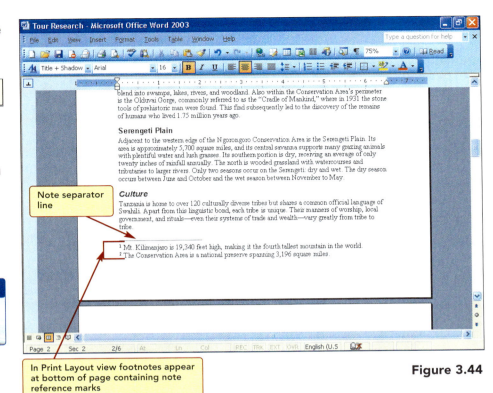

Figure 3.44

The footnotes are displayed immediately above the bottom margin separated from the text by the note separator line. They appear at the bottom of the page containing the footnote reference mark.

Inserting a Footnote in Print Layout View

As you continue to check the document, you decide you want to explain the CE abbreviation following the date 1300 in the Historical Culture section. While in Print Layout view, you can insert, edit, and format footnotes just like any other text. After using the command to insert a footnote, the footnote number appears in the footnote area at the bottom of the page, ready for you to enter the footnote text.

1 ● **Display the Document Map and move to the Historical Culture section.**

● **Move the insertion point after "CE" in the second sentence.**

● **Insert a footnote at this location.**

● **Type Common Era (CE) is the period dating from the birth of Christ.**

● **Click** 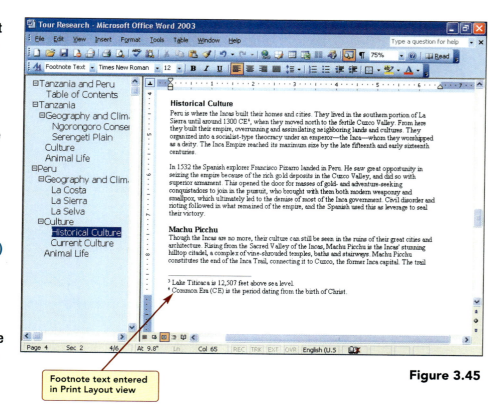 **Save to save the changes you have made to the document.**

Your screen should be similar to Figure 3.45

Footnote text entered in Print Layout view

Figure 3.45

Formatting Picture Layout

Next you want to add a picture in the report to complement the subject of the first topic. You want the text in the document where the picture will be inserted to wrap around the picture. To do this, you change the text-wrapping layout for the picture.

Concept 4

Text Wrapping

4 You can control the appearance of text around a graphic object by specifying the **text wrapping** style. The text in the paragraph may wrap around the object in many different ways as shown below.

| Inline with Text | Square | Tight | Through | Top and Bottom | Behind Text | In Front of Text |

When a picture is inserted into a Word document, it is an **inline object**. This means it is positioned directly in the text at the position of the insertion point. It becomes part of the paragraph, and any paragraph alignment settings that apply to the paragraph also apply to the picture.

By changing a graphic to a **floating object**, it is inserted into the **drawing layer**, a separate layer from the text that allows graphic objects to be positioned precisely on the page. You can change an inline object to a floating picture by changing the wrapping style of the object.

You will insert a picture of a giraffe next to the second paragraph on page 2.

1 • Use the Document Map to move to the Geography and Climate head under Tanzania.

• Move to the beginning of the second paragraph.

• Close the Document Map and change the zoom to Text Width.

• Insert the picture wd03_Giraffe from your data files.

• Reduce the size of the picture to approximately 2 by 2 inches.

Additional Information
Additional Information: Dragging the corner handle maintains the original proportions of the picture.

Your screen should be similar to Figure 3.46

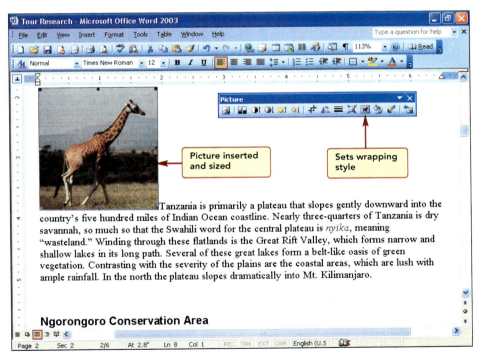

Figure 3.46

The picture has been inserted using the wrap default setting as an inline object and appears at the beginning of the paragraph like the first text characters of the paragraph. The text continues to the right of the picture.

The Picture toolbar is also automatically displayed. Its buttons (identified below) are used to modify the selected picture object. Your Picture toolbar may be floating or may be docked along an edge of the window, depending on its location when last used.

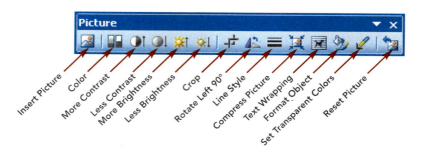

Wrapping Text Around Graphics

You want the text to wrap to the right side of the picture. To do this, you will change the wrapping style to Square.

1 ● Click 📷 **Text Wrapping on the Picture toolbar.**

Another Method

The menu equivalent is **F**ormat/**P**icture/Layout/ Wrapping Style.

default wrapping style →

- In Line With Text
- Square
- Tight
- Behind Text
- In Front of Text
- Top and Bottom
- Through
- Edit Wrap Points

● **Click 📷 Square.**

● **If necessary, resize the picture until the text wraps around it as in Figure 3.47.**

Your screen should be similar to Figure 3.47

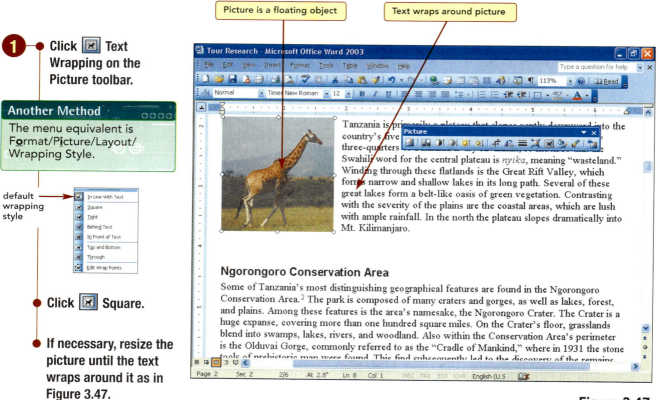

Figure 3.47

2 ● **Move the picture to the center of the paragraph to see how the text wraps around it.**

Your screen should be similar to Figure 3.48

The picture is changed to a floating object that can be placed anywhere in the document, including in front of or behind other objects including the text.

Because the picture is aligned with the left margin, the text wraps to the right side of the object. If you moved the picture, because the wrapping style is Square, the text would wrap around the object on all sides.

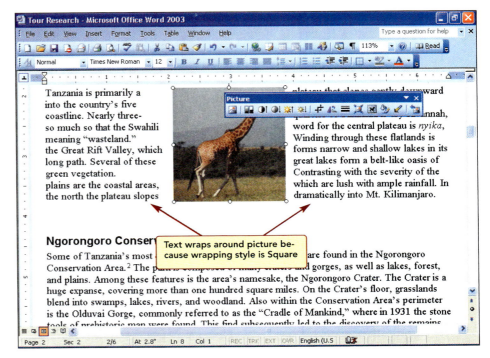

Figure 3.48

The text wraps on all sides of the object, depending on its location in the text. You will align this picture with the left margin again. Then you will add a second picture in the Peru Animal Life section.

3. • **Move the picture back to the left margin and aligned with the top of the paragraph (see Figure 3.47).**

• **Move to the beginning of the first paragraph in the Peru Animal Life section.**

• **Insert the picture wd03_Parrots to the left of the first paragraph.**

• **Change the wrapping style to Square.**

• **Position the picture as in Figure 3.49.**

• **Click 🖫 to save the document.**

Your screen should be similar to Figure 3.49

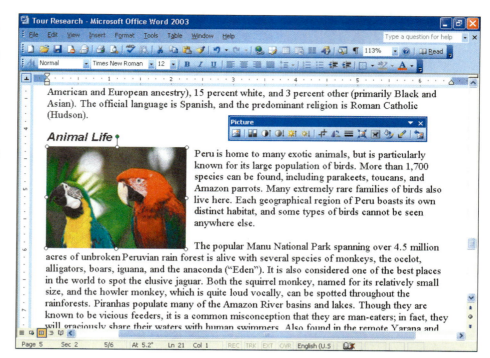

Figure 3.49

Referencing Figures

After figures and other illustrative items have been added to a document, it is helpful to include figure references to identify the items. Figure references include captions and cross-references. If the reader is viewing the document online, the captions and cross-references become hyperlinks to allow the reader to jump around in the document.

Concept 5

Captions and Cross-References

5 Using captions and cross-references in a document identifies items in a document and the helps the reader locate information quickly. A **caption** is a numbered label for a figure, table, picture, or graph. Word can automatically add captions to graphic objects as they are inserted, or you can add them manually. The caption label can be changed to reflect the type of object to which it refers, such as a table, chart, or figure. In addition, Word automatically numbers graphic objects and adjusts numbering when objects of the same type are added or deleted.

A **cross-reference** is a reference from one part of a document to related information in another part. Once you have captions, you can also include cross-references. For example, if you have a graph in one part of the document that you would like to refer to in another section, you can add a cross-reference that tells the reader what page the graph is on. A cross-reference can also be inserted as a hyperlink, allowing you to jump to another location in the same document or in another document.

Adding a Figure Caption

Next, you want to add a caption below the picture of the giraffe.

1 **Move to the blank line below the giraffe picture in the Tanzania section.**

Having Trouble?

If the blank line is not below the figure, make the figure smaller so the line does not wrap to the side of the figure.

● **Select the Giraffe picture.**

● **Choose Insert/ Reference/Caption.**

Your screen should be similar to Figure 3.50

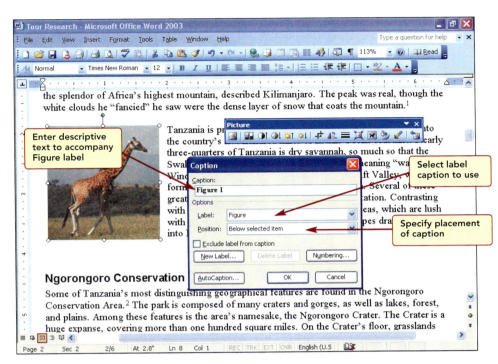

Figure 3.50

The Caption options are described in the following table.

Option	Description
Label	Select from one of three default captions: Table, Figure, or Equation.
Position	Specify the location of the caption, either above or below a selected item. When an item is selected, the Position option is available.
New Label	Create your own captions.
Numbering	Specify the numbering format and starting number for your caption.
AutoCaption	Turns on the automatic insertion of a caption (label and number only) when you insert selected items into your document.

The default caption label, Figure, followed by the number 1 because it is the first figure in this document, appears in the Caption text box. You want to use this caption and to add additional descriptive text. The default setting of "Below selected item" is also correct.

2 In the Caption text box, following "Figure 1," type **- Giraffe in Serengeti**.

● Click [OK].

Your screen should be similar to Figure 3.51

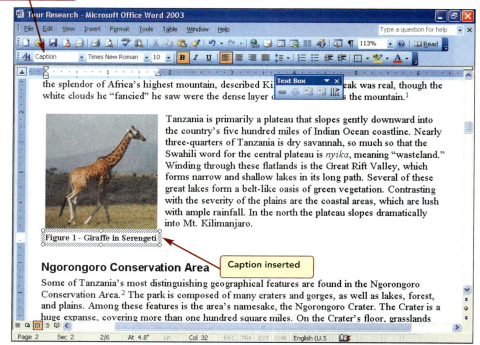

Style applied to caption text

Caption inserted

Figure 3.51

The caption label appears below the figure. It is inserted as a text box, a container for text and other graphic objects, that can be moved like any other object.

Adding a Cross-Reference

In the Animal Life section of the report, you discuss the animals found in the Serengeti. You want to include a cross-reference to the picture at this location.

While working in long documents, it is helpful to split the document window into two separate viewing areas.

Concept 6

Splitting Windows

6 To view different parts of the document at the same time, you can create a **split window** by dividing the document window into two horizontal sections. Each section is displayed in a pane that can be scrolled and manipulated independently. You can also display the document in different views in each pane. For example, you can display the document in Print Layout view in one pane and Normal view in the other.

Splitting the document window is most useful for viewing different sections of the document at the same time and allows you to quickly switch between panes to access information in the different sections without having to repeatedly scroll to the areas.

You will split the document window so you can see the figure you will reference in the upper pane and the text area where you will enter the cross-reference in the lower pane. When you create a split, the location of the split can be adjusted by dragging the pane divider line.

1 ● Click outside the text box to deselect it.

● Choose **W**indow/**S**plit.

● Drag the split bar to the position shown in Figure 3.52.

● Click to position the split at that location.

Another Method

You can also drag the split box located above the vertical scroll bar to create a split.

Your screen should be similar to Figure 3.52

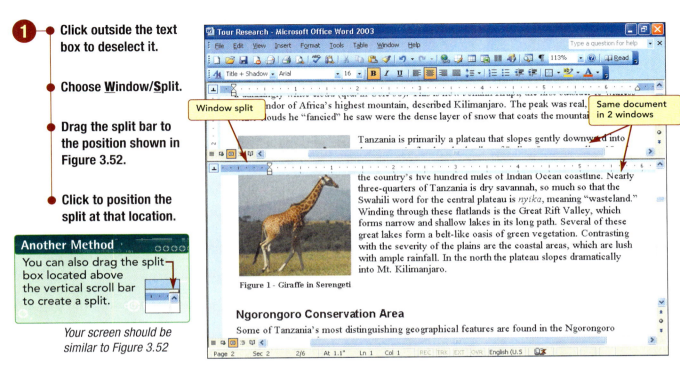

Figure 3.52

The document is divided into two horizontal panes. Next, you will scroll the document in the panes to display the areas you want to view. While using panes, the insertion point and the ruler are displayed in the active pane or the pane in which you are currently working.

2 ● Scroll the upper pane to display the Figure 1 caption below the giraffe picture.

● Scroll the lower pane to display the third paragraph in the Tanzania Animal Life section (page 3, section 2).

Your screen should be similar to Figure 3.53

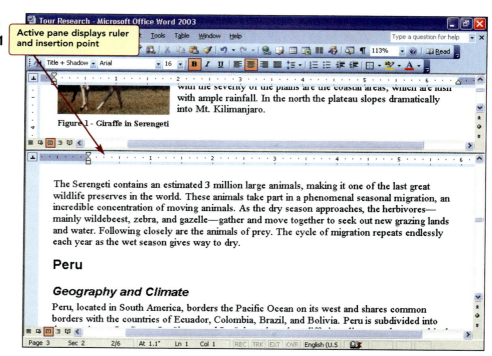

Figure 3.53

Now you can conveniently see both areas of the document while you enter the cross reference.

3 ● Move to after the word "water" (before the period) in the third paragraph in the Tanzania Animal Life section.

● Press [Spacebar].

● Type (see and press [Spacebar].

● Choose Insert/ Reference/Cross-reference.

Your screen should be similar to Figure 3.54

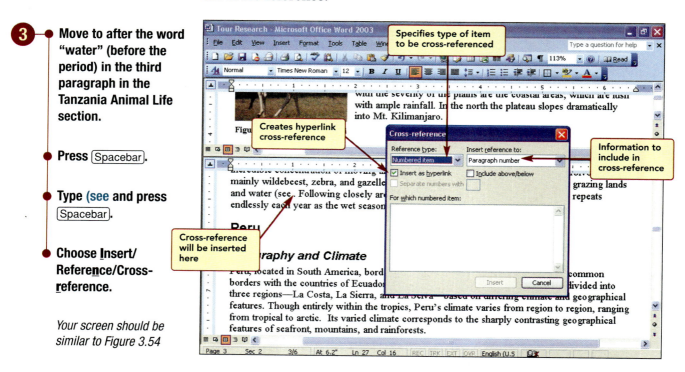

Figure 3.54

In the Cross-reference dialog box, you specify the type of item you are referencing and how you want the reference to appear. You want to reference the giraffe picture, and you want only the label "Figure 1" entered in the document.

4 From the Reference Type drop-down list box, select Figure.

From the Insert Reference To drop-down list box, select Only label and number.

Your screen should be similar to Figure 3.55

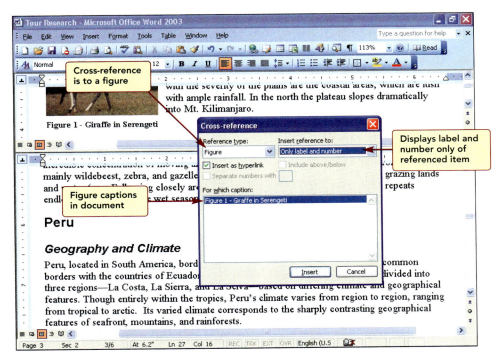

Figure 3.55

The For Which Caption list box lists all figure captions in the document. Because this document has only one figure caption, the correct figure caption is already selected. Notice that the Insert as Hyperlink option is selected by default. This option creates a hyperlink between the cross-reference and the caption. The default setting is appropriate.

5 Click **Insert**.

Click **Close**.

Type **)**.

Click on the Figure 1 cross-reference.

Your screen should be similar to Figure 3.56

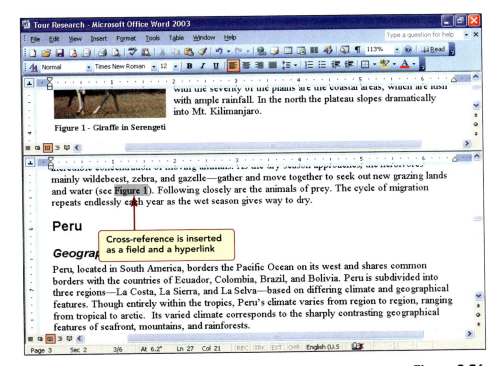

Figure 3.56

The cross-reference to Figure 1 is entered into the document as a field. Therefore, if you insert another picture or item that is cross-referenced, the captions and cross-references will renumber automatically. If you edit, delete, or move cross-referenced items, you should manually update the cross-references using Update Field. When you are working on a long document with several figures, tables, and graphs, this feature is very helpful.

Using a Cross-Reference Hyperlink

The cross-reference field is also a hyperlink, and just like a table of contents field, can be used to jump to the source it references.

1 ● **Hold down** Ctrl **and click on the Figure 1 cross-reference.**

Your screen should be similar to Figure 3.57

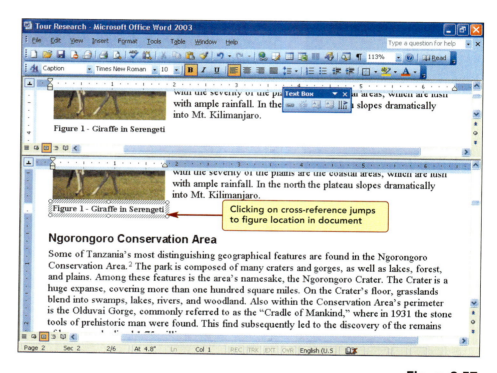

Figure 3.57

The document in the lower pane jumped to the caption beneath the figure. You will clear the split and save the document next.

2 ● **Choose** <u>W</u>indow/Remove <u>S</u>plit.

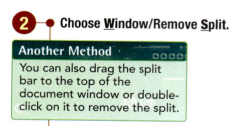

Another Method

You can also drag the split bar to the top of the document window or double-click on it to remove the split.

● **Save the document.**

The split is removed and the document window returns to a single pane.

Creating a Simple Table

Next, you want to add a table comparing the rainfall and temperature data for the three regions of Peru.

Concept 7

Table

7 A **table** is used to organize information into an easy-to-read format of horizontal rows and vertical columns. The insertion of a row and column creates a **cell** in which you can enter data or other information. Cells in a table are identified by a letter and number, called a **table reference**. Columns are identified from left to right beginning with the letter A, and rows are numbered from top to bottom beginning with the number 1. The table reference of the top leftmost cell is A1 because it is in the first column (A) and first row (1) of the table. The second cell in column 2 is cell B2. The fourth cell in column 3 is C4.

	A	B	C	D	E
1	(A1)	Jan	Feb	Mar	Total
2	East	7 (B2)	7	5	19
3	West	6	4	7	17
4	South	8	7 (C4)	9	24
5	Total	21	18	21	60

Tables are a very effective method for presenting information. The table layout organizes the information for readers and greatly reduces the number of words they have to read to interpret the data. Use tables whenever you can to make your documents easier to read.

The table you want to create will display columns for regions, rainfall, and temperature. The rows will display the data for each region. Your completed table will be similar to the one shown below.

Region	Annual Rainfall (Inches)	Average Temperature (Fahrenheit)
La Costa	2	68
La Sierra	35	54
La Selva	137	80

Inserting a Table

Word includes several different methods you can use to create tables. One method (Table/Convert/Text to Table) will quickly convert text that is arranged in tabular columns into a table. Another uses the Draw Table feature to create any type of table, but is most useful for creating complex tables that contain cells of different heights or a varying number of columns per row. The third method, which you will use, initially creates a simple table consisting of the same number of rows and columns.

1 ● **Click La Selva in the Document map.**

● **Close the Document map.**

● **Move to the second line of blank space below the paragraph on La Selva.**

● **Click**  **Insert Table (on the Standard toolbar).**

Your screen should be similar to Figure 3.58

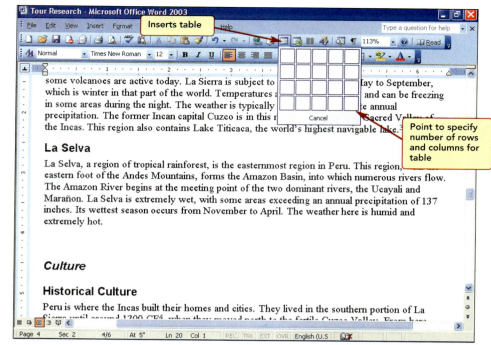

Figure 3.58

The Insert Table drop-down menu displays a grid in which you specify the number of rows and columns for the table. Moving the mouse pointer over the grid highlights the boxes in the grid and defines the table size. The dimensions are reflected in the bottom of the grid.

2 ● **Point to the boxes in Insert Table drop-down grid to highlight a 3-by-3 section.**

● **Click on the lower right corner of the selection.**

Your screen should be similar to Figure 3.59

Table of rows and columns is inserted →

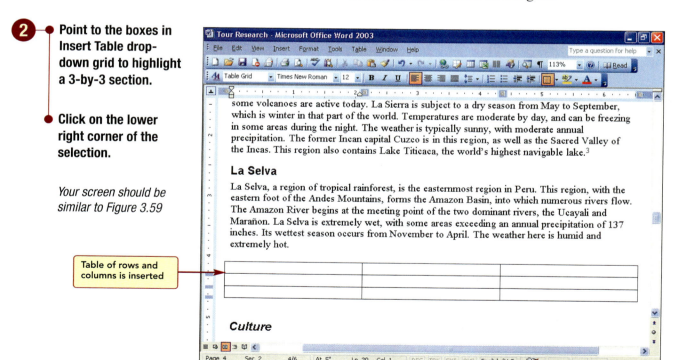

Figure 3.59

A table the full width of the page is drawn. It has equal sized columns and is surrounded by a black borderline.

Entering Data in a Table

Now you are ready to enter information in the table. Each cell contains a single line space where you can enter data. You can move from one cell to another by using the arrow keys or by clicking on the cell. In addition, you can use the keys shown in the table below to move around a table.

To Move To	Press
Next cell in row	Tab
Previous cell in row	Shift + Tab
First cell in row	Alt + Home
Last cell in row	Alt + End
First cell in column	Alt + Page Up
Last cell in column	Alt + Page Down
Previous row	↑
Next row	↓

The mouse pointer may also appear as a solid black arrow when pointing to the table. When it is a ↓, you can click to select the entire column. When it is ↗, you can click to select a cell. You will learn more about this feature shortly.

You will begin by entering the information for La Costa in cells A1 through C1. You can type in the cell as you would anywhere in a normal document.

1 ● **If necessary, click cell A1.**

● **Type La Costa.**

● **Press [Tab⇥].**

● **In the same manner, type 2 in cell B1 and 68 in cell C1.**

● **Continue entering the information shown below, using [Tab⇥] to move to the next cell.**

Cell	Entry
A2	La Sierra
B2	35
C2	54
A3	La Selva
B3	137
C3	80

Your screen should be similar to Figure 3.60

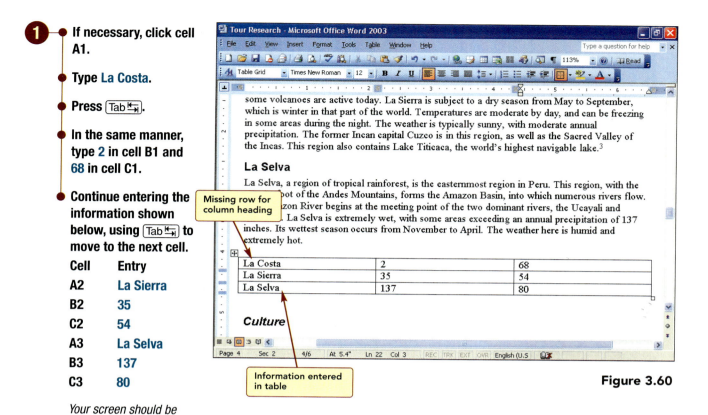

Figure 3.60

Inserting a Row

After looking at the table, you realize you forgot to include a row above the data to display the column headings.

1 ● **Move to any cell in row 1.**

● **Choose Table/Insert/Rows Above.**

● **Click in the new row to deselect the row.**

Your screen should be similar to Figure 3.61

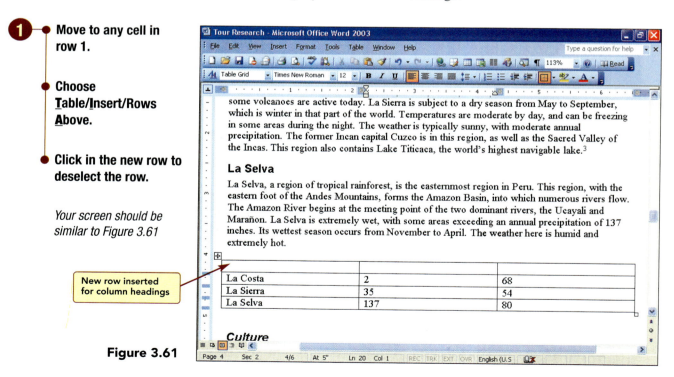

Figure 3.61

Now, you are ready to add the text for the headings.

2 In cell A1 type **Region**.

In cell B1 type **Annual Rainfall**.

Press ⟵Enter to insert a second line in the cell.

Type **(Inches)**.

In cell C1 type **Average Temperature** on the first line and **(Fahrenheit)** on the second.

Your screen should be similar to Figure 3.62

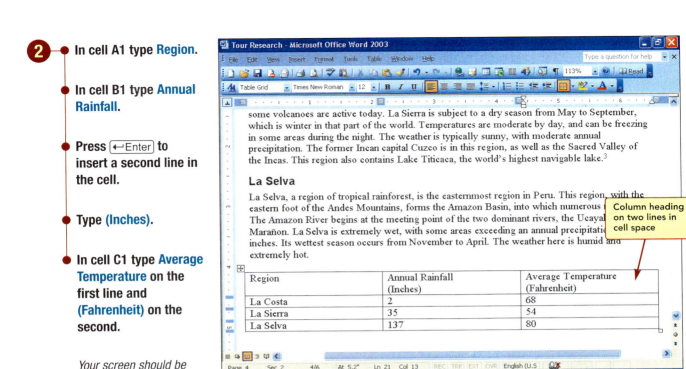

Figure 3.62

Sizing a Table

The table is much larger than it needs to be. To quickly reduce the overall table size, you can drag the resize handle □. This handle appears in the lower right corner whenever the mouse pointer rests over the table. Once the table is smaller, you will select the entire table by clicking the ⊞ move handle and center it between the margins.

1 Drag the □ resize handle to decrease the width of the table to 5 inches (see Figure 3.63).

Click ⊞ to select the entire table.

Click ≡ Center.

Your screen should be similar to Figure 3.63

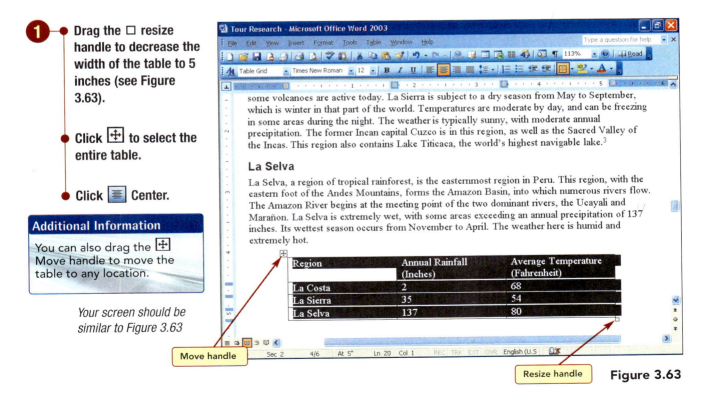

Figure 3.63

Formatting a Table

To enhance the appearance of the table, you can apply many different formats to the cells. This process is similar to adding formatting to a document, except that the formatting affects the selected cells only.

You want the entries in the cells A1 through C1, and B2 through C4, to be centered in their cell spaces. As you continue to modify the table, many cells can be selected and changed at the same time. You can select areas of a table using the Select command on the Table menu. However, it is often faster to use the procedures described in the table below.

Area to Select	Procedure
Cell	Click the left edge of the cell when the pointer is ↗.
Row	Click to the left of the row when the pointer is ↗.
Column	Click the top of the column when the pointer is ↓.
Multiple cells, rows, or columns	Drag through the cells, rows, or columns when the pointer is ↓, or select the first cell, row, or column and hold down ⇧ Shift while clicking on another cell, row, or column.
Contents of next cell	Press Tab ⇄.
Contents of previous cell	Press ⇧ Shift + Tab ⇄.
Entire table	Press Alt + 5 (on the numeric keypad with NumLock off) or click ⊞.

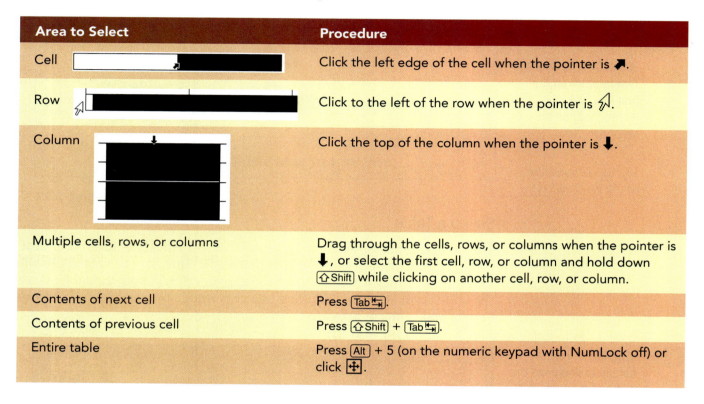

1 Select cells A1 through C1.

Click ≣ Center.

In the same manner, center cells B2 through C4.

Click on any cell of the table.

Your screen should be similar to Figure 3.64

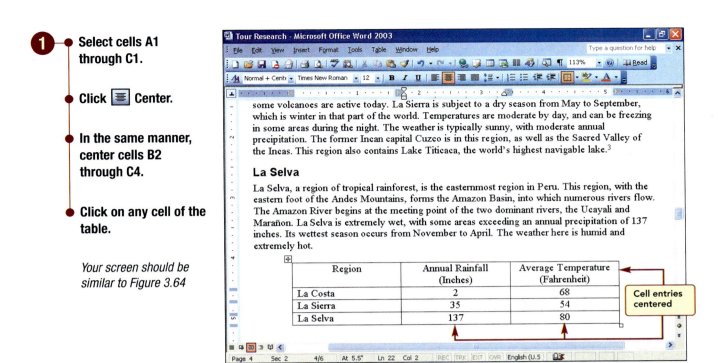

Figure 3.64

A quicker way to apply formats to a table is to use the table AutoFormat feature. This feature includes built-in combinations of formats that can be applied to a table. The AutoFormats consist of a combination of fonts, colors, patterns, borders, and alignment settings.

2 Choose Table/Table AutoFormat.

Your screen should be similar to Figure 3.65

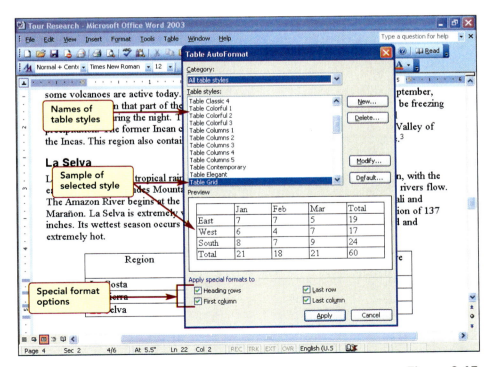

Figure 3.65

From the AutoFormat dialog box, you select the format design you want to apply to the table. The Table Grid style is the default selection. In addition, all the sections of the table that will receive special formatting, such as the heading row and last row, are selected. These settings allow you to emphasize different areas of the table, such as the last row and column where total values are frequently displayed. The Preview area shows how the selected format will look.

Since this table does not include any special information in the last column or the last row, you do not want any special formats applied to them.

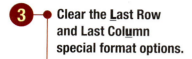

- Clear the **L**ast Row and Last Col**u**mn special format options.

- Select several names from the Table styles list and look at the samples in the Preview box.

- Select Table Colorful 1.

- Click  Apply .

- Select the table and center it again.

- Click outside the table to deselect it.

- Click 💾 Save.

Your screen should be similar to Figure 3.66

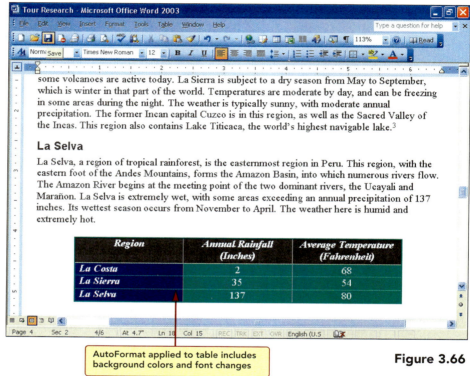

AutoFormat applied to table includes background colors and font changes

Figure 3.66

The table is reformatted to the new design. Different color backgrounds are applied to the entire table along with a change in the text color and italics. Using AutoFormat was much faster than applying these features individually.

Sorting a List

The last page of the report contains the list of works cited in the report. According to the MLA style, each work directly referenced in the paper must appear in alphabetical order by author's last name. Additionally, they must be formatted as hanging indents—the first line is even with the left margin, and subsequent lines of the same work are indented .5 inch. This page needs to be alphabetized and formatted. To quickly arrange the references in alphabetical order, you can sort the list.

8   Word can quickly arrange or **sort** text, numbers, or data in lists or tables in alphabetical, numeric, or date order based on the first character in each paragraph. The sort order can be ascending (A to Z, 0 to 9, or earliest to latest date) or descending (Z to A, 9 to 0, or latest to earliest date). The following table describes the rules that are used when sorting.

Sort By	Rules
Text	First, items beginning with punctuation marks or symbols (such as !, #, $, %, or &) are sorted.
	Second, items beginning with numbers are sorted. Dates are treated as three-digit numbers.
	Third, items beginning with letters are sorted.
Numbers	All characters except numbers are ignored. The numbers can be in any location in a paragraph.
Date	Valid date separators include hyphens, forward slashes (/), commas, and periods. Colons (:) are valid time separators. If unable to recognize a date or time, Word places the item at the beginning or end of the list (depending on whether you are sorting in ascending or descending order).
Field results	If an entire field (such as a last name) is the same for two items, Word next evaluates subsequent fields (such as a first name) according to the specified sort options.

When a tie occurs, Word uses the first nonidentical character in each item to determine which item should come first.

First you will change the format of the list of works to hanging indent and then you will rearrange the order. You will use the default Sort Text settings that will sort by text and paragraphs in ascending order.

1
- Move to the last page of the document.
- Select the list of references.
- Drag the ⬚ Hanging Indent marker on the ruler to the .5 inch position.

Having Trouble?
Click and drag on the triangle section of the Hanging Indent marker.

Another Method
You could also apply the Body Text Indent style or press Ctrl + T to create hanging indents.

- Choose Table/Sort.
- Click [OK].
- Deselect the list of references.

Your screen should be similar to Figure 3.67

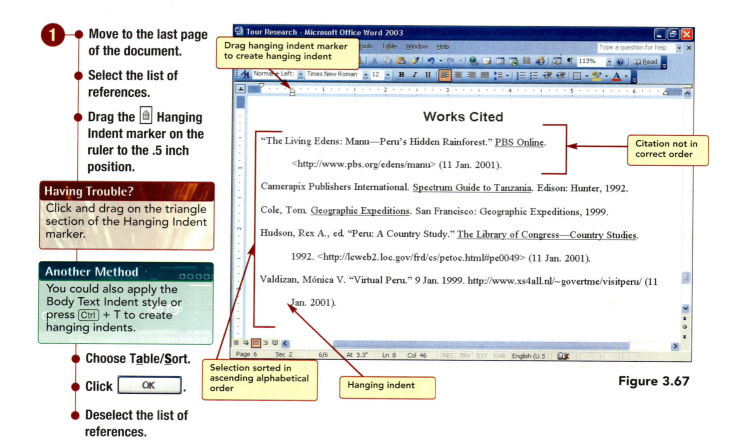

Drag hanging indent marker to create hanging indent

Citation not in correct order

Selection sorted in ascending alphabetical order

Hanging indent

Figure 3.67

The list is in ascending alphabetical order. Entries that are longer than one line appear with a hanging indent. Notice, however, that the citation for "The Living Edens . . ." is still at the top of this list. This is because Word sorts punctuation first. You will need to move this item to below the citation for Hudson.

2
- Select the entire "The Living Edens . . ." citation and drag it to below the Hudson citation.

Your screen should be similar to Figure 3.68

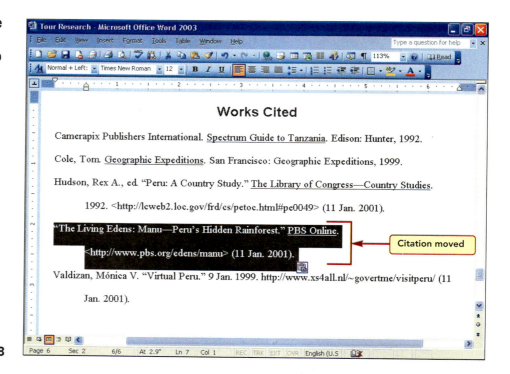

Citation moved

Figure 3.68

Creating Headers and Footers

Next you want to add information in a header and footer to the report.

Concept 9
Header and Footer

9 Headers and footers provide information that typically appears at the top and bottom of each page in a document and helps the reader locate information in a document. A **header** is a line or several lines of text in the top margin of each page. The header usually contains the title and the section of the document. A **footer** is a line or several lines of text in the margin space at the bottom of every page. The footer usually contains the page number and perhaps the date. Headers and footers can also contain graphics, such as a company logo.

The same header and footer can be used throughout a document, or a different header and footer can be used in different sections of a document. For example, a unique header or footer can be used in one section and a different one in another section. You can also have a unique header or footer on the first page, or omitted entirely from the first page, or use a different header and footer on odd and even pages.

Adding a Header

You want the report header to display your name and the page number.

1 Move to the Tanzania heading on page 2.

Choose **V**iew/**H**eader and Footer.

Your screen should be similar to Figure 3.69

Header begins .5 inches from top edge of page

Header area active so you can enter text

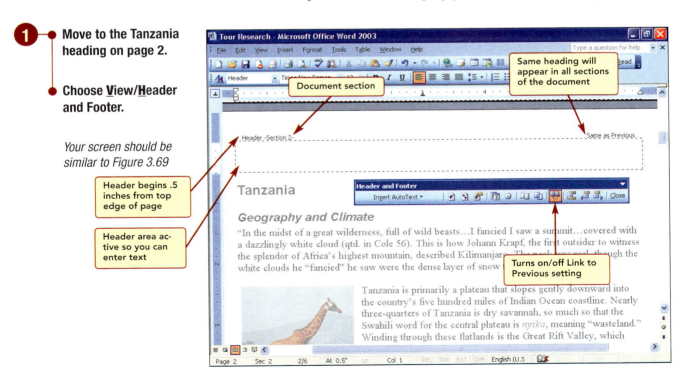

Figure 3.69

The document dims, and the header area becomes active. The Header and Footer toolbar is automatically displayed. Its buttons, identified below, are used to add items to the header and footer and to navigate between headers and footers.

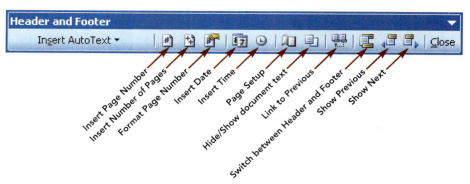

Notice that the information above the header area identifies the section location of the document where the insertion point is positioned, in this case, section 2. In addition, in the upper right corner the message "Same as Previous" is displayed. When this setting is on, the header in the sections before and after the section in which you are entering a header will have the same header. Because you do not want the title page in section 1 to have a header, you will break the connection between sections by turning off this option.

2 ● Click  **Link to Previous.**

Your screen should be similar to Figure 3.70

Additional Information

MLA style requires that headers and footers be placed .5 inch from the top and bottom of the page. This is the default layout for the normal document. The header includes the page number preceded by the author's name.

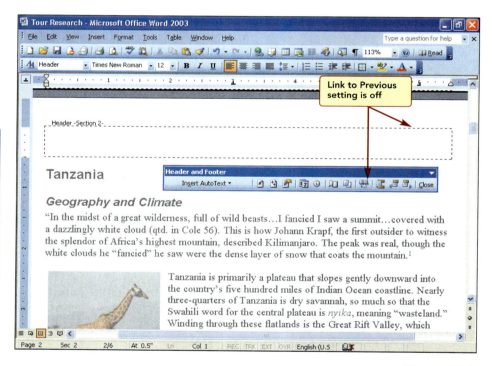

Figure 3.70

You type in the header as if it were a mini-document. The header and footer text can be formatted just like any other text. In addition, you can control the placement of the header and footer text by specifying its alignment: left-aligned, centered, or right-aligned in the header or footer space. You will enter your name followed by the page number, right-aligned.

3 • Type **your name**.

• Press [Spacebar].

• Click [#] **Insert Page Number**.

• Click [≡] **Align Right**.

Your screen should be similar to Figure 3.71

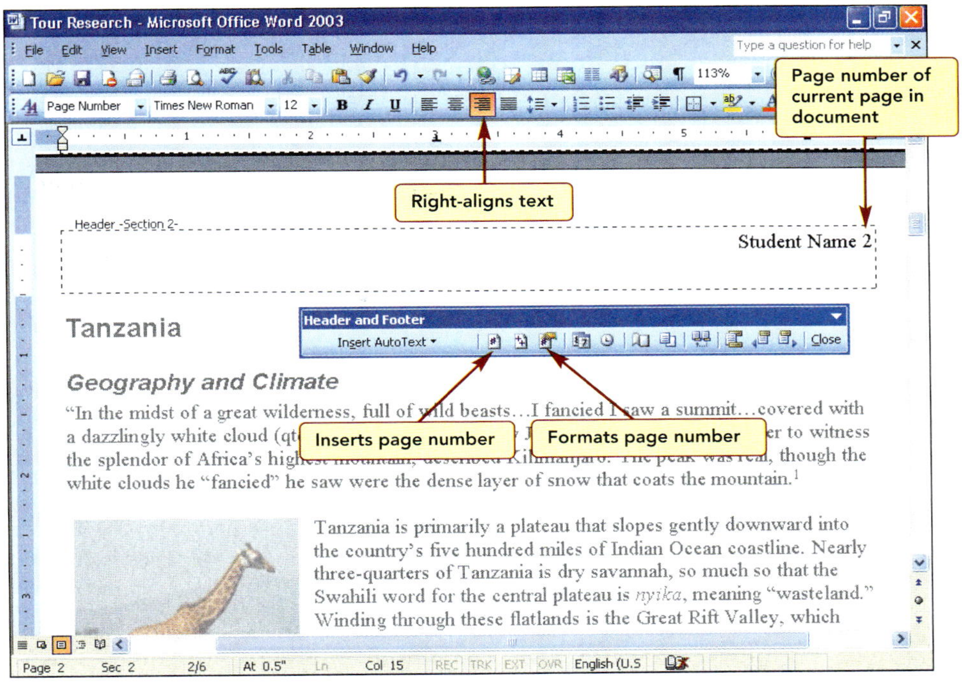

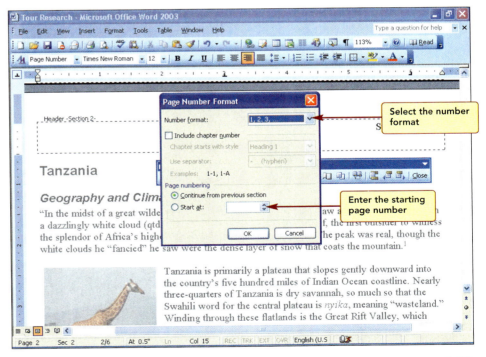

Figure 3.71

The page number "2" is displayed, because that is the current page in the document. You do not want the title page included in the page numbering, but instead want to begin page numbering with the first page of section 2.

4 • Click [📄] **Format Page Number**.

Your screen should be similar to Figure 3.72

Figure 3.72

The Page Number Format dialog box is used to change the format of page numbers, to include chapter numbers, and to change the page numbering sequence. The default page numbering setting continues the numbering from the first section. You will reset the page number sequence to begin section 2 with page 1.

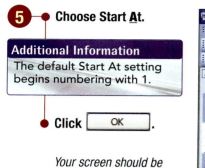

5 ● Choose Start **At**.

Additional Information
The default Start At setting begins numbering with 1.

● Click [OK].

Your screen should be similar to Figure 3.73

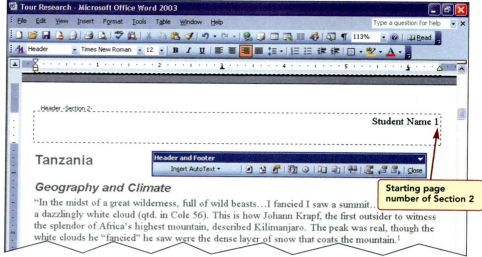

Figure 3.73

The header now displays "1" as the current page number.

Adding a Footer

You want to display the date in the footer. To quickly add this information, you will use an AutoText entry.

1 ● Click 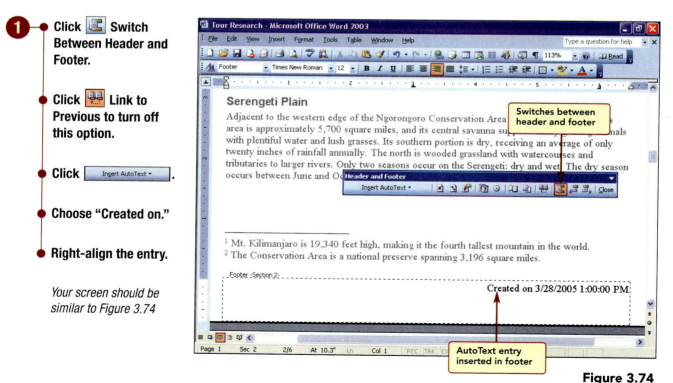 Switch Between Header and Footer.

● Click [icon] Link to Previous to turn off this option.

● Click [Insert AutoText ▾].

● Choose "Created on."

● Right-align the entry.

Your screen should be similar to Figure 3.74

Figure 3.74

The AutoText entry is displayed followed by the date and time.

2 ● Close the Header and Footer toolbar.

● In section 2, scroll down to see the bottom of page 1 and the top of page 2.

Your screen should be similar to Figure 3.75

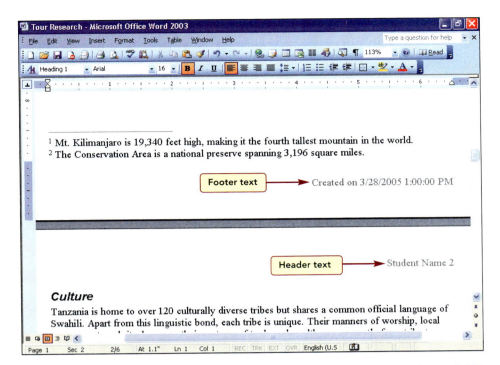

¹ Mt. Kilimanjaro is 19,340 feet high, making it the fourth tallest mountain in the world.
² The Conservation Area is a national preserve spanning 3,196 square miles.

Footer text ──→ Created on 3/28/2005 1:00:00 PM

Header text ──→ Student Name 2

Culture

Tanzania is home to over 120 culturally diverse tribes but shares a common official language of Swahili. Apart from this linguistic bond, each tribe is unique. Their manners of worship, local

Figure 3.75

The document area is active again, and the header and footer text appears dimmed. The header and footer can only be seen in Print Layout view and when the document is printed.

Checking the Document

Before you print the report, you want to quickly read the entire document. You will do this using the Reading Layout view. Then you will do a final check for spelling and grammar errors in the document, including the footnotes, header, and footer. You also want to check the formatting of the document for consistency. Many times when creating a long document, it is easy to format areas differently that should be formatted the same. For example, if your headings are mostly formatted as Heading 2 styles, but you accidentally format a heading with a Heading 3 style, Word can locate the inconsistent formatting and quickly make the appropriate correction for you. Using the formatting consistency checker can give your documents a more professional appearance.

Using Reading Layout View

To make documents easier to read, Word includes a Reading Layout view that displays the document like pages in a book.

1 ● **Click** [📖 Read].

Another Method

You can also check ▢ in the scrollbar or press [Alt] + R to switch to Reading Layout view.

● **If necessary, click** ▢ **Allow Multiple Pages to display two screen pages.**

● **If the Document Map is displayed, click** [Document Map] **to close it.**

Your screen should be similar to Figure 3.76

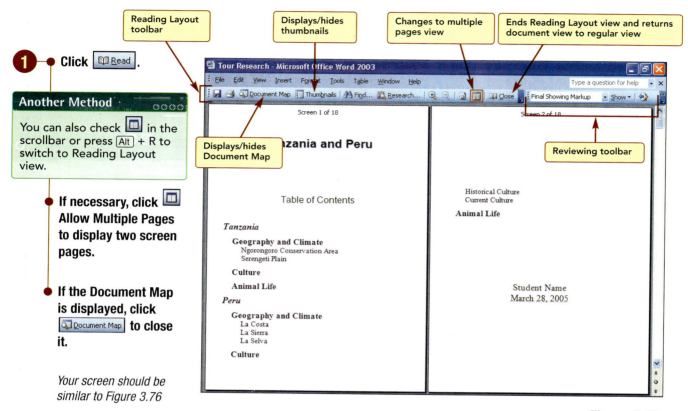

Figure 3.76

The body of the document is displayed as screen pages that are sized to fit your screen and that are easy to browse. These pages do not represent the pages you would see when you print the document. Because Reading Layout view is not designed for editing and creating a document, unnecessary features, such as the Standard and Formatting toolbars and the status bar, are hidden to provide more space on the screen to display the document in pages.

The Reading Layout toolbar is displayed and contains buttons to access reading-related activities. In addition the Reviewing toolbar is displayed and includes features to help you to annotate the document with comments and highlighting.

Using Reading Layout view you can quickly review the entire manuscript as if reading a book. You can use the scroll bar to browse the document two screen pages at a time. To jump quickly to different sections of the document you can display the Document Map. You can also display thumbnail images of each screen page in a separate pane and click on the thumbnail to display that page. A single page is displayed when thumbnails or the Document Map are displayed.

2 • Click the ▾ scroll arrow several times to read several pages of the document.

• Click 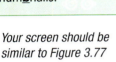.

• Click on thumbnail image 8.

Your screen should be similar to Figure 3.77

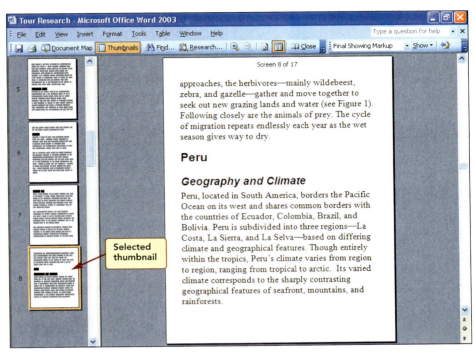

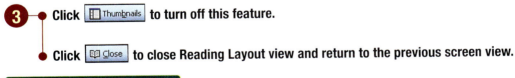

Figure 3.77

The selected thumbnail is surrounded by a gold border and the selected screen page is displayed.

3 • Click 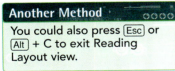 to turn off this feature.

• Click 📖 Close to close Reading Layout view and return to the previous screen view.

Redisplaying Spelling and Grammar Errors

Now you will turn on the display of spelling and grammar errors again and then spell and grammar check the document.

1 ● Move to the top of page 1 of section 2.

● Choose **T**ools/**O**ptions/Spelling and Grammar.

● Clear the checkmark from Hide **s**pelling errors in this document.

● Clear the checkmark from Hi**d**e grammatical errors in this document.

● Click [OK].

● Click [🗹] Spelling and Grammar.

● Choose **I**gnore All for all proper names, special terms and abbreviations. Respond appropriately to any other located errors.

● Click [OK] to end spelling and grammar checking.

Your screen should be similar to Figure 3.78

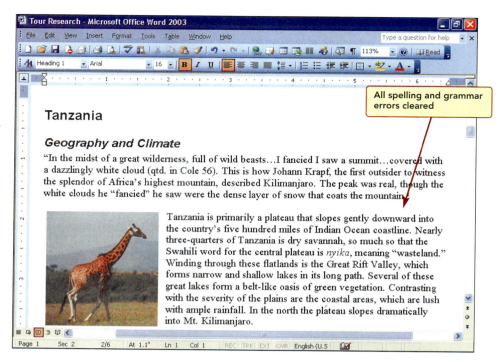

Figure 3.78

The Spelling and Grammar Checker first checked the document text for errors, then footnotes, and finally headers and footers.

Checking Formatting Inconsistencies

Next, you will turn on the Formatting Consistency Checker feature to check for formatting inconsistencies. Word identifies inconsistencies with a blue wavy underline.

1 **Choose Tools/Options.**

From the Edit tab, select Mark formatting inconsistencies.

Click OK .

Right-click on the word Nyika in the second paragraph.

Your screen should be similar to Figure 3.79

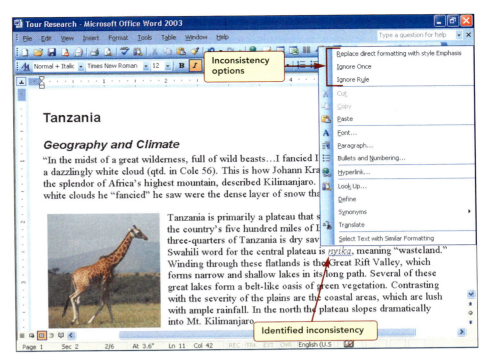

Figure 3.79

The first identified formatting inconsistency is for the italics applied to the word "nyika." When checking for formatting inconsistencies, Word looks for occurrences of similar formatting that you have applied directly to text, of styles that contain additional direct formatting, and of direct formatting that matches styles that are applied elsewhere in the document. If two occurrences of formatting are markedly different, then they are not identified as inconsistent. However, in cases where the formatting is very similar, they are identified as inconsistent. In this case, the identified inconsistency is because the formatting was applied directly to the word using the italics feature, and the same result could be obtained by using the style Emphasis. Because changing this formatting will not affect the appearance of the word, you will ignore the suggestion.

2 • Choose **I**gnore Once.

• Scroll to page 4 to see the next located occurrence in the Machu Picchu heading.

• Right-click on Machu Picchu.

Your screen should be similar to Figure 3.80

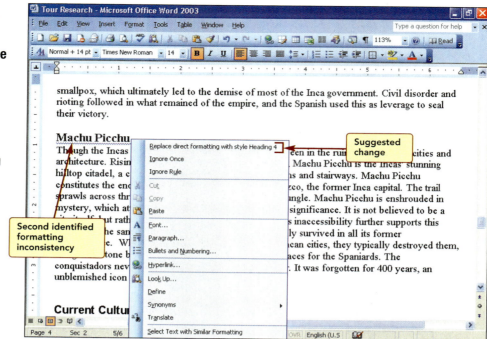

Figure 3.80

The suggested change is to replace the direct formatting of this text (14 points and bold) with the equivalent heading style. Because you want the topic to appear in the table of contents, you will replace the formatting with the Heading 4 style. Then you will move to the last located inconsistency.

3 • Choose **R**eplace direct formatting with style Heading 4.

• Move to the Works Cited page.

• Right-click on the Works Cited title.

• Right-click on any of the referenced works.

Your screen should be similar to Figure 3.81

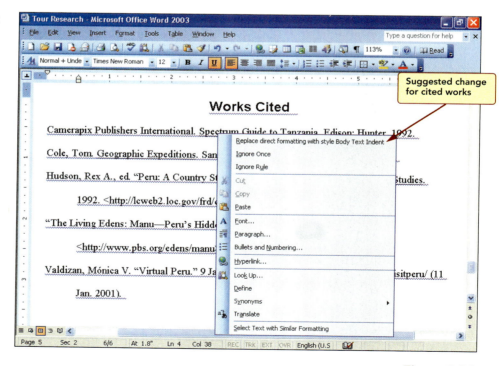

Figure 3.81

The suggested change for all the cited works is to use the Body Text Indent style. You will not make this change since it will not affect the appearance of the text. The suggested style change for the title was to use the Title style. In this case, you want to change it to a Heading 1 style so it will appear in the table of contents. You will need to make this change directly.

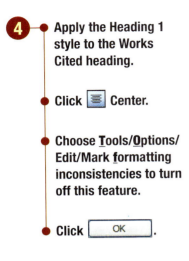

4 ● Apply the Heading 1 style to the Works Cited heading.

● Click ▤ Center.

● Choose **T**ools/**O**ptions/ Edit/Mark **f**ormatting inconsistencies to turn off this feature.

● Click OK .

Your screen should be similar to Figure 3.82

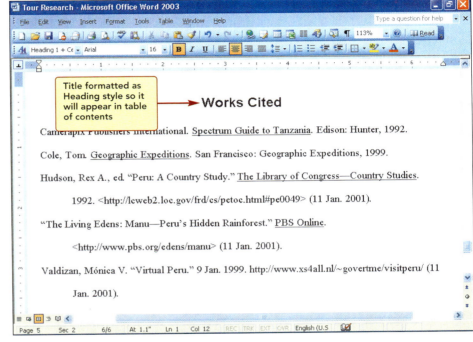

Figure 3.82

Updating a Table of Contents

You have made many modifications to the report since generating the table of contents, so you want to update the listing. Because the table of contents is a field, if you add or remove headings, rearrange topics, or make other changes that affect the table of contents listing, you can quickly update the table of contents. In this case, you have added pictures and a table that may have affected the paging of the document, and you changed two headings to heading styles. You will update the table of contents to ensure that the page references are accurate and that all headings are included.

1 • Move to the top of the document.

• Right-click on the table of contents to display the shortcut menu.

• Choose **U**pdate Field.

Another Method

You can also press F9 to quickly update a field.

• Choose Update **e**ntire table.

• Click [OK] .

• Click outside the table of contents to deselect it.

• Scroll the window to see the entire table of contents.

Your screen should be similar to Figure 3.83

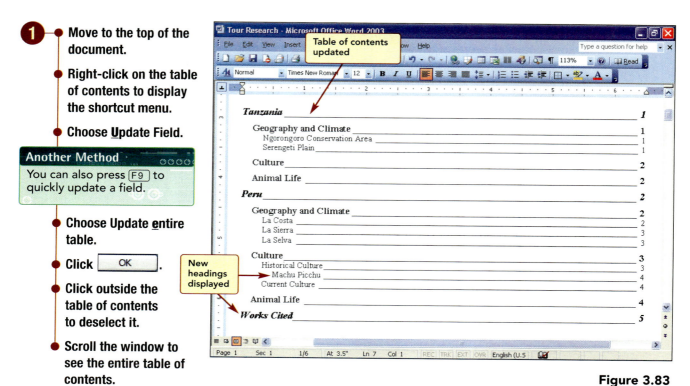

Figure 3.83

The page numbers referenced by each table-of-contents hyperlink have been updated as needed and the two new topics are listed.

Printing Selected Pages

You are now ready to print the report.

1 • Click 🖫 Save.

• Print preview the report.

• Click 🎛 Multiple Pages and select 2x3 Pages to display six pages.

Another Method

The menu equivalent is **V**iew/**Z**oom/**M**any Pages.

Your screen should be similar to Figure 3.84

Figure 3.84

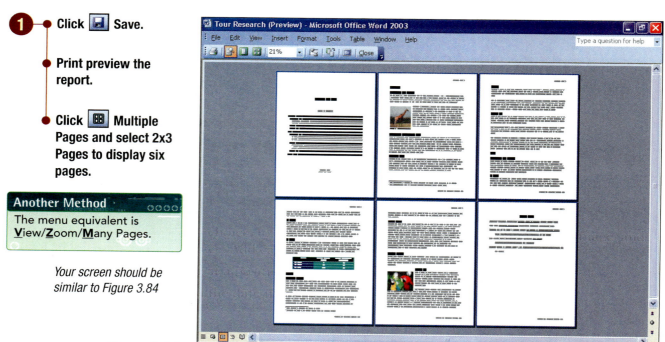

You would like to print only the first, second, fourth, and sixth pages of the document. To do this, you use the Print dialog box to select the pages you want to print. When printing pages in different sections, the page number and section number (p#s#) must be identified in the page range.

2 ● Choose File/Print.

● If necessary, select the appropriate printer for your computer system.

● Type p1s1, p1s2, p3s2, p5s2 in the Pages text box.

● Click [OK].

● Click [▣] One Page to return the preview display to a single page.

● Close Print Preview.

● Change to Normal view, if necessary, turn off Document Map, and set the zoom to 100%.

● Close the file and exit Word.

Your printed output should be similar to that shown in the Case Study at the beginning of the lab.

Focus on Careers

EXPLORE YOUR CAREER OPTIONS

Market Research Analyst

Have you ever wondered who investigates the market for new products? Ever thought about the people who put together phone surveys? Market research analysts are responsible for determining the potential sales for a new product or service. They conduct surveys and compile statistics for clients or their employer. These reports usually include report features like a table of contents, cross-references, headers and footers, and footnotes for references. Market research analysts may hold positions as faculty at a university, work for large organizations, or hold governmental positions. The salary range for market research analysts is $37,000 to $52,000 and demand is high in a strong economy.

Concept Summary

LAB 3
Creating Reports and Tables

Style (WD3.7)

Applying a style, a predefined set of formatting characteristics, to a selection allows you to quickly apply a whole group of formats in one simple step.

Section (WD3.33)

To format different parts of a document differently, you can divide a document into sections.

Footnote and Endnote (WD3.37)

A footnote is a source reference or text offering additional explanation that is placed at the bottom of a page. An endnote is also a source reference or long comment that typically appears at the end of a document.

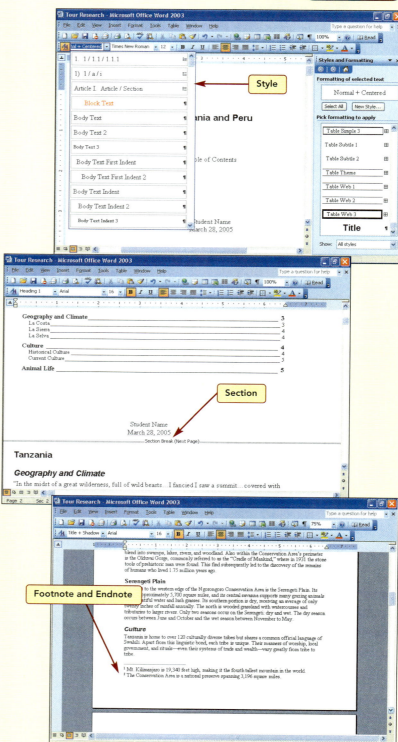

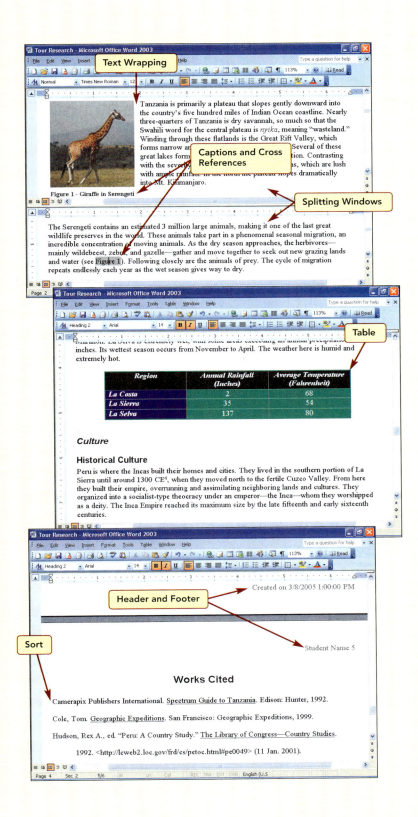

Text Wrapping (WD3.45)

You can control the appearance of text around a graphic object by specifying the text wrapping style.

Captions and Cross References (WD3.48)

A caption is a numbered label for a figure, table, picture, or graph. A cross-reference is a reference from one part of a document to related information in another part.

Splitting Windows (WD3.50)

To view different parts of the document at the same time you can create a split window by dividing the document window into two horizontal sections.

Table (WD3.55)

A table is used to organize information into an easy-to-read format of horizontal rows and vertical columns.

Sort (WD3.63)

Word can quickly arrange or sort text, numbers, or data in lists or tables in alphabetical, numeric, or date order based on the first character in each paragraph.

Header and Footer (WD3.65)

A header is a line or several lines of text in the top margin of each page. A footer is a line or several lines of text in the margin space at the bottom of every page.

lab review

LAB **3**

Creating Reports and Tables

key terms

caption   WD3.48
cell   WD3.55
Click and Type   WD3.18
cross-reference   WD3.48
Document Map   WD3.30
drawing layer   WD3.45
endnote   WD3.37
floating object   WD3.45
footer   WD3.65

footnote   WD3.37
header   WD3.65
heading style   WD3.7
inline object   WD3.45
note pane   WD3.38
note reference mark   WD3.37
note separator   WD3.37
note text   WD3.37
section   WD3.33

section break   WD3.33
sort   WD3.63
split window   WD3.50
style   WD3.7
table   WD3.55
table reference   WD3.55
text box   WD3.15
text wrapping   WD3.45

mos skills

The Microsoft Office Specialist (MOS) certification program is designed to measure your proficiency in performing basic tasks using the Office 2003 applications. Getting certified demonstrates that you have the skills and provides a valuable industry credential for employment. After completing this lab, you have learned the following Microsoft Office Word Specialist skills:

Skill	Description	Page
Creating Content	Insert frequently used and predefined text	WD3.68
Organizing Content	Insert and modify tables	WD3.55
	Create bulleted and numbered lists and outlines	WD3.4
Formatting Content	Format text	WD3.7
	Insert and modify content in headers and footers	WD3.65
	Modify document layout and page setup	WD3.34
Formatting and	Organize documents using file folders	WD3.14
	Print documents, envelopes, and labels	WD3.76
	Preview documents and Web pages	WD3.76
	Change and organize document views and windows	WD3.16, WD3.70

command summary

Command	Shortcut Keys	Button	Action
File/Page Set**u**p/**L**ayout/ **V**ertical Alignment			Aligns text vertically on a page
View/**D**ocument Map		▣	Displays or hides Document Map pane
View/Thum**b**nails		▤	Displays miniature representations of each page
View/**H**eader and Footer			Displays header and footer areas
View/Foot**n**otes			Hides or displays note pane
View/**Z**oom/**M**any Pages		▦	Displays two or more pages in document window
Insert/**B**reak/**N**ext Page			Inserts a section break
Insert/Page N**u**mbers			Specifies page number location
Insert/Refere**n**ce/Foot**n**ote	Alt + Ctrl + F		Inserts footnote reference at insertion point
Insert/Refere**n**ce/**C**aption			Creates figure captions
Insert/Refere**n**ce/Cross-**r**eference			Creates figure cross-reference
Insert/Refere**n**ce/In**d**ex and Tables/Table of **C**ontents			Generates a table of contents
F**o**rmat/P**i**cture/Layout/ Wrapping Style		▣	Specifies how text will wrap around picture
Tools/**O**ptions/Edit/Mark **F**ormatting Inconsistencies			Checks for formatting inconsistencies
Tools/**O**ptions/Spelling & Grammar			Changes settings associated with Spelling and Grammar checking feature
T**a**ble/**I**nsert Table		▦	Inserts table at insertion point
T**a**ble/**I**nsert/Rows **A**bove			Inserts a new row in table above selected row
T**a**ble/Sele**c**t			Selects different table objects
T**a**ble/Con**v**ert/Te**x**t to Table			Converts selected text to table format
T**a**ble/Table Auto**F**ormat			Applies predesigned formats to table
T**a**ble/**S**ort			Rearranges items in a selection into sorted order
Window/**S**plit			Divides a document into two horizontal sections

lab exercises

matching

Match the item on the left with the correct description on the right.

1. split window	_____	**a.**	combination of fonts, type sizes, bold, and italics used to identify different levels of headings in a document
2. table reference	_____	**b.**	divides document into two areas you can view and scroll independently
3. inline image	_____	**c.**	graphic positioned directly in the text
4. Document Map	_____	**d.**	feature used to quickly insert items in a blank area of a document
5. tight wrap	_____	**e.**	letter and number used to identify table cells
6. section break	_____	**f.**	uses headings to navigate through the document
7. cross-reference	_____	**g.**	text closely follows contours around a graphic
8. note pane	_____	**h.**	reference from one part of the document to another part
9. Click and Type	_____	**i.**	instructs Word to end one set of format settings and begin another
10. heading style	_____	**j.**	additional explanatory information at the bottom of a page
11. footnote			

multiple choice

Circle the correct response to the questions below.

1. A(n)_____ displays information in horizontal rows and vertical columns.
   a. Document Map
   b. cell reference
   c. object
   d. table

2. _____ are lines of text at the top and bottom of a page outside the margin lines.
   a. characters and paragraphs
   b. headers and footers
   c. tables and text wrappers
   d. styles and sections

3. A _____ allows you to see two parts of the same document at the same time.
   a. divided window
   b. split window
   c. sectioned window
   d. note pane

4. A _____ is inserted automatically when a new page is created in a document.
   a. hard page break
   b. section break
   c. soft page break
   d. page division

5. You can control how text appears around a graphic with _____ styles.
   a. sorting
   b. text wrapping
   c. section
   d. caption

6. A(n) _____ is a predesigned set of formats that can be applied to characters and paragraphs.
   a. AutoFormat
   b. effect
   c. style
   d. font

7. A _____ is a title or explanation for a table, picture, or graph.
   a. statement
   b. cross-reference
   c. caption
   d. footnote

8. A _____ is a reference from one part of a document to related information in another part of the same document.
   a. Document Map
   b. note
   c. heading
   d. cross-reference

9. Text sorted in _____ order appears alphabetically from A to Z.
   a. ordered
   b. descending
   c. ascending
   d. rescending

10. _____ displays a document like pages in a book.
   a. Reading Layout view
   b. Print preview
   c. Print Layout
   d. Multiple page view

lab exercises

true/false

Circle the correct answer to the following questions.

1. Paragraph styles are a combination of any character formats and paragraph formats that affect all text in a paragraph.   True   False
2. Word automatically applies styles to the text in an outline as it is entered.   True   False
3. AutoCaption selects one of three default captions.   True   False
4. The Document Preview pane displays the headings in your document.   True   False
5. The drawing layer is separate from the text in a document.   True   False
6. A section break identifies the end of a section and stores the document format settings.   True   False
7. When a tie occurs in a sort, Word sorts text by numerical characters.   True   False
8. A style is a combination of character formats.   True   False
9. A cross-reference can be placed within a document to refer back to a figure or other reference in the document.   True   False
10. An endnote is a source reference that typically appears at the end of a document.   True   False

fill-in

1. The _____ identifies the end of a section and stores the document format settings.

2. A(n) _____ is a set of formats that is assigned a name and can be quickly applied to a selection.

3. The _____ for a footnote appears at the bottom of the page on which the reference mark appears.

4. By changing a graphic to a(n) _____ it is inserted into the drawing layer.

5. The intersection of a row and column creates a(n) _____.

6. You can arrange, or _____, numbers or data in lists or tables in Word.

7. A(n) _____ is a line or several lines of text at the top of each page in a document.

8. A(n) _____ is used to organize information into horizontal rows and vertical columns.

9. _____ are source references or long comments that usually appear at the end of a document.

10. Specifying _____ controls how text appears around a graphic object.

Hands-On Exercises

step-by-step

Creating a Table ★

1. You work for the Animal Rescue Foundation and are putting together a list of the donation sites to give to local pet stores along with a map showing the location of each site. You would like to put the donation site list in a table. Your completed table is shown here.

   a. Open a new document and use Click and Type to enter the title **Animal Rescue Foundation Donation Sites** at the top of the document. Apply the Title style. Include a blank line below the title.

   b. Insert a simple table with 3 columns and 10 rows. Enter the following information into the table:

3	Pets 'R Us	Sally Lee
1	Reptile House	Suhas Daftuar
6	Exotic Bird Co.	Chirag Shah
5	Animal House	James Smith
4	Aimee's Pets	AJ Guerin
2	Aquarium Emporium	Mendi Gault
7	Cats & Kittens	Alicia McKellan
8	Fancy Fins	William Hertzler
10	Bird's the Word	Helen Bunch
9	Ma's Paws	Susanna Dickson

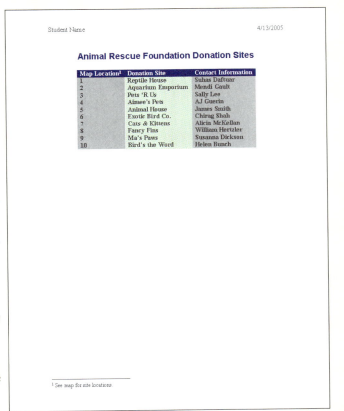

   c. Change the order of the list so that it is sorted by the numbers in ascending order.

   d. Insert a new row above the first entry and enter the following headings:

   Map Location   Donation Site   Contact Information

   e. Apply a table AutoFormat of your choice to the table.

   f. Center the table.

   g. Color the title to match colors used in the table.

   h. Include a footnote, "See map for site locations" with the reference mark next to the Map Locations table heading.

   i. Add a header to the document that displays your name left-aligned and the current date right-aligned.

   j. Save the document as Donation Sites.

   k. Preview and print the document.

lab exercises

Creating and Modifying an Outline ★

2. The Downtown Internet Café provides handouts to customers on different topics related to coffee. You are just starting work on a new handout about selecting the right beans. To help organize your thoughts, you decide to create an outline of the main topics to be included. Your completed outline is shown here.

a. Open a new blank document. Switch to Outline view. Turn on formatting marks.

b. The topics you want to discuss are shown below. Enter these topics at the outline level indicated, pressing ⏎Enter at the end of each.

Aroma (Level 1)
Traditional Blends (Level 2)
Colombian Supremo (Level 3)
French Roast (Level 3)
Sumatra French Roast (Level 4)
Viking French Blend (Level 4)
Espresso Roast (Level 3)
Guatemala Antigua (Level 3)
Brazil Santos (Level 3)
Body (Level 1)
African Coffees (Level 2)
Ethiopian Yirgacheffe (Level 2)
Ethiopian Harrar (Level 2)
Tanzanian Peaberry (Level 3)
Acidity (Level 1)
Asian Coffees (Level 2)
Sumatra Mandheling (Level 3)
Hawaiian Coffees (Level 2)
Hawaiian Kona Fancy (Level 3)
Maui Kaanapali (Level 3)
Flavor (Level 1)
Central and South American Coffees (Level 2)
Costa Rican Tarrazzu (Level 3)
Jamaican Blends (Level 3)
Jamaican Blue Mountain (Level 4)
Jamaica Prime (Level 4)

Student Name—November 12, 2005

Aroma
Traditional Blends
French Roast
Sumatra French Roast
Viking French Blend
Colombian Supremo
Espresso Roast
Brazil Santos
Body
African Coffees
Ethiopian Yirgacheffe
Ethiopian Harrar
Tanzanian Peaberry
Flavor
Central and South American Coffees
Costa Rican Tarrazzu
Jamaican Blends
Jamaican Blue Mountain
Jamaica Prime
Acidity
Asian Coffees
Sumatra Mandheling
Celebes Kalossi Toraja

Student Name—November 12, 2005

Hawaiian Coffees
Hawaiian Kona Fancy
Maui Kaanapali

c. Move the Flavor topic and all subtopics above the Acidity topic.

d. In the Body topic, change the subtopics Ethiopian Yirgacheffe and Ethiopian Harrar to level 3.

e. In the Aroma topic, move Colombian Supremo below Viking French Blend.

f. Insert a new level 3 line, Celebes Kalossi Toraja as the last subtopic under Asian Coffee.

g. Delete the Guatemala Antigua topic under Aroma.

h. Turn off formatting marks. Switch to Normal view.

i. Enter your name and the date centered in a header.

j. Print page 1 of the outline.

k. Save the outline as Coffee Outline in a new folder name Cafe. Close the file.

Designing a Flyer ★ ★

3. The Sports Company is introducing a new line of kayaking and equipment. It is holding a weekend promotional event to familiarize the community with paddling equipment. You have already started designing a flyer to advertise the event, but it still needs additional work. Your completed flyer is shown below.

a. Open the file wd03_Kayaking Flyer.

b. Change the left and right margins to 1 inch.

c. Create the following table of data below the ". . . boat giveaway!" paragraph.

TIME	EVENT
12:00 p.m.	Freestyle Whitewater Panel Discussion
1:15 p.m.	Kids Canoe Relay Race
1:30 p.m.	Becky Andersen & Brad Ludden Autographed Boats Charity Auction
2:30 p.m.	Drawing for Extrasport Joust Personal Flotation Device
3:00 p.m.	Team Dagger Autograph Session
5:00 p.m.	Free BBQ dinner

d. Use Table/AutoFit/AutoFit to Contents to size the table to the cell contents.

e. Apply an AutoFormat of your choice to the table. Center the table.

f. Insert the picture wd03_Kayacker from your data files to the right of the text "Meet Team Dagger." If necessary, size the graphic as shown in the example. Apply the Tight wrapping style and right horizontal alignment.

g. Add a caption of Eli Herbert, World Champion Rodeo Freestyler below the image.

h. Add formatting and styles of your choice to the document. Center the page vertically.

i. Preview the document. Make any editing changes you feel are appropriate.

j. Enter your name and the date centered in the footer.

k. Save the document as Kayaking Flyer.

l. Preview and print the document.

The Sports Company
Annual Boat Show
& Kayaking Exposition

Meet Team Dagger *at the 15th Annual Sports Company Kern Festival Events!*

Figure 1 Eli Herbert, World Champion Rodeo Freestyler

April 24th From Noon to 6 P.M.
The Sports Company River Plaza Location

Informative Paddling Seminars
Learn new tips and techniques! Get expert advice from Eli Hebert, World Champion Kayaker.

Come See the Latest Gear
Boats and equipment from Dagger, Perception and many more...

Boat Giveaway!
Win a Dagger FX 5.7 Freestyle boat!

TIME	EVENT
12:00 p.m.	Freestyle Whitewater Panel Discussion
1:15 p.m.	Kids Canoe Relay Race
1:30 p.m.	Becky Andersen & Brad Ludden Autographed Boats Charity Auction
2:30 p.m.	Drawing for Extrasport Joust Personal Flotation Device
3:00 p.m.	Team Dagger Autograph Session
5:00 p.m.	Free BBQ Dinner

Student Name 11/14/2005

Writing a Report ★ ★ ★

4. As a senior trainer at Lifestyle Fitness Club, you are responsible for researching new fitness trends and sharing your findings with other trainers and clients. You have written a Beginner's Guide to Yoga to distribute to club members. Pages two through three contain the body of your report. Several pages of your completed report are shown here. Use the features presented in this lab to add the following to the report.

a. Open the file wd03_Yoga Practice.

b. Create a new page at the beginning of the document to be used as a title page. Enter the report title, **Beginner's Guide to Yoga**, your name, and the date centered on separate lines. Format the report title using the Title style.

c. Apply a Heading 1 style to the five topic headings.

d. Create a table of contents on the title page below the date with a style of your choice.

e. Remove the hard page break and replace it with a next page section break, then center the title page vertically.

f. Insert the graphics wd03_History and wd03_Yoga Pose as shown in the example. Wrap the text around the graphics using a text wrapping method of your choice. Include captions below the graphic.

1

What is Yoga?

If you are beginning to think that Americans everywhere "do yoga"—you are right! Celebrities, the young, and the old, are spending time in the yoga studio. Over 18 million Americans practice one of the many styles of yoga for health, fitness, and spiritual well-being. Perhaps it seems like a new fad—the latest in a long line of abdominal crunch machines, aerobic dance routines, or martial arts hybrids. But yoga is not another dance routine requiring leg warmers; yoga has been a powerful mind and body therapy for thousands of years. While it first made an appearance in the United States in the 1800s, but it took the peace loving youth of the 1960s to bring it to popular attention. Today you can find yoga classes at the local YMCA, or as an extension of the New Age community, in nearly every city in the US.

There are many types of yoga, but yoga practice usually consists of a series of poses. These poses, called asanas, are designed to stretch and strengthen the body; most asanas are practiced in pairs to balance opposites. Yoga practice usually emphasizes breathing exercises and meditation in addition to series of asanas. Many consider yoga meditation in action. However, most Americans do not practice yoga as part of a specific spiritual tradition, rather they seek stress reduction, relaxation, and general health benefits of yoga. Regardless of your spiritual beliefs, yoga practice is designed to strengthen the link between mind and body.

Figure 1--Yoga emphasizes breathing and meditation.

History of Yoga

The roots of yoga are found in India, more than 5000 years ago, before written language even existed. Ceramics from this period include images of yoga poses.[1] Many people mistakenly attribute the origins of yoga to Hinduism, but Yoga actually predates Hindu practices. In fact, the term "yoga" is a Sanskrit, one of the world's oldest languages, meaning to connect the mind, body, and spirit.

The main branches of yoga as we know them today began to appear in India at approximately the same time as the Christian era began in the Middle East. In the 1960s when Western celebrities, like the Beatles, sought out the magnetic yogis like Maharishi Mahesh Yogi, yoga reconnected with the West.

Figure 2--Yoga's roots lie in ancient India.

Benefits

As alternative therapies, like acupuncture, massage, and meditation, have become more popular options for those with chronic pain, interest in yoga has also increased. However, Western medicine has only recently begun to

[1] Ancient ceramics found in the caves of Mojendro-Daro and Harappa depict recognizable yoga positions.

Student Name   10/23/2005

Beginner's Guide to Yoga

Student Name
October 23, 2005

Table of Contents

Beginner's Guide to Yoga _____ 1
What is Yoga? _____ 1
History of Yoga _____ 1
Benefits _____ 1
Types _____ 2
Getting Started _____ 2
Works Consulted _____ 2

Student Name   10/23/2005

---

g. Apply additional formats of your choice to the report.

h. Under the section History of Yoga, move to the end of the second sentence in the first paragraph after the word "poses" and add the following text as a footnote:

Ancient ceramics found in the caves of Mojendro-Daro and Harappa depict recognizable yoga positions.

i. In the Ashtanga (Power Yoga) description, move to the end of the second sentence after the word "style" and add the following text as a footnote:

Vinyasa is a flow or sequence of poses.

j. At the end of the document, create a Works Consulted page following the example in the lab. Apply a Heading 1 style to the page title. Sort the list and use a .5 inch hanging indent. Enter the following four reference sources:

Iyengar, B.K.S. *Yoga: The Path to Holistic Health.* Los Angeles: DK Publishing, 2001.

Sparrowe, Linda. *Yoga.* New York: Hugh Lautner Levin Associates, 2002.

Phillips, Kathy. *The Spirit of Yoga.* Los Angeles: Barrons Educational Series, 2002.

Wilber, Ken. The *Yoga Tradition: History, Religion, Philosophy and Practice Unabridged.* Philadelphia: Hohm Printers, 2001.

k. Update the table of contents and adjust any formatting as necessary.

l. In the header, add right-aligned page numbers. Do not number the title page. Add your name and the date centered in the footer.

m. Use Reading Layout view to review the document. Run a style consistency check.

n. Save the document as Yoga Guide in a new folder. Preview the document. Print the table of contents and pages one and four of the report.

Writing a Report ★ ★ ★

5. The marketing coordinator at Adventure Travel Tours has recently completed a study of market trends. She has concluded backpacking tours are a growing specialty. You have been asked to compose a report on some new tours and lightweight backpacking for distribution to some key customers. You have already started working on the report and just have some finishing touches to add. The table of contents will appear on the first page of the document. Pages two through four contain the body of your report. Several pages of your completed report are shown here. Use the features presented in this lab to add the following to the report.

   a. Open the file wd03_Triple Crown.

   b. Create a new page at the beginning of the document to be used as a title page. Enter the report title, **Lightweight Backpacking Adventures**, your name, and the date centered on separate lines. Format the report title only using the Title style.

   c. Apply level 1 headings to the six topic headings.

   d. On the title page below the date enter the text **Table of Contents** and format it using the Subtitle style. Create a table of contents using the Formal style. Display one level of headings and exclude the Title style.

Lightweight Backpacking Adventures

Student Name

September 15, 2005

Table of Contents

TRIPLE CROWN CHALLENGE 1
WHY GO LIGHTWEIGHT? 1
PRINCIPLES OF LIGHTWEIGHT BACKPACKING 2
PREPARING FOR YOUR TRIP 2
LEARN MORE! 2
READY TO GO? 2
QUALIFYING HIKES 2
WORKS CONSULTED 2

Student Name - September 15, 2005

1

Triple Crown Challenge

Adventure Travel Tours, your premier active adventure vacation planner, is proud to announce three new adventure tours: Lightweight Backpacking Expeditions on the Pacific Coast Trail, Appalachian Trail, and Continental Divide Trail. Beginning in 2004 Adventure Travel Tour Guides will begin leading expeditions to complete each of these long distance hiking undertakings. At over 2000 miles long each, these three trails represent some of the greatest adventures available in the United States![1]

Figure 1 Hiking the PCT

In order to guarantee your success on these challenging adventures, Adventure Travel Tours is embarking on several qualifying lightweight backpacking trips. We invite you to join us on these exciting adventures and find out if the Triple Crown is the quest for you! Tracey Lynne, our Continental Divide Trail expert, has composed this introduction to lightweight backpacking to whet your appetite for the adventures ahead. (See Figure 4 ATT Guide Tracey Lynne) Please feel free to contact Tracey at Adventure Travel Tours to learn more about lightweight backpacking and the upcoming hikes!

Why Go Lightweight?

Any hiker will tell you: cutting weight is of utmost importance when you plan on hiking miles in the wilderness with all of your possessions strapped to your back. Accordingly, there are many "tricks of the trade" diehard backpackers use to cut weight from their packs. Some cut the handles from their toothbrushes, others trim the margins from their maps, and other hikers have been known to hike 2000 miles on granola and candy bars to avoid the weight of a cook stove and fuel. Yet most hikers don't flinch when it comes to buying the latest heavyweight hiking boots. Marketers have convinced those who love the outdoors that it is a dangerous world out there and we will need the heaviest and most durable backpacks, clothing, shoes, and equipment to survive. Traditional backpacking gear is designed to survive everything you can put it through—and more. Most gear is heavy and heavy duty, but all of this durability adds weight to our gear.

Figure 2 Jack Denae Goes "Lightweight"

Backpackers have begun to rethink their actual needs when out in the wilderness with an eye on reducing weight. Even with all the

[1] The Pacific Coast Trail is 2,650 miles long. The Appalachian Trail is 2,155 miles long. The Continental Divide Trail is approximately 2,800 miles long.

Student Name - September 15, 2005

e. Remove the hard page break and replace it with a next page section break, then center the title page vertically.

f. In this step you will be inserting several graphics. For each of these, size the graphic appropriately and add captions of your choice. Wrap the text around the picture using whatever text wrapping method you prefer. Insert the following pictures at the specified location:

- Insert the graphic wd03_PCT to the right of the first paragraph of the report.
- Insert the graphic wd03_Lightweight to the left of the first paragraph of the Why Go Lightweight? section.
- Insert the graphic wd03_Backpack to the right of the second paragraph in the Principles of Lightweight Backpacking section.
- Insert wd03_Tracey to the left of the last paragraph in the last section of the report.

g. In the second paragraph of the Triple Crown Challenge section, after the word "Lynne," add a cross-reference, with the Figure number and caption, for the photo of Tracey. Use the split window feature to add the cross-reference.

h. Apply additional formatting of your choice to the report. An example may be adding color to the title and headings.

i. Under the section Triple Crown Challenge in the last sentence of the first paragraph, after the word "States!," add the following text as a footnote: **The Pacific Coast Trail is 2,650 miles long. The Appalachian Trail is 2,155 miles long. The Continental Divide Trail is approximately 2,800 miles long.**

j. Under the section Principles of Lightweight Backpacking after the fourth sentence of the first paragraph, after the word "weight," add the following text as a footnote: **For example, a lightweight titanium stove weighs approximately three ounces, where the traditional stove may weigh as much as three times that weight.**

k. Add a new section titled **Qualifying Hikes**, with the following information in a table following the last paragraph in the Ready to Go? section:

Hike	Location	Distance	Date	Guide
Death Valley	California	35 miles	August 29, 2005	Logan Thomas
Paria Canyon	Page, Arizona	40 miles	September 12, 2005	Logan Thomas
Bryce To Zion	N. Arizona	120 miles	October 15, 2005	Tracey Lynne
Brian Head	Utah	95 miles	November 5, 2005	Jack Denae
Capitol Reef Park	Utah Desert	65 miles	February 23, 2006	Jack Denae

l. Apply formatting of your choice to the new table. Apply a Heading 1 style to the title.

m. At the end of the document, create a works consulted page following the example in the lab with a hanging indent. Enter the following five reference sources:

Jardine, Ray. *Beyond Backpacking: Ray Jardine's Guide to Lightweight Hiking. Arizona: AdventureLore Press, 1992.*

Berger, Karen. *Hiking the Triple Crown: Appalachian Trail — Pacific Crest Trail — Continental Divide Trail — How to Hike America's Longest Trails.* NY: Mountaineers Books, 2000.

Gibson, John. *Go Light: The Complete Guide to Lightweight Equipment for Hiking and Backpacking Eastern America!* New York, Thorndike Press, 2002.

Ridley, Tom. *Power Packing: Principles of Lightweight Long Distance Backpacking.* New York: Puffin, 1999.

lab exercises

Bryson, Bill. *A Walk in the Woods: Rediscovering America on the Appalachian Trail.* New York: Broadway Books, 1999.

n. Sort the list of references. Apply a Heading 1 style to the page title.

o. Update the table of contents and adjust formatting as needed.

p. In the header, add right-aligned page numbers. Do not number the title page. Enter your name and the date centered in the footer.

q. Use Reading Layout view to review the document. Run a style consistency check.

r. Save the document as ATT Triple Crown in a new folder. Preview the document. Print the table of contents and pages 1, 4, and 5 of the report.

on your own

Creating an Information Sheet ★

1. You work for a small camera repair and retail shop. You have fielded many different questions about digital cameras lately and have decided to compile these questions in an information sheet. Your completed document will offer your customers answers to the most common questions about digital technology and help them make informed choices when they buy new cameras. Use the features presented in this lab to add the following to your information sheet:

- Open the file wd03_Digital Cameras.

- Use the Document Map to locate the headings in the document and apply appropriate heading levels.

- Create a bulleted list in the Advantages of Digital Cameras section. Use Format Painter to add bold and underlines to the beginning of each sentence, before the semicolon. Do the same for the Disadvantages of Digital Cameras section.

- Use the following information to create a simple table. Apply an AutoFormat of your choice to the table.

Number of Pixels	Print Size
Less than 1 megapixel	Good for e-mail
1 megapixel	4X6-inch prints
2 megapixels	5X7-inch prints
3 megapixels	8X10-inch prints
4 megapixels	11X14-inch prints
5 megapixels	16X20-inch prints

- Add graphics of your choice to the document. Wrap the text around each image and use alignments of your choice. Add captions to the images.

- Display a page number at a position of your choice in the footer.

- Include your name and the date in the header.

- Save the document as Digital Cameras. Preview and print the document.

Using an Outline to Create a Report ★ ★

2. You are continuing your work on the Downtown Internet Café coffee bean flyer. Your outline includes the main characteristics of coffee beans, with examples of different beans that emphasize these characteristics. Create a report using this outline that discusses the four characteristics of coffee beans: acidity, flavor, aroma, and body. Discuss the different regions coffee comes from and the characteristics regional coffee emphasizes. Include the following features in your report:

- Open the file Coffee Outline you created in Step-by-Step Exercise 2 of this lab.
- Create a title page and table of contents. Center the title page vertically.
- The body of the report should include at least three footnotes and two cross-referenced images.
- Include a works cited page with an alphabetical list of your reference sources.
- Add page numbers to the report, excluding the title page.
- Include your name and the date in the footer.
- Save the report as Coffee Report in a new folder. Preview and print the title page, the first page, and the works cited page.

Preparing for a Job Search ★ ★

3. You are graduating next June and want to begin your job search early. To prepare for getting a job, locate three sources of information on this topic. Use your school's career services department, the library, newspaper, and magazine articles as sources. Begin by creating an outline of the topics you will include in the report. Using the outline, write a brief report about your findings. Include the following features in your report:

- A title page that displays the report title, your name, the current date, and a table of contents. Center the page vertically. Use appropriate text formatting.
- The body of the paper should include at least two levels of headings and a minimum of three footnotes.
- The report layout should include page numbers on the top right corner of every page (excluding the title page). The title page should be vertically aligned.
- Include at least one picture with a caption and cross-reference.
- Include a table that compares the jobs you are interested in.
- Include a works cited page with an alphabetical list of your reference sources.
- Save the report as Job Search in a new folder. Preview and print the document.

Writing a Research Paper ★ ★ ★

4. Create a brief research report (or use a paper you have written in the past) on a topic of interest to you. The paper must include the following features:

- A title page that displays the report title, your name, the current date, and a table of contents.
- The body of the paper should include at least two levels of headings and a minimum of three footnotes.
- The report layout should include page numbers on the top right corner of every page (excluding the title page). The title page should be vertically aligned.
- Include at least one picture with a caption and cross-reference.

- Include a table of information.
- Include a works cited page with an alphabetical list of your reference sources.
- Save the document as Research in a new folder. Preview and print the title page and last page of the report.

Creating a Research Report ★ ★ ★

5. Computer viruses can strike at any time and can cause serious problems. Use the Web as a resource to learn more about them, then write a brief report defining computer viruses. Describe three viruses, what they do, and the effect they could have on a large company. The paper must include the following features:

- A title page that displays the report title, your name, the current date, and a table of contents.
- The body of the paper should include at least two levels of headings and a minimum of three footnotes.
- The report layout should include page numbers on the top right corner of every page (excluding the title page). The title page should be vertically aligned.
- Include at least one picture with a caption and cross-reference.
- Include a table of information.
- Include a works cited page with an alphabetical list of your reference sources.
- Save the document as Computer Viruses. Preview and print the document.

Working Together 1: Word 2003 and Your Web Browser

Case Study

Adventure Travel Company

Adventure Travel Tours has a World Wide Web (WWW) site through which it hopes to be able to promote its products and broaden its audience of customers. In addition to the obvious marketing and sales potential, it wants to provide an avenue for interaction between the company and the customer to improve customer service. The company also wants the Web site to provide articles of interest to customers. The articles, with topics such as travel background information and descriptions, would change on a monthly basis as an added incentive for readers to return to the site.

You believe that the flyer you developed to promote the new tours and presentations could be used on the Web site. Office Word 2003 includes Web-editing features that help you create a Web page quickly and easily. While using the Web-editing features, you will be working with Word and with a Web browser application. This capability of all Office 2003 applications to work together and with other applications makes it easy to share and exchange information between applications. Your completed Web pages are shown here.

Note: The Working Together tutorial is designed to show how two applications work together and to present a basic introduction to creating Web pages.

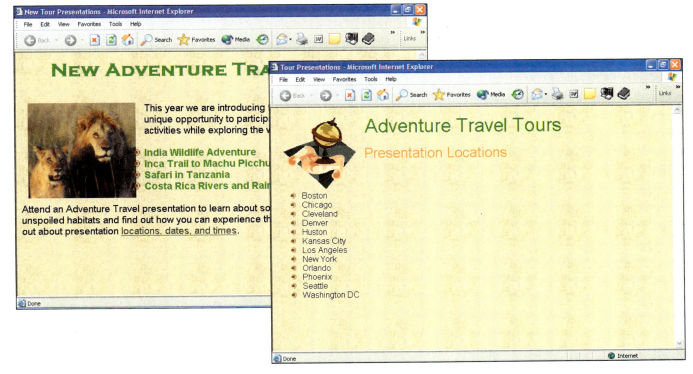

Saving a Word Document as a Web Page

You want to create a Web page to be used on the company's Web site. A **Web page** is a document that can be used on the WWW. The Web page you create will provide information about the tour presentations. Word offers three ways to create or **author** Web pages. One way is to start with a blank Web page and enter text and graphics much as you would a normal document. Another is to use the Web Page Wizard, which provides step-by-step instructions to help you quickly create a Web page. Finally, you can quickly convert an existing Word document to a Web page.

Because the tour flyer has already been created as a Word document and contains much of the information you want to use on the Web page, you will convert it to a Web page document. You made a couple of changes to the flyer, giving it a title that is more appropriate for the Web page and removing the AutoShape banner. You will use the modified version of the flyer as the basis for the Web page.

1
- **Start Office Word 2003.**

- **Open the file** wdwt_Presentations **from the appropriate location.**

- **Close the Getting Started task pane.**

Your screen should be similar to Figure 1

Revised flyer document

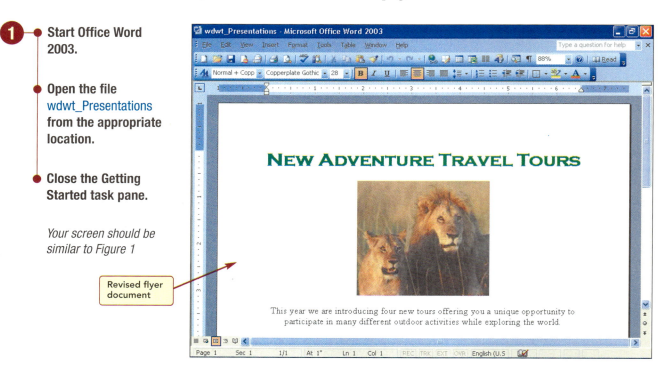

Figure 1

Word converts a document to a Web page by adding HTML coding to the document. **HTML (HyperText Markup Language)** is a programming language used to create Web pages. HTML commands control the display of information on a page, such as font colors and size, and the way an item will be processed. HTML also allows users to click on hyperlinks and jump to other locations on the same page, other pages in the same site, or other sites and locations on the WWW. HTML commands are interpreted by the browser software you are using. A **browser** is a program that connects you to remote computers and displays the Web pages you request.

When a file is converted to a Web page, the HTML coding is added and it is saved to a new file with an .html file extension.

2 **Choose File/Save as Web Page.**

Your screen should be similar to Figure 2

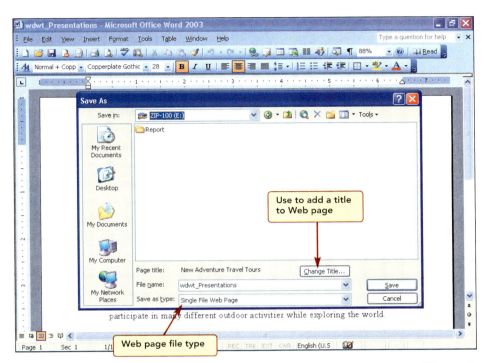

Figure 2

The file type of Web Page is automatically specified. You want to save the Web page using the file name New Tour Presentations in a new folder. You also need to provide a title for the page. This is the text that will appear in the title bar of the Web browser when the page is displayed. You want the title to be the same as the file name.

3 If necessary, change the location to save to the appropriate save location.

● Create a new folder named ATT Web Page.

● Change the file name to New Tour Presentations.

● Click [Change Title...].

● Change the title to **New Tour Presentations**.

● Click [OK].

● Click [Save].

● If an informational box appears, click [Continue].

Your screen should be similar to Figure 3.

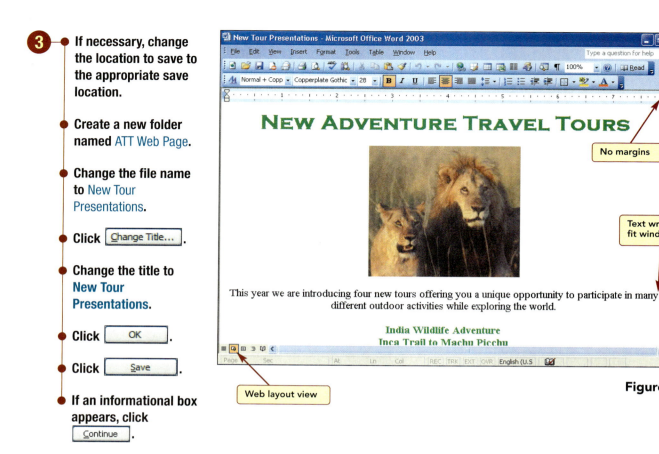

No margins

Text wraps to fit window

Web layout view

Figure 3

The flyer has been converted to an HTML document and is displayed in Web Layout view. Although the menu bar contains the same menus, Word customizes some menus, commands, and options to provide the Web page authoring features. This view displays the document as it will appear if viewed using a Web browser. This document looks very much like a normal Word document. In fact, the only visible difference is the margin settings. A Web page does not include margins. Instead, the text wraps to fit into the window space. However, the formatting and features that are supported by HTML, in this case the paragraph and character formatting such as the font style, type size, and color attributes, have been converted to HTML format.

Web Layout view does not display the HTML codes that control the formatting of the Web page. To view these codes, you will switch to HTML Source view.

④ **Choose View/HTML Source.**

Having Trouble?

If the HTML Script Editor is not installed on your system, you will not be able to use this feature.

● If necessary, maximize the window.

HTML tags

Your screen should be similar to Figure 4

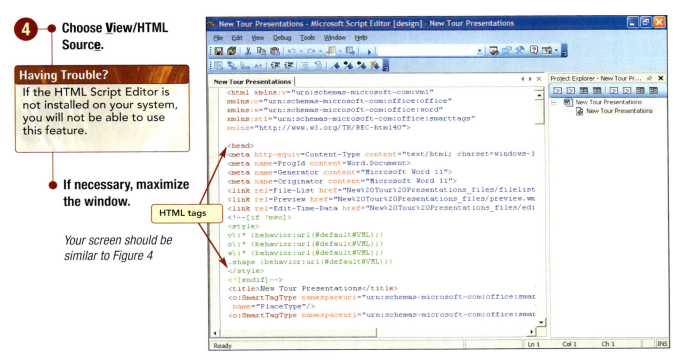

Figure 4

Every item on a Web page has properties associated with it that are encoded in HTML tags. **Tags** are embedded codes that supply information about the page's structure, appearance, and contents. They tell your browser where the title, headings, paragraphs, images, and other information should appear on the page. Converting this document to HTML format using Word was much easier than learning to enter the codes yourself.

⑤ **Click ✖ in the title bar to close the Microsoft Script Editor window.**

The Web page is displayed in Web Layout view again.

Making Text Changes

Next, you want to change the layout of the Web page so that more information is displayed in the window when the page is viewed in the browser. To do this, you will delete any unnecessary text and change the paragraph alignment to left-aligned.

1 ● **Delete the last two paragraphs in the flyer.**

● **Select all the text below the picture.**

● **Click ▤ Left.**

● **Add bullets preceding the list of four tours.**

● **Move to the top of the document.**

Your screen should be similar to Figure 5

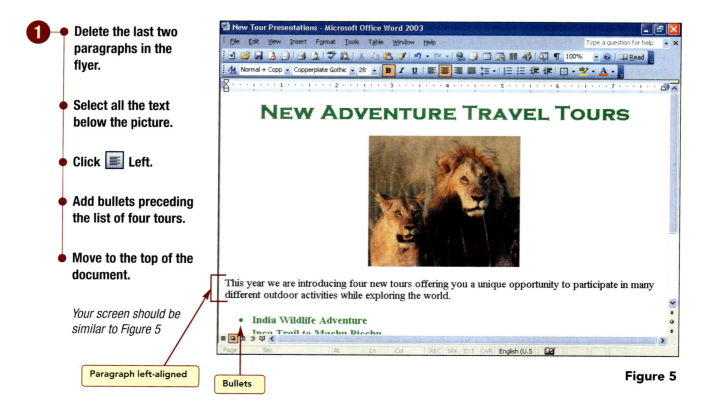

NEW ADVENTURE TRAVEL TOURS

This year we are introducing four new tours offering you a unique opportunity to participate in many different outdoor activities while exploring the world.

● **India Wildlife Adventure**
● **Inca Trail to Machu Picchu**

Paragraph left-aligned

Bullets

Figure 5

Changing the Picture Layout

Additional Information

When graphic files are added to a Web page, they are copied to the same folder location as the Web page. The graphic files must always reside in the same location as the HTML document file in which they are used.

You still cannot view all the information in a single window. To make more space, you will move the picture to the left edge of the window and wrap the text to the right around it. Unlike a normal Word document, a Web page document does not have pictures and other graphic elements embedded in it. In an HTML file, each graphic object is stored as a separate file that is accessed and loaded by the browser when the page is loaded. In an HTML file, each graphic object is stored as a separate file that is accessed and loaded by the browser when the page is loaded. Word creates a link to the object's file in the HTML file. The link is a tag that includes the location and file name of the graphic file.

Additionally, graphics are inserted into a Web page document as inline objects. You can change the wrapping style and move, size, and format graphic objects in a Web page just like embedded objects in a Word document.

1

- Click on the picture to select it.

- If necessary, display the Picture toolbar.

- Drag the graphic to the "T" in "This" at the beginning of the first paragraph.

- Click 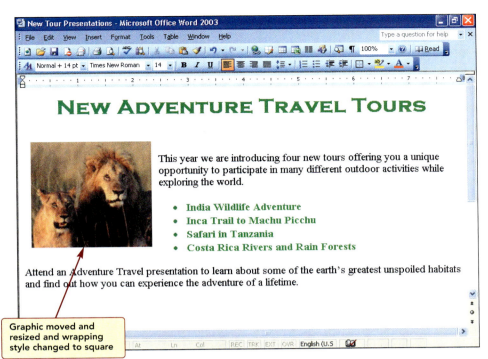 Text Wrapping.

- Select Square.

- Reduce the picture size slightly as in Figure 6.

- Deselect the picture.

Your screen should be similar to Figure 6

Graphic moved and resized and wrapping style changed to square

Figure 6

Now all the information is visible. Next, you will make a few other adjustments to improve the appearance.

Applying a Theme

Because color and design are important elements of Web pages, you can add a background color and other special effects to a Web page. Many of these special effects are designed specifically for Web pages and cannot be used in printed pages. Like styles, Word includes many predesigned Web page effects, called **themes**, which you can quickly apply to a Web page.

1 ● **Choose Format/Theme.**

Your screen should be similar to Figure 7

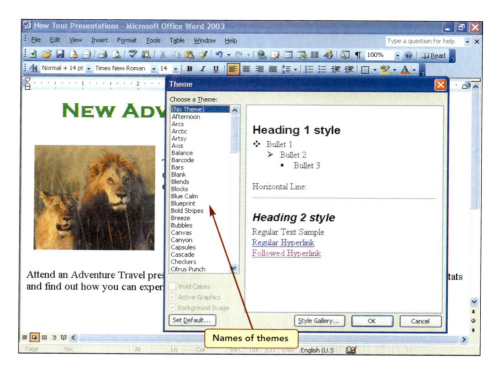

Figure 7

The Choose a Theme list displays the names of all the themes that are provided with Word. The preview area displays a sample of the selected theme showing the background design, bullet and horizontal line style, and character formats that will be applied to headings, normal text, and hyperlinks.

2 ● **Select several themes to preview them.**

● **Select the Tabs and Folders theme.**

Having Trouble?
If the Tabs and Folders theme is not available, try Expedition or Artsy.

● **Click** OK .

● **If necessary, readjust the picture.**

● **Click** 💾 **Save to save the changes you have made to the Web page.**

Your screen should be similar to Figure 8

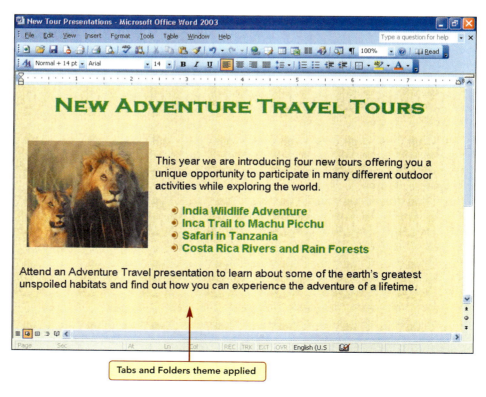

The formatting settings associated with the selected theme are applied to the Web page. The two obvious changes are the addition of a background design and graphical bullets.

Creating a Hyperlink

Next, you want to create another Web page that will contain a list of presentation locations. You will then add a hyperlink to this information from the New Tour Presentations page. As you have learned, a hyperlink provides a quick way to jump to other documents, objects, or Web pages. Hyperlinks are the real power of the WWW. You can jump to sites on your own system and network as well as to sites on the Internet and WWW.

The list of tour locations has already been entered as a Word document and saved as a file.

1 • **Open the file** wdwt_Locations.

• **Save the document as a Web page to the ATT Web Page folder with the file name** Locations **and a page title of** Tour Presentation Locations.

• **Apply the same theme to this page.**

• **Save the page again.**

Your screen should be similar to Figure 9

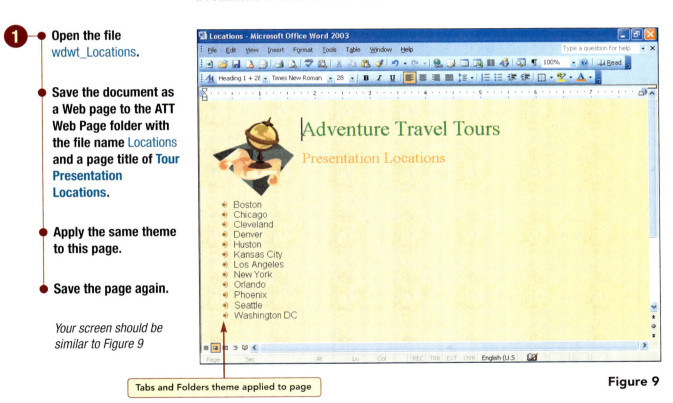

Tabs and Folders theme applied to page

Figure 9

Now you are ready to create the hyperlink from the New Tour Presentations page to the Locations page.

2 ● **Switch to the New Tour Presentations window.**

● **Add the following text to the end of the last paragraph: Find out about presentation locations, dates, and times.**

● **Select the text "locations, dates, and times."**

● **Click 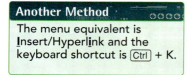 Insert Hyperlink (on the Standard toolbar).**

Another Method ○○○○

The menu equivalent is Insert/Hyperlink and the keyboard shortcut is Ctrl + K.

Your screen should be similar to Figure 10

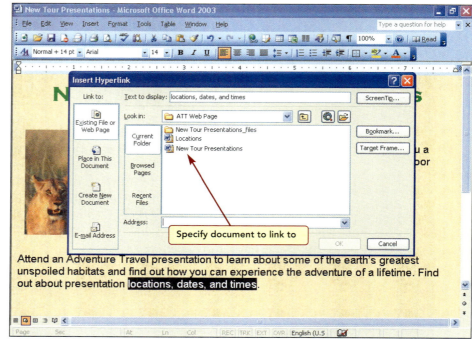

Specify document to link to

Figure 10

From the Insert Hyperlink dialog box, you need to specify the name of the document you want the link to connect to.

3 ● **Select Locations from the file list.**

● **Click OK.**

Your screen should be similar to Figure 11

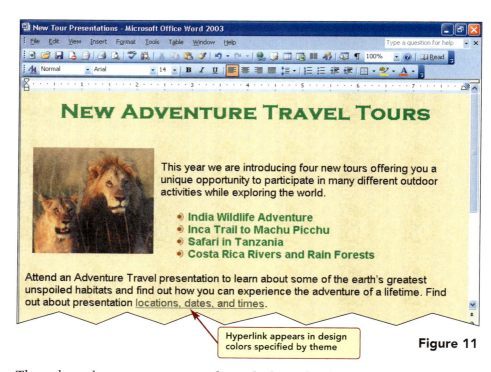

NEW ADVENTURE TRAVEL TOURS

This year we are introducing four new tours offering you a unique opportunity to participate in many different outdoor activities while exploring the world.

● India Wildlife Adventure
● Inca Trail to Machu Picchu
● Safari in Tanzania
● Costa Rica Rivers and Rain Forests

Attend an Adventure Travel presentation to learn about some of the earth's greatest unspoiled habitats and find out how you can experience the adventure of a lifetime. Find out about presentation locations, dates, and times.

Hyperlink appears in design colors specified by theme

Figure 11

The selected text appears as a hyperlink in the design colors specified by the theme.

4 Hold down Ctrl and click the hyperlink.

Your screen should be similar to Figure 12

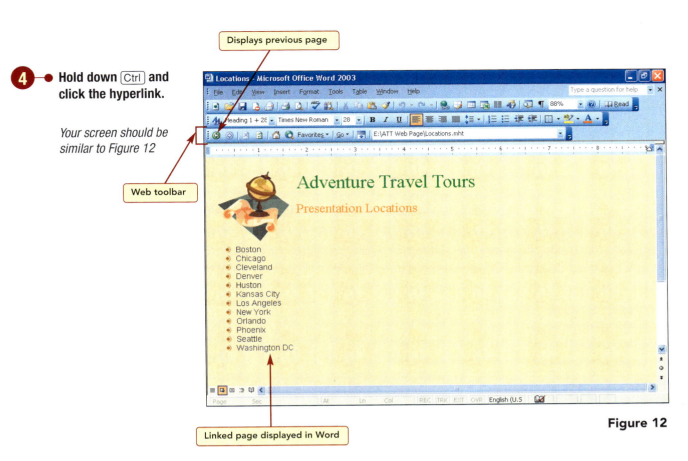

Displays previous page

Web toolbar

Linked page displayed in Word

Figure 12

Because the Locations document is already open in a window, clicking the hyperlink simply switches to the open window and displays the page. In addition, the Web toolbar is displayed. Its buttons are used to navigate and work with Web pages.

You plan to add hyperlinks from each location to information about dates and times for each location at a later time.

Previewing the Page

To see how your Web page will actually look when displayed by your browser, you can preview it.

1 Click  Back on the Web toolbar to view the previous page.

• Choose **F**ile/We**b** Page Preview.

• If necessary, maximize the browser window.

• If Internet Explorer is your default browser and any of the Explorer bars are open, click ☒ in the bar to close it.

Your screen should be similar to Figure 13

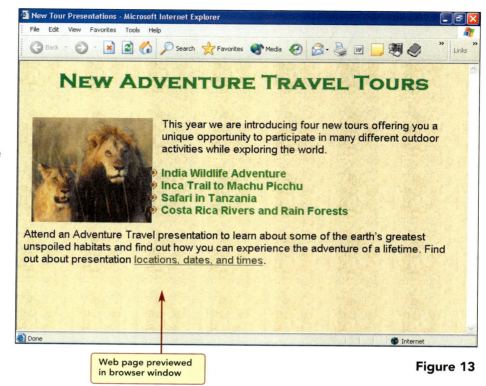

Web page previewed in browser window

Figure 13

The browser on your system is loaded offline, and the Web page you are working on is displayed in the browser window. Sometimes the browser may display a page slightly differently from the way it appears in Web Page view. In this case, the bullets overlap the edge of the picture. If you do not like the change, you can return to Word and adjust the layout until it displays appropriately in the browser. You will leave it as it is for now.

2 • **Click on the hyperlink.**

Your screen should be similar to Figure 14

Linked page displayed in browser

Figure 14

The associated page is displayed in the browser. This page also looks fine and does not need any additional formatting.

3 ● Click ✖ in the title bar to exit the browser program.

● Exit Word, saving the changes you made to both documents.

Making a Web Page Public

Now that you have created Web pages, you need to make them available on the Internet for others to see them. The steps that you take to make your pages public depend on how you want to share them. There are two main avenues: on your local network or intranet for limited access by people within an organization, or on the Internet for access by anyone using the WWW. To make pages available to other people on your network, save your Web pages and related files, such as pictures, to a network location. To make your Web pages available on the WWW, you need to install Web server software on your computer or to locate an Internet service provider that allocates space for Web pages.

lab review

WORKING TOGETHER 1
Word 2003 and Your Web Browser

key

author   WDWT1.2

browser   WDWT1.3

HTML (Hypertext Markup Language)   WDWT1.2

tag   WDWT1.5

theme   WDWT1.7

Web page   WDWT1.2

mos skills

The Microsoft Office Specialist (MOS) certification program is designed to measure your proficiency in performing basic tasks using the Office 2003 applications. Getting certified demonstrates that you have the skills and provides a valuable industry credential for employment. After completing this lab, you have learned the following Microsoft Office Word Specialist skills:

Skill	Description	Page
Organize Content	Insert and modify hyperlinks	WDWT1.9
Formatting and Managing Documents	Preview documents and Web pages	WDWT1.11
	Save documents in appropriate formats for different uses	WDWT1.3

command summary

Command	Shortcut Keys	Button	Action
File/Save as Web Pa**g**e			Saves file as a Web page document
File/We**b** Page Preview			Previews Web page in browser window
View/HTML Sour**c**e			Displays HTML source code
Insert/Hyper**l**ink	Ctrl + K		Inserts hyperlink
F**o**rmat/Th**e**me			Applies a predesigned theme to Web page

step-by-step

Adding a New Web Page ★

1. You want to continue working on the Web pages about the new tour presentations for the Adventure Travel Web site. Your next step is to create links from each location to information about each location's presentation date and times. Your completed Web page for the Los Angeles area is shown here.

a. In Word, open the Web page file Locations you created in this lab.

b. Open the document wdwt_LosAngeles. Save the document as a Web page to the ATT Web Page folder with the file name LosAngeles and a page title of **Los Angeles Presentation Information**.

c. Apply the Tabs and Folders design theme to the new page. Change the first title line to a Heading 1 style and the second title line to a Heading 2 style. Change the

title lines color to the same colors used on the Locations page. Add color to the table headings. Enhance the Web page with any features you feel are appropriate.

d. Two lines below the table add and bold the text **Contact [your name] at (909) 555-1212 for more information.**

e. On the Locations page, create a link from the Los Angeles text to the Los Angeles page. Test the link.

f. Resave both Web pages and preview them in your browser. Print the Los Angeles Web page.

g. Exit the browser and Word.

lab exercises

Converting a Flyer to a Web Page ★ ★

2. The Animal Rescue Foundation has asked you to modify the Volunteers Needed article you created and convert the article into a Web page to add to the Foundation's Web site. Your completed Web page is shown here.

a. Open the file Volunteers Needed you created in Step-by-Step Exercise 2 in Lab 1.

b. Convert the article to a Web page and save it as Volunteers Needed in a new folder. Include an appropriate page title.

c. Apply a theme of your choice to the page.

d. Change the list to left-aligned. Add bullets to the list.

e. Change the text wrapping style of the graphic to square. Move the graphic to the left of the bulleted list. Increase the size of the picture so that all the bulleted items appear next to the graphic.

> **\\LINDA-DESKTOP\SharedDocs\McGraw-Hill\Office 2003\Word2003 Brief\Data&Solutions\Solutions\WDWT - Micr...**
>
> File Edit View Favorites Tools Help
>
> Back · · Search Favorites Media
>
> ## Volunteers Needed!
>
> The Animal Rescue Foundation is in need of your help. Over the past 6 months, we have seen a **20 percent** increase in the number of rescued animals. With the increase in animals, we need more people to join Animal Angels, our volunteer group.
>
> Our volunteer program is both diverse and flexible; no matter how hectic your schedule, we can find a place for you. It is our goal to have volunteers actively involved in many areas of our organization--from providing direct care for the animals to contributing to the every day functioning of our shelter and programs to furthering animal welfare and our mission of finding a loving home for each animal. Here are just some of the opportunities that await you.
>
> - Foster parent
> - Work at adoption fairs
> - Socialize the cats
> - Provide obedience training
> - Pet grooming specialists
> - Repair, organize, and distribute donations
> - Greeters and matchmakers
> - Adoption counselor
> - Kennel and animal care assistants
> - Special event volunteers
>
> Done   Local intranet

f. Change the color of the title line to dark red and a Heading 1 style. Center the title.

g. Delete your name and the date from the document. Replace "us" in the last line with your name.

h. Save the Web page. Preview the page in your browser. Adjust the layout as needed. Close your browser. Resave the Web page.

i. Use Print Preview to see how the page will appear when printed. Change the layout as needed. Print the Web page.

j. Exit Word without saving your changes to the page.

Advertising on the Web ★ ★ ★

3. You would like to advertise the grand opening of the Internet Café on the Web. You plan to use the information in the advertisement flyer you created as the basis for the Web pages. Your completed Web page is shown here.

a. Open the file Grand Opening you created in Step-by-Step Exercise 3 in Lab 1. Convert the document to a Web page and save it as Café Flyer in a new folder. Delete the graphic. Insert the image wdwt_Coffee Cup. Change the picture text wrapping style to square. Move the picture to the right, as shown in the example.

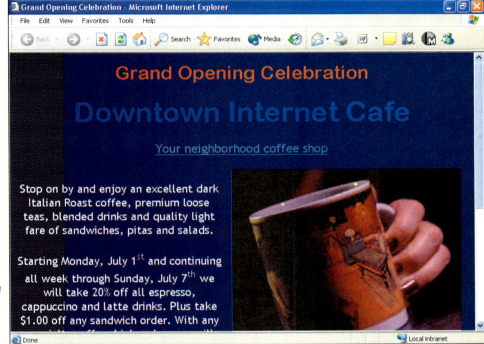

b. Open the file wdwt_Café Locations. Save the document as a Web page to your Web Page folder with the file name Locations and a page title of **Your Neighborhood**.

c. Create a link from the text "Your Neighborhood Coffee Shop" to the Locations page. Add a theme of your choice to the pages. Enhance the pages with any features you feel are appropriate.

d. Test the link. Resave the Web pages and preview them in your browser.

e. Print the pages.

lab exercises

on your own

Learning About Web Design

1. Use Word Help to learn more about Web pages and making Web pages public.

   a. Search in Help for information on Web page design, Web layout, Web sites, and publishing Web pages.

   b. Print the Help pages that might be appropriate for writing a report on using Word to create a Web site.

   c. Write a one-page report in Word summarizing the information you found.

   d. Include your name and the date in a header.

   e. Save the report as Web Design. Print the report.

Command Summary

Command	Shortcut Key	Button	Voice	Action
File/**N**ew	Ctrl + N	📄	New file	Opens new document
File/**O**pen	Ctrl + O	📂	Open	Opens existing document file
File/**C**lose	Ctrl + F4	✖	Close Document	Closes document
File/**S**ave	Ctrl + S	💾	Save	Saves document using same file name
File/Save **A**s				Saves document using a new file name, type, and/or location
File/Save as Web Pa**g**e				Saves file as a Web page document
File/Ve**r**sions				Saves, opens, and deletes document versions
File/We**b** Page Preview				Previews Web page in browser window
File/Page Set**u**p				Changes layout of page including margins, paper size, and paper source
File/Page Set**u**p/Layout/**V**ertical Alignment				Aligns text vertically on a page
File/Print Pre**v**iew		🔍	Preview	Displays document as it will appear when printed
File/**P**rint	Ctrl + P	🖨	Print	Prints document using selected print settings
File/Propert**i**es				Displays file statistics, summary, and property settings
File/E**x**it	Alt + F4	✖		Exits Word program
Edit/**U**ndo	Ctrl + Z	↩	Undo	Restores last editing change
Edit/**R**edo	Ctrl + Y	↪	Redo	Restores last Undo or repeats last command or action
Edit/Clea**r**/**C**ontents	Delete			Deletes characters you do not want
Edit/Cu**t**	Ctrl + X	✂	Cut	Cuts selection to Clipboard

Command	Shortcut Key	Button	Voice	Action
Edit/**C**opy	Ctrl + C		Copy	Copies selection to Clipboard
Edit/**P**aste	Ctrl + V		Paste	Pastes item from Clipboard
Edit/Select A**ll**	Ctrl + A			Selects all text in document
Edit/**F**ind	Ctrl + F			Locates specified text
Edit/R**e**place	Ctrl + H			Locates and replaces specified text
View/**N**ormal			Normal View	Shows text formatting and simple layout of page
View/**W**eb Layout			Web Layout View	Shows document as it will appear when viewed in a Web browser
View/**P**rint Layout			Print Layout View	Shows how text and objects will appear on printed page
View/**O**utline				Shows structure of document
View/Tas**k** Pane				Displays or hides task pane
View/**T**oolbars			Task Pane	Displays or hides selected toolbar
View/F**u**ll Screen			View full screen	Displays document only, without application features such as menu bars or toolbars
View/**R**uler				Displays/hides horizontal ruler bar
View/**D**ocument Map				Displays or hides Document Map pane
View/Thum**b**nails				Displays a miniature representation of each page
View/**H**eader and Footer				Displays header and footer areas
View/Foot**n**otes				Hides or displays note pane
View/**Z**oom/**W**hole Page				Fits entire page on screen
View/**Z**oom/**M**any Pages				Displays two or more pages in document window
View/HTML Sourc**e**				Displays HTML source code
Insert/**B**reak/**P**age break	Ctrl + ↵Enter			Inserts hard page break
Insert/**B**reak/**N**ext Page				Inserts new page break
Insert/Page N**u**mbers				Specifies page number location
Insert/Date and **T**ime				Inserts current date or time, maintained by computer system, in selected format

Command	Shortcut Key	Button	Voice	Action
Insert/**A**utoText				Enters predefined text
Insert/**A**utoText/AutoTe**x**t				Creates new AutoText entries
Insert/**A**utoText/AutoTe**x**t/Show/ AutoComplete suggestions				Turns on AutoComplete feature
Insert/Refere**n**ce/Foot**n**ote	Alt + Ctrl + F			Inserts footnote reference at insertion point
Insert/Refere**n**ce/**C**aption				Creates figure captions
Insert/Refere**n**ce/Cross-reference				Creates figure cross-reference
Insert/Refere**n**ce/In**d**ex and Tables/Table of **C**ontents				Generates a table of contents
Insert/**P**icture/**C**lip Art		🖼		Accesses Clip Organizer and inserts selected clip
Insert/**P**icture/**F**rom File		🖼		Inserts selected picture
Insert/**P**icture/**A**utoShapes		AutoShapes ▾		Inserts selected AutoShape
Insert/Hyper**l**ink	Ctrl + K	🌐		Inserts hyperlink
Format/**F**ont/Font/**F**ont		Times New Roman ▾		Changes typeface
Format/**F**ont/Fo**n**t/Font Style/Bold	Ctrl + B	**B**	On bold	Makes selected text bold
Format/**F**ont/Font/**S**ize		12 ▾		Changes font size
Format/**F**ont/Font/**C**olor		**A** ▾		Changes text to selected color
Format/**F**ont/F**o**nt/ **U**nderline style/Single	Ctrl + U	**U**		Underlines selected text with a single line
Format/**P**aragraph/**I**ndents and Spacing/Ali**g**nment/Center	Ctrl + E	≡	Centered	Centers text between left and right margins
Format/**P**aragraph/**I**ndents and Spacing/Ali**g**nment/Justified	Ctrl + J	≡		Aligns text equally between left and right margins
Format/**P**aragraph/**I**ndents and Spacing/Ali**g**nment/Left	Ctrl + L	≡	Left justify	Aligns text to left margin
Format/**P**aragraph/**I**ndents and Spacing/Ali**g**nment/Right	Ctrl + R	≡	Right justify	Aligns text to right margin
Format/**P**aragraph/**I**ndents and Spacing/Special/First Line				Indents first line of paragraph from left margin
Format/**P**aragraph/**I**ndents and Spacing/Line Spacing	Ctrl + #			Changes amount of white space between lines
Format/Bullets and **N**umbering		≣ ≣		Creates a bulleted or numbered list
Format/**T**abs				Specifies types and position of tab stops

Command	Shortcut Key	Button	Voice	Action
F**o**rmat/Change Cas**e**				Changes case of selected text
F**o**rmat/Th**e**me				Applies a predesigned theme to Web page
F**o**rmat/P**i**cture				Changes format settings associated with selected picture
F**o**rmat/P**i**cture/Layout/Wrapping Style		[button]		Specifies how text will wrap around picture
F**o**rmat/Re**v**eal Formatting	⇧Shift + F1			Opens Reveal Formatting task pane
Tools/**S**pelling and Grammar	F7	[ABC]		Starts Spelling and Grammar tool
Tools/**L**anguage/Thesaurus	⇧Shift + F7			Starts Thesaurus tool
Tools/**W**ord Count				Reviews document statistics
Tools/**A**utoCorrect Options/**E**xceptions			Options button	Option to exclude words from automatic correction
Tools/**O**ptions/Edit/O**v**ertype Mode	Insert	OVR		Switches between Insert and Overtype modes
Tools/**O**ptions/View/**A**ll	Ctrl + S + *	¶		Displays or hides formatting marks
Tools/**A**utoCorrect Options/S**h**ow AutoCorrect Options buttons			Options button	Displays or hides AutoCorrect option buttons
Tools/**C**ustomize/**O**ptions/**S**how Standard and Formatting toolbar				Displays Standard and Formatting toolbars on two rows
Tools/**O**ptions/View/**A**ll	Ctrl + ⇧Shift + *	¶	Show formatting marks	Displays or hides formatting marks
Tools/**O**ptions/Edit/O**v**ertype Mode	Insert	OVR		Switches between Insert and Overtype modes
Tools/**O**ptions/Spelling & Grammar				Changes settings associated with the Spelling and Grammar checking feature
T**a**ble/**I**nsert Table		[button]		Inserts table at insertion point
T**a**ble/**I**nsert/Rows **A**bove				Inserts a new row in table above selected row
T**a**ble/Con**v**ert/Te**x**t to Table				Converts selected text to table format
T**a**ble/Table Auto**F**ormat				Applies pre-designed formats to table
Table/Sort				Rearranges items in a selection into sorted order
Window/**S**plit				Divides a document into two horizontal sections

Glossary of Key Terms

active window The window containing the insertion point and that will be affected by any changes you make.

alignment How text is positioned on a line between the margins or indents. There are four types of paragraph alignment: left, centered, right, and justified.

antonym A word with the opposite meaning.

author The process of creating a Web page.

AutoComplete A feature that recognizes commonly used words or phrases and can automatically complete them for you if chosen.

AutoCorrect A feature that makes basic assumptions about the text you are typing and automatically corrects the entry.

AutoFormat A feature that makes certain formatting changes automatically to your document.

AutoShape A ready-made shape that is supplied with Word.

AutoText A feature that provides commonly used words or phrases that you can select and quickly insert into a document.

browser A program that connects you to remote computers and displays the Web pages you request.

bullet A dot or other symbol that is placed before text.

bulleted list Displays items that logically fall out from a paragraph into a list, with items preceded by bullets.

caption A title or explanation for a table, picture, or graph.

case sensitive The capability to distinguish between uppercase and lowercase characters.

cell The intersection of a column and row where data is entered in a table.

character formatting Formatting features, such as bold and color, that affect the selected characters only.

Click and Type A feature available in Print Layout and Web Layout views, that is used to quickly insert text, graphics, and other items in a blank area of a document, avoiding the need to enter blank lines.

cross-reference A reference in one part of a document to related information in another part.

cursor The blinking vertical bar that shows you where the next character you type will appear. Also called the insertion point.

custom dictionary A dictionary of terms you have entered that are not in the main dictionary of the spelling checker.

default The initial Word document settings that can be changed to customize documents.

destination The location to which text is moved or copied.

docked toolbar A toolbar fixed to an edge of the window and displays a vertical bar called the move handle, on the left edge of the toolbar.

Document Map Displays the headings in the document in a separate pane.

document window The area of the application window that displays the contents of the open document.

drag and drop A mouse procedure that moves or copies a selection to a new location.

drawing layer The layer above or below the text layer where floating objects are inserted.

drawing object A simple object consisting of shapes such as lines and boxes.

edit   The process of changing and correcting existing text in a document.

embedded object   An object, such as a picture graphic, that becomes part of the Word document and that can be opened and edited using the program in which it was created.

endnote   A reference note displayed at the end of the document.

end-of-file marker   The horizontal line that marks the end of a file.

field   A placeholder that instructs Word to insert information in a document.

field code   The code containing the instructions about the type of information to insert in a field.

field result   The results displayed in a field according to the instructions in the field code.

file property   A setting associated with a file.

floating object   A graphic object that is inserted into the drawing layer and which can be positioned anywhere on the page.

floating toolbar   A toolbar that appears in a separate window and can be moved anywhere on the desktop.

font   A set of characters with a specific design. Also called a typeface.

font size   The height and width of a character, commonly measured in points.

footer   The line or several lines of text at the bottom of every page just below the bottom margin line.

footnote   A reference note displayed at the bottom of the page on which the reference occurs.

format   To enhance the appearance of the document to make it more readable or attractive.

Format Painter   The feature that applies formats associated with the current selection to new selections.

formatting marks   Symbols that are automatically inserted into a document as you enter and edit text and that control the appearance of the document.

Formatting toolbar   The toolbar that contains buttons representing the most frequently used text-editing and text-layout features.

grammar checker   The feature that advises you of incorrect grammar as you create and edit a document, and proposes possible corrections.

graphic   A non-text element in a document.

hard page break   A manually inserted page break that instructs Word to begin a new page regardless of the amount of text on the previous page.

header   The line or several lines of text at the top of each page just above the top margin line.

heading style   A style that is designed to identify different levels of headings in a document.

HTML (HyperText Markup Language)   The programming language used to create Web pages.

hyperlink   A connection to locations in the current document, other documents, or Web pages. Clicking a hyperlink jumps to the specified location.

indent   To set in a paragraph from the margins. There are four types of indents: left, right, first line, and hanging.

inline object   An object that is inserted directly in the text at the position of the insertion point, becoming part of the paragraph.

Insert mode   Method of text entry in which new characters are inserted into existing text, which moves to the right to make space for the new characters; the text on the line is reformatted as necessary.

insertion point   The blinking vertical bar that shows you where the next character you type will appear on the line. Also called the cursor.

leader characters   Solid, dotted, or dashed lines that fill the blank space between tab stops.

line spacing   The vertical space between lines of text.

main dictionary   The dictionary of terms that comes with Word 2003.

menu bar   Located below the title bar, this bar displays the application's program menu.

note pane   Lower portion of the window that displays footnotes.

note reference mark   A superscript number or character appearing in the document at the end of the material being referenced.

note separator   The horizontal line separating footnote text from main document text.

note text   The text in a footnote.

numbered list   Displays items that convey a sequence of events in a particular order, with items preceded by numbers or letters.

object   An item that can be sized, moved, and manipulated.

Office clipboard   A temporary Windows storage area in memory.

outline numbered list   Displays items in multiple outline levels that show a hierarchical structure of the items in the list.

Overtype mode   Method of text entry in which new text types over the existing characters.

page break   Marks the point at which one page ends and another begins.

page margin   The blank space around the edge of the page.

paragraph formatting   Formatting features, such as alignment, indentation, and line spacing, that affect an entire paragraph.

picture   An illustration such as a scanned photograph.

Reading Layout view   Displays a document like pages in a book.

ruler   The ruler located below the Formatting toolbar that shows the line length in inches.

sans serif font   A font, such as Arial or Helvetica, that does not have a flair at the base of each letter.

scroll bar   Used with a mouse to bring additional lines of information into view in a window.

section   A division into which a document can be divided that can be formatted separately from the rest of the document.

section break   Marks the point at which one section ends and another begins.

select   To highlight text.

selection cursor   A colored highlight bar that appears over the selected command.

selection rectangle   The rectangular outline around an object that indicates it is selected.

serif font   A font, such as Times New Roman, that has a flair at the base of each letter.

shortcut menu   By right clicking on an item, this menu displays only the options pertaining to that item.

sizing handles   Black squares around a selected object that can be used to size the object.

Smart Tag   A feature that recognizes data such as names, addresses, telephone numbers, dates, times, and places as a particular type. The recognized item can then be quickly added to a Microsoft Outlook feature.

soft page break   A page break automatically inserted by Word to start a new page when the previous page has been filled with text or graphics.

soft space   A space between words automatically entered by Word to justify text on a line.

sort   To arrange alphabetically or numerically in ascending or descending order.

source   The location from which text is moved or copied.

source program   The program in which an object was created.

spelling checker   The feature that advises you of misspelled words as you create and edit a document, and proposes possible corrections.

split window   A division of the document window into two horizontal sections making it easier to view different parts of a document.

Standard toolbar   The toolbar that contains buttons for the most frequently used commands.

status bar   A bar displayed at the bottom of the document window that advises you of the status of different program conditions and features as you use the program.

style   A named combination of character and paragraph formats that can be applied to a paragraph.

synonym   A word with a similar meaning.

system Clipboard   Where a selection that has been cut or copied is stored.

tab stop   A marked location on the horizontal ruler that indicates how far to indent text when the ⎯Tab⎯ key is pressed.

table   Displays information in horizontal rows and vertical columns.

table reference   The letter and number (for example, A1) that identify a cell in a table.

tag   Embedded codes that supply information about a Web pages structure, appearance, and contents.

task pane   Displayed on the right side of the document window, it provides quick access to features as you are using the application.

text box   A container for text and other graphics.

text wrapping   Controls how text appears around a graphic.

theme   Predesigned Web page effects.

thesaurus   Word feature that provides synonyms and antonyms for words.

thumbnail   A miniature representation of a picture.

toolbar   A bar of buttons below the menu bar that are shortcuts for many commonly used commands.

TrueType   A font that is automatically installed when you install Windows.

typeface   A set of characters with a specific design. Also called a font.

URL   The address that indicates the location of a document on the World Wide Web. URL stands for Uniform Resource Locator.

version   A "snapshot" of a document at a specific time, that is saved with the file.

Web page   A document that can be used on the World Wide Web and viewed in a browser.

word wrap   A feature that automatically determines where to end a line and wrap text to the next line based on the margin settings.

Data File List

Supplied/Used	Created/Saved As
Lab 1	
wd01_Flyer1	Flyer
wd01_Lions	Flyer1
Step-by-Step	
1.	Web Site Memo
2.	Volunteers Needed
3. wd01_Coffee	Grand Opening
4. wd01_Note Taking Skills	Note Taking Skills
5. wd01_Conserve Water	Water Conservation
wd01_Water Hose	
On Your Own	
1.	Hawaii Cruise Flyer
2.	Lab Rules
3.	CPR Classes
4.	Computer Cleaning
5.	Career Report
Lab 2	
wd02_Tour Letter	Tour Letter2
wd02_Flyer2	Flyer 2 Versions
Step-by-Step	
1. wd02_Conservation Tips	Water Conservation2
Water Conservation (Lab 1)	
2. Note Taking Skills (Lab 1)	
wd02_Note Taking Tips	Note Taking Skills2
3. wd02_Yoga Flyer	Yoga Flyer
4. Volunteers Needed (Lab 1)	Orientation Schedule
	Volunteers Needed2
5. wd02_Coffee Flyer	Coffee Flyer2
On Your Own	
1.	Reference Letter
2.	Phone Rates
3.	For Sale Flyer
4. wd02_New Orleans	New Orleans2
5.	Election Results
Lab 3	
wd03_Tour Research	Tour Research
wd03_Giraffe	Research Outline
wd03_Parrots	

Supplied/Used	Created/Saved As
Step-by-Step	
1.	Donation Sites
2.	Coffee Outline
3. wd03_Kayaking Flyer	Kayaking Flyer
wd03_Kayacker	
4. wd03_Yoga Practice	Yoga Guide
wd03_History	
wd03_Yoga Pose	
5. wd03_Triple Crown	ATT Triple Crown
wd03_PCT	
wd03_Lightweight	
wd03_Backpack	
wd03_Tracey	
On Your Own	
1. wd03_Digital Camera	Digital Cameras
2. Coffee Outline (Lab 3)	Coffee Report
3.	Job Search
4.	Research
5.	Computer Viruses
Working Together 1	
wdwt_Presentations	New Tour Presentations
wdwt_Locations	Locations
Step-by-Step	
1. Locations (from WT lab)	
wdwt_LosAngeles	LosAngeles
2. Volunteers Needed (Lab 2)	Volunteers Needed
3. Grand Opening (Lab 1)	Locations
	Cafe Flyer
wdwt_Coffee Cup	
wdwt_Café Locations	
On Your Own	
1.	Web Design

Reference 2

MOS Certification Guide

Office Word 2003 Specialist Certification

Standardized Coding Number	Skill sets and objectives	Lab	Page	Lab Exercises Step-By-Step	On Your Own
WW03S-1	**Creating Content**				
WW03S-1-1	Insert and edit text, symbols, and special characters	1	1.11	1,2,3,4,5	1,2,3,5
		2	2.12	1,2,3,4,5	1,4,5
WW03S-1-2	Insert frequently used and predefined text	1	1.21	1	3
		2	2.53	1,2,3,4,5	1,2,5
		3	3.68		
WW03S-1-3	Navigate to specific content	2	2.22	1,2,3,4,5	
WW03S-1-4	Insert, position, and size graphics	1	1.60	3,4,5	1,2,4
		2	2.50	2,3,4,5	2,3,4,5
WW03S-1-5	Create and modify diagrams and charts				
WW03S-1-6	Locate, select, and insert supporting information				
WW03S-2	**Organizing Content**				
WW03S-2-1	Insert and modify tables	3	3.55	1,3,5	1,3,4,5
WW03S-2-2	Create bulleted and numbered lists and outlines	2	2.50	1,2,3	3,4,5
		3	3.4	2	2
WW03S-2-3	Insert and modify hyperlinks	2	2.58	1,4,5	1,2,3,4
		WT1	WT1.9	1,2,3	1
WW03S-3	**Formatting Content**				
WW03S-3-1	Format text	1	1.50	1,2,3,4,5	1,2,3,4,5
		2	2.45	1,2,3,4,5	3,4,5
		3	3.7	3,4,5	4,5
WW03S-3-2	Format paragraphs	1	1.57	1,2,3,4,5	1,2,3,4,5
		2	2.33	3,4,5	2,3,4,5
WW03S-3-3	Apply and format columns				
WW03S-3-4	Insert and modify content in headers and footers	3	3.65	1,2,3,4,5	1,2,3,5
WW03S-3-5	Modify document layout and page setup	2	2.29	2,4,5	
		3	3.34	3,4,5	1,2,3,4,5
WW03S-4	**Collaborating**				
WW03S-4-1	Circulate documents for review				
WW03S-4-2	Compare and merge document versions				
WW03S-4-3	Insert, view, and edit comments				
WW03S-4-4	Track, accept, and reject proposed changes				
WW03S-5	**Formatting and Managing Documents**				
WW03S-5-1	Create new documents using templates				
WW03S-5-2	Review and modify document properties	1	1.69	1,2,3,4,5	1,2,3,4,5
WW03S-5-3	Organize documents using file folders	3	3.14	3,4,5	2,3,4

Standardized Coding Number	Skill sets and objectives	Lab Exercises				
		Lab	Page	Step-By-Step	On Your Own
WW03S-5-4	Save documents in appropriate formats for different uses	WT1	WT1.3	1,2,3	1
WW03S-5-5	Print documents, envelopes, and labels	1	1.67	1,2,3,4,5	1,2,3,4,5
		2	2.64	1,2,3,4,5	1,2,3,4,5
		3	3.76	1,2,3,4,5	1,2,3,4,5
WW03S-5-6	Preview documents and Web pages	1	1.67	1,2,3,4,5	1,2,3,4,5
		2	2.61	1,2,3,4,5	1,2,3,4,5
		3	3.76	1,2,3,4,5	1,2,3,4,5
		WT1	WT1.11	1,2,3	1
WW03S-5-7	Change and organize document views and windows	1	1.8	1,2,3,4,5	
		2	2.18	1,2,4,5	
		3	3.16,3.70	4,5	

Reference 2: MOS Certification Guide

www.mhhe.com/oleary

Index

Active window, WD2.18
Alignment, WD1.57–WD1.59
All caps, WD1.55
Antonyms, WD2.10
APA style, WD3.18
Applying styles, WD3.21–WD3.23
AutoComplete, WD1.22
AutoComplete ScreenTip, WD1.22
AutoCorrect, WD1.25–WD1.27
AutoCorrect Options button, WD1.26
AutoCorrect Options menu, WD1.27
AutoFormat, WD2.59, WD3.61–WD3.62
AutoFormat dialog box, WD3.62
AutoRecover, WD1.30
AutoShape, WD2.55–WD2.61
    adding text, WD2.58–WD2.60
    filling, with color, WD2.57
    inserting, WD2.56–WD2.57
    moving an autoshape, WD2.60–WD2.61
AutoText, WD1.22
AutoText entries, WD2.53–WD2.55

Backspace key, WD1.12
Bitmap files, WD1.60
Black text, WD1.56
Blank line, WD1.13
Block of text, WD1.43
.bmp, WD1.60
Bold, WD1.55
Break dialog box, WD3.34
Bulleted list, WD2.50, WD2.53
Bullets and Numbering dialog box, WD2.51

Caption, WD3.48–WD3.50
Caption options, WD3.49
Case sensitive, WD2.24
Cell, WD3.55
Centered, WD1.58
Centering a page vertically, WD3.35–WD3.36
Change Case command, WD1.48
Change Case dialog box, WD1.49
Changing case, WD1.48–WD1.50
Character effects, WD1.55–WD1.56
Character formatting, WD1.50, WD2.44–WD2.50
    color highlighting, WD2.45
    Format Painter, WD2.48
    Styles and Formatting task pane, WD2.48–WD2.50
    underlining text, WD2.46–WD2.47
Character size, WD1.8
Character style, WD3.7, WD3.21
Checking grammar, WD1.18–WD1.21
Checking the document, WD3.69–WD3.75
    formatting inconsistencies, WD3.72–WD3.75
    Reading Layout view, WD3.69–WD3.71
    redisplaying spelling/grammar errors,
    WD3.71–WD3.72

Clear Formatting, WD3.25
Click and Type, WD3.18–WD3.20
Click and Type pointer, WD3.19
Clip art, WD1.60–WD1.62
Clip Art task pane, WD1.61
Clip Organizer, WD1.60
Clipboard, WD2.12
Closing a file, WD1.33–WD1.34
Color, WD1.55
Color highlighting, WD2.45
Command summary
    Lab 1, WD1.75–WD1.77
    Lab 2, WD2.71–WD2.72
    Lab 3, WD3.81
Compare Side by Side toolbar, WD2.18
Copy. *See* Moving and copying selections
Copying between documents, WD2.17–WD2.19
Copying formats, WD2.48
Correcting errors, WD1.18–WD1.30
    AutoComplete, WD1.22
    AutoCorrect, WD1.25–WD1.27
    AutoText, WD1.22
    grammar/spelling. *See* Spelling and grammar errors
    smart tag, WD1.29–WD1.30
    word wrap, WD1.28
Create
    AutoText entry, WD2.54–WD2.55
    custom style, WD3.24–WD3.25
    document, WD1.7–WD1.11
    section break, WD3.34–WD3.35
    version, WD2.65–WD2.66
Cross-reference, WD3.48. *See also* Referencing figures
Cross-reference dialog box, WD3.52
Cross-reference hyperlink, WD3.54
Cursor, WD1.5
Custom dictionary, WD1.23
Custom mark, WD3.38
Custom style, WD3.24–WD3.25
Cut and paste, WD2.15–WD2.16

Date and Time command, WD2.26–WD2.29
Date and Time dialog box, WD2.27
Default caption label, WD3.49
Default document settings, WD1.9
Delete
    graphic, WD1.64–WD1.65
    section break, WD3.33
    select, and, WD1.43–WD1.45
    word, WD1.42–WD1.43
Delete key, WD1.12
Destination, WD2.12
Developing a document, WD1.10–WD1.11
Dictionary, WD1.23
Dimmed menu option, WD1.19
Directional keys, WD1.16

Document
    checking, WD3.69–WD3.75
    creating, WD1.7–WD1.11
    developing, WD1.10–WD1.11
    editing, WD1.39–WD1.50
    formatting, WD1.50–WD1.59
    navigating, WD1.36–WD1.39
    previewing, WD1.67
    printing, WD1.68–WD1.69
    revising, WD2.4–WD2.12
    scrolling, WD1.36–WD1.39
    viewing/zooming, WD1.8–WD1.10
Document formatting. *See* Formatting documents
Document Map, WD3.30–WD3.32
Document Map pane, WD3.31
Document paging, WD2.20–WD2.21
Document sections, WD3.32–WD3.36
Document versions, WD2.64–WD2.67
Document views, WD1.8
Document window, WD1.5
Documenting a file, WD1.69–WD1.71
Double strikethrough, WD1.55
Drag and drop, WD2.16–WD2.17
Drawing Canvas toolbar, WD2.57
Drawing layer, WD3.45
Drawing object, WD1.60
Drawing toolbar, WD2.56, WD2.57

Editing, WD1.11
Editing documents, WD1.39–WD1.50
    changing case, WD1.48–WD1.50
    deleting a word, WD1.42–WD1.43
    ignoring spelling errors, WD1.40
    inserting text, WD1.40–WD1.42
    selecting text, WD1.43–WD1.45
    undoing changes, WD1.46–WD1.48
Editing while previewing, WD2.61–WD2.64
Embedded object, WD1.60
End-of-file marker, WD1.5
Ending a line, WD1.13
Endnote, WD3.37. *See* also Source references
Enter key, WD1.13
Entering text, WD1.11–WD1.15
Errors. *See* Correcting errors
Exiting Word, WD1.71

Field, WD2.27
Field code, WD2.27–WD2.29
Field result, WD2.27
Field shading, WD2.29
Figure caption, WD3.49–WD3.50
Figure references. *See* Referencing figures
File
    closing, WD1.33–WD1.34
    documenting, WD1.69–WD1.71
    opening, WD1.34–WD1.36
    saving, WD1.30–WD1.33
File properties, WD1.69–WD1.71
Fill color, WD2.56, WD2.57
Find and Replace, WD2.21–WD2.26
Find and Replace dialog box, WD2.22–WD2.24
Finding text, WD2.22–WD2.24
Floating object, WD3.45
Font, WD1.51–WD1.55
Font size, WD1.51–WD1.54
Footer, WD3.65–WD3.69
Footnote, WD3.37. *See* also Source references

Footnote and Endnote dialog box, WD3.37
For Which Caption list box, WD3.53
Format Painter, WD2.48
Formatting, WD1.11
    AutoFormat, WD2.59
    character, WD2.44–WD2.50
    document, WD1.50–WD1.59, WD3.18–WD3.25
    document sections, WD3.32–WD3.36
    paragraph, WD2.33–WD2.44
    picture layout, WD3.44–WD3.48
    table, WD3.60–WD3.62
Formatting documents, WD1.50–WD1.59
    automatic formatting, WD3.18–WD3.25
    character effects, WD1.55–WD1.56
    character/paragraph formatting, WD1.50
    font/font sizes, WD1.51–WD1.55
    paragraph alignment, WD1.57–WD1.59
    reveal formatting, WD1.50–WD1.51
Formatting documents automatically, WD3.18–WD3.25
    applying styles, WD3.21–WD3.23
    Click and Type, WD3.18–WD3.20
    creating custom style, WD3.24–WD3.25
Formatting inconsistencies, WD3.72–WD3.75
Formatting marks, WD1.14–WD1.15
Formatting toolbar, WD1.5, WD1.53
Formatting zones, WD3.19
Full Screen view, WD1.8

Getting Started task pane, WD1.6
Grammar. *See* Spelling and grammar errors
Grammar checker, WD1.19, WD2.5–WD2.9
Grammar dialog box, WD1.20
Grammar error, WD1.18–WD1.21. *See* also Correcting errors
Grammar shortcut menu, WD1.19
Graphics, WD1.60–WD1.66
    captions/cross-references, WD3.48–WD3.54
    clip art, WD1.60–WD1.62
    defined, WD1.60
    deleting, WD1.64–WD1.65
    inverting a picture, WD1.60–WD1.64
    sizing, WD1.66
    text wrapping, WD3.44–WD3.48
    thumbnails, WD1.62
Green wavy underline, WD1.18
Gutter margin, WD2.30

Hard page break, WD2.20, WD2.21
Header, WD3.65–WD3.69
Header and Footer toolbar, WD3.66
Heading styles, WD3.7
Hidden, WD1.55
Hiding
    spelling/grammar errors, WD3.16–WD3.18
    white space, WD3.16
Hiding white space, WD3.16
Highlighting, WD2.45
Horizontal ruler, WD1.9
Hyperlink, WD2.58–WD2.60, WD3.29

I-beam, WD1.6, WD1.17
Indent, WD2.33–WD2.38
Indents and Spacing tab, WD2.35
Inline object, WD3.45
Insert mode, WD1.40–WD1.41
Insert Table drop-down menu, WD3.56
Inserting text, WD1.40–WD1.42

Insertion point, WD1.5
Italic, WD1.55

.jpg, WD1.60
Justified, WD1.58

Keyboard directional keys, WD1.16

Leader characters, WD2.41
Line spacing, WD2.42–WD2.44
List style, WD3.7
Lists, WD2.50–WD2.53

Main dictionary, WD1.23
Margin setting, WD2.30–WD2.33
Match Case, WD2.23, WD2.24
Mirror margins, WD2.30, WD2.32
MLA style, WD3.18, WD3.36, WD3.62
Mouse pointer
    arrow, as, WD1.6
    drag and drop, WD2.16
    hide white space, WD3.16
    I-beam, as, WD1.6, WD1.7
Moving and copying selections, WD2.12–WD2.19
    copy and paste, WD2.13–WD2.15
    copying between documents, WD2.17–WD2.19
    cut and paste, WD2.15–WD2.16
    drag and drop, WD2.16–WD2.17
    moving an autoshape, WD2.60–WD2.61
Moving through text, WD1.15–WD1.18

Navigating a document, WD1.36–WD1.39
Navigating by headings, WD3.29–WD3.32
    Document Map, WD3.30–WD3.32
    table of contents hyperlink, WD3.29–WD3.30
New documents, WD1.7–WD1.11
New folder, WD3.14–WD3.15
New Folder dialog box, WD3.15
New Style dialog box, WD3.24
Normal view, WD1.8
Note reference mark, WD3.37
Note separator, WD3.37
Note text, WD3.37
Num Lock, WD1.16
Numbered list, WD2.50–WD2.52
Numbered mark, WD3.38
Numeric keypad, WD1.16

Object, WD1.60
Office Clipboard, WD2.12
Open dialog box, WD1.34
Opening a file, WD1.34–WD1.36
Options dialog box, WD3.17
Outline, WD1.55, WD3.4–WD3.14
    changing outline levels, WD3.7–WD3.9
    collapsing/expanding, WD3.11–WD3.14
    moving/inserting topics, WD3.9–WD3.11
    Outline view, WD3.5–WD3.7
Outline levels, WD3.7–WD3.9
Outline numbered list, WD2.50
Outline symbol, WD3.5, WD3.6, WD3.8
Outline toolbar, WD3.5, WD3.8
Outline view, WD1.8, WD3.4–WD3.5
Overtype mode, WD1.41–WD1.42

Page break, WD2.20–WD2.21
Page layout, WD2.29–WD2.33
Page margin, WD2.30–WD2.33

Page Number Format dialog box, WD3.67
Page Setup command, WD2.31
Page Setup dialog box, WD2.32
Pane, WD1.6
Paragraph, WD1.50
Paragraph alignment, WD1.57–WD1.59
Paragraph formatting, WD1.50, WD2.33–WD2.44
    indenting, WD2.33–WD2.38
    line spacing, WD2.42–WD2.44
    tab leaders, WD2.41–WD2.42
    tab stops, WD2.38–WD2.41
Paragraph indent, WD1.9
Paragraph style, WD3.7, WD3.21
Parenthetical source references, WD3.36
Paste, WD2.13–WD2.16
Paste Options button, WD2.13
.pcx, WD1.60
Photographs. See Graphics
Pick Formatting to Apply list box, WD2.49
Picture, WD1.60. See also Graphics
Picture toolbar, WD1.65, WD3.46
Preview
    document, WD1.67
    editing in print preview, WD2.62–WD2.64
    multiple pages, WD2.61–WD2.62
Preview/Properties dialog box, WD1.63
Preview window, WD1.67
Print
    document, WD1.68–WD1.69
    selected pages, WD3.76–WD3.77
Print dialog box, WD1.68
Print Layout view, WD1.8, WD1.9, WD3.16, WD3.19
Print preview. See Preview
Print Preview window, WD1.67
Properties, WD1.69–WD1.71

Reading Layout toolbar, WD3.70
Reading Layout view, WD1.8, WD3.69–WD3.71
Reading Mode Markup toolbar, WD3.70
Red wavy line, WD1.23
Redo, WD1.47–WD1.48
Referencing figures, WD3.48–WD3.54
    adding a cross-reference, WD3.50–WD3.54
    adding a figure caption, WD3.49–WD3.50
    cross-reference hyperlink, WD3.54
Related words, WD2.10
Replace With text box, WD2.25
Replacing text, WD2.25–WD2.26
Research task pane, WD2.11
Resizing. See Sizing
Reveal Formatting task pane, WD1.50–WD1.51
Revealing formatting marks, WD1.14–WD1.15
Revising a document, WD2.4–WD2.12
Right paragraph indent, WD1.9
Ruler, WD1.5, WD1.9–WD1.10

Sans serif fonts, WD1.51
Save As, WD1.30–WD1.31
Save As dialog box, WD1.31
Save In drop-down, WD1.31
Saving a file, WD1.30–WD1.33
Saving to new folder, WD3.14–WD3.15
ScreenTip
    AutoComplete, WD1.22
    dragging a scroll box, WD3.29
    footnote, WD3.42
    thumbnail, WD1.62
Scrolling, WD1.36–WD1.39

Section, WD3.33–WD3.35
Section break, WD3.33–WD3.35
Selecting a style, WD3.22
Selecting text, WD1.43–WD1.45
Selection rectangle, WD1.65
Serif fonts, WD1.51
Shadow, WD1.55
Shortcut menus, WD1.19
Show/Hide button, WD1.14
Sizing
    Document Map pane, WD3.31
    graphic, WD1.66
    table, WD3.59
Sizing handles, WD1.65
Small caps, WD1.55
Smart Tag, WD1.29–WD1.30
Soft page break, WD2.20
Sort, WD3.62–WD3.64
Source, WD2.12
Source program, WD1.60
Source references, WD3.36–WD3.44
    adding footnotes, WD3.37–WD3.42
    converting footnotes to endnotes, etc., WD3.41
    inserting footnote in Print Layout view, WD3.43–WD3.44
    viewing footnotes, WD3.42–WD3.43
Spelling and Grammar dialog box, WD2.6
Spelling and grammar errors
    checking grammar, WD1.18–WD1.21
    checking spelling, WD1.22–WD1.25
    hiding, WD3.16–WD3.18
    ignoring spelling errors, WD1.40
    redisplaying, WD3.71–WD3.72
    revising the document, WD2.5–WD2.9
Spelling and Grammar Status icon, WD1.18, WD1.21, WD1.25
Spelling checker, WD1.22–WD1.25, WD1.40, WD2.5–WD2.9
Spelling error, WD1.22–WD1.25. *See also* Correcting errors
Split window, WD3.50–WD3.52
Standard block of text, WD1.43
Standard toolbar, WD1.5, WD1.14
Starting Word, WD1.4–WD1.5
Status bar, WD1.6–WD1.7
Strikethrough, WD1.55
Style, WD3.7, WD3.21–WD3.25
Style drop-down menu, WD3.23
Style of report formatting, WD3.18
Styles and Formatting task pane, WD2.48–WD2.50, WD3.21
Subscript, WD1.55
Superscript, WD1.55
Synonyms, WD2.10
System Clipboard, WD2.12

Tab leaders, WD2.41–WD2.42
Tab stop, WD2.36, WD2.38–WD2.41
Tab types, WD2.38
Table, WD3.55–WD3.62
    AutoFormat, WD3.61–WD3.62
    defined, WD3.55
    entering data, WD3.57–WD3.58
    formatting, WD3.60–WD3.62
    inserting, WD3.55–WD3.56
    inserting a row, WD3.58–WD3.59
    navigating/moving, WD3.57
    selecting rows/columns, etc., WD3.60
    sizing, WD3.59

Table of contents, WD3.25–WD3.29, WD3.75–WD3.76
Table of contents hyperlink, WD3.29–WD3.30
Table of Contents Options dialog box, WD3.28
Table reference, WD3.55
Table style, WD3.7
Tabs dialog box, WD2.41
Text
    block of, WD1.43
    entering, WD1.11–WD1.15
    finding/replacing, WD2.21–WD2.47
    inserting, WD1.40–WD1.42
    moving through, WD1.15–WD1.18
    selecting, WD1.43–WD1.45
    typing, WD1.11–WD1.12
    wrapping, around graphics, WD3.46–WD3.48
Text alignment, WD1.57–WD1.59
Text wrapping, WD3.45
Thesaurus, WD2.10–WD2.12
Thumbnails, WD1.62
Toolbar
    Compare Side by Side, WD2.18
    Drawing, WD2.56
    Drawing Canvas, WD2.57
    Formatting, WD1.53
    Header and Footer, WD3.66
    Outline, WD3.5
    Picture, WD1.65, WD3.46
    Reading Layout, WD3.70
    Reading Layout Markup, WD3.70
    Standard, WD1.14
TrueType, WD1.52
Typeface, WD1.51
Typing text, WD1.11, WD1.12

Underline, WD1.55
Underlining text, WD2.46–WD2.47
Undo, WD1.46–WD1.48
Uniform resource locator (URL), WD2.58
Updating a table of contents, WD3.75–WD3.76
URL, WD2.58

Version, WD2.64–WD2.67
Versions dialog box, WD2.66
Vertical alignment, WD3.35–WD3.36
Vertical Alignment drop-down list box, WD3.35
Vertical ruler, WD1.9, WD1.10
View menu, WD1.8

Web Layout view, WD1.8
White space, hiding, WD3.16
White text, WD1.56
Word 2003 window, WD1.5–WD1.7
Word wrap, WD1.28

Zoom button, WD1.7–WD1.9